MOYNIHAN'S MOMENT

MOYNIHAN'S MOMENT

AMERICA'S FIGHT AGAINST
ZIONISM AS RACISM

GIL TROY

OXFORD
UNIVERSITY PRESS

OXFORD
UNIVERSITY PRESS

Oxford University Press is a department of the University of Oxford.
It furthers the University's objective of excellence in research,
scholarship, and education by publishing worldwide.

Oxford   New York

Auckland   Cape Town   Dar es Salaam   Hong Kong   Karachi
Kuala Lumpur   Madrid   Melbourne   Mexico City   Nairobi
New Delhi   Shanghai   Taipei   Toronto

With offices in

Argentina   Austria   Brazil   Chile   Czech Republic   France   Greece
Guatemala   Hungary   Italy   Japan   Poland   Portugal   Singapore
South Korea   Switzerland   Thailand   Turkey   Ukraine   Vietnam

Oxford is a registered trademark of Oxford University Press
in the UK and certain other countries.

Published in the United States of America by Oxford University Press
198 Madison Avenue, New York, NY 10016

Library of Congress Cataloging-in-Publication Data
Troy, Gil.
Moynihan's moment : America's fight against Zionism as racism / Gil Troy.
p.   cm. Includes bibliographical references and index.
ISBN 978–0–19–992030–3
1. United Nations—United States.   2. Moynihan, Daniel P. (Daniel Patrick), 1927–2003.
3. World politics—1975–1985.   4. Antisemitism—History—20th century.
5. United States—Foreign relations—20th century.
6. Zionism—Government policy—United States.   I. Title.
JZ4997.5.U6T76 2012 320.54095694—dc23   2012013808

Grateful acknowledgment is made for permission to quote lyrics from the following:

Bad Blood (Words and Music by Neil Sedaka and Phil Cody). ©1974 (Renewed 2002). EMI Sosaha Music Inc., EMI
Jemaxal Music Inc., Songs of SJL-RSL Music Co. and SJL-RSL Songs Company. International Copyright Secured. All
Rights Reserved. Used by Permission. Reprinted by permission of Hal Leonard Corporation.

Won't Get Fooled Again (Words and Music by Peter Townshend). ©1971 Towser Tunes, Inc., Fabulous Music Ltd., and
ABKCO Music, Inc. Copyright Renewed. All Rights for Towser Tunes, Inc., Administered by Universal Music Publishing
International MGB Ltd. All Rights for Universal Music Publishing International MGB Ltd. in the U.S. Administered by
Universal Music—Careers. International Copyright Secured. All Rights Reserved. Used by Permission. Reprinted by
permission of Hal Leonard Corporation.

3 5 7 9 8 6 4 2

Printed in the United States of America
on acid-free paper

To my parents, Bernard Dov and Elaine Gerson Troy,
children of Daniel Patrick Moynihan's New York,
for repeatedly facing up to their most challenging
moments with a Moynihanesque grit, while teaching us
his enduring lesson, that "words matter."

Few events have so offended the American people as the "Zionism-is-racism" resolution of November 10, 1975. It was as if all America stood to affirm the response of our chief delegate, Daniel Patrick Moynihan: "The United States rises to declare before the General Assembly of the United Nations and before the world that it does not acknowledge, it will never abide by, it will never acquiesce in this infamous act." The U.S., under the leadership of three different Presidents, has remained true to that pledge. Today, I am proud to reaffirm that promise and further, to pledge my support for the removal of this blot from the UN record.

—President Ronald Reagan, November 10, 1985

CONTENTS

MOYNIHAN'S MOMENT

INTRODUCTION: "JUST A MATTER OF DECENCY"

On November 10, 1975, the United Nations General Assembly passed Resolution 3379 with 72 delegates voting "yes," 35 opposing, 32 abstaining, and 3 absent. In the world parliament's dry, legalistic language, the resolution singled out one form of nationalism, Jewish nationalism, for unprecedented vilification. "Recalling" UN resolutions in 1963 and 1973 condemning racial discrimination, and "taking note" of recent denunciations of Zionism from the International Women's Year Conference, the Organization of African Unity meeting, and the Non-Aligned Conference in Peru that summer, the General Assembly concluded that "Zionism is a form of racism and racial discrimination."

After the resolution passed, America's ambassador to the United Nations, Daniel Patrick Moynihan, rose to speak. With his graying hair and matching gray suit, a white handkerchief in his breast pocket, from afar the forty-eight-year-old American looked like every other middle-aged Western diplomat. Up close, the 6-foot 5-inch professor made a different impression. His hair was a little long and untamed, more Harvard Yard than Turtle Bay, the fashionable New York neighborhood where the UN is located. Strands of hair drooped over the right side of his prominent forehead, compelling him to brush back the errant hair periodically. With a no-nonsense scowl reinforced by arched eyebrows on his oblong face, Moynihan undiplomatically denounced the very forum he was addressing.

"The United States rises to declare," Moynihan began his formal address, swaying gently, both hands clutching the podium, "before the General Assembly of the United Nations, and before the world, that it does not acknowledge"—he paused—"it will not abide by"—he paused again—"it will never acquiesce in this infamous act." Later on, he proclaimed, "The lie is that Zionism is a form of racism. The overwhelmingly clear truth is that it is not."

Soviet-engineered, absolutist, and impervious to changing conditions, the Zionism-is-racism charge fused long-standing anti-Semitism with anti-Americanism, making it surprisingly potent in the post-1960s world, despite being a political chimera. In the *Iliad*, a Chimera is a grotesque animal jumble, "lion-fronted and snake behind, a goat in the middle." To make Israel as monstrous, Resolution 3379 grafted allegations of racism onto the national conflict between Palestinians and Israel. This ideological hodge-podge racialized the attack on Israel and stigmatized Zionism, for race had been established as the great Western sin and the most potent Third World accusation thanks to Nazism's defeat, America's Civil Rights' successes, the Third World's anti-colonial rebellions, and the world's backlash against South African apartheid.

Criminalizing Zionism turned David into Goliath, deeming Israel the Middle East's perpetual villain with the Palestinians the perennial victims. This great inversion culminated a process that began in 1967 with Israel's imposing Six-Day War victory, followed by the Arab shift from conventional military tactics to guerilla and ideological warfare, especially after the 1973 Yom Kippur War. Viewing Israel through a race-tinted magnifying lens exaggerated even minor flaws into seemingly major sins.

The vote shocked many, especially in the United States, the country largely responsible for founding the UN and justifiably proud of hosting the UN's main headquarters in New York. The prospect of this non-Jewish society rising with such unity and fury against anti-Semitism provided a rare sight in Jewish history. Only in America, it seemed, would so many non-Jews take Jew hatred so personally. The reaction to Resolution 3379 further demonstrates American exceptionalism, expressed in this case by the extraordinary welcome Jews, Judaism, and Zionism have enjoyed in the United States, particularly after World War II.

This pure, passionate reaction also proves that America's alliance with Israel was organic, popular, deep, and enduring. Daniel Patrick Moynihan became the symbol of the relationship's authenticity and intensity. He supported Israel and Zionism as natural extensions of his love for America and for liberal democracy. In confirming this overlap of values, Moynihan reaffirmed Justice Louis Brandeis's equation between Zionism and Americanism that first made Zionism palatable to many American Jews during World War I.

Moynihan, the respected but eccentric Harvard professor, policy wonk, and White House adviser to presidents John Kennedy, Lyndon Johnson, Richard Nixon, and, now, Gerald Ford, was new to the UN. He was an entrancing talker, a fluid writer, encyclopedically literate, perpetually witty, and frequently prophetic. "Pat was colorful, delightful, smart, and so well informed," recalls Donald Rumsfeld, the White House Chief of Staff when Ford appointed Moynihan. "He brightened up the room." "It was good of you to tell me about my inaudibility in the Senate chamber," Moynihan retorted once when told he mumbled while testifying. "But on the other hand, it is from being heard that I have mostly got in trouble."

Moynihan was surprised he stumbled into this particular pack of UN trouble, because, he emphasized, "Israel was not *my* religion." He backed Israel "for reasons that had almost nothing to do with it." He wanted to defend democracy and decency. "The accused" interested him less than "the accusers." Resolution 3379, with its perverse Soviet-orchestrated distortions of language, history, and reality, he said, "reeked of the totalitarian mind, stank of the totalitarian state."

Moynihan's strategy of equating protecting Israel with opposing America's enemies initially left him feeling as lonely and unpopular as the country he was defending. A most undiplomatic diplomat, he was charming enough to "spend an evening with," as the British correspondent Henry Fairlie sniffed in the *Washington Post*. "But would anyone in his senses appoint him to be the ambassador to the United Nations?" Fairlie feared "a new form of gunboat diplomacy, his words, his guns." The *New York Times* was also skeptical—as were many of his new colleagues, at the UN and even at the US mission to the UN. "Pat couldn't trust many of the American mission staff," recalls his widow Elizabeth Moynihan, universally known as Liz. Most were busy guarding Secretary of State Henry Kissinger's more accommodating détente policy. UN ambassador R. K. Ramphul of Mauritius would charge that delegates "lived in positive dread" of Moynihan's "manners, his language, and his abuse."

To his surprise, Moynihan's stand made him an instant political celebrity. Suddenly reprieved from two race-tinged controversies, which haunted him during the Johnson and Nixon years, Moynihan became America's great champion: honorable and honest, unlike Nixon; elegant and eloquent, unlike Ford; aggressively patriotic, unlike Kissinger; and a household name, unlike most cabinet colleagues. But the fight cost Moynihan his job. His fury alienated America's allies and adversaries, along with much of America's foreign policy establishment, including Kissinger. Less than three months later, Moynihan, feeling sabotaged, resigned. He served only eight months as ambassador, what he would call "an abbreviated posting," from June 30, 1975, through February 1976.

Nearly four decades later, Moynihan's speech remains a high point in what was, for most Americans, a depressing decade. Moynihan recognized the attack on Zionism as a totalitarian assault against democracy itself, motivated by anti-Semitism and anti-Americanism. Fighting it was "just a matter of decency," his UN colleague Leonard Garment explained. Barely six months after Vietnam fell, with American morale sagging, inflation climbing, revelations about CIA assassination plots mounting, and the embattled new president, Gerald Ford, supposedly telling a bankrupt New York City to "Drop Dead," an American leader defended America proudly. "It was the beginning of a national reassertion," the columnist George Will—who became one of Moynihan's closest friends—recalls.

Fans responded to the emotion in his voice as much as the words on his lips. Moynihan essentially said what Peter Finch, the fictional anchorman in the Academy Award–winning movie *Network*, would say a year later: "I'm as mad as hell and I'm not going to take this anymore." "Did I make a crisis out of this obscene resolution?" Moynihan would bellow, responding to criticism that he picked a fight. "Damn right I did!"

Resolution 3379 struck many Americans as not just an affront but absurd. "It struck one as implausible," Will says. "Zionism already had a half-century or more of momentum behind it. Americans knew it was not an expression of something ugly." The comedian Chevy Chase mocked the resolution on fall 1975's edgy new hit, *Saturday Night* (it became *Saturday Night Live* in 1977). On "Weekend Update," his must-see news satire, Chase first ridiculed Gerald Ford's clumsiness by mimicking America's president pouring a glass of water in his ear instead of down his throat. Then, Chase reported: "The United Nations General Assembly proclaimed Zionism to be racism. The black entertainer Sammy Davis, Jr., who recently converted to Judaism, said: 'What a breakthrough, I can finally hate myself.'"

When the world parliament demonized Zionism, it traumatized many of America's 5.8 million Jews, who deeply identified with American blacks, sharing wounds from historic bigotry, feeling the anguish of otherness. Dr. Leonard Cole, a civil rights activist like many of his Jewish friends, was finishing his first book, *Blacks in Power*, celebrating emerging black electoral success. He recalls thinking: "With 3379, the UN seemed to be saying I was a racist. Huh?" After the vote, Stephen Solarz, a thirty-five-year-old antiwar freshman Democratic congressman from Brooklyn, put in his wallet a credit-card-sized "scorecard" showing how the countries voted. He carried it around for more than a decade, to remember "who our friends are."

For "anybody on the Left who had illusions about the UN, they were shattered," the Princeton political philosopher Michael Walzer recalls. Alan Dershowitz, a Harvard Law School professor best known then for defending antiwar protesters and pornographers against censorship, remembers feeling "galvanized." "It was the turning point. I quit the UN Association over that issue," recalled Dershowitz. Many Jews, including the feminist icon Betty Friedan, became more protective of Israel and more reflective about their own Jewish identities.

Most major civil rights leaders were equally outraged, including Vernon Jordan, Cesar Chavez, and Eldridge Cleaver, the Black Panther who, from his jail cell, said: "to condemn the Jewish survival doctrine of Zionism as racism is a travesty upon the truth." The legendary labor leader, A. Philip Randolph, founded the Black Americans to Support Israel Committee, BASIC, with Bayard Rustin. More than two hundred leading African Americans signed an advertisement rejecting the racism charge, including athletes like Hank Aaron, Roy Campanella, and Arthur Ashe, politicians like Los Angeles mayor Tom Bradley and Congressman Andrew Young, and civil rights icons like Coretta Scott King and the Reverend Martin Luther King Sr.

Farther left politically, the anti-poverty activist Michael Harrington, a Moynihan critic, nevertheless condemned Resolution 3379. "If one preposterously charges that Zionism is racist, then so are all nationalisms which joined to condemn it at the UN," Harrington said. "And that is to drain the concept of racism of any serious meaning." Harrington feared the rancor doomed the agenda of economic change UN delegates advanced weeks earlier. He also warned that "By inventing a nonexistent racism in Israel, the UN has undermined the effectiveness of mobilizing serious action against the real racism of Southern Africa."

Resolution 3379's passage was a consciousness-raising moment for many Americans, heralding a changing world. This burgeoning anti-Americanism engulfing the UN, following the Vietnam War, unnerved many patriots. "Approximately half our associates in the world parliament dislike our policies as a matter of principle," C. L. Sulzberger glumly concluded in his influential "Foreign Affairs" column in the New York Times during the resolution fight.

Hence the reason that Moynihan's speech struck a chord. More than 70 percent of Americans surveyed applauded Moynihan's assertiveness. "A FIGHTING IRISHMAN AT THE U.N. TALKS TOUGH—AND MANY AMERICANS FEEL, TALKS SENSE TOO," People magazine proclaimed in later designating Moynihan one of 1975's "25 Most Intriguing People." Others included Betty Ford, Anwar Sadat, Werner Erhard, and Woody Allen. Affirming the people's sentiments, General Matthew Ridgway, the tough World War II hero of the Eighty-second Airborne Division who then redeemed the US-UN Korean war effort, called Resolution 3379 "A deplorable action." Donald Rumsfeld called it "outrageous," launching the UN's ritualistic assaults on Israel. UNICEF would sell two million fewer greeting cards during the 1975 Christmas season, attributing this nearly 10 percent drop to Americans' anti-UN backlash. On the flagship network news show, the CBS Evening News with Walter Cronkite, Eric Sevareid commented: "The country is simply tired of feeling self-disgust. That explains the almost joyous response to Moynihan's passion and candor at the UN."

Moynihan became "the most celebrated intellectual in US politics," the historian James Patterson writes, and, after resigning, one of the "most sought-after speakers in the world," according to Don Walker, whose Harry Walker Agency represented Moynihan. By January 1977, Moynihan, who entered the UN with limited political prospects, became New York's Democratic senator. He would serve four terms, loyal to liberals yet surprisingly popular with conservatives, partially thanks to a sustained, post-UN halo effect.

A decade after the resolution passed, on November 12, 1985, that unerring receptor of popular opinion, Ronald Reagan, declared, "Few events have so

offended the American people as the 'Zionism is racism' resolution."
Addressing the General Assembly that fall, Reagan blasted the "infamous"
resolution's "total inversion of morality." Resolution 3379 had remained for
over a decade what the New York Times called the UN's "nadir" and the resolution that "pushed many Americans toward full-scale disillusionment"
with that world body.

Still, popular memory—even of dramatic water-cooler moments that
captured the nation's attention and sparked many conversations—is fickle.
Some historical events, like cataclysmic earthquakes, destroy contemporary
structures, rattling everyone. Others may not register as high on the historical equivalent of the Richter scale, even as they transform the topography
while leaving significant fault lines. Just as they forget boom times during
economic busts, many Americans lost faith in the UN, with fewer and fewer
remembering its initial promise. Resolution 3379 is not as well remembered
today as the Yom Kippur War, which preceded it, or the 1978 Camp David
Peace Accords between Israel and Egypt, which followed. But its aftershocks
nevertheless persist with surprising strength.

The aftershocks from Moynihan's defiance also anticipated broader shifts
in American politics and culture that would shape the 1980s' Reagan
Revolution, while marking the loss of most Americans' respect for the UN.
For the many baby boomers who were raised Trick-or-Treating for UNICEF
and participating in Model UNs, the disillusion with the UN was distress-
ing, another blow to their once-innocent worldview. Moynihan's politics of
patriotic indignation inspired many, including Ronald Reagan, who attracted
loud applause when quoting Moynihan's speeches during the 1976
presidential contest—which he narrowly lost to the incumbent Gerald Ford.
With mixed emotions, the liberal commentator Max Lerner noted that rid-
ing this "wave of nationalist feeling" made Moynihan a "hot political
property."

Moynihan's indignation attracted bipartisan approval, from liberals such
as Senator Frank Church and Congressman Ed Koch to conservatives such
as Senator Barry Goldwater and the economist Milton Friedman. "You have
voiced—with courage and arresting rhetoric—convictions that most
Americans long have held, and which so often have been muted," the
Supreme Court Justice Lewis F. Powell would write in one of 26,000 overwhelmingly positive letters that reached Moynihan that fall and winter.
Gallup Polls confirmed near universal support, from Left to Right. Asked if

Moynihan should remain candid or be more diplomatic, 72 percent of liberals, 76 percent of conservatives, and 80 percent of independents polled, wanted candor.

Moynihan's anger was patriotic but not personal, populist but not partisan, offering confident leadership when most leaders dithered. He paved the way for a more muscular, idealistic, foreign policy, one which began to be called "neoconservative"—a label Michael Harrington had popularized, starting in 1973—and one which Moynihan rejected his entire public life. Remembering Moynihan's eloquent defense of America and its foreign policy, along with the enthusiasm it generated, adds nuance to the simplistic narrative of the "Morning in America" 1980s by suggesting that the 1970s were not as defeatist as many recall today. Historians are recognizing that America's rightward shift began in the 1970s. Reagan himself acknowledged that America's patriotic spirit had begun to revive even before his 1981 inauguration.

By the 1990s Moynihan was vindicated, even though as senator he often broke with President Reagan. The Soviet Union fell. More and more politicians Left and Right echoed Moynihan's politics of patriotic indignation. In 1991 the General Assembly revoked the "Zionism is racism" finding. Newly freed Eastern European countries apologized for collaborating on this Cold War relic. Moynihan's "standing up and being responsible for the rescission of the Zionism is racism resolution of the UN was an act far more important than anything I have done," New York's mayor Ed Koch would say. Two years later, Israelis and Palestinians embraced, if awkwardly, on the White House lawn, seeking peace through the Oslo Accords.

Yet now, a decade after Moynihan's death in 2003 at the age of seventy-six, and nearly forty years after Resolution 3379 passed, America and Israel seem to be reliving the 1970s. In the traditional oscillation between realism and idealism in American foreign policy, the idealists are flagging. President George W. Bush's ideological, confrontational stance, followed by economic recession, has led many Americans to doubt America's clout, repudiating both neoconservatism and Woodrow Wilson's faith in disseminating democracy worldwide, which Moynihan shared. The Israeli-Palestinian stalemate looks chronic. And the libel that Zionism—a nationalist movement like hundreds of others—is racist and creating a form of apartheid seems more ubiquitous than ever.

The Soviet-Arab propaganda outlasted the Soviet Union, especially in the UN. In December 2011, shortly after Basher al-Assad's Syria, having already killed five thousand of its own citizens, was elected to two UNESCO human rights committees, America's UN ambassador Susan Rice, picking up Moynihan's mantle, deplored the "unfair treatment" and "double standards" Israel suffered at the UN "daily." "It's obsessive. It's ugly. It's bad for the UN. It's bad for peace. And it must stop."

Soviet propagandists understood the power of manipulating words to trigger "Pavlovian" responses, the Princeton kremlinologist Robert Tucker observed. For them, the "ultimate weapon of political control would be the dictionary." Terms like "racism," "colonialism," and "imperialism" came straight out of the Communist playbook for demonizing enemies. These terms effectively obscured what was really occurring—a clash of nationalisms between two nations emerging following the collapse of two imperial powers, first the Ottoman Empire, then Great Britain. Indeed, "Zionism is racism" became the most famous slogan to emerge from more than six decades of UN life, more popular than the lovely but ineffectual catchphrases the United Nations Postal Administration has tried launching, including "Live Together in Peace" and "A Mine Less Is a Victim Less."

Well into the twenty-first century, the words cast their spell as opponents of Israel in the United States and abroad continued echoing the charge. The Palestine Liberation Organization covenant still called Zionism "racist and fanatic in its nature, aggressive, expansionist, and colonial in its aims"—a proposition that predated Resolution 3379 but was reinforced by it. In 2001, the "Programme of Action" the NGO forum passed at the World Conference against Racism, Racial Discrimination, Xenophobia, and Related Intolerance, meeting in Durban, South Africa, demanded "the reinstitution of UN Resolution 3379 determining the practices of Zionism as racist practices." "Zionism is racism" was emblazoned on signs at anti-Israel protest rallies in 2009 and on folders used by some Arab delegates to the UN's Durban II review conference in Geneva—with a swastika added as background. "My amended dictionary entry explains why Zionism is racism and why Zionists are racists," Ahmed Moor, a twenty-four-year-old activist writes in a blog posting on The Electronic Intifada. "Zionism is racism," Dr. Mark Braverman proclaims as he lectures to enthusiastic audiences on American campuses.

For many Palestinians, frustrated, harassed, disappointed, bereft, exiled, feeling abandoned by the world, Resolution 3379 was a cure-all, the UN's remedy for their suffering. Many advocates for Israel believed the Zionism-is-racism charge was the ideological equivalent of crack cocaine for

Palestinians. It gave this depressed people a rush, made this powerless people feel strong. But its nasty side effects included endorsing a terrorist crime spree and encouraging an unhealthy zero sum approach on both sides. When one people's poison is another's antidote, the conflict feels irreconcilable.

Some radical ideas radicalize discourse subtly, even if most people consciously reject the notions as extreme. Reflecting the national preference for familiar references, even some pro-Israeli politicians used the chimerical Zionism-racism charge to cast the Palestinians as blacks and the Israelis as rednecks. Both President Barack Obama and George W. Bush's secretary of state Condoleezza Rice compared the Palestinian quest for independence with the African American quest for civil rights. Although Obama affirmed that "we will always reject the notion that Zionism is racism," this analogy reduced the story to one of racial oppression, rather than what it is—national conflict. This reading implicitly sanctioned Palestinian terrorism, given the immorality of racial tyranny. It linked the United States and Israel as the sinning successors to South Africa's apartheid regime in leftist demonology—echoed in Israel-Apartheid weeks on American campuses, and bestselling polemics like President Jimmy Carter's 2006 *Palestine: Peace not Apartheid*. It realized the civil rights activist Bayard Rustin's fear of the term *racism* becoming an all-purpose, meaningless epithet "in international discussions" like s.o.b. is "in personal relations."

Thus, even in the United States, which remained overwhelmingly pro-Israel, the liberal Protestant churches, the Middle East Studies departments, the civil rights and human rights organizations—most of whose leaders cheered Moynihan, defended Israel, and denounced the UN in 1975—now had more and more ideologues labeling Zionism racism and Israel an apartheid state. This essentialist attack damned Israel's existence, not its actions. Building on the Zionism-racism charge as the foundation, the inevitable rubble that emerges in national struggles like the bitter Israeli-Palestinian conflict reinforced the growing pile-on against Israel. With the blackening of the Palestinians and the whitening of Israelis, extremist critics saw the religious-nationalist settlements as racist; the post-Oslo, terror-induced security infrastructure of checkpoints, bypass roads, walls, and fences as replicating apartheid; and the hawkish governments under Ariel Sharon and Benjamin Netanyahu as justifying Israel's illegitimacy, even as Sharon withdrew from Gaza, then Netanyahu endorsed a two-state solution.

What had been a punch line in 1975 became a tagline decades later. Israel stood accused of a crime considered characteristic of Western powers but also deemed particularly Jewish, with "chosenness" misread as a pretension to genetic superiority not a spur to added moral responsibility. The UN accepted all countries "as equally legitimate," Moynihan subsequently explained: "Only regimes based on racism and racial discrimination were held to be unacceptable." This made Resolution 3379's threat a mortal one—and even more harmful to Israel's legitimacy than being expelled from the UN would have been.

Even the MIT professor Noam Chomsky, a harsh critic of Israel, acknowledged Resolution 3379's "profound hypocrisy, given the nature of the states that backed it (including the Arab states)," as well as the unfair repudiation of Israel's legitimacy by "referring to Zionism as *such* rather than the policies of the State of Israel." Similarly, the leading Palestinian academic Edward Said, in his 1980 manifesto *The Question of Palestine*, called the accusation too "vague," and said that Israel's achievements should "not sloppily be tarnished with the sweeping rhetorical denunciation associated with racism." Deeming 3379 counterproductive, Said would confess: "I was never happy with that resolution."

Of course, some criticisms of Israel and Zionism are anti-Semitic, some are not. There is a legitimate anti-Zionist critique among Jews and non-Jews with both an established intellectual tradition and valid contemporary arguments. The contemporary Israeli-Palestinian stalemate is too complex for simplistic judgments yet nevertheless constantly clouded by them.

The Zionism-is-racism charge emerged from two such crude condemnations: the Soviet attempt to demean the Jewish people, and the Arab desire to destroy the Jewish state. Hadassa Ben Itto, an Israeli jurist who served in Israel's UN delegation, recalls that in October 1965, when Soviet delegates first injected the charge against Zionism into a UN resolution to block American attempts to condemn anti-Semitism as a form of racism, they never bothered making the case intellectually. She recalls, "it was almost a joke. They said that they were only suggesting the idea to get the Americans off their anti-Semitism kick." Years later, Moynihan would emphasize Resolution 3379's Soviet pedigree by calling it the "Big Red Lie."

The totalitarian anti-Zionism that resulted, the categorical Zionism-racism charge, its anti-Semitic roots, its exterminationist logic, and its distorting impact on Middle East discourse, justify the decision to follow the story of this ideological reading without exploring all the rights and wrongs of the Arab-Israeli conflict, including Israeli settlement policy. This book is not a history of Israeli racial attitudes or Arab-related policies. Rather it assesses the impact, in the United States particularly, of the fight Daniel Patrick Moynihan led against totalitarian anti-Zionism, expressed in Resolution 3379.

Clearly, some of the hatred against Israel is blind—which is what this book addresses. Yet anyone who sincerely hopes to move beyond the conflict cannot be blinded by the blindness. There are thwarted dreams, broken lives, bad actors, wrong moves, missed opportunities, crushed peoples, individual and collective traumas on both sides, which other books examine, and peacemakers will ultimately have to take into account. In his 1968 classic, *White Over Black: American Attitudes toward the Negro, 1550–1812*, the historian Winthrop Jordan analyzed the "process of debasement" creating a "we" against a "they" in early America, which turned the "Negro" into a slave. Similarly, this book analyzes how the Zionism-is-racism charge demonized Israel, Zionism, often the Jewish people, and occasionally the American people, trying to make the Jewish state a pariah.

The fight over Resolution 3379 represents a turning point in history— American history, Jewish history, Cold War history, UN history, the history of the Arab-Israeli conflict, and the history of liberalism and conservatism. Nearly four decades later we can assess the resolution's impact, including evaluating what Moynihan's opposition accomplished. Questions persist about the diplomatic struggle surrounding the resolution, especially regarding the initial quiet of the Israeli government and the American Jewish establishment when the Soviet-Arab alliance proposed the resolution, as well as Henry Kissinger's attitude toward his outspoken Harvard and cabinet colleague. Moynihan resigned two months after his big speech, convinced that Kissinger had encouraged the British ambassador to the UN, Ivor Richard, to denounce Moynihan's cowboy diplomacy as too "Wyatt Earp." Kissinger denied the charge, insisting he and Moynihan cooperated closely. Moynihan eventually accepted that Richard had acted independently but still felt undermined by Kissinger's maneuverings. "We are conducting foreign policy," Kissinger had grumbled behind Moynihan's back. "This is not a synagogue."

Moynihan felt cursed to live in what he called "the worst of times, the age of the totalitarian state." The murderous regimes of Adolf Hitler, Joseph

Stalin, and Mao Zedong disgusted him, while the cowardly callousness of their fellow travelers and appeasers on the Left alarmed him. Watching these world criminals and their enablers made Moynihan "a hard anti-Marxist, anti-totalitarian," as he wrote to Richard Nixon. Moynihan worried about a generalized "failure of nerve" among America's "interconnected elites." He mourned: "Like New York City bonds, American promises to pay in the assorted coinage of international relations are said to have lost their 'A' rating." During his first staff briefing at the US mission to the UN, he warned that democracy was losing, catastrophe was looming.

Moynihan considered the singling out of Zionism, meaning Jewish nationalism, as the one illegitimate form of nationalism in a world using nationalism as its organizing rationale, an "insult to his intelligence," the writer Elie Wiesel recalls, an affront to his seriousness and the UN's. In combating Resolution 3379, Moynihan fought "a tangle of pathology" in America and the world, just as he had diagnosed a "tangle of pathology" in America's ghettoes in the 1960s. In characterizing the UN, he would quote James Joyce, invoke *Alice in Wonderland*, and, most frequently, channel George Orwell, viewing the UN as a postmodern dystopia that, to describe, required the literary skills of a Thomas Pynchon or a Kurt Vonnegut—two mid-1970s superstars.

Moynihan was defying two groups of domestic opponents. The first he usually called "liberals," but we might call "adversarials," because even those who were no longer that political absorbed the New Left compulsion to self-criticize. They reflected American elites' post-1960s skepticism about America itself. To Moynihan, those launching this "neototalitarian assault" on "liberal dissenters" such as himself included spoiled students, hypercritical reporters, hypocritical professors, and appeasing diplomats. Many of these internal critics "believe that our assailants are motivated by what is wrong about us," Moynihan thundered. "*They* are wrong. We are assailed because of what is right about us. We are assailed because we are a democracy."

These adversarials enabled an angrier group whom Moynihan called the "totalitarian Left" or the "authoritarian Left." His friend Norman Podhoretz called them "anti-Americans." Encouraged by Frantz Fanon and other postcolonial, postmodern, Marxist ideologues, hard-Left radicals indulged Third World prerogatives, even justifying terrorism and other violence. Moynihan was also fighting European leftists, Soviet propagandists, Arab anti-Semites, and Third World dictators whose anti-Zionism and anti-Americanism intermingled.

A proud New Deal and Great Society liberal, Moynihan hoped to save liberalism from the authoritarian Left. But the ugly political civil wars he witnessed as a student in City College of the 1940s, followed by the tumult of the 1960s, made him a "liberal antiradical," in the words of Dr. Tevi Troy. He felt betrayed by what his assistant Suzanne Weaver Garment would call, "them, *them*," his own camp's extremists. He resented how those he saw as self-hating Westerners undermined liberalism and distorted the international legal climate, exaggerating democracies' imperfections while excusing Third World and Communist sins. In his notebook he scribbled: "Zionism issue is attempt to induce guilt, as is colonialism generally."

By 1975 the New Left had started betraying its defining ideals, especially regarding human rights. Traditional liberalism spread enlightenment by operating consistently, rationally, fairly. The totalitarian post-sixties leftism worshiped the new god of identity, valorizing racial and colonial victimhood as proof of virtue. Who you were determined the justice you deserved. The hard Left became reactionary, often choosing positions to oppose the United States or Israel. Democracy seemed embattled, autocracy empowered: "There will be more campaigns. They will not abate." Moynihan warned, "for it is sensed in the world that democracy is in trouble. There is blood in the water and the sharks grow frenzied."

Throughout the late 1960s and early 1970s anti-Zionism and anti-Americanism increasingly overlapped, not just in the UN but throughout Europe and the Third World. In the General Assembly in November 1975, the PLO's Farouk Kaddoumi led delegates in ritualistically slamming "the organic and total link between Washington's policy and that of Tel Aviv." Both hatreds were exported to the Third World and imported by American radicals.

Particular incidents inflamed the anti-Israel and anti-American rhetoric, ranging from Israel's war with the PLO in Lebanon in 1982 to the two Palestinian upheavals of the late 1980s and the early 2000s to America's Iraq invasion in 2003. Yet the spread of the Zionism-racism critique in the universities and among radicals during the Oslo peace-processing in the 1990s reveals that such bigotry transcends current events. This baseline contempt was constant, frequently disproportionate, and occasionally lethal—especially during the wave of suicide bombings in Israel that began in September 2000 and on September 11, 2001, in the United States. In exploring 9/11's origins, historians should more carefully examine Resolution 3379 as an early warning of the growth of anti-Americanism and Western self-hatred.

Moynihan wanted to end this era of American—and Western—breast-beating. He believed that "this is a society worth defending," in the phrase Suzanne Weaver Garment coined for his 1976 senatorial campaign. He embodied a traditional ideal of civil courage that Betty Friedan and other feminists who fought anti-Zionism embraced too. "You sound like the first real American that we have heard in years," a couple from Houston wrote to Moynihan. "You make us feel proud once again." In forging an early response to America's loss in Vietnam, Moynihan had a critical early role in a national recovery process and quest for understanding that nearly four decades later remains incomplete.

The assault on Israel damaged the prospects for peace. Part of Resolution 3379's toxic quality was to attack Israel's honor, a "crucial topic modern moral philosophy has neglected," as the Princeton philosopher Kwame Anthony Appiah teaches. Accusations of dishonor demonize and demoralize, making it difficult to compromise. In passing the resolution, the UN inflamed extremists from both sides. In 1980 the General Assembly's temporary president, Salim Ahmed Salim of Tanzania, would insist that there was "no basis for compromise on the inhuman policies of apartheid in South Africa," or with Israel.

As Moynihan predicted, selective condemnation of Israel tainted the entire human rights revolution. Historians now appreciate the Soviet, American, and European signing of the Helsinki Accords in August 1975, midway between Saigon's fall and the Zionism-racism fight that year, as a turning point in the world's developing sensitivity to human rights. Over the next decade and a half, the Soviet Union's failure to fulfill the human rights pledges it made unthinkingly at Helsinki made it look like an Evil Empire, hastening its collapse. Yet, just as this governmental and nongovernmental human rights infrastructure became broadly accepted, the UN politicized once-universal standards. Communists and anti-colonialists valued their collective agendas over individual rights. Dictators learned to accuse Israel of human rights abuses in international forums even while committing worse abuses against their own citizens. This ritualized hypocrisy demeaned the human rights community and the UN. "There are those of us who have not forsaken these older words" of human rights and democratic ideals, "still so new to the world," Moynihan told the General

Assembly on November 10, 1975, "Not forsaken them now, not here, not anywhere, not ever."

Although Moynihan was not much of a churchgoer, he still worshiped at the shrine of John Kennedy's activist Democratic liberal Irish Catholicism. Moynihan's great, deeply American faith in human rights became even more zealous thanks to Pope John XXIII's April 1963 peace on earth encyclical, *Pacem in Terris*, which placed human rights at the heart of world politics. In embracing Israel through the medium of human rights, Moynihan was not just fulfilling a duty to which he was religiously devoted; he was providing a platform for Christians to move beyond their anti-Semitic past by supporting Israel and Zionism.

The UN's human rights hypocrisy violated America's civil religion and emergent Judeo-Christian ethic. Alan Dershowitz recalls that in 1975, "while the UN is debating 'Zionism is racism', three million Cambodians are being murdered. The Left is saying 'nothing bad is happening in Cambodia,'" while the UN ignored the start of a genocide. This moral blindness, Dershowitz contends, "transformed the United Nations from an institution that even plausibly could be concerned about human rights to a facilitator of human wrongs, and an attacker of human rights."

Suddenly, anti-Semites found welcome homes on the Left. Singling out Israel for disproportionate, demonizing criticism echoed traditional attacks on Jews. In 1984, the Iranian delegate Said Rajaie-Khorassini predicted that the "final solution of the problem of the Middle East" would be to replace Israel with a Palestinian state. Israel's UN Ambassador at the time, Benjamin Netanyahu, observed, "No one in the hall batted an eyelash," despite the Hitlerian echo. The *New Republic's* James Kirchik, analyzing "the delusion, paranoia, and cynicism of the Jewish state's most earnest detractors" in 2011 would lament, for "an increasingly large swath of the international left, there really is no good Israel can do, short of disappear."

"There will be time enough to contemplate the harm this act will have done the United Nations," Moynihan said after the resolution passed. "Historians will do that for us, and it is sufficient for the moment only to note one foreboding fact"—he started shaking his finger—"a great evil has been loosed upon the world." This book is a historian's attempt to understand the 1970s—and today—by focusing on this dramatic moment and exploring what it "loosed upon the world."

Moynihan resented the many entreaties he received to "tone down" his approach. "What is this word toning down; when you are faced with an outright lie about the United States and we go in and say this is not true. Now, how do you tone that down? Do you say it is only half untrue?" he asked. "What kind of people are we? What kind of people do they think we are? They know it's not true. They want to know how much of this stuff they can make us eat, you know."

One conundrum fascinated Moynihan, as both academic and statesman: whether individuals shape history or history's tide overwhelms individuals. Moynihan had long hoped "to affect history," his friend Leonard Garment recalled. In his initial charge to his US mission colleagues, Moynihan warned that "the danger" of the moment was "compounded" by the lack of awareness to the threat. Nevertheless, he said "be of good cheer," for "it has fallen to you to play an important role in the life of your country." Moynihan relished the role, part Paul Revere alerting the citizenry, part Winston Churchill fighting totalitarianism with bombast not bombs. By defending Israel, America, and the West, by refuting what his friend Israel's ambassador to the UN Chaim Herzog called this new "dangerous anti-Semitic idiom," Daniel Patrick Moynihan made an impact and should be remembered for it, even as the forces he opposed persist.

FROM "WE THE PEOPLES OF THE UNITED NATIONS" TO "THE UNITED STATES IN OPPOSITION"

The United States goes into opposition. This is our
circumstance. We are a minority. We are outvoted.
—DANIEL PATRICK MOYNIHAN, *COMMENTARY*, MARCH 1975

On Friday, October 17, 1975, at its 2,134th meeting, the United Nations' Social Humanitarian and Cultural Committee, also known as the "Third Committee," debated Draft Resolution A/C.3/L2159. Leonard Garment, the US representative to the United Nations Human Rights Commission, addressed the committee. For weeks already, Garment and colleagues in the US mission had been researching what lay behind the resolution—the UN's fight against racism, the growing tendency to demonize Israel, and the ways in which Arab diplomats were throwing their new oil money around, intimidating poorer countries that might have considered opposing the resolution or abstaining. Now, Garment warned his colleagues that this "obscene act" would place "the work of the United Nations in jeopardy."

This was one of Garment's—and Ambassador Daniel Patrick Moynihan's—signal contributions to the debate. They argued that by passing the resolution the UN risked devaluing the currency of human rights. Since World War II, through its Universal Declaration of Human Rights, the Convention on the Prevention and Punishment of the Crime of Genocide, and its moral authority, the United Nations had advocated "equal and inalienable rights" for all. Now, just months after the Soviet Union, the United States, and thirty-three other countries signed the Helsinki Accords that ultimately would help spread freedom worldwide, the language of human rights was being politicized and demeaned in New York.

Finally, shortly after Garment's speech, Israel's ambassador to the United Nations, the elegant, Irish-born, future president of Israel, Chaim Herzog, rose to speak. "Mr. Chairman," he began, with his birthplace's upbeat lilt in his voice somehow amplifying his anger, "we have listened to the most unbelievable nonsense on the subject of Zionism from countries who are the archetypes of racists." Herzog deemed this "a sad day for the United Nations," declaring that "we, the Jewish people will not forget. We shall not forget those who spoke up for decency and civilization." Then, finishing by shouting his words, Herzog repeated: "We shall not forget those who voted to attack our religion and our faith. We shall never forget."

The room momentarily fell silent. The results from the vote emerged: 70 in favor of advancing the resolution to the General Assembly, 28 against, 27 abstaining. "A long, mocking applause broke out," Moynihan recalled. "The Israeli delegation, clearly on instructions, showed not the least emotion."

The tall, red-faced, bearish American ambassador straightened his tie and lumbered across the room, looming over his Israeli colleague. Moynihan embraced Herzog and loudly muttered: "Fuck 'em!"

Thirty years earlier, those Americans who founded the UN would never have imagined an American ambassador could utter such a condemnation. On April 25, 1945—five days before Adolf Hitler committed suicide in Berlin—delegates met in San Francisco to establish the United Nations Organization. They came from fifty nations representing close to 80 percent of the world's population. The Second World War persisted. Europe was in ruins. Americans—and their allies—were mourning President Franklin D. Roosevelt's recent death, on April 12.

Nevertheless, the 850 delegates, aided by 2,600 staffers, and watched by more than 2,500 press, radio, and newsreel reporters, were optimistic. The United Nations would be one of the few happy outcomes of the great and terrible war. The phrase "United Nations" had first entered common parlance in early 1942, referring to twenty-six nations combating the Axis powers together. Now, three years later, these and other nations were establishing the United Nations Organization to build peace. Just as Americans were learning the full extent of the Nazi horrors, and months before Americans themselves would drop the first two atomic bombs, the founding of the UNO—as it was known then—restored some faith in humanity.

Roosevelt had watched his mentor President Woodrow Wilson flounder in establishing the League of Nations after World War I, losing political support while spawning an impotent organization. Roosevelt wanted to avoid Wilson's mistakes. His United Nations was less representative, more muscular, and much more popular with Americans.

His passing infused the UN with the aura of presidential martyrdom, Roosevelt having seemingly worked himself to death for the cause. His UN address, which he was still drafting when he died, envisioned "peace; more than an end of this war—an end to the beginning of all wars." Carrying the torch, guaranteeing the UN's goodness and popularity, would be the newly widowed First Lady, Eleanor Roosevelt.

The delegates worked hard for the next two months, drafting a charter and defining new institutions: the Security Council, the General Assembly, the International Court of Justice. Not everything was going smoothly. Smaller nations opposed the power of the "Big Five" to veto decisions in the Security Council. For months already, US intelligence agencies had been intercepting diplomatic cables telegraphing resentment. Typically, one Turkish diplomatic communication in March 1945 warned that "the small states are inevitably going to be reduced to the status of satellites of the great." Nevertheless, the convening powers—the United States, the Soviet Union, China, Great Britain, and France—insisted. These countries would enjoy the right to exercise a veto in the Security Council, while ten other countries would serve with them temporarily on a rotating basis. By contrast, in the weaker General Assembly, every country had one equal vote.

Time magazine estimated that the final charter contained only a quarter of what the Big Powers initially proposed after meeting earlier in the spring at Dumbarton Oaks in Washington, DC. "That 25 percent was still the backbone of the charter and of the new United Nations organization," but the message was clear. This organization would require give and take.

On June 25, the delegates filed into San Francisco's Opera House for their final session. Lord Halifax—Edward Frederick Lindley Wood, 1st Earl of

Halifax—the British ambassador presiding in rotation, told the delegates as they voted on the charter: "This issue upon which we are about to vote, is as important as any we shall ever vote in our lifetime."

The preamble to the UN charter, signed the next day, echoed America's own Constitution, while rhapsodizing about the future. "We the peoples of the United Nations," the nations proclaimed, were determined "to save succeeding generations from the scourge of war...to reaffirm faith in fundamental human rights...to establish conditions under which justice and respect for the obligations arising from treaties and other sources of international law can be maintained, and to promote social progress and better standards of life in larger freedom."

It was a remarkable achievement. Out of the ashes of the most brutal war in history, its embers still smoldering, wounds still healing, and its graves still fresh, the victors constructed an international mechanism with peace as its aim and human rights for all at its heart. It was an injection of the liberal democratic idealism generated by the American Revolution into the international bloodstream.

Most Americans were ecstatic, expecting the United Nations to be redemptive. Barbara Hartman née Willner, a twelve-year-old girl attending PS 64 in East New York in 1945, remembers the "messianic" excitement generated by the UN's founding. Her teachers assumed there would be no war anymore. "[T]here is now a reasonable chance that this is the last war of this sort," the *New York Times* editorialized on June 17, five weeks after Nazi Germany surrendered and barely two months before Japan followed. "Men are dying for something better than glory. They are dying for a just peace." Five weeks later, on July 24, the paper's editors declared the UN's aim: "TO STOP A THIRD WORLD WAR." By July 1946, 54 percent of America's once-isolationist population supported strengthening the UN to make it "a world government with power to control the armed forces of all the nations, including the US." One year later, 91 percent of Americans surveyed considered it "very important" or "fairly important" to "try to make the United Nations a success." Some skeptics, such as the diplomat and future secretary of state Dean Acheson, considered these aspirations "unrealistic." Still, he understood that Americans had long dreamed of "universal law and internationally enforced peace."

America's Jews, beginning to realize how many millions of their people Adolf Hitler's Nazis had slaughtered, were particularly thrilled—and hopeful. Most trusted that in the future, this "battlefield of ideas," as Pittsburgh's *Jewish Criterion* put it, would replace history's more brutal combat zones as the world's arena for resolving conflicts. Indeed, from its birth, the UN followed the dictum "Never Again," long before it became a popular phrase, let alone a cliché. In early January 1946, Secretary of State James F. Byrnes, addressing the General Assembly, attributed the UN's founding to the resolve "to bind together in peace the free nations of the world so that never again would they find themselves isolated in the face of tyranny and aggression." That year, the American Jewish leader Rabbi Stephen S. Wise proclaimed at a pro-Zionist rally that the "least that Christian civilization can do for us now in memory of our martyred dead is to say 'never again shall there be a Hitler or Mussolini.'" A quarter of a century later, the militant Jewish Defense League—founded by Rabbi Meir Kahane in 1968—embraced the slogan, whose popularity soon transcended that of the organization itself.

The UN was therefore to be the architect of a post-Holocaust world, guaranteeing that never again would countries charge down the path of mass genocide. This collective promise to Nazism's victims, and especially to the devastated Jewish people, was expressed most dramatically in November 1947 when the UN recognized the need for a Jewish state in Palestine. "It is the greatest thing that has happened to the Jewish people in 1900 years," Sam Surkis, a Jewish leader in Los Angeles, would rejoice after the vote.

In 1947 most Jews viewed their national narrative through four different lenses. Their most sweeping telescopic perspective looked back more than three thousand years to the patriarch Abraham who started the Jewish story by founding the Jewish nation with a tie to the land of Israel. Since then, the Jews had worshiped the same god, spoken the same language, developed a common culture, and remained bound to the same land, making them "the original aboriginal people," as McGill University law professor Irwin Cotler today calls them. Jews also remembered 70 CE, nearly 1,900 years earlier, as a traumatic turning point in their history, when the Romans destroyed the Second Temple and the millennia of exile and powerlessness began, even though a remnant always remained in the land of Israel.

Counting recent history in decades rather than centuries or millennia, the modern push to redeem Palestine began in the late nineteenth century, when Zionism emerged as the Jewish movement of national liberation, amid other romantic nationalist movements, East and West. As Moynihan would explain, European nationalism became "an exercise in matching a 'people' with a state." Most immediately, in 1947 Jews were reeling from a miserable eleven years in Europe and Palestine. Arab riots in Palestine from 1936 to 1939 triggered British limits on immigration there, just as Hitler's war against the Jews turned deadly. Millions of Jews died because they had nowhere to go. No country welcomed an influx of Jews, including Palestine, despite being the national Jewish homeland and an incipient Jewish state thirsting for more immigrants.

The British White Paper of 1939 restricting Jewish immigration to Palestine as well as land sales to Jews demoralized the Palestinian Jews. Palestine's chief rabbi, Isaac Ha-Levi Herzog, denounced these restrictions as "a sin against the spirit of God and the soul of man" in a letter to the London Sunday *Times*. Protesting in front of the Yeshurun synagogue on Jerusalem's King George Street, the learned, dignified, Sorbonne-educated, top-hatted rabbi tore up a copy of the White Paper.

The Arab riots from 1936 to 1939 reinforced the sobering realization for Jews that control over their homeland was contested. There were voices on both sides seeking coexistence, but fiery Arab leaders, especially the grand mufti of Jerusalem, Haj Amin el Husseini, sabotaged any compromise. Fueled by a Hitlerite anti-Semitism, tapping Islam's radical potential, the mufti expected to win. "We shall be fighting on our own ground and shall be supported not only by 70,000,000 Arabs around us, but also by 400,000,000 Muslims," he proclaimed. Husseini told British officials in September 1947, "We do not fear the Jews.... They will eventually crumble into nothing."

An irony both antagonists often ignored was that in this national conflict, the Arab response to Zionism sharpened Palestinian Jews' Zionist identity, just as the Zionists' advance in Palestine sharpened Palestinian Arabs' national identity. At the time, both Jews and Arabs in Palestine called themselves "Palestinian." Palestinian nationalism also emerged, as the Columbia University professor Rashid Khalidi explains, from the "universal process [that] was unfolding in the Middle East during this period, involving an increasing identification with the new states created by the post–World War I partitions," of which the British Mandate over Palestine was one.

After the war, growing Arab-Jewish enmity prompted even the Soviets and Americans to cooperate, despite the emerging Cold War. Both superpowers supported General Assembly Resolution 181, the UN plan to end the British mandate by dividing the area into a Jewish state and an Arab state, while internationalizing Jerusalem. "[I]f these two people that inhabit Palestine, both of which have deeply rooted historical ties with the land, cannot live together within the boundaries of a single State, there is no alternative but to create, in place of one country, two States—an Arab and a Jewish one," the Soviet Ambassador to the UN, Andrei Gromyko, explained during the Partition debate on November 26, 1947. Rejecting Arab complaints, he insisted "the decision to partition Palestine is in keeping with the high principles and aims of the United Nations. It is in keeping with the principle of the national self-determination of people." Reflecting the logic that most compelled the vote of 33 to 13 in favor of partition, with 10 abstentions, Gromyko said: "the Jewish people has been closely linked with Palestine for a considerable period in history" and that "the Jews, as a people, have suffered more than any other people."

The dramatic vote—broadcast on radio from the UN's temporary headquarters on the World's Fair grounds in Flushing Meadows' Corona Park in Queens, New York, built in 1939—reflected the UN's political power and moral standing. Moshe Shertok, the head of the political section of the Jewish Agency, the Palestinian Jews' government-in-formation, said: "My first feeling is that not only has our cause triumphed at Flushing Meadows, but the UN has triumphed through our cause. This is the first time that the UN and the civilized world have decided to create a new state."

The partition question vexed Palestine's Jewish leaders. In July 1937 Lord Peel's royal commission proposed dividing Palestine, using what the report called the "peculiarly English proverb" that "Half a loaf is better than no bread." Ten years later, the mass murder of six million Jews, the yearning for a Jewish state, a utopian faith in compromise balanced by a pragmatic sense that borders could be redrawn, led the Jewish Agency to approve the plan, despite the sacrifices.

The vote triggered mass dancing in the streets of Jerusalem and Tel Aviv, as well as in Jewish neighborhoods worldwide, reflecting the great faith Jews, Americans, and many in the postwar world had in the UN's mediating ability. The American Zionist leader Rabbi Abba Hillel Silver celebrated this "turning point in Jewish history" as "an impressive reaffirmation of the just claim of the Jewish people to rebuild its national life in its ancestral home." The decision's wisdom validated the new organization. Silver predicted: "This noble decision to re-establish and restore the Jewish people to its rightful place in the family of nations will redound to the everlasting credit of the United Nations."

The Palestinian Arab leadership rejected the compromise, as did most of the Arab world, which condemned the UN along with the Jews of Palestine. "Today's resolution destroys the Charter and all previous covenants," said Emir Feisal al-Saud of Saudi Arabia. Faris el-Khouri of Syria, responding to many Arabs who claimed the organization's move was self-destructive, said "No," the UN had "not died." It was "Murdered."

Nevertheless, if there was a postwar covenant between the Jewish people and the world, it was sealed November 29, 1947, the day the UN approved the Palestine partition plan. Many Americans looked with pride at their creation, feeling especially protective in the coming years as the UN's thirty-nine-story, blue-green modernist headquarters on the East River became an icon of postwar New York, postwar liberalism, and the benign postwar Pax Americana. The resulting state of Israel enjoyed its special status as a state voted into being by the UN, not simply accepted as a member in 1949. The mostly secular Jews who founded Israel believed that their country and this new world parliament could help solve global problems. In so many ways, in those days, Zionism was UNism—a belief in universal, liberal, democratic, communal ideals redeeming the world through the particularist political entity of the enlightened nation-state. The strong bond between the UN and Israel would not last, nor would Americans' faith in their extraordinary creation.

In crushing Nazi Germany and totalitarian Japan, the United States created an intoxicating foreign policy brew mixing idealism and power. The Convention on the Prevention and Punishment of the Crime of Genocide and the Universal Declaration of Human Rights, both adopted by the General Assembly on two days back-to-back in December 1948, established a language and a legal structure for advancing human rights. UN peacekeepers, with their distinctive blue helmets, were famous for calming the world's most volatile flashpoints, patrolling in the Sinai, Cyprus, Kashmir, separating Arabs from Israelis, Turks from Greeks, Indians from Pakistanis.

The United Nations quickly developed a reputation for do-gooding worldwide. The UN was also the most effective international social service agency the world had ever seen, pushing economic reform, spreading literacy, fighting parasitic diseases, pressing for universal immunization, ultimately halving child mortality rates while reducing birthrates. By 1975 the

World Health Organization would be midway through a thirteen-year mission that would virtually eradicate smallpox.

Many Americans took pride in these accomplishments, knowing that visionary American leaders shaped the institution while generous American taxpayers bankrolled it. Throughout the 1950s and 1960s, Americans' faith in the UN grew. Americans polled in 1946 were split, with many doubting the UN's actual accomplishments "to date" despite their hopes. By the mid-1950s, three-quarters of those polled praised the UN's progress.

The Korean War increased the UN's popularity among Americans. Even though they lost confidence in 1951 when the Chinese counterattacked, most Americans enthusiastically supported the initial cooperation between United States and UN forces in June 1950, as well as the signing of a Korean armistice agreement in 1953.

Actually, the great confluence of American and UN goals during the Korean War was a fluke. In what became a legendary miscalculation, the Soviet Union had been protesting the UN's refusal to seat the Chinese delegate for six months prior to the North Korean invasion of South Korea. As a result, on June 25, 1950, there were no Soviet delegates to veto the Security Council Resolution adopted 9 to 0, uniting the American and UN forces in a joint military effort.

Chastened, the Soviets learned to manipulate the UN rather than boycott it. Soviet diplomacy focused on wooing Third World delegates, building a front against the Western, imperialist powers. Following World War II, dozens of new nation states came into existence, many forged in revolution against colonialist powers. The organization expanded from the original 51 members in 1945, to 99 members by 1960, to 142 members by 1975. Continuing their rebellion—if only diplomatically and rhetorically—gave developing countries an identity and the Soviets an opportunity, in the seemingly perennial conflict with the United States and its allies: the Cold War.

Support for the UN jumped again and remained consistently high for most of the decade after November 1956, when the UN Emergency Forces (UNEF) created a buffer zone between Israeli and Egyptian troops after the Suez crisis. Throughout this period, from 1947 through 1970, whenever asked, approximately nine out of ten Americans polled said it was important that the UN succeed.

By getting bogged down in the Vietnam War in the 1960s, the United States lost its standing as champion to this developing "Third World." The turnaround from the Peace Corps–style idealism greeting John Kennedy's administration to the Vietnam-generated cynicism toward Lyndon Johnson's administration, beginning in 1966 and building, was staggering, domestically and internationally. Rather than seeing the United States of America as their friend and role model, leaders in these new postcolonial states viewed America as the enemy.

Ironically, idealistic Americans helped the world sour on American idealism. What the liberal literature critic Lionel Trilling called the "adversary culture," just then emerging in the media and the New Left, fashioned a devastating critique of the American character, placing many in permanent opposition to their country. Just as the United States was demonstrating tremendous ability to change, many of America's most privileged young people deemed their country unredeemable. The Yippie leader Jerry Rubin claimed that the iconic Argentine revolutionary leader Che Guevara told a delegation of American radicals visiting Cuba in 1964: "You North Amerikans are very lucky"—spelling America with a "k" was a Rubinesque twist. "You live in the middle of the beast. You are fighting the most important fight of all, in the center of the battle."

Extremists in the civil rights movement and the anti-Vietnam war movement reinforced each other, spawning a hard-Left ideology that denounced the West, idealized the Third World, and alternated between supporting Communism or simply ignoring Soviet and Chinese oppression. By July 1967 Stokely Carmichael was integrating America's Black Power movement into the worldwide struggle against "white Western imperialist society."

As their anger against the system spiraled, activists became radicalized. Recoiling from America's napalming in Vietnam, radicals viewed the black ghettos as oppressed domestic colonies, linked in a chain of imperialist oppression from Harlem and Watts to Hanoi and Hai Phong. When Columbia University students protested that a new gymnasium being built in Morningside Park disrespected their neighbors, one black student, William Sales, saw just "one oppressor—in the White House, in [Columbia's] Low Library, in Albany, New York. You strike a blow at the gym, you strike a blow for the Vietnamese people. You strike a blow at Low Library, you strike a blow for the freedom fighters in Angola, Mozambique, Portuguese Guinea, Zimbabwe, South Africa."

The anger against Western racism proved politically potent—and distort-ing. Many activists in the West and the developing world made race the great dividing line. Whites were considered to be inherently privileged, powerful, oppressive, and usually in the wrong when confronting minorities who were considered marginalized, powerless, oppressed, and virtuous. The fights against racism, colonialism, and imperialism were packaged together, even if that simplified some conflicts. At the UN and other flashpoints worldwide, Western powers were often deemed to be automatically guilty.

The developing countries caucused as the "Group of 77" that would grow by 2011 to encompass 132 members, when the Micronesian Republic of Nauru joined. Going far beyond Cold War politics, most of the Group of 77 also belonged to the Non-Aligned Movement, even though they were increasingly hostile to the United States and influenced by the Soviet Union through its Cuban satellite. These countries rallied around what their founding document in June 1964 called "the basic problems of development," meaning the countries still felt exploited, humiliated, and dependent on the Western economies.

At the UN, America's increasing reliance on its Security Council veto symbolized its turnaround from champion to target. For the first quarter-century of the UN's existence, until March 1970, the United States had never vetoed any Security Council decisions. But the Soviets did, frequently. Vetoing 79 initiatives in the first ten years of the UN's existence, Andrei Gromyko and his successors as UN representatives were nicknamed "Mr. Nyet." After 1970 the records reversed. The Americans started vetoing and the Soviets no longer needed to.

Even before Resolution 3379, the UN power balance had shifted. In 1971 the UN expelled Taiwan and gave the People's Republic of China full mem-bership, overcoming decades of American support for the Chinese national-ists controlling the island of Formosa. Encouraged by the Soviets and emboldened by their successful oil embargo in the West, Arab states began bashing Israel in UN forums and boosting the Palestine Liberation Organization from an outlaw terrorist organization to the sole legitimate representative of the Palestinian people. Particularly after the Non-Aligned Movement's Algiers Summit in September 1973, attacking Israel as racist became a way of uniting the Communist bloc, the Arab countries, and sub-Saharan Africa. *Time* magazine and other mainstream media sources described a desultory "War of Words" on Manhattan's East Side, with UN organs "repeating" one "familiar, futile ritual" condemnation after another.

When on May Day, 1974, the General Assembly passed its Declaration on the Establishment of a New International Economic Order, the UN formally targeted the powers that had founded the organization. The declaration celebrated the great achievement of colonial liberation while condemning "the remaining vestiges of alien and colonial domination, foreign occupation, racial discrimination, apartheid, and neocolonialism." With developing countries constituting 70 percent of the world's population but earning only 30 percent of the world's income, the world's economic and political structures had to change. The New Economic Order entailed restricting multinational corporations while indulging sovereign states, no matter what economic or political system they adopted.

The UN had undergone a rhetorical transplant. In 1945 the UN Charter "reaffirm[ed] faith in fundamental human rights, in the dignity and worth of the human person, in the equal rights of men and women and of nations large and small," seeking justice for all. Three decades later, the rhetoric was of neocolonialism and racial discrimination, of developing countries pitted against developed countries and multinationals. The language shifted from individual rights to national grievances, from aspirational to confrontational, from universal to categorical, from echoing the Declaration of Independence and the Constitution to sounding like a Soviet tract or a guerilla communiqué.

Many of the Americans most hopeful about the UN were increasingly disillusioned. John Scali recalled believing "deeply in the United Nations since 1945 when, as a young reporter just returned from the war, I observed the birth of this organization." Scali became an ABC-TV news correspondent in the days when network news was king. In 1962, a KGB operative in Washington approached him to convey to his State Department contacts the face-saving agreement that ultimately ended the Cuban Missile Crisis. In 1973 Scali succeeded George H. W. Bush as America's ambassador to the United Nations.

Once established, Scali increasingly felt compelled to warn his fellow delegates. On December 6, 1974, after watching mounting popular and congressional anger at such moves as the banning of South Africa, limiting Israel to one speech during a debate about Palestinians, and welcoming Yasir Arafat to the General Assembly, Scali warned against seeking "paper triumphs" that reflect the "tyranny of the majority"—echoing a phrase President Ford had used. Scali still believed in trying "to meld and reflect the views of all" the nations rather than the bloc warfare emerging. "The only victories with meaning are those which are victories for us all," he proclaimed, warning against rhetorical posturing and "one-sided, unrealistic resolutions that cannot be implemented"—and would make the UN irrelevant.

Scali's uncharacteristic rebuke of his colleagues thrilled Westerners, and unnerved the Third World. The *New York Times* reprinted his speech while even the Swedish representative Olof Rydbeck echoed Scali's "frustration and disenchantment." Publicly, Third World delegates scoffed, as the Jordanian delegate Sherif Abdul Hamid Sharaf did, that "the old power elite," having lost its majority, was now resisting progress by "downgrading" the United Nations. Privately, reporters noted that worried delegates cabled back home "long excerpts" of the dissenting delegates' addresses.

Scali was right. Americans were forsaking the UN. Although in 1954, 58 percent of Americans approved of the UN's performance, and in 1967, 50 percent remained satisfied, by August 1970 the figured dipped to 44 percent. Pollsters recorded a dramatic reversal in American public opinion in October 1971 when barely a third of the American people surveyed—35 percent—approved of the UN while 43 percent did not. The disappointment was intense because 87 percent in August 1970 agreed we should "try to make the United Nations a success." Gallup would not again record a majority pleased with the UN until October 1990, when 54 percent of Americans surveyed gave the UN high marks amid George H. W. Bush's efforts to develop an international coalition against Saddam Hussein after Iraq invaded Kuwait.

This disillusionment with the UN, though driven by its transformation, played into Americans' broader crisis of confidence. By 1975, thirty years after the UN's founding, the situation for the UN—and the United States—looked grimmer than it had in 1945. The moral clarity backed by superpower muscle America enjoyed when World War II ended vanished. America's world standing was slipping—as was the UN's standing in America. America seemed on the verge of a collective meltdown with the UN increasingly a forum for bashing America.

President Nixon launched his second administration in January 1973 feeling vindicated by his re-election landslide over George McGovern.

Partnering with the popular National Security Adviser, Henry Kissinger, Nixon was hailed as a foreign policy genius, having penetrated the Iron Curtain with his trips in 1972 to China and the Soviet Union. Kissinger became America's patron saint of foreign policy realism, eschewing the moral high ground to engage with America's adversaries. Now, Nixon and Kissinger could toast the recent ceasefire agreement with North Vietnam, their latest foreign policy triumph—or so they thought.

That August, Nixon promoted Kissinger to secretary of state. For a Jewish refugee from Nazi Germany, who had worked his way through Harvard, Kissinger's was an extraordinary achievement. At his swearing in, to which his Orthodox Jewish parents walked because it occurred on a Saturday, Kissinger exulted "there is no country in the world where it is conceivable that a man of my origin could be standing here."

By the time he had nominated Kissinger, however, Nixon was in crisis, humiliated after a summer of Senate hearings exposing White House chicanery in the Watergate scandal. Nixon frequently felt upstaged by his popular, megalomaniacal subordinate who was as egotistical as he was brilliant. Nixon would later admit that "the Watergate problem" compelled him to promote Kissinger. "Do you prefer to be called Mr. Secretary or Dr. Secretary," one reporter asked Kissinger shortly after his nomination. "I do not stand on protocol," Kissinger responded, feeling triumphal but acknowledging his reputation for self-puffery. "If you just call me Excellency, it will be okay."

As Nixon's administration imploded, Kissinger's standing rose. By December 1973 he was America's most admired man. Watching his sometime friend, sometime rival, dominate Washington, America's ambassador to India Daniel Patrick Moynihan marveled at Kissinger's unprecedented power. "The powers of the very Presidency have been accorded him: by desire; in order that the incumbent should *not* have them." Moynihan was always wary of Kissinger, whom he thought a thin-skinned egotist addicted to "secrecy and surprise." "If I am to function I shall do so as a courtier," Moynihan noted in his diary. The famously contrarian Moynihan, who enjoyed fencing with President Nixon, confessed "I should do this with extreme caution respecting the Secretary of State."

Less than a year after Kissinger's promotion, in August 1974, Nixon had resigned in disgrace, replaced by the kind, straightforward Gerald Ford, the first president in history not to have faced the national electorate. Ford first was appointed as vice president to replace Spiro Agnew. Ford avoided the competitive Kissinger-Nixon pathology. "Ford has just got to realize there are times when Henry has to be kicked in the nuts," Nixon would tell one staffer during the transition. "Because sometimes Henry starts to think he's president. But at other times you have to pet Henry and treat him like a child." Instead, White House counselor Robert Hartmann would recall that Ford recognized "Henry's vanity" and "compulsion to crow" as "part of this total ability to perform well. If he needed more reassurance than the rest of us, Ford gladly gave it."

While perhaps less fraught, the Ford-Kissinger partnership was less productive. By spring 1975, Kissinger was flailing as American foreign policy seemed to be failing. The most public fiasco at the time was in the Middle East. Following the October 1973 Yom Kippur War, Kissinger's indefatigable shuttle diplomacy had given him mythological "Super K" status. Hopscotching between Jerusalem, Cairo, and Damascus, Kissinger pieced together a ceasefire agreement.

Yet stopping the fighting and arranging a prisoner exchange was only the start. The war had not only increased American and Israeli interdependence, it strained the alliance. Baring teeth with the Soviet Union during the war had resulted in American forces shifting to a higher alert status, "Defcon Three," which made the Middle East, for the first time, a central, ongoing policy-making obsession for an American administration. Kissinger tried but failed to parlay the chaos of the war into a lasting peace. Israel refused to give up certain strategic assets gained in 1967 without "an overall settlement" or at least a non-belligerency pact, which Egypt rejected. Kissinger was furious, warning the Israelis "we're losing control," with the Palestinian issue gaining traction, the Arab world collaborating together, Egypt's moderate President Anwar Sadat undermined, and the Soviets preparing to "Step back onto the stage."

The Arab oil embargo following the 1973 war terrified Kissinger. As the price of oil quadrupled from $3 a barrel to $12 within a few months, inflation began and Exxon's chairman Ken Jamieson warned the secretary of state that the United States faced "the possible breakdown of the economy." In one of his first briefings to Ford, days after Nixon resigned, Kissinger warned: "The Middle East is the worst problem we face. The oil situation is the worst we face. We . . . can't afford another embargo. If we are faced with that, we may have to take some oil fields."

Kissinger also feared that the Europeans, Soviets, and Arabs, through the UN, would impose a Geneva conference on the Middle East. Such a multinational conference would isolate Israel, sideline the United States, and risk another war. Considering that the impasse concerned the strategic Giddi and Mitla passes in the Sinai desert, the president and secretary of state were dumbfounded that, as Kissinger said, the Israelis were "bringing the world to the edge of war for three kilometers in the Giddi and eight kilometers in the Mitla."

In March 1975, the Israeli foreign minister Yigal Allon, stalling, proposed a two-week break. Kissinger was "outraged at the Israelis," he informed the president. He accused them and America's Jewish community of strongarming the administration, of being "irresponsible," of fomenting anti-Semitism. In one of many Oval Office tantrums denouncing the Israelis as "fools," "common thugs," and "the basic cause of the trouble," he confessed, "This is terribly painful to me....I am Jewish. How can I want this? I have never seen such cold-blooded playing with the American national interest."

Kissinger's anger ran deep as a conflicted Jew, a proud American, and a driven perfectionist. When issues involving Israel crossed his desk, Kissinger felt contradictory tugs. He had built his career as the German intellectual, not the striving Jew. His status as a Nazi refugee and a US Army sergeant who helped denazify Germany during World War II made his Germanic manner proof of brilliance rather than a mark of Cain. In the Nixon White House, he had to endure the president's anti-Semitic rants, which included calling him a Jew-boy, and initially trying to bar all Jews including Kissinger from Middle East matters. Yet when he visited Israel, Kissinger had to endure the same contemptuous cries of Jew-boy from harsh critics there.

To the extent that he felt any ethnic solidarity, Kissinger felt Israel was acting foolishly and dangerously. At one point, he condemned Israel's leaders as "a sick bunch"; another time he called them "the world's worst shits," for some of their backstage maneuvering to mobilize members of Congress and influential journalists against him. Moreover, as an ambitious American leader, he resented this small country's disdain for his country's big picture needs, while brooding over his failure in this arena, when just months before he had been touted as the genius peacemaker, shuttling step-by-step toward the Middle East peace that eluded mere mortals.

As both courtier and careerist, Kissinger absorbed the anti-Semitism around him and encouraged it, to prove his independence from his "co-religionists." Mid-1970s America was far more welcoming to Jews than it had been thirty years earlier. Still, a waspish distaste lingered regarding Jews as foreign, as disloyal, even when they had Kissinger's government credentials or lacked his heavy accent and exotic résumé.

The Arab oil embargo convinced some Americans that US interests now clashed with Israel's needs and American Jews' desires. In October, 1974, the chairman of the Joint Chiefs of Staff, Air Force general George S. Brown, publicly speculated that another oil embargo might encourage Americans to "get tough-minded enough to set down the Jewish influence in this country and break that lobby." Brown attributed American support for Israel—and Jewish power—to "where the Jewish money is," saying, "They own, you know, the banks in this country, the newspapers." President Ford reprimanded his top general but retained him.

A month after the media exposed Brown's remarks, Kissinger echoed them while briefing the president aboard Air Force One. Speaking of American Jews, Kissinger said: "Their power in the United States derives from campaign financing. It is not easy to explain to the American people why we must oppose 115 million Arabs who possess all the world's oil, permanently, on behalf of a nation of 3 million."

Such toadying, while contagious, did not inoculate the supplicant against similar treatment. In December, Max Fisher, an American Jewish tycoon and power broker from Ford's home state of Michigan, would describe Israeli skittishness, mistrust, and feelings of isolation following Resolution 3379 by telling the president in the Oval Office: "you know how they are—like Henry is as a person. It is a national trait."

Ford lacked Nixon's crude anti-Semitism. Still, the president shared a subtle, generalized discomfort with "the Jews," along with the secretary of state's anger and desire to punish the Israelis, considering that, as Ford grumbled, "such a tiny people can raise so much havoc here." "The effect on our policy in the Middle East is devastating. The radicals are vindicated; Sadat is jeopardized," Kissinger advised the president in March, urging a freeze on relations with Israel: "Every Department should put Israeli activities at the bottom of the list."

Ford agreed. "Henry and I have spent more time on this than on any other foreign policy issue. We put my credibility on the line and it was a hell of a disappointment," he told Max Fisher. "You are a good friend," the president continued, "and I had to tell you on a personal basis that nothing has hit me so hard since I've been in this office." Trying to prove he was no anti-Semite, Ford exaggerated about both the emotional cost and the time investment, considering his tenure began with Betty Ford's mastectomy and his pardon of Nixon, the latter proving extremely unpopular.

Ford reminded his advisers that in Congress his record on Israel "was so close that I had a black reputation with the Arabs." He instructed his cabinet members that, in dealing with Israeli officials, "be business-like but arms-length and aloof." The president expected pushback. "I know they will hit us," Ford told Kissinger, "but I kind of enjoy a fight when I know I am right."

Desperation—and perhaps guilt—fed Kissinger's anger. "We are responsible in large part," he told the president, watching his hard-fought peace in Vietnam collapse that same spring. Weakness fed weakness. "No one thought the North Vietnamese would attack this year," Kissinger admitted. "They did it based on their assessment of American weakness"—which was now proving contagious. Kissinger wanted to blame Congress. But he understood what was happening—America looked weak. King Faisal of Saudi Arabia told him, Kissinger reported, "you have let Cambodia go, Vietnam, Portugal, Turkey—you will let Israel go also." Kissinger's rival, Secretary of Defense James Schlesinger, warned of Israel's "Vietnamization."

In March, as President Ford announced a formal "reassessment" of American policy toward Israel, the world situation deteriorated. What would turn out to be the final North Vietnamese offensive began, as the imperial city of Hue fell quickly on March 26. The American-backed government in Cambodia was also under attack, and soon doomed. A failed coup against Portugal's left-leaning government triggered fears of a pro-Soviet Marxist regime. In Angola, civil war raged. Turkey punished America for embargoing aid due to the Cypriot crisis by closing all American military installations except one air base. And one of Kissinger's greatest achievements, détente with the Soviet Union, was threatened by the political fight over the Jackson-Vanik amendment imposing human rights concerns about Soviet Jews and other oppressed minorities into the already strained Strategic Arms Limitation Talks, SALT.

Post-Vietnam and post-Watergate America was an unhappy place, with Americans questioning their government, culture, society, and themselves. The Watergate scandals had ended in Nixon's resignation. The Vietnam War triggered massive demonstrations accompanied by mass alienation. The economic mess included Arab embargo-induced oil shortages, growing inflation, and job stagnation. All made America's government look impotent. The relentless cascade of social criticism had Americans wondering whether theirs was "a sick society." And the culture became adversarial, shifting from peddling a soporific sentimentality to indulging a paralyzing cynicism.

In mid-October 1975, as the Zionism is racism resolution advanced in the UN, President Ford was busy explaining why he would not bail out New York City financially. Telescoping America's descent in the 1960s and 1970s into one unhappy metaphor, Ford's press secretary Ron Nessen compared America's flagship city "to a wayward daughter hooked on heroin," saying "You don't give her $100 a day to support her habit. You make her go cold turkey." The United Nations, once the inspiration to democracies, was turning on its founders, rapidly becoming the Third World dictators' debating society. Turtle Bay no longer symbolized American glory but reflected America's eclipse.

In such a climate, with America's collective psyche strained, moviegoers felt more drawn to *The Exorcist* and *The Godfather* than to Walt Disney or screwball comedies. Readers embraced the absurdist, postmodernist, "So it goes" sensibility of a Kurt Vonnegut. The top five television programs in 1974 also reflected these tensions: *All in the Family* pivoted on the generational divide; *Sanford and Son, Chico and the Man,* and *The Jeffersons* pivoted around racial and class divides; *M*A*S*H* pivoted on the Hawk versus Dove divide. Viewers watched a more diverse America but a more depressed and divided America. Rather than celebrating the opened doors of the civil rights movement, the greater freedoms from the youth revolt, these shows often mocked the broken dreams of an America gripped by malaise.

It was a time of long gas lines and a growing crime wave, of rising divorce rates and increasing drug use. "We'll be fighting in the streets, with our children at our feet, and the morals that they worship will be gone," The Who sang in one of the decade's defining songs. Yet, rather than welcoming revolution, hope degenerates into resignation, "Meet the new boss, same as the old boss." For that reason the songwriter Pete Townshend vowed, we "Won't Get Fooled Again."

As ambassador to India from 1973 to 1975, Moynihan certainly did not want to get fooled. After concentrating on domestic policy for more than a decade as an adviser in the John Kennedy, Lyndon Johnson, and Richard

Nixon administrations, Moynihan returned to his first academic love, international relations, when Nixon sent him to India. Moynihan's relations with his Indian hosts were sufficiently warm that he helped reorient American foreign policy away from America's tilt toward Pakistan. But his close look at India's role in the increasingly anti-American, non-aligned Third World movement dismayed him.

Transcending the Cold War's simplistic Americans versus Soviets, capitalism versus communism, democracy versus totalitarianism dualities, Moynihan decided the real culprit was British socialism. The post–World War II independence movements resulted in dozens of countries run by elites like India's prime minister Indira Gandhi who viewed the world through the parlor socialism that British universities had taught them, especially the London School of Economics. In the UN and elsewhere, Moynihan argued, they speak English not American.

British socialists viewed Western progress as exploitative—disdaining Western freedoms but most especially Western wealth. They imbued the ascending postcolonial leaders with a strong redistributionist bias, an impressive chip on their collective shoulders and demands for reparations. With an overarching narrative of liberation after colonial exploitation, their defining mission involved extracting concessions, politically, economically, and diplomatically from the West. And, coached by their British mentors, encouraged by their Soviet patrons, these new powers on the world scene had imbibed a particular anti-American bias.

As a result, Moynihan argued in the March 1975 issue of *Commentary* that the United States is in opposition—and must recognize that fact. Currently, he continued, Americans, like most Westerners, blithely hosted conferences at the UN and elsewhere that bashed them and their values. The United States had to defend the values of liberal democracy, free economy, and honest dialogue. "*The United States goes into opposition,*" Moynihan wrote. "This is our circumstance. We are a minority. We are outvoted. This is neither an unprecedented nor an intolerable situation. The question is what do we make of it? So far we have made little—nothing—of what is in fact an opportunity."

Moynihan knew the history of the UN and acknowledged that "Such a reversal of roles would be painful to American spokesmen," but he believed "it could be liberating also." Then, rejecting the conventional wisdom dominant both in the United States and throughout much of the world, Moynihan proclaimed: "It is past time we ceased to apologize for an imperfect democracy. Find its equal."

In pitching his foreign policy on proud, non–Cold War, but nevertheless ideological terms, Moynihan was repudiating Kissinger's worldview. Having written his Harvard doctoral dissertation on the nineteenth-century Austrian Prince Metternich and the balance of power, Kissinger sought to teach America foreign policy realism. In classic realpolitik fashion, he believed that countries have no friends, only interests. Moynihan was suggesting that America could only find salvation by remembering core democratic values and expressing them in foreign policy as well as domestic policy.

Moynihan soon had an opportunity to try translating his vision into policy. His *Commentary* article attracted attention in the White House, and within months he was off to New York, to represent the United States at the United Nations. There, he would discover that his analysis was partially correct. Yes, the United States was now outnumbered. Yes, the United States had to go on the offensive. Yes, the so-called Third Worlders did have a coherent worldview rooted in a British-honed—and often British-induced—sense of injury. But Moynihan's analysis missed a central characteristic of the new ideology. It was not just a class war and a regional war, it was a race war. Considering his experiences in Washington before he became a diplomat, that Daniel Patrick Moynihan missed the racial dimension in this story is ironic. It was a mistake he would not repeat; he would not be fooled again.

THE ULTIMATE
WARRIOR-DIPLOMAT

Pat was so witty, that you never felt as witty, as when you were
with Pat. You never laughed so hard, as when you were with Pat.
—NORMAN PODHORETZ TO GIL TROY

Daniel Patrick Moynihan became the US ambassador to the United Nations
by having declared himself ready to fight the status quo and restore American
pride. Moynihan lived the American dream, partially by studying it.
Celebrating his unique rise from New York's Hell's Kitchen to Harvard,
Moynihan's "American Dream" story also updated the classic mythical trajectory from a log cabin to the White House.

Even if Moynihan's true biography is a little more nuanced than his legend,
his was an extraordinary trajectory. He joined the wave of hardscrabble ethnics who "made it" in America in the 1960s and 1970s thanks to their service in World War II, the GI Bill's generosity, and American society's opening
up. Grateful to the country and the elite institutions that embraced him,
serving as an aide in the Kennedy, Johnson, Nixon, and Ford administrations, Moynihan dismissed the 1960s student rebels as nihilistic, while crusading for democracy and against totalitarianism.

Yet, for all his bluster, ever conscious of the miracle of his ascent to the once unreachable WASP strongholds of the Harvard faculty club and the Oval Office, Moynihan was hypersensitive to slights. When admiring Henry Kissinger's diplomatic magic in negotiating a cease-fire after the October 1973 Middle Eastern war, Moynihan noted that in Kissinger, "A massive ego and a pervading fear combine somehow to inform him as to what it is that moves other persons, and then to pose alternatives that lead them of their own accord to move as he desires." Moynihan had a similar combination of vanity and "vulnerability," as his friend, the Harvard sociologist David Riesman termed it. Riesman saw this fragility as "the source of some of his strength: it makes him extraordinarily sensitive to the nuance of social affairs, personal relations, works of art and architecture."

Moynihan was also extraordinarily, flamboyantly smart. "I don't think I've ever known anybody smarter than Pat," the longtime editor of *Commentary* and New York intellectual Norman Podhoretz says. "They used to say he was the sort of Irishman who could charm the birds out of the trees." As he matured from working class tough to intellectual whirling dervish, Moynihan frequently felt inadequate. "God I wish I were more entertaining," he would write in his twenties while studying in London. "I am never up to sustaining a real conversation with anyone. I would like to be an English novel character—full of stories and odd bits of fascinating info."

Moynihan's efforts at self-improvement succeeded. As both talker and writer, he sparkled. "Pat was so witty," Podhoretz recalls, "that, like Shakespeare's Falstaff in *Henry IV, Part II,* he was not only witty in himself 'but the cause that wit is in other men.' You never felt as witty, as when you were with Pat. You never laughed so hard, as when you were with Pat."

Still, despite his brilliant conversation, sociological sophistication, and keen insight, Moynihan had certain blind spots. He never anticipated, never quite understood, and never fully recovered from the two firestorms his controversial comments about blacks triggered. And while he gave graduate courses in ethnicity at Harvard University, nothing prepared him for the complexity of the politics he would encounter when defending Zionism.

Being a newcomer to America's elite freed Moynihan to think boldly, unconstrained by the conventional wisdom. This open-mindedness also caused him trouble, as he warned about the crisis in the black family during the Kennedy-Johnson years, joined Nixon's White House, despite so many colleagues' disdain and his own wife's discomfort, then courageously advised

Americans to stop obsessing about racial issues during the Nixon years. On foreign policy, he instinctively doubted the euphoria surrounding détente—and refused to join the Western chorus of apologies the Third World demanded. In the 1960s, and, more crucially in 1975, Moynihan's ability to think what we now call outside the box served his country well and launched his unexpected leap into the American political stratosphere.

Born in 1927 to a lower-middle-class family in Tulsa, Oklahoma, Daniel Patrick Moynihan was of the GI Joe generation that had great faith in the UN when it began. The son of John H. Moynihan and Margaret Phipps, he spent much of the first ten years of his life in comfortable, middle-class enclaves, first in the Midwest, then in the New York area. In 1937 Jack Moynihan, a hard-drinking, sloppy-gambling, skirt-chasing journalist and advertising copywriter, abandoned his wife and three young children. Pat was the oldest. "Marriage broke up," Moynihan would recall, "and down we went."

The blow was psychological, not just economic. His father's abandonment was "intensely painful" and darkened all his childhood memories. Like so many members of his generation, living through the Great Depression and World War II collectively, Moynihan had an intimacy with catastrophe that would be foreign to their children. It made him particularly tuned to outsiders' opinions and vulnerable to their criticism. He feared whatever he achieved could disappear as quickly as his family's status had. Moynihan would subsequently believe that "almost everything that has happened to me has taken place by chance." At the same time, this anxiety fed a blustery self-confidence, as he recognized that he had talked or written his way from one achievement to another, into one seemingly impenetrable inner American sanctum after another.

These experiences also sharpened Moynihan's appreciation for the underdog, be it single mothers or embattled states. Defending the United States and President Franklin Roosevelt against sophomoric British attacks when he was studying in London after the war, he admitted he "loved arguing for something bigger than myself which I thought was right." Moynihan, like so many of his generation, internalized Roosevelt's optimistic, problem-solving, liberal outlook. He shared Roosevelt's faith in government, but he also honed an outsider's skepticism that made him quicker than most to see when government or the conventional wisdom failed.

The Moynihans bounced around after Jack Moynihan left. Margaret Phipps Moynihan had another, shorter, marriage two and a half years after her first marriage broke up. Pat shined shoes on the northeast corner of Broadway and West Forty-third Street to help the family, graduated from Holy Name, a Catholic parochial school on Manhattan's Upper West Side, then attended two different high schools, Yorktown Heights High School in Westchester and Benjamin Franklin High School in East Harlem, from which he graduated as valedictorian and class secretary.

In 1943 he enrolled in City College of New York (CCNY) and, among other jobs, before and after college worked as a newsboy and a longshoreman. During this period his mother would purchase the lease on a tavern in Hell's Kitchen—"Moynihan's Bar"—which would become so significant in the Moynihan legend. Never one to miss a chance to self-dramatize, Moynihan would later tell reporters he took the CCNY exam with his "longshoreman's loading hook sticking out of my back pocket. I wasn't going to be mistaken for any sissy kid."

By 1944 Moynihan had enrolled in an officer training program in the US Navy; he would remain on active duty until 1947. Dispatched as a trainee to more exclusive schools than his native City College, Moynihan took college courses at Middlebury College, and then Tufts University, graduating from Tufts, class of 1948. At these schools and in his program in America's most aristocratic service branch, Moynihan encountered upper-class peers for the first time. Moynihan envied yet disdained them, believing most "needed a good swift kick in their blue-blood asses."

Moynihan also felt the allure of the life of the mind—and the good life. As his naval service ended, he continued studying, working on his master's at Tufts. In 1950, having failed the Foreign Service exam the year before, he received a Fulbright grant to study trade unionism at the London School of Economics. As the initial nine months stretched to three years, Moynihan blossomed into an intellectual—and something of a dandy.

As he cultivated a taste for Saville Row suits, rococo conversational riffs, and Churchillian oratory, Moynihan tempered his newly acquired British airs with his gruff, inbred New York bluster. Politically he insisted that "nothing and no one at LSE ever disposed me to be anything but a New York Democrat who had some friends who worked on the docks and drank beer after work." In that spirit, on returning to the United States in September 1953, Moynihan plunged into New York politics. The first of his many miracle mentors, Jonathan Bingham, eventually placed him in 1954 with the well-connected, aristocratic governor of New York, Averill Harriman.

While working for Harriman, Moynihan befriended Bingham's secretary Elizabeth Brennan. They married in 1955 and by 1960 had three young children, a son, Tim, born in 1956, a daughter, Maura, born in 1958, and a son, John, born two years later. Liz and Pat developed an exceptional partnership, a true working marriage, with Liz often serving as Pat's primary advisor and campaign manager as well as his toughest critic and best friend.

When Harriman lost his re-election bid, he hired Moynihan to write an official history of his administration. While spending two years on this project at Syracuse University, which housed Harriman's papers, Moynihan completed his PhD in International Relations at Tuft University's Fletcher School of Law and Diplomacy. He also began writing articles in the *Reporter*, an intellectual, left-leaning magazine. The exposure eventually led to his work on the *Public Interest* with Irving Kristol and to his biggest academic break, his productive partnership with the sociologist Nathan Glazer.

Glazer was working on a manuscript, which became the classic *Beyond the Melting Pot*, published in 1963. Fascinated by ethnic culture's enduring power despite all the talk about America's powerful assimilatory mechanism, Glazer wrote four chapters about New York's Jews, African Americans (then called Negroes), Puerto Ricans, and Italians. Moynihan wrote about the Irish and drafted most of the book's conclusion.

The delicate dance between Americanism and ethnic particularism Moynihan and Glazer depicted captured Moynihan's own elaborate Irish American jig. As an Irish Catholic New Yorker who would gain fame as a social scientist and a public intellectual, Moynihan reflected the sociological revolution that was transforming America's elites. He delighted in both his professorial status and his Irish Catholic background. Like so many high achievers of his generation, he was proud of how far he—and his people—had come. Moynihan's letters are peppered with references to his Irishness. Many newspaper profiles emphasized what Nixon's press secretary Ron Ziegler pointedly called his "Gaelic charm." Beyond his impressive erudition as lecturer, reader, and writer, his ethnicity was a tool for advancement, supplemented by a quick wit, a genius for phrase-making, a talent for flattery, and a love of the literary bon mot that reflected his membership in America's once exclusively WASPy intellectual elite.

Yet, as with so many successful ethnics, group pride in his and his kinsmen's achievements mixed with tribal hostilities and rivalries. "Moynihan was a contrarian. There was almost an oppositional element to his temperament," his former aide Chester Finn recalls. As a result, Moynihan kept his outsider's chip on his shoulder toward powerful and influential people, even as he became an insider himself.

The ethnic, religious and class consciousness reinforced one another. Moynihan expressed this in a strong affinity toward the working class as reflecting the solid, patriotic, Irish Catholic sensibility, along with a continuing fascination with the Jewish people as a phenomenon. Moynihan was intrigued by Jews and Jewish idiosyncrasies, awed by American Jewish smarts, "hyper-aware of Jewish power," Glazer notes, and disdainful of the many Jewish limousine liberals and faculty club radicals. "He was very much a Catholic liberal," Glazer says, even as his widow Liz Moynihan remembers that "probably most of our friends were Jewish."

John Kennedy's successful, cosmopolitan New Frontier liberalism dazzled Moynihan, making him proud as the first Irish Catholic president swept into Washington with a vanguard of idealistic intellectuals. That was one club Moynihan desperately wanted to join. He spent the first few months of Kennedy's administration working every contact he could. Eventually, a friend from the London days, the NBC newsman Sander Vanocur, introduced Moynihan to the undersecretary of labor W. Willard Wirtz. In July 1961 Moynihan arrived with his family in Washington as a special assistant to the secretary of labor Arthur Goldberg.

When President Kennedy was assassinated in November 1963, Moynihan captured both dimensions of his political love affair with Camelot—the ethnic and the idealistic. He would recall that along with Speaker of the House John McCormack and Mrs. McCormack, he was among the first to see the president lying in state in the White House, being "Catholics, with a claim on that moment." Shortly thereafter, speaking on television, using his ethnic patois, Moynihan said "I guess there's no point in being Irish if you don't know the world will break your heart some day."

In the emerging Kennedy hagiography, that bon mot competed with another one of Moynihan's lightning-quick lines. His reporter friend Mary McGrory phoned him hours later. Heartbroken, she said, "We'll never laugh again." "No, Mary," Moynihan replied. "We'll laugh again, but we'll never be young again." Moynihan marveled "that for weeks after people would touch me in the street, and say that is what they had felt, and move away immediately."

Thereafter, remembering the Kennedy years frequently made Moynihan wistful. In 1973 Moynihan reflected that since then, "Very little has gone well for us: almost nothing as we would have wished. Not *all* bad. The high school rhetoric has been knocked out of us: no more torches. Yet no more dreams and not much courage either."

Moynihan viewed the turmoil of the sixties from an extraordinary vantage point. In addition to witnessing the campus chaos in Cambridge, Massachusetts, toward the end of the decade, Moynihan served in various domestic policy posts in the Kennedy, Johnson and Nixon administrations. "I don't know *anyone* else who could testify on behalf of the Ford Admin. in the a.m. and dine with the Coalition for a Democratic Majority that same night," Chester Finn would remark in 1975 when Moynihan was already UN ambassador under his fourth president, Gerald Ford. As a Democrat who worked for Nixon, as a liberal unsettled by the Left's excesses, and as the buddy of other intellectuals such as Glazer, Podhoretz, and Irving Kristol, Moynihan would become a leading "neoconservative," although he disliked the term, knowing it was "coined in epithet."

While the Social Democrat Michael Harrington indeed meant to dismiss Moynihan and his colleagues when labeling them "neoconservatives" in 1973, Irving Kristol, for one, embraced it. Kristol insisted, however, that it was more a "tendency" or a "persuasion," than a movement—and a quite varied one at that. Still, in 1976 he identified five key neoconservative tenets: accepting the idea of a welfare state but not the "Great Society version"; respecting "the power of the market"; championing "traditional values and institutions"; believing in equality but not the rigid dehumanizing doctrine of "egalitarianism"; and fearing a new post-Vietnam isolationism or American defeatism in a dangerous world, hostile to democracy. In the persistent "tension between liberty and equality," Moynihan believed that he and his closest friends tended toward "liberty," which is why he preferred to see himself as a Wilsonian progressive, a Roosevelt liberal, a liberal asking "What happened to liberalism?" or, more simply, an American patriot.

Ambitious, loquacious, and disputatious, Moynihan developed a knack for being noticed—for better and worse. Stunned by the array of policy debates Moynihan shaped, the journalist Nicholas Lemann would say Moynihan "practically invent[ed] the role of the social welfare intellectual in government." Moynihan's "extraordinary radar," Lemann explained, helped him identify key issues and "dramatize his findings in a way that would get the attention of high government officials."

In 1965, as Lyndon Johnson's War on Poverty gained momentum, Moynihan analyzed the challenges facing the black family. "We have to do something. We have to be different," he wrote, trying to galvanize America. Moynihan's detailed analysis warned with characteristically pungent phrasing about the epidemic of illegitimate births in the black community. The "deterioration of the Negro family" ensnared blacks in a "tangle of pathology."

Even years later Willard Wirtz, who became secretary of labor when Arthur Goldberg joined the Supreme Court, would recall his "almost physical excitement" upon reading Moynihan's memo. Moynihan was tackling taboo subjects. Anticipating the next half-century of social tensions, Moynihan noted that establishing legal rights was not enough; the challenge was ensuring equal opportunity. "The most difficult fact for white Americans to understand," he wrote, was that economically and even socially "the circumstances of the Negro American community in recent years has probably been getting *worse, not better*." When forwarding Moynihan's "Case for National Action" to the White House, Wirtz called the memo "nine pages of dynamite about the Negro situation."

Unfortunately for Moynihan, the dynamite detonated later that fall. Though his report inspired President Johnson's stirring civil rights speech at Howard University on June 4, 1965, calling for equal opportunity because "freedom is not enough," many liberals and black radicals attacked Moynihan. They accused him of "blaming the victim," of racist stereotyping. The riots in the Watts ghetto of Los Angeles in August raised tensions regarding race relations in America and fed the critics' anger.

"I am now known as a racist across the land," Moynihan wrote bitterly to the civil rights leader Roy Wilkins in January 1966. "If Pat is a racist, I am," said the leading black sociologist Kenneth Clark. "Is a doctor responsible for a disease simply because he diagnoses it?"

The attacks soured Moynihan on the Left. He was increasingly incensed that the rational, problem-solving liberalism he championed had spawned this fanatic, self-righteous, nihilistic, identity-driven aberration. His reactionary fury only furthered the gap between him and his critics. "It was the worst thing that ever happened to him," Liz Moynihan acknowledged, still wincing more than four decades later.

The controversy also seemed to kill Moynihan's dream of running for office. Earlier, in July 1965, he had left the Johnson administration to run for

New York City Council president. Taking a ward heeler's approach to New York politics, he viewed it as a clash between Irish get-out-the-vote drives and Jewish fund-raising. He lost in a crowded field, which divided the Irish vote and saw the influential Jewish vote go elsewhere. The attacks against the report later that fall, following his defeat for this minor office, crushed Moynihan, making him appear unelectable.

Instead of shaping New York politics, he studied it. After a year at the Center of Advanced Studies at Wesleyan University, Moynihan became director of the Harvard-MIT Joint Center for Urban Studies. In Cambridge, Moynihan secured the ultimate academic credential by getting tenure at the Harvard School of Education. Even though he spent few years actually being that, he was defined as a Harvard professor for the rest of his life, the model of the scholar-politician.

Watching the sixties rebels unleash a destructive anger against America, its values, and its institutions, Moynihan became even more disgusted with the New Left. All the chips lined up on Moynihan's shoulder, as he viewed the "liberal-left," and the "totalitarian-left" as disproportionately upper class, Jewish, elitist, unpatriotic, unreasonable, and illiberal. Calling himself a "liberal dissenter," Moynihan would describe President Johnson's forced retirement in 1968 as making him "the first American President to be toppled by a mob. No matter that it was a mob of college professors, millionaires, flower children, and Radcliffe girls." Moynihan's indignation and self-righteous anger freed him to accept a White House job offer from the liberals' bête noire, Richard Nixon, in 1969.

Nixon essentially hired Moynihan to be Moynihan. The president liked having a "Harvard" on the domestic side, paralleling the Harvard government professor Henry Kissinger running foreign policy. Sporting the ambiguous title of "counselor to the President," enjoying a cabinet seat, Moynihan was a roving troubleshooter and intellectual troublemaker. Among his tasks was serving as ambassador from academe and resident expert on race relations— called "urban affairs."

Moynihan was amazed at the "nihilist terrorism" he witnessed on campuses and dismayed by "the crisis of confidence, the erosion of authority." These phenomena, he insisted, "had to be raised to the highest level of policy concern." His memos described the sixties rebellion as a broader social, cultural, political, and ideological breakdown. The "educated elite of the American middle classes have come to detest their society, and their detestation is rapidly diffusing to youth in general," Moynihan warned in one memo. "The effects of this profound movement of opinion will be with us for generations," he predicted, including constraining America internationally.

Moynihan enjoyed his status as the iconoclastic genius in the straitlaced Nixon White House and one of Nixon's token Democrats—with his new friend, Nixon's liberal Jewish former law partner Leonard Garment. Moynihan considered the Vietnam War disastrous and squabbled with those in the White House who tried to undermine him. Even the *Washington Post's* normally skeptical Jack Anderson fed the Moynihan legend, reporting that the Harvard professor simply would "shrug off" the West Wing sniping "with a fast quip and a bit of Irish blarney."

Unfortunately for Moynihan, he could not sweet talk his way out of another debacle caused by yet another colorfully worded memo about race relations leaked by a critic.

Moynihan decided to mark a year into the Nixon presidency with one of his big-picture looks at "the position of Negroes" in America and under Nixon. He detailed the rising problems of "Social Pathology" and "Social Alienation." He speculated that much of the crime committed by blacks had "become quasi-politicized. Hatred—revenge—against whites is now an acceptable excuse for doing what might have been done anyway."

Such candid discussion was edgy under any circumstances. But in proposing strategies for the Nixon administration, Moynihan's language became explosive. He suggested that "the issue of race could benefit from a period of 'benign neglect.' The subject has been too much talked about. The forum has been too much taken over to hysterics, paranoids, and boodlers on all sides."

Moynihan proposed a cooling-down period "in which Negro progress continues and racial rhetoric fades." But critics read the memo as proposing that Nixon ignore civil rights. "Benign neglect" became shorthand for Moynihan's and Nixon's racist insensitivity. Referring back to the 1965 Moynihan Report, reflecting their distrust of Nixon and anyone who worked for him, critics pilloried both men.

Once again Moynihan felt betrayed, especially by liberals, blacks, and academics. "Benign neglect" became as tethered to Moynihan's biography as "Harvard professor" and "Hell's Kitchen." The fallout made him politically radioactive for years. It also increased suspicions about the president's

Family Assistance Plan. Eventually, Congress killed this visionary welfare reform plan proposing minimum income for all adult American citizens.

The controversy sapped Moynihan, who was already drained by shuttling between his family in Cambridge and his work in Washington, as well as by the carping from Nixon-haters in Cambridge and Nixon-loyalists in Washington. On May 8, 1970, Moynihan's despair increased when SDS— Students for a Democratic Society—radicals protesting America's invasion of Cambodia threatened to trash his house in Cambridge. That same, terrifying week of the Kent State shootings and cross-country protests, anything seemed possible.

Moynihan's family went into hiding, after Liz Moynihan moved all their possessions away from the windows, covering them with sheets, and a big peace sign. Liz Moynihan told her husband to remain in Washington, as he would only be a target in Cambridge. Not the type to abandon her post, she contemplated defending her homestead with a baseball bat. Six Harvard Divinity students guarded the house on Francis Avenue—soon reinforced by government agents Nixon sent. Moynihan stayed in Washington, telling the president guiltily the next day "I am choosing the interests of the administration over the interests of my children." The threat passed. Nevertheless, Moynihan drafted a resignation letter days later, which he never submitted.

In late November, Nixon offered Moynihan the post of ambassador to the United Nations. Moynihan initially said yes, and word of the appointment leaked to the press. But Liz Moynihan objected as did Harvard, which refused to extend his two-year leave of absence. At the last minute, Moynihan decided to return to Cambridge. When he called his wife to tell her the news, she sobbed with relief, Moynihan later told his biographer Godfrey Hodgson.

Although Moynihan resumed teaching in January 1971, he remained a consultant on domestic matters. He also served as a Public Delegate to the UN, part of the ceremonial five-person (two senators, two representatives, and one citizen who did not hold elective office) delegation accompanying Ambassador George H. W. Bush to the General Assembly. The intellectual sloppiness at the UN appalled Moynihan. He mocked the UN's 1970 "Report on the World Social Situation" as reading "like the work of a harassed undergraduate hoping against reason that his senior thesis, compiled in three horrendous nights of scissors, paste and black coffee, will be accepted on grounds that he will otherwise not graduate."

Moynihan also blasted the State Department when bureaucrats there suggested using Soviet Jewry to counter Syrian and Hungarian attacks on American racism. While sympathetic to Soviet Jews prevented from emigrating, Moynihan refused to enter "the same dreary pissing match with the totalitarians." It was demeaning to compare America's open democratic culture with closed Communist societies. He told Ambassador Bush: "It is incomprehensible to me that a State Department that would take the nation into a hopeless and disastrous war in Asia in defense of abstract principles about democracy is not able—or in some perverse way—not willing—to summon the intellectual competence to defend democracy in a United Nations debate." Four years later, Moynihan would have similar complaints.

Moynihan's return to Cambridge was rough. His fury at the "Authoritarian Left" was matched by its disdain for him. He emphasized that he opposed Vietnam—but opposed even more the antiwar radicals who had lost perspective. Moynihan himself lost faith when protestors hung a Viet Cong flag from Peace Corps headquarters in Washington, DC, during that same turbulent day that threatened his family, May 8, 1970. That one vile gesture defiled Kennedy's legacy and the American patriotic enterprise. Criticizing your country was acceptable, even during war; identifying with the enemy was treason. In a 1972 letter to the novelist Saul Bellow, who was trying to woo him to the University of Chicago, Moynihan admitted "It was probably a mistake to come back" to Harvard. "Here I found nothing" beyond politics, pettiness, and a surprising hostility from many colleagues and students.

The resentment would build. "The students hate the likes of me, and it is a struggle, and a costly one, not to hate back," he would confess. Feeling injured, he took perverse pleasure as crime "ravaged" Cambridge. The "undergraduates are learning what we pigs have tried to tell them about the uses of order, as against their beloved disorder," Moynihan would note in his journal in 1974. Mixing in doses of class resentment, Moynihan concluded, with a ghastly one-liner reflecting his fury: "Nothing like a little rape to teach the children of the rich what it means to be poor."

In late 1972 Nixon nominated Moynihan to serve as ambassador to India, having offered him a choice between India and the UN. Moynihan believed the UN "corpse had already begun to decompose.... The spirit of liberty had seeped out of that institution. A Death of a Thousand Cuts had occurred." India had cachet, especially because another Harvard luminary, John Kenneth Galbraith, had served there under Kennedy.

Both Moynihans were ambivalent about the posting. India was hot, smelly, dirty, chaotic, instinctively anti-American, hell on their digestive systems, and unappealing to their teenage children, one of whom remained in America. "Is it true you were constantly sick in New Delhi?" a reporter asked him years later. "I was only sick *once!*" Moynihan insisted. "It lasted two and a half years!"

Moynihan admitted to being a New York provincial, willing to venture north to Cambridge, south to Washington, and occasionally to London—but only if necessary. He most liked the Anglo touches in India. Feeling lonely, he—only half-jokingly—told his friends Norman Podhoretz and Midge Decter, Podhoretz's wife "that the only people I cared about in the world were the Jews and the Irish."

Nonetheless, Moynihan proved to be an effective ambassador. He appreciated India's role as the world's most populous democracy. He improved relations by breaking a logjam regarding a huge debt India incurred for food. Negotiations resulted in his writing a check for $2.2 billion to the Indian government, as America's representative, the largest check ever written to date.

Moynihan appreciated his safe distance from America's erupting campuses and Nixon's self-destructing White House. He was enough of an egotist—and bureaucratic climber—to recognize that while "I *like* to think the Ehrlichmans"—his shorthand for Nixon's slavish Germanic aides—"assumed I wouldn't go along" with the Watergate crimes, he dodged that disaster because "it was simply that I wasn't trusted."

Still, Moynihan "felt out of the loop," his friend Bernard Weinraub, the *New York Times* India correspondent recalls, and felt guilty for not saving Nixon from himself. He was also embarrassed that he had vouched for Nixon during the 1972 re-election campaign. "Have I been a fool or a whore or both?" Moynihan wondered. "What do you call such a person? A Moynihan, I suppose. A term suggestive of moral and political failing."

Nixon's weakness dismayed Moynihan further when the Egyptians and Syrians surprised Israel by attacking during the Jews' holiest day, Yom Kippur, October 6, 1973. Despite his many Jewish friends, Moynihan was not an Israel enthusiast. He admired the country's democratic government but found it too Russian and too Marxist. From the Nixon White House, Moynihan acquired what Podhoretz would call "a semi-secret bias against Israel." Although he opposed the Vietnam War, Moynihan nevertheless shared the Nixonites' frustration that so many Jews could be, as Henry Kissinger sharply called them, "Hawks on Israel but Doves on Vietnam."

This time, with the American presidency in crisis and watching the Indian press blame Israel for the war while delighting in Israel's weakness, Moynihan despaired. "I have been thinking of you repeatedly these past three days, and recalling those tense days of 1967 when you were staying with us, glued to the radio and terribly worried to the end," Moynihan wrote Nathan Glazer. "I fear this time it is I who am most probably the most worried. From this perspective it is so clear almost the whole world has turned on Israel. The imbalance seems to be ominous in the utmost degree."

After Nixon and Kissinger arranged to resupply Israel, Moynihan again despaired that "We were alone with Israel. Almost alone." Portugal was the lone NATO ally that permitted American cargo planes to land and refuel while flying to Israel. Moynihan also noted Jewish liberals' hypocrisy, as those professors who were so proudly pacifist in the 1960s rallied, demanding the president send Israel weapons and ammunition. Resenting the damage these antiwar warriors imposed on America, the "obscene" contradiction "hurt" Moynihan. "I admire Israel as much as a man can who has never been there; I scurried about in 1967 getting signatures for advertisements in the *Times*," he noted in his diary. Still, the moral inconsistencies suggested that "American elites" believed "Smart bombs *may* be used on Arabs."

A few weeks later, in mid-December, the Moynihan family tasted Middle East madness more personally, when the Egyptian ambassador insisted on meeting Moynihan. Moynihan was surprised, as they never socialized. The ambassador delivered a warning from President Anwar Sadat that the PLO sought to disrupt the Geneva Middle East peace conference, slated to start on December 21. The plans included attacking Rome's Leonardo da Vinci airport and dispatching a PLO hit squad to assassinate or kidnap Moynihan.

Two days later, on December 17, Palestinian terrorists swarmed Rome's airport, murdering thirty-two people. That same week, a New Delhi cab driver told police he had driven three Arab tourists who timed repeated runs between the airport, their hotel, the train station, and the American embassy complex, which included Roosevelt House, the ambassador's residence. The Arabs, who had a picture of the tall, distinctive-looking, US ambassador to India, asked the driver to pick them up later that afternoon. Instead, detectives arrived to arrest them.

Securing the embassy, the police recommended cancelling all social events. Liz Moynihan was responsible for hosting the annual embassy Christmas party. Pat deferred to his wife's judgment. She proceeded with the party. "One doesn't change one's plan," the elegant, steely Liz Moynihan explains.

Moynihan rarely mentioned the terrorist threat—despite being what subsequent generations might call a drama king. Later, after Puerto Rican FALN terrorists blew out fifty-five windows and damaged an entrance door by bombing the US mission to the UN on Forty-fifth Street and the United Nations Plaza early on October 27, 1975, the State Department dispatched two security guards to shadow him. "He found it bothersome and after about two weeks asked that they be reassigned," Liz Moynihan recalls. Echoing John Kennedy's fatal insouciance, Moynihan said, "if someone wants to get you they will," reasoning that "having security meant three people would be hurt instead of one." Pat was toughened by the fact that "He'd already had threats to his life from Black radicals following the Moynihan Report," Liz Moynihan explains. "That troubled him more—because his views were so totally misinterpreted." Besides, "because he grew up poor on the West Side, worked on the docks and was in the Navy, physical threats did not seem to register much."

Although she courageously continued with the Christmas party, Liz Moynihan took the threat more seriously. Two years later, the elegant, aristocratic yet thuggish Permanent PLO Observer to the UN Zehdi Terzi approached her in the UN galleries during the Zionism is racism controversy. "I don't remember exactly how he phrased it," Liz Moynihan says, "but he said something ominous like 'you must have mixed feelings about remembering events in New Delhi.'...It wasn't a casual remark asking 'did you like touring all those sites in India, Mrs. Moynihan.' No I didn't take it that way."

Just as the radical threats made Moynihan feel embattled in the United States, the PLO threat may have intensified his resentment of Indian anti-Americanism. Moynihan scoffed when an Indian minister described Israel "as a stooge of imperialism," calling it "an inventive term from the poetic mind." He noticed that India "has got itself so ideologically committed to the political causes of the Arabs that it just can't deal with the economic consequences of Arab actions on India itself."

Moynihan summarized his two years in India by saying, "I came here thinking that liberty was losing in the world. I leave thinking that liberty may well be lost." Europe's cowardice and America's demoralization amid growing Third World effrontery made him fear that freedom was an "endangered species." Fed up with Western groveling expressed through excessive but unappreciated generosity, he grumbled: "The more we do for them, the more they will hate us."

Living in India had reinforced Moynihan's fear that a pinched and resentful British socialist worldview was shaping this Third World rebellion against the West. Moynihan recognized the problem in India's leader, the formidable Indira Gandhi. A wealthy Brahmin steeped in "this leftist, 'anti-colonial' political culture" with its "anti-American" rhetoric, she had no qualms imposing emergency decrees, which undermined Indian democracy.

A world with America demoralized and Third World nations on the offensive pleased the Soviets but terrified Moynihan. He began studying the problem of Western and American weakness, integrating his frustrations with the totalitarian Left and Third World autocrats. One 1972 article, "Moralism and Foreign Policy," by Ernest W. Lefever, diagnosed the new inverted sensibility Moynihan detested. Lefever denounced the Left's "sham morality" and "soft moralism," which "associates virtue with weakness, just as it associates vice with power."

In late November 1974, the Berkeley political scientist Paul Seabury wondered about "the powerful upsurge of the so-called Afro-Arab-Asian-Communist bloc, and the passivity of so many Western countries in responding to it." Seabury believed the problem went beyond Israel. And he predicted that "this coalition may prove to be the death of the United Nations." He encouraged Norman Podhoretz to commission Moynihan to analyze this issue "after he escapes India."

Moynihan, who was resigning as of January 6 because he faced another two-year-leave-of-absence deadline from Harvard, loved the idea. A month later, he telegrammed Podhoretz, "PAPER GOING WELL." Moynihan was ready to identify the "IDEOLOGICAL COHERENCE" uniting the Third World, with its "POWERFUL BRITISH BASE.... WE CAN'T DEAL WITH THIS WORLD IF WE DO NOT RECOGNIZE ITS IDEOLOGY."

As *Commentary*'s editor, Podhoretz was used to getting impressive essays in the mail from leading American thinkers such as Saul Bellow and Daniel Bell, Alfred Kazin and Irving Kristol. By 1975 the dapper, intense, occasionally vehement forty-six-year-old Podhoretz was one of America's leading intellectual *provocateurs*. "Norman Podhoretz is very simply the finest literary-intellectual editor of this age. And he has, of course, paid for it," Moynihan told one journalist friend.

One day, in early 1975, Podhoretz received from Moynihan a "huge manuscript that must have been easily sixty pages, maybe more, although it was typed triple-spaced." Podhoretz immediately recognized the "unwieldy" manuscript's power, even while shrinking it. "His organization wasn't necessarily all that good, and sometimes points were not made sufficiently clear. . . . I had to cut it, condense, write in transitions," Podhoretz recalls.

The cuts made the editor nervous. "I had never edited him that much." Podhoretz feared Moynihan might resist. Moynihan "was very, very smart, but like a lot of people—in fact, like most people—he could not take criticism," Podhoretz remembers.

Although Moynihan was back in the United States, Podhoretz suggested mailing the manuscript back rather than risking a blowup face to face. Moynihan insisted they meet at New York's Century Club for lunch. After arriving, Podhoretz watched anxiously as Moynihan read the revised manuscript through, pen in hand. After only "three little corrections," Moynihan pronounced himself "Delighted."

Podhoretz was too. For the first time since becoming *Commentary's* editor in chief in 1960, he called a press conference to promote a particular article. "And a lot of reporters did, in fact, show up," Podhoretz recalls. Moynihan "was famous, and he was a figure to be reckoned with by this time. So it got a lot of coverage and it was a huge hit. It was all over the place, which was great for *Commentary*. It was great for him."

The article, "The United States in Opposition," published in *Commentary's* March 1975 issue was a sensation. Moynihan told White House Chief of Staff Donald Rumsfeld that he had never triggered such a response "in all my scribbling." He received "Hundreds of letters. . . . All say one thing. Yes, we *should* 'go into opposition,' raise hell, state our case, present alternatives, stop apologizing for a merely imperfect democracy. The message is unmistakable. People are tired of our being ashamed of ourselves." Pushing his point, Moynihan emphasized: "If we were to start making our case, the first effect might be that the American people might once more come to realize that we have one."

The article attracted President Ford's attention too. During his farewell meeting with Ford in late January, Moynihan had already started pitching the idea. "Mr. President, we have learned to deal with Communism in the

World. We are now going to have to learn to deal with Socialism," Moynihan said. He loved wowing powerful people by saying smart things they could not comprehend but nevertheless considered profound. "I can't imagine he had the least idea what I was talking about," Moynihan noted in his diary, "but it got Kissinger on the subject of my cables—entirely generous, as he always has been."

Weeks later, Kissinger started reading the essay in his limousine, then continued reading it through an afternoon appointment. Bestowing a jealous scholar's highest compliment, he wished he had written the essay. When Kissinger proposed that Moynihan "head a group about behaving more aggressively at the UN," Ford responded: "How about appointing Pat at the UN?" Rumsfeld, knowing Moynihan's tendency to agonize over these appointments, urged his friend: "Do what Henry and the President ask you to. We need you."

Kissinger approved the appointment, albeit reluctantly. Kissinger would insist in his memoirs that he "had long been an admirer" of Moynihan and recommended his colleague for the United Nations post. Ford would recall: "Henry was not in favor of sending Moynihan to the UN and warned that he might use it as a political stepping stone." For his part, Moynihan would open his memoirs about his UN tenure by quoting Helmut Sonnenfeldt, Kissinger's State Department counselor: "You do not understand," Sonnenfeldt would say when Moynihan insisted he would not serve if the secretary of state lied to him. "Henry does not lie because it is in his interest. He lies because it is in his nature."

Moynihan's ascendance threatened Kissinger. Kissinger enjoyed his status as the Harvard wunderkind, dazzling bureaucrats and reporters; he did not want to share the spotlight with another articulate intellectual with a crimson glow. Kissinger's star was already in eclipse due to the "reassessment" with Israel in March and the collapse of South Vietnam weeks later. Moreover, Moynihan's confrontational and idealistic approach contrasted with Kissinger's more conciliatory, amoral, and realist foreign policy strategy.

Idealists and realists had been clashing over American foreign policy for decades, and in fact this tug-of-war persists. Moynihan considered himself a Wilsonian, a believer in Woodrow Wilson's vision of spreading democracy and American values around the world. "And to say no more," George Will explains archly, Henry Kissinger did not. Moreover, Will adds, "the durability of ethnicity as a force in history was a great theme in Moynihan's life," and another flashpoint with Kissinger. The ideological rift between the UN ambassador and the secretary of state guaranteed constant institutional tension between Moynihan's camp in Turtle Bay and Kissinger's camp in Foggy Bottom.

On April 12, 1975, when President Ford and Secretary Kissinger greeted their newly appointed UN ambassador in the Oval Office, Kissinger proclaimed: "That *Commentary* article is one of the most important articles in a long time." The *New York Times* summarized Moynihan's views melodramatically: "MOYNIHAN CALLS ON U.S. TO START 'RAISING HELL' IN UN."

Essentially, the Social Democratic activist Carl Gershman would note, Moynihan was declaring ideological war—or at least mounting an ideological counterattack. Gershman, along with a growing group of intellectuals and activists, deemed Henry Kissinger's Nixon-Ford détente policies a failure because, by ignoring Soviet human rights abuses they overrode defining American principles. Five years before the anti-Communist trinity of Ronald Reagan, Pope John Paul, and Margaret Thatcher put Western policy on a more moralistic footing—and encountered hostility—Moynihan blazed the trail. Contrary to the conventional wisdom, not all of these anti-Communists were neoconservatives, abandoning their leftist values. Some like Bayard Rustin, Gershman, and the labor leader Lane Kirkland remained Progressives, but were tough, unsentimental, freedom-loving liberals who recognized the evils lurking in Communism.

With the United States of America perceived as flagging, Moynihan's message was timely at home and abroad. "We must play hard ball," Moynihan told President Ford, saying, rather crudely, that "there is nothing like exposure to others pissing on your country" to spur some patriotism. Both Ford and Kissinger knew what they were getting with Moynihan. "Would he carry out orders?" Ford asked Kissinger regarding Moynihan. Kissinger replied cryptically: "You—and the press—would know when he disagreed. He would basically be with us and basically [be] okay." A few weeks later, when Kissinger noted that the assistant secretary of state William Buffum called John Scali's usually quiet performance at the UN "a disgrace," Ford replied that he hoped Moynihan "is as obnoxious up there as he has propensity to be." Kissinger predicted: "He will give us fits, but he will do well."

Amid America's hurricane of humiliations in the 1970s, the fall of Saigon at the end of April 1975 hurt most. The United States had never lost a war before. And most Americans had convinced themselves that the peace treaty Kissinger helped negotiate during the Nixon administration had solved the problem. Few noticed South Vietnam rotting from within, victimized by internal corruption, as North Vietnam mobilized. The final, heartbreaking scenes of American helicopters lifting off amid chaos, leaving behind thousands of loyal South Vietnamese friends, teetering as some locals desperately clung to the choppers, was seared into the national memory. The violence so intensified that as the last helicopter took off from the American embassy's roof, marines set off a tear gas container in the stairwell. They forgot that a helicopter sucks up the air as it ascends. Tellingly, the last Americans leaving South Vietnam left temporarily blinded.

"It is a moral collapse of the United States," Kissinger told the president histrionically. Crestfallen, he told Ford he was returning the Nobel Peace Prize "but the money is in a trust fund so I will have to borrow to return the money." "By our self indulgence," Kissinger would conclude, "we damaged the fabric of freedom everywhere" and "ushered in a period of American humiliation" stretching from Angola to Ethiopia to Iran to Afghanistan.

The fall of Saigon depressed most Americans, even those who had opposed the war. Senator Hubert Humphrey, who lost the presidency in 1968 because of Vietnam, captured the country's gloomy mood when he concluded: "What we've learned is that there aren't American answers for every problem in the world."

As the president and secretary of state briefed their new appointee, the Vietnam disaster—and the continuing tensions with Israel—predominated. "I have no illusions…" Moynihan reassured Kissinger and Ford. "The only consensus now" in the world "is screw the United States." "I want strong statements and the guts to veto," Ford said, noting this would please Congress and the public. The president exulted, "I am delighted, Pat. We are on the same wave length."

As they left the Oval Office, that Saturday, April 12, Kissinger invited Moynihan into his West Wing office. Podhoretz recalls Moynihan reporting that there, in his awkward, imperious way Kissinger barked—jokingly—"On your knees, Moynihan." Getting serious, but having made his point, Kissinger warned, the now-declassified transcripts show: "One major problem you will have is on Israel. We must dissociate ourselves a bit from Israel—not to destroy them but to prevent them from becoming a Sparta, with only military solutions to every problem." Kissinger was worried. "They are desperately looking for a spokesman and they will work on you...I don't want Israel to get the idea that our UN mission is an extension of theirs....We have to show Israel they don't run us."

Like Moynihan, Kissinger saw the shadow of Vietnam. "You can't maintain that selling out Vietnam has no impact on Israel—as the Jewish community thinks. It can't be." Playing the courtier, reflecting back Kissinger's tone, Moynihan agreed: "The American Jews have got to be Americans."

If nothing else, Moynihan's crack about American Jews proves he did not take the UN job to woo the Jews or run for office, as critics later charged. His close friend from India, Bernard Weinraub, was never aware of any political ambitions, only recalling "intellectual ambitions," book ideas, and professorial visitors not politicos. Moynihan knew how politically unpopular he still was, having dueled as recently as late November 1974, with his old friend—and one-time defender against charges that the Moynihan Report was racist—the black sociologist Kenneth Clark. Clark called Moynihan's "benign neglect" memorandum "one of the most disturbing and dangerous publicly stated positions in an incredibly regressive Nixon administration." Such attacks still stung and probably made Moynihan more comfortable sticking to foreign policy matters.

Ford and Kissinger were hiring Moynihan to be Moynihan—with "Moynihan" now meaning bravery not knavery, as Moynihan feared it might mean during the Watergate traumas. Conservatives speculated Ford hired him "to shore up the right flank without having to pay too much for it." The UN posting "was harmless," Podhoretz explains. "So you send this guy in and he makes a few speeches, that's great." And you can then "pursue your policies with some camouflage."

Moynihan would use the posting to his advantage, however—to become the ultimate Warrior-Diplomat, elegant, intellectual, witty, charming but also blunt, blustery, explosive, aggressive. At the UN, Moynihan would play the Irish pol, downing whiskey and dropping bon mots here and there. He would play the professor, quoting great thinkers while thinking great thoughts expressed in ten-dollar words and complex sentences. He would play the pinstriped envoy, with his Saville Row suits and his addiction to talk. But he would also play America's White Knight, battling for his country, his values, and, in his mind, freedom itself. And he would play to the American people, many of whom sought some way past the Vietnam humiliation.

Yet being a magnet for controversy came at a price. Those closest to Moynihan knew how tormented he was by critics and conflict, despite his bravado. Moreover, Ford and Kissinger would soon realize that Moynihan would be far more "obnoxious" than they ever expected. No diplomat had ever stirred up so much trouble from the US mission to the UN—Moynihan emphasized that he spoke "in public only four times in two years" as ambassador to India. He would speak much more frequently and loudly in Turtle Bay. As a result, his moment in office would last only eight months—enough time, it turns out, to change the national conversation and its mood.

THE "FASHIONABLE ENEMY"

If, as is not impossible, the racist is at some future time replaced
by some other fashionable enemy, then no doubt the
denunciation of Zionism will be adjusted accordingly.
—BERNARD LEWIS, *FOREIGN AFFAIRS*, OCTOBER 1976

Daniel Patrick Moynihan "was not interested in power," his widow, Liz
Moynihan, recalls, "Pat was interested in access for his ideas. Pat was always
trying to get people to talk about or do something about an idea he had—
that is what interested him"—and what frequently got him into trouble. As a
social scientist, a teacher, a public intellectual, and a contrarian, Moynihan
particularly enjoyed defying the conventional wisdom.

In that spirit, Moynihan and his UN colleague Leonard Garment always
insisted that Resolution 3379's "source" was not the Arab states but the
Soviet Union, which, Garment said, "was actively promoting the idea that
Zionism was a US plot, all Jews were Zionists, and all Soviet Jews could
therefore be seen as a pro-American fifth column." Even among "the organized American Jewish community," this "argument of ours met with considerable skepticism," Garment recalled. The misunderstanding emerged,
Garment believed, because "Americans, and other 'decent' societies, tend
again and again to forget the existence of such deep-rooted sentiments of
racial, ethnic and religious bitterness and hatred." Arab enmity—focused on

Palestine—had a logic Westerners could understand; Soviet hatred was irrational. The "conflation of targets—Jews, Zionists, Israel, America—used in varying combinations" was absurd; the result, Garment concluded, "not of specific grievances but of an attempt to induce a generalized paranoia." This paranoia built on what Garment called "the most savage single phenomenon in all history: The hatred of Jews and the never-ending manipulation of that hatred for both rational and insane purposes." More succinctly, Moynihan called the Zionism is racism resolution the "Big Red Lie," a Communist—Red—totalitarian updating of Adolf Hitler's "Big Lie" technique.

The Soviet-Arab weakness in 1967 strengthened the Soviet-Arab alliance. Although the Arab world had been hostile to the State of Israel since its founding in 1948, Israel's Six-Day War triumph triggered a major shift ideologically, not just geopolitically. Israel-the-strong was a more popular target than Israel when considered weak. Anti-Semitism and anti-Zionism, considered after the Holocaust to be right-wing and lower-class phenomena, appeared on the New Left and among some Western elites. The growing opposition to Israel and Zionism added a racial component, with opponents calling Zionism racist while accusing Israel of practicing apartheid like the despised South African regime. The Soviet propagandists hit an ideological gusher. "It was these two ideas—the Israelis as Nazis and the Israelis as white imperialists—which were brought together with such brazen neatness in the identification of Zionism with racism," Norman Podhoretz would write in *Commentary*.

The Princeton historian Bernard Lewis noted that in making Israel into a "fashionable enemy," the charge resonated with the times even as it deviated from the truth. After colonialism collapsed, and America's civil-rights movement succeeded, Moynihan noted, "racism was the one offense international society universally condemned." The Holocaust made labeling Zionism as racism particularly perverse. After the Nazis used their Volkish Master Race ideology to murder six million Jews they deemed subhuman, most Jews recoiled from calling themselves a race. Still, the Zionism-racism charge stuck, outlasting the revoking of 3379 and the Soviet Union's collapse, within weeks of each other in 1991.

Central to the *Judenfrage*, "the Jewish Question" of the late 1800s and early 1900s—what to do with the Jews as a stateless people in a Europe of growing nation-states—was the question, as the German anthropologist

THE "FASHIONABLE ENEMY" • 65

Carl Heinrich Stratz put it in 1903: *Was sind Juden*: "What are the Jews...Are they a religion, tribe, nation, people, race?" Jews were not like Christians, united only by a common theology. Jews were bound by a common history, which they traced back three thousand years, a common language Hebrew, a common land Israel, a sense of interconnectedness, which some friends and foes believed had a biological basis after years of inbreeding.

Most Zionists used "race" occasionally, but often sloppily, as a synonym for nation rather than a separate biological category. A few minority voices, like those of Arthur Ruppin, a German-trained sociologist, had a Teutonic timbre that based their Zionism—meaning Jewish nationalism—on Jewish biological separateness. But modern Zionism's founder, Theodor Herzl in *The Jewish State*, published in 1896, blurred race, nation, and religion. He celebrated "our national teachers" in one sentence then continued with "Our community of race is peculiar and unique, for we are bound together only by the faith of our fathers." Similarly, James Joyce called his masterwork, *Ulysses*, serialized two decades later, "the epic of two races (Israel-Ireland)." Herzl's messianic dream included saving African blacks after saving the Jews. He believed that "only a Jew can fathom" African slavery, in all its "horror."

To Herzl and most Zionists, Jews' religious bonds outweighed their occasional race rhetoric. Defined by the mother's religion or an individual's conversion, Jews were a "peculiarly" permeable biological grouping. Yehiel Michael Pines, the Russian-born Hebraist and religious Zionist who moved to Jerusalem in 1878, emphasized Judaism's unique "combination of religion with nationality." This made Jewish nationalism less about "race and soil" but about "a group professing a separate faith and bound in a mutual covenant to observe that faith."

Zionists usually conceived of the Jews as a people or a nation, not a biological race. David Ben-Gurion, Israel's first premier, envisioned Jewish national fulfillment as a first step in unifying the "human race," saying "We consider that the United Nations' ideal is a Jewish ideal." Israel's proclamation of independence offered equality to all citizens, regardless of "race, color or creed." By 1950, visitors to Israel noted its diversity as a veritable "United Nations"—as the popular saying went—with a broad palate of skin colors as Jews from around the world returned "home."

Despite the religious definition and the Jewish genius for assimilation making Jews a particularly ambiguous biological category, anti-Semites condemned Jews as a race apart. This distinction gave their hatred a veneer of scientific sophistication. In fifteenth-century Spain "Purity of Blood Statutes" discriminated racially against Jewish converts to Christianity and their descendants. The early-twentieth-century forgery, *The Protocols of the Elders of Zion*, called Jews "the peculiar and chosen race," but it emphasized Jews' thirst for world domination. The Nazis pushed the biological classification farthest, constructing their ideology on notions of Aryan racial superiority threatened by contamination from Jewish racial inferiority. Targeting Jewish blood, not belief or belonging, and using their perverse logic, murder became the final solution.

As race talk became anathema to Zionists, American Jews experienced their own identity shift. Historically, Jews posed an American "racial conundrum," not fitting into the usual racial peg holes, the historian Eric Goldstein notes. In the late 1800s, talk of the "Jewish race" and "Hebrew blood" distinguished Jews from "Negroes" and "Christian whites." Initially, white Christian Americans viewed Jews as whites practicing a different religion, although some bigots considered Irish immigrants and Jews racially inferior. The influx of 23 million European immigrants starting in 1880, mostly from southern and eastern Europe, coincided with Social Darwinism's rise. Suddenly, Americans facing foreigners flooding their cities explained gaps in breeding and behavior with racial stereotyping. Even humane Progressives like Theodore Roosevelt warned Anglo-Saxons against "race suicide."

Although European Jews spoke of the Jewish "race" to be different, many American Jews spoke of the Jewish "race" to belong, refuting claims that the Jewish "nation" was disloyal to the American nation. "Israel has disappeared as a nation," the radical reform rabbi David Einhorn taught in 1870, describing his people "as a race with certain qualities of soul and mind which form the life-giving condition and root of its own peculiar historical mission." In 1934 Max Baer, a half-Jewish boxer sporting a Star of David on his trunks, called himself the "first bona fide heavyweight champion of the Hebrew race."

Even before the Holocaust, Franz Boas and other academics demolished the biological determinism that would underpin Nazi racism. Rejecting claims that Jews were distinct biologically, the pioneering anthropologist focused on human variation through culture and social structure, not physiology. In 1938 the American Anthropological Society, swayed by Boas, passed a resolution proclaiming that terms such as "Aryan" and "Semite" had "no racial significance whatsoever."

For most American Jews, "peoplehood," emphasizing a distinct national experience with a safer, more red-white-and-blue ethnic dimension, began replacing "race" well before the Nazi horror. The land of the "melting pot" was about social mobility and cultural fluidity, not biological rigidity. Rabbi Mordechai Kaplan in his monumental 1934 book *Judaism as a Civilization* emphasized culture and peoplehood over race or nationhood, as did the great bard of "cultural pluralism," Horace Kallen.

Classifying Jews as a race apart increasingly seemed un-American, while "whitening" Jewish identity became a part of the assimilation process. Jews felt welcomed into the New Deal, as they rallied around President Franklin Roosevelt's broad nationalistic vision. In realizing the American dream, massing into the middle class as the Great Depression ended, Jews appeared less exotic and more American—meaning white.

During World War II, Jews appeared in war movies like *Operation Burma* (1945) as colorful ethnics along with Italians and the Irish, who by the last reel overcome minor cultural differences to fight and sometimes die together as Americans. Postwar talk of the "Judeo-Christian ethic," as Jews commuted to and from suburbia, treated Judaism as a parallel religion to Christianity, with Jews neither a race nor a people. The growing sensitivity regarding black-white relations also collapsed the racial categories. By the 1970s, amid celebrations of "Irish Power," "Italian Power," and "Polish Power," the Jews, too, were classed as "unmeltable ethnics" in Michael Novak's resonant phrase, but clearly white—using a word, "ethnicity," that few would have applied to Jews or Christians before World War II. Ethnics traditionally were "gentiles, heathens and pagans—not Jews," Brandeis University professor Jonathan D. Sarna explains.

President Lyndon Johnson's expansive 1965 immigration legislation completed the transformation. As the new law welcomed in more people of color from Africa, Asia, and South America, the next generation of assimilated and frequently successful Jews seemed "normal." The Jews, the anthropologist Karen Brodkin notes, "became white folks."

Jews' solidifying status in America paralleled Jews' solidifying status in the world. Just as the Holocaust seemed to bury the twin demons of racism and anti-Semitism, Israel's establishment introduced a new, powerful, redeemed Jew. Despite being attacked by six Arab armies in May 1948, this small country won its war of independence, increasing its territory by about 30 percent.

The Arab rejection of the 1947 UN partition plan proved catastrophic for what were still called the Palestinian Arabs. Israel's territory became more contiguous, with its borders following a more natural logic. Rather than being internationalized, Jerusalem was divided between Israel and Jordan. And the undefined Arab entity was never formed. Egypt controlled Gaza, while Jordan controlled the area on the Jordan River's west bank. An estimated 600,000 Palestinian Arabs suddenly became refugees. Some fled voluntarily, thinking it was temporary; others left involuntarily, displaced by the chaos of war, personal panic, Arab calls to evacuate, and fear of Israeli actions. In a cover story celebrating Israel's prime minister David Ben-Gurion as a prophet with a pistol, *Time* magazine declared these mighty new Jews "too tough, too smart and too vigorous for the divided and debilitated Arab world to conquer."

Still, Israelis felt vulnerable after this victory. Six thousand Jews died in the 1948 war, in a country of only 600,000 still stunned by the Holocaust. The war ended in an armistice, not peace. Israel was surrounded by 639 miles-worth of unfriendly borders, with Jerusalem's Old City inaccessible, and the middle of the country only nine miles wide at its narrowest point. The Zionist dreams of the Jews returning to history and defending themselves had resulted in a traumatized country that still seemed captive to historic events and hostile forces.

Nevertheless, throughout the 1950s and 1960s, Israel was the UN's poster child, the best of the post–World War II postcolonial states. Here was the land of the successful socialist experiment, the kibbutz; the land where the desert bloomed, yielding succulent Jaffa oranges. When nineteen Arab and Muslim countries expelled hundreds of thousands of Jews, Israel absorbed them, making the refugees citizens upon arrival. But the destruction of these communities, most centuries old, highlighted the ongoing Israeli challenge—and tragedy. For all Israel's accomplishments, it lacked peace with its Arab neighbors.

The respite Jews thought they earned from anti-Semitism after the Holocaust proved fleeting, just as hopes that the Nazis' demise defeated racism worldwide proved delusional. Haj Amin al-Husseini, the grand mufti of Jerusalem, linked traditional European anti-Semitism with the new Islamist, anti-Zionist anti-Semitism. Building on classic motifs of Jews as wicked, greedy, and dishonest, the Arab repudiation of Israel was visceral and comprehensive. Arab and Muslim countries refused to recognize Israel, to transact business with Israel, even to communicate with Israel. As the political scientist Gil Carl Alroy observed, "The thought of the Jews as rulers suggests cosmic disorder," which is why Arabs depicted "Jewish statehood as 'abnormal', 'unnatural,' 'artificial.'"

When Gamal Abdul Nasser seized power in Egypt in the 1950s, he denounced "Zionist Nazism" as a form of colonialism and imperialism. Nasser muscled through a resolution at the African nations' 1961 Casablanca Conference condemning Israel as "the pillar of imperialism in Africa." His Muslim Brotherhood rivals framed their anti-Semitism in traditional Islamic terms. Nasser also stirred trouble along Israel's southern Negev-Sinai border, as attacks by Bedouin smugglers, returning Palestinians, greedy brigands, Egyptian soldiers, and local Fedayeen, the so-called self-sacrificers, became routine. In response, Israel counterattacked. Hundreds died in thousands of incidents between 1949 and 1956.

In late October 1956, with the violence from both sides worsening, Israel allied with France and Great Britain against Egypt to conquer the Sinai Peninsula and the Suez Canal. The Israelis sought stability in the south. The French and British wanted to retake the Suez Canal, which Nasser nationalized in June. Militarily, the operation went smoothly. Israel conquered the Sinai quickly. Diplomatically, it was disastrous. Blindsided, the United States forced an Israeli retreat. France and Great Britain lost standing in the Middle East. And Israel was now cast as the imperialists' "stooge," a colonial presence that occupied the Sinai, what Africans considered "African" territory.

Although the 1956 campaign intimidated the Arab armies and calmed the Egyptian and Jordanian borders, Nasser and other Arab leaders demanded a "third round" to crush Israel. Calls for exterminating the "Zionist entity" intensified throughout the 1960s. "We want a full-scale, popular war of liberation...to destroy the Zionist base in Palestine," President Nureddin al-Atassi of Syria instructed his soldiers.

Meanwhile, Palestinians also issued a new call for armed struggle. The scholar Rashid Khalidi insists that Palestinian national consciousness began in 1920s, not in the 1960s as many scholars believe. But Palestinians were dispirited after 1948 and engaged in the kind of identity juggling normally associated with Jews. Even today, Khalidi explains, "it would be normal for a Palestinian...to identify *primarily* as an Arab in one context, as a Muslim or Christian in another, as a Nablusi or Jaffan in yet another, and as a Palestinian in a fourth."

When Palestinian guerilla movements in 1964 merged together into the Palestine Liberation Organization, its founding covenant targeted Israel as a foreign and illegitimate intrusion into the Middle East. The PLO's main strike force would be al-Fatah, whose first attack targeted Israel's National Water Carrier, in January 1965.

Palestinian leaders understood the potency of playing to Third World, postcolonial solidarity, pitching their movement as yet another national liberation movement. This people, long feeling particularly invisible, unpopular, marginalized in the West—and deeply wronged by Israel—found legitimacy among Westerners through this anti-Western rhetoric. Article 22 of the PLO covenant called Zionism "racist and fanatic in its nature, aggressive, expansionist and colonial in its aims, and fascist in its methods." The term "racist" appeared but was not central to the PLO's ideological assault against the Jewish state, at least initially.

Spurred by Nasser's pan-Arab nationalism, Syria, Jordan, and Egypt terrorized Israel in spring 1967. Nasser expelled the UN forces that had been deployed in the Sinai as a buffer and flooded the Sinai with more than 80,000 troops. He vowed to wipe out the Jewish state, threats Jews took seriously so soon after the Holocaust. The PLO's founder Ahmad al-Shuqayri anticipated Israel's "complete destruction" predicting "practically no Jewish survivors."

With reserve soldiers digging out graves in public parks, preparing for as many as 10,000 deaths, Israelis felt embattled and lonely. "It is about time we realized that nobody is going to come to our rescue," Chief of Staff Yitzhak Rabin told his generals on May 19. Impatience with the plodding civilian leadership had Israelis speculating that when a waiter asked Prime Minister Levi Eshkol whether he wanted tea or coffee, Eshkol answered, tentatively, "half of both." Growing desperate, Israelis predicted a sign hanging near Lod Airport's boarding gate would ask the last one out of the country "to turn off the lights."

An urbane and eloquent radio broadcaster, Chaim Herzog, calmed the public by analyzing the Arab military threat nightly, providing just enough information to reassure his listeners. During his fifth broadcast, Herzog explained why Israel was not threatened by a London-style blitz. "If I had to choose tonight," he concluded, "between being an Egyptian pilot attacking Tel Aviv and being a citizen in the city of Tel Aviv, I would in the interests of self-preservation prefer to be in the city of Tel Aviv." This epigram instantly became iconic and soon appeared prophetic.

On the morning of June 5, Israel launched a preemptive strike against the planned, multifront Arab attack, justifying the move by international legal standards because the Egyptians blocked the Straits of Tiran. Within hours, Israel had destroyed 304 of the Egyptian Air Force's 419 planes, all of Jordan's Air Force, and half of Syria's. The result was Israel's Six-Day War triumph, which added territory three-and-a-half times larger than Israel itself. Israel took over the Sinai Desert, the Golan Heights, and the entire West Bank of the Jordan, while reuniting Jerusalem. Israel also now controlled one million more Palestinians, most of whom lived in the West Bank and Gaza. Feeling cocky, Israelis joked that one morning an officer proposed: "Let's conquer Cairo." His colleague wondered: "What will we do after lunch?"

This overwhelming victory, and overweening arrogance, transformed Israel's relationship to the world. Israel lost its "David" status and became a "Goliath" overnight, able to defeat Arab armies with ease—and an "occupier" responsible for more than one million unhappy Palestinians. Israel shifted from feeling a part of the Third World to becoming a client state of the United States. These shifts were ill-timed, as the social, cultural and political eruption of the sixties made the world much less amenable to victors, especially those easily cast as white Western winners. As in 1956, Israel's occupation of the Sinai infuriated many postcolonial Africans as an imperialist intrusion into Africa—despite being technically in Asia. And the shellacking Israel administered to the Arab armies humiliated and enraged their Soviet patrons.

At the UN the Soviet premier Alexei Kosygin denounced Israel before the General Assembly. Kosygin hit all the usual notes, attacking "Israeli aggression," darkly pointing to the "imperialist circles" supporting Israel and condemning Israel's "policy of conquests and territorial expansion." Kosygin also compared the actions of "Israeli troops" to "the heinous crimes perpetrated by the fascists during World War II." This was the first time a Soviet premier compared Israelis to Nazis. A secret CIA assessment nonetheless noted that Kosygin's speech "combined a severe attack on Israel with an effort to appear statesmanlike and generally moderate."

That analysts viewed Kosygin's speech as not "resorting to bombast" reflected how routine attacks on Israel were becoming—and their higher levels of hysteria. The Egyptian representative Mahmoud Fawzi, at the same special session, sounded apoplectic. He attacked "the unfolding of the Zionorama [sic] picture.... Just look at the motley crowd," he sputtered, "the misguided, the frightened, the Zionism-drugged, and their Uncle Sam, cajoling, arm-twisting, their ubiquitous, omnipresent Uncle Sam, with his steamroller, gold bag and all, leading the band." A representative from one of Kosygin's satellite states, the Albanian ambassador Halim Budo, denounced "the American imperialists in their hateful intransigence...and the Zionist racists in their vanity and covetousness and their defiance of world public opinion." Racism was becoming part of the critics' vocabulary but not yet central to the assault.

Israel's triumph thus stirred its enemies in profound ways. The Palestinians emerged more galvanized—and more popular in a world increasingly sympathetic to the underdog, especially if the conflict could be cast as people of color under the yoke of Western whites. Disappointed by the Arab states' failures, disillusioned by Pan-Arabism as their hope for salvation, Palestinian leaders became more autonomous and more aggressive. They also became angrier. The numbers of Palestinians under Israeli rule had grown. The Palestinians in the West Bank and Gaza Strip were in legal limbo, not citizens like their Israeli Arab cousins within the "Green Line," the original 1949 armistice borders. Israel did not annex the West Bank or Gaza Strip, although it did annex East Jerusalem and, eventually, the Golan Heights. "Israel became an occupying power," not "simply a Jewish state," the Palestinian intellectual Edward Said would note, and thus had become an easier target.

Under the leadership of the charming, ruthless Yasir Arafat, the Palestinians hijacked, kidnapped, and bombed their way onto the world's agenda. In this conflict of dueling narratives, Palestinians and Israelis also had dueling timelines. The Israeli chronology of Palestinian history in the early 1970s was a litany of violence: September 1970, Dawson's Field, Jordan— Palestinian terrorists hijacked then blew up three jumbo jets, although they spared the hostages' lives; May 1972, at Lod Airport, Israel, three Japanese terrorists sympathizing with the Palestinians killed twenty-six including sixteen Christian pilgrims from Puerto Rico; September 1972, at the Munich Olympics, eleven Israeli athletes and coaches were held hostage and then killed; April 1974, in Kiryat Shmona, Israel, eighteen hostages died; May 1974, in Ma'alot, Israel, Palestinians killed twenty-five, including twenty-two high school students. As the PLO celebrated these moments as victories, the movement focused on other dates, including "Black September," 1970, when King Hussein of Jordan cracked down on the Palestinian guerillas operating in his country, and October 1974, when the Arab summit meeting in Rabat recognized the PLO "as the sole legitimate representative of the Palestinian people."

Beyond terror attacks and diplomatic moves, Arafat and his allies fought an ideological war to shape world opinion. Exploiting the rise of a global mass media, and what Edward Said called the twentieth century's "generalizing tendency," the Palestinians framed their local narrative as part of a global struggle. They invested heavily in research centers, think tanks, and publishing houses to tell their story—and thus link it to broader trends. As a result, Said noted in 1979, "the Palestinians since 1967 have tended to view their struggle in the same framework that includes Vietnam, Algeria, Cuba, and black Africa," joining "the universal political struggle against colonialism and imperialism."

This language of worldwide anti-colonial rebellion, of Third World solidarity, made race more central to Palestinian rhetoric. In critiquing Zionism, ideologues went from wallowing in their feelings of being dispossessed to charging discrimination. According to Said, this transformed "The Zionist settler in Palestine...from an implacably silent master into an analogue of white settlers in Africa."

As a bonus, calling Zionism racism furthered the Palestinian argument that Jews were not a nation. Judaism to Palestinian propagandists was just a religion; anti-Semitism a Zionist delusion; and the Jewish ties to the land mere illusion. They viewed any distinctions between Arab and Jew in Israel as racial, along the lines of whites and blacks in South Africa, rather than the legitimate national distinctions all UN member states drew between, say, Americans and Canadians or Germans and Poles.

Many PLO propagandists steered away from the crass anti-Semitism characterizing the Arab or Soviet anti-Zionist campaigns. "I have never made the mistake of attacking the Jews [verbally]," Arafat said in 1992. "As far as we are concerned, the Jews are our cousins." He pitched a "secular democratic state," he said, as "a humanitarian plan which will allow the Jews to live in dignity, as they have always lived, under the aegis of an Arab state." This statement ignored the Jews' historic, humiliating, second-class "dhimmi" status under Islam, while again negating any national component to Judaism or tie to the land of Palestine. Moreover, beneath the intellectual veneer ran a cancerous Jew hatred. Arafat confessed to the Italian journalist Oriana Fallaci in 1970, "Our goal is the destruction of Israel." *Mein Kampf* was required reading in some Fatah training camps, where former Nazis trained Palestinian guerillas to continue their war against the Jews.

The Palestinian national movement mastered this dual-track strategy, trying to defeat Israel through a combination of terrorist attacks and assaults on its legitimacy, wrapped in the modern rhetoric of national liberation. As the PLO chairman and its public face, Yasir Arafat was tough enough to control unruly factions but shrewd enough to become palatable to Westerners. As fighter and propagandist, Arafat mastered the two sides of the terrorist's sword, wherein violence could be justified in an increasingly polarized and relativistic world if sheathed in the right message.

Gradually, Arafat's strategy succeeded. Despite the standard rhetoric denouncing terrorism as futile, attacks against Olympic athletes and school kids, in airports and on buses, publicized Palestinian demands. This violence against Israel helped create the great inversion. Israel, once considered by many to be above reproach, was increasingly viewed as being beneath contempt. In October 1973, when Egypt and Syria attacked Israel on Yom Kippur, Moynihan and other observers would notice the many newspapers blaming Israeli aggression for the violence.

The Soviet Union viewed Palestinian misery, propaganda, and terrorism as opportunities to outmaneuver the United States in the Cold War. Smoldering after the 1967 victory—and worried about the inspiration Israel's victory provided to three million Soviet Jews—the Soviets declared a propaganda war. Internationalist Communism had long rejected Jewish nationalism, meaning Zionism, with particular vehemence. Early Soviet denunciations of anti-Semitism had degenerated into harsh anti-religious and anti-capitalist campaigns scapegoating Jews during Joseph Stalin's day. Still, the Soviets supported the establishment of Israel, hoping to recruit another socialist ally, then began inching away almost immediately. In the early 1950s, propagandists started using "Zionist" as pejorative for "Jew." To woo Third World postcolonial movements and the Arab world, at America's expense, the Soviets starting denouncing Zionism as imperialist, especially after the 1956 Suez campaign.

The Soviets intensified their anti-Semitic and anti-Zionist campaign in the early 1960s, especially with the publication of Trofim Kichko's 1963 book, *Judaism without Embellishment*. "What is the secular God" of the Jews, Kichko asked. "Money. Money. Money, that is the jealous God of Israel." In 1965, when the UN Commission on Human Rights debated what would become the "International Convention on the Elimination of All Forms of Racial Discrimination," the United States and Brazil proposed an amendment condemning anti-Semitism. Fearing that the charter could be used against them, considering what Soviet Jews were enduring, Soviet delegates sabotaged the amendment. Their counterproposal read: "State parties condemn anti-Semitism, Zionism, Nazism, neo-Nazism and all other forms of the policy and ideology of colonialism, national and race hatred and exclusiveness." The initiative was dropped but the precedent was set.

Furious after the Six-Day War, further humiliated because the United States and Israel were now closely allied, the Soviets launched a comprehensive campaign against Zionism, including labeling Soviet Jews as American or Israeli agents. The next year, the UN's twentieth anniversary celebration of the Universal Declaration of Human Rights would be derailed in Tehran as the Soviets and the Arabs attacked Israel mercilessly during the International Conference on Human Rights, the centerpiece of "International Human Rights Year."

The formal Soviet campaign debuted with an article "What is Zionism" depicting the Zionist movement as a vast conspiracy. At first, the attack was the standard one against the corporate Jew, the international Jew, the cosmopolitan Jew—all seeking to dominate the world. Eventually, the Soviets mobilized the state media, demonizing Zionism in books and newspapers, on radio and television, in schools and in popular lecture halls. Zionism would be "equated with every conceivable evil," Dr. William Korey would note, "racism, imperialism, capitalist exploitation, colonialism, militarism, crime, murder, espionage, terrorism, prostitution, even Hitlerism. No ideology, no 'enemy' had received as much attention or been subjected to so much abuse." In his definitive history of anti-Semitism, Professor Robert Wistrich argues that "Only the Nazis in their twelve years of power had ever succeeded in producing such a sustained flow of fabricated libels as an instrument of their domestic and foreign policy."

As the Soviet authorities invested more in creating what Korey called this "new official demonology," they shifted from attacking Zionism as colonialism and imperialism to treating Zionism as a form of Jewish Nazism. Propagandists targeted the biblical notion of Jews as the chosen people, distorting an attempt to elevate Jews toward godliness by entering a special covenant with the Lord, marked by obligations and constraints, into an attempt to denigrate non-Jews. "Everyone who believes in Zionism admits that a non-Jew in the Jewish state is a sub-human," Radio Moscow declared. And Israeli policy toward the Palestinians—as depicted by the Soviets and the Palestinians themselves—seemed to prove the charge.

In 1971 the anti-Zionist campaign intensified as the movement within the Soviet Union demanding free emigration rights for Soviet Jews progressed. Moynihan would blame a two-part article in *Pravda* that February 1971, as the origin of Resolution 3379, presenting "a proposition that has changed our times, literally." A propagandist named Vladimir Viktorovich Bolshakov labeled Zionism "an enemy of the Soviet people," while accusing Zionists of collaborating with the Nazis. The article soon appeared as an English-language pamphlet *"Anti-Sovietism—Profession of Zionists."* Some Soviet Jews were subjected to political trials, while the Political Literature Publishing House churned out tens of thousands of copies of other anti-Zionist pamphlets. To Moynihan, by linking Zionism with their greatest enemy, Soviet propagandists demonstrated their willingness to libel Zionism promiscuously, to maximize damage. But the Soviets had been trying to Nazify Zionism for four years at least already.

In September 1971, the Soviet Ambassador to the UN Yakov A. Malik shocked his Security Council colleagues when he lambasted the Israeli Ambassador Yoseph Tekoah—telling him "Don't stick your long nose into our Soviet garden.... The chosen people: is that not racism?" Malik added. "What is the difference between Zionism and Fascism, if the essence of its ideology is racism, hatred towards other people? The chosen people," he repeated the phrase, sarcastically. "The people elected by God. Where in the second half of the twentieth century does one hear anyone advocating this criminal absurd theory of the superiority of the one race and one people over others?"

Three years later, in 1974, the highest levels of the Communist Party advanced the campaign. The Party Central Committee embraced a seven point "Plan of Measures to Strengthen Anti-Zionist Propaganda and Improve Patriotic and National Education of the Workers and Youth." The Party distributed the plan to every one of its district committees. In the seven years since the Six Day War, the number of anti-Zionist tracts floating through the Soviet system increased by 600 percent.

Calling Zionism racism played well in Africa too. Linking Zionism with apartheid, and Israel with South Africa, made the Soviet Union look attentive to African needs. At the Algiers Summit in September 1973, Fidel Castro of Cuba and Muammar Qaddafi of Libya had resolved their power struggle over leadership of the Non-Aligned Movement by uniting against Israel. Castro agreed to sever diplomatic ties with the Jewish state and Qaddafi agreed to veer closer toward the Soviet orbit. Encouraged by the Soviets, responding to appeals to Islamic solidarity or Marxist-Leninist discipline, lured by millions of Arab petrodollars, many sub-Saharan nations broke diplomatic ties with Israel following the Yom Kippur War in October 1973. Qaddafi claimed responsibility for bankrolling seventeen countries' decisions to break with Israel. By 1974, after nearly two decades of warm ties in some cases, only Lesotho, Malawi, Mauritius, and Swaziland still had formal relations with Israel. In severing relations, African countries deprived themselves of Israeli coaching and technology.

Israel's new image as a regional strongman in America's orbit, rather than a postcolonial success story, made it easier for adversaries to cast it as the Middle Eastern equivalent of South Africa, a colonialist intrusion. The Arab-Soviet move to estrange Israel from Africa also pushed Israel toward South Africa commercially and militarily. In the 1960s, Israel had not even opened an embassy there, dismaying the large, active, yet vulnerable South African Jewish community. In the 1970s, Israeli leaders still tried keeping some distance, limiting Israel's economic ties to a fraction of most other countries' trade with the apartheid regime, even as the military links multiplied. Nevertheless, this equation of Israel with South African apartheid would outlast the Soviet Union.

The apartheid analogy was absurd because the conflict between Israelis and Palestinians was national, not racial. Not only were there dark-skinned Israelis and light-skinned Palestinians, there was no legalized discrimination based on race in Israel or the disputed territories, which is what defined South African apartheid. In 1948 the Afrikaner National Party had instituted a series of laws segregating the races, including restricting certain jobs to "whites only," and prohibiting marriage between whites and non-whites. Two years later, the Population Registration Act empowered the government's Department of Home Affairs to classify every South African racially, as either white, black (African), or colored (of mixed descent).

By the 1970s, opposition to apartheid within the international community was growing and even some domestic dissent was stirring, but the National Party still controlled the country. The international community intensified the pressure. In May 1970 the International Olympic Committee withdrew recognition of the South African National Olympic Committee. Within the United States, the NAACP began demanding major corporations boycott South Africa. And within the UN, South Africa was attacked constantly. In October 1970 the UN condemned white-dominated nations. In November 1972, with Israel voting "yes" and the United States voting "no," the General Assembly recognized the "legitimacy" of anti-colonial armed struggles. On April 2, 1973, the UN Human Rights Commission approved a draft convention deeming apartheid a "crime against humanity." That winter, in resolution 3151 G (passed December 14, 1973), the General Assembly denounced "the unholy alliance" between South African racism, Zionism, and Israeli imperialism. Burundi—of all countries—had added "Zionism and Israeli imperialism" to the mix. This amendment, which passed 88 to 7, with 28 abstaining, anticipated Resolution 3379. Now it became common to denounce apartheid and Zionism simultaneously. The General Assembly suspended South Africa's UN membership on November 12, 1974. Racism was the crime that made a country unworthy of belonging to the UN, actually, unworthy of existing.

With the Soviets pushing to make their vulgar anti-Semitism seem virtuous, the charge of racism became an increasingly popular libel against the Jewish state. Communists were experts at demonization, wielding libelous labels with the deftness of Samurai swordsmen. Underlying the theatrics was genuine Palestinian pain and a growing Israeli quagmire. In the modern postcolonial world especially, having more than one million mostly non-white people under military rule, their collective rights to self-determination unfulfilled, their dignity frequently assailed, was unacceptable. Israelis themselves struggled with their conflicting commitments to democratic values, differing definitions of their historic homeland, and varying risk assessments in terms of Israelis' security and Israel's soul.

The push to legitimize the PLO—and delegitimize Israel—had also accelerated in 1974. That year the PLO received observer status in the UN, Arafat addressed the General Assembly, and the Soviet-Arab alliance sought to expel Israel from the United Nations. Arafat's ninety-minute speech brilliantly tailored the Palestinian narrative to suit Third World sensibilities and the new realities at what he called "the United Nations of today," which "is not the United Nations of the past, just as today's world is not yesterday's world."

Arafat integrated the claim that Zionism was racism into his appeal and into his formulation of the Palestinian story as one of many among "the peoples of Asia, Africa and Latin America" craving freedom. The world's central challenge was the "struggle...to be victorious over colonialism, imperialism, neocolonialism, and racism in all its forms, including Zionism." Arafat began his story in the "closing years of the 19th century...the era of colonialism and settlement," with Europeans colonizing Palestine and Africa. He equated "the racism practiced both in South Africa and in Palestine" on "behalf of world imperialism" and "settler colonialism." Playing to the UN's anti-Americanism, he also blasted particular "Israeli stands: its support of the Secret Army Organization in Algeria, its bolstering of the settler-colonialists in Africa—whether in the Congo, Angola, Mozambique, Zimbabwe, Tanzania or South Africa—and its backing of South Vietnam against the Vietnamese revolution."

Brashly claiming that Zionism was anti-Semitism rather than a response to it, Arafat hailed the PLO as more pro-Jewish than the Anti-Defamation League. The Zionist notion of welcoming Jews from all over the world back to the homeland was wrong. It was anti-Semitic, he charged, to uproot "adherents of the Jewish faith" from "their national residence" and sequester them from their fellow "non-Jewish citizens." In the guise of championing equality for all, Arafat denied that Jews were a people and rejected Zionism's "artificially created nationality."

Finally, Arafat rationalized the PLO's methods. "Whoever stands by a just cause and fights for liberation from invaders and colonialists cannot be called terrorists," he insisted. "Those who wage war to occupy, colonize and oppress other people are the terrorists."

Arafat was articulating what we could call Che Guevera Rules with some postmodern Frantz Fanon added, glorifying guerillas, hailing anticolonialist movements, and relativizing once universal laws. Those deemed oppressed asserted a near absolute right to use violence or any other tactic. In his book *Guerilla Warfare*, Che preached that doctrine of romantic relativism, arguing that "When the forces of oppression come to maintain themselves in power against established law, peace is considered already broken." Reinforcing his point—and ending his speech—Arafat said ominously: "I have come bearing an olive branch and a freedom fighter's gun. Do not let the olive branch fall from my hand."

While Arafat used race to link Israeli oppression with the most contemptible forms of oppression and Palestinian suffering with the noblest forms of suffering, the spectacle of his speech upstaged the contents. Headlines emphasized the anomaly of a gun-toting terrorist mounting the world's greatest podium for peace—although he only wore an empty holster. Arafat's speech showed that the UN had turned reflexively anti-Zionist. Still, there was not yet a popular understanding of this, nor did the speech elicit the broad reaction Resolution 3379 would trigger. In many ways, Arafat's appearance was more a Jewish event—when many Jews lost faith in the UN—and less of an American or universal turning point.

Meanwhile, the Palestinian and Soviet strategy to woo the Arab world and the rest of the Third World found surprising resonance on the American Left too. The 1967 war had transformed attitudes in the New Left and within parts of the African American community regarding Israel. Black radicals took the lead, feeling the greatest sense of solidarity with the Third World, and with the Palestinians in particular. While most of the black leadership supported Israel in 1967, SNCC—the Student Non-violent Coordinating Committee—repudiated Israel.

A SNCC pamphlet circulated just weeks after the Six-Day War asked a series of "Do you know" questions, including: "Do you know" that "Israel was Planted at the Crossroads of Asia and Africa Without the Free Approval of Any Middle-Eastern, Asian, or African Country?" The pamphlet—echoing a 1966 PLO diatribe—featured gruesome photos from the 1956 Suez war, which SNCC called the "Gaza Massacres 1956." The caption condemning "Zionist Jewish terrorists" read: "Zionists lined up Arab victims and shot them in the back in cold blood. This is the Gaza Strip, Palestine, not Dachau, Germany." One cartoon depicted a hand marked with both a Jewish star and a dollar sign, tightening a rope fastening around the necks of Gamel Nasser of Egypt and the controversial African American boxer Muhammad Ali. This caricature blurred anti-Zionism with anti-Semitism, as greedy Jews replaced southern rednecks in the lynching with an iconic black figure and an iconic Arab leader the target. SNCC's program director Ralph Featherstone insisted that the message was not anti-Semitic but was "only" targeting Jewish oppressors—both those in Israel and "those Jews in the little Jew shops in the [Negro] ghettos." Featherstone celebrated this emerging "third world alliance of oppressed people all over the world—Africa, Asia, and Latin America."

While developing a sense of Third World solidarity, black radicals were using attacks on Zionism to determine whether whites would let blacks "assume leadership." The summer ended with a National Convention on

New Politics, held in Chicago's plush Palmer House hotel—and largely bankrolled by Marty Peretz, a liberal Harvard professor and civil rights activist. Peretz was already starting to recoil from the New Left and black radicals, having been awakened in his own Cape Cod cottage, while hosting a convention planning session, by some radicals singing—by "habit"—deep into the night an anti-Semitic ditty about rent-gouging Jewish landlords. Meanwhile, James Forman of SNCC and other radicals tried imposing a thirteen-point policy statement providing 50 percent of the vote at the conference to blacks and denouncing "the imperialistic Zionist war."

"The importance of this demand is that it puts leadership in the hands of the dispossessed, where it belongs," James Forman proclaimed as he crowned himself "dictator," mocking what he called the weak "liberal-labor" moderates. Meanwhile, the anti-Semitic rhetoric, using "Zionist" to mean unappealing American Jew, escalated. The power struggles between whites and blacks—but particularly between black radicals and Jewish liberals—intensified. A year later, during the New York City teachers' strike, black radicals wondered whether "the Middle East murderers of colored people" could teach young blacks effectively, while denouncing the union leader Albert Shanker and his colleagues as "racist, ruthless, Zionist Bandits." In 1968, the Black Panther Eldridge Cleaver also attacked the judge presiding over his friend Huey Newton's trial by threatening "If the Jews like Judge Friedman are going to be allowed to function and come to their synagogues to pray on Saturdays, or do whatever they do down there, then we'll make a coalition with the Arabs, against the Jews." Similarly, the Black Panthers' weekly newspaper frequently called greedy Jewish slumlords "racist Zionists."

SNCC's leading ideologue, Stokeley Carmichael, linked tensions in the Middle East with tensions in American ghettos. The "same Zionists that exploit the Arabs also exploit us in this country," he raged. In September 1967 he would travel through the Arab world and come back proclaiming "Egypt is in Africa and Africa is our homeland" making the fight to liberate the African land that Israel occupied essential to fighting "imperialism." His 1971 book *Stokeley Speaks* included a chapter on "The Black American and Palestinian Revolutions"—and Carmichael would regularly visit American campuses well into the 1980s denouncing Zionism as racism.

As New Leftists embraced the Manichaean Che Guevara Rules and as the US-Israel friendship warmed, American—and European—radicals soured on Israel. Bashing Israel became "the litmus test," according to Alan

Dershowitz. It allowed authoritarian leftists—especially the many radical Jews—to prove their ideological purity, as others like Dershowitz and Peretz broke with the movement over the issue. Peretz recognized this growing link between radical anti-Americanism and anti-Zionism. Peretz also sensed the particular "biological" zeal that children of Communists and radical Jews brought to their Israel-bashing. Those raised to idolize Joseph Stalin or Fidel Castro had an easier time idolizing Yasir Arafat, just as those repudiating their Jewish heritage took special delight in renouncing Israel.

With New Left posters claiming: "ZIONISM (KOSHER NATIONALISM) + IMPERIALISM = FASCISM," a lynch-mob mentality against Zionists grew. The Weathermen leader Eric Mann wrote in the *Guardian* in 1970, "Israeli embassies, tourist offices, airlines and Zionist fund-raising and social affairs are important targets for whatever action is decided to be appropriate." At an anti-nukes, pro-peace rally in August 1970, Paul O'Dwyer, a leading liberal activist, was booed off the podium because of his support for Israel—which he never mentioned at that rally.

It was difficult to quantify the extent of New Left anti-Zionism, but the attacks on Israel were building among the small cadre of vocal extremists. The 1973 War triggered another wave of denunciations from the Far Left, even as mainstream American public opinion rallied around Israel. On October 19, 1973, the Jesuit priest Daniel Berrigan described Israel as "a criminal Jewish community" that has committed "crimes against humanity," has "created slaves," and espouses a "racist ideology" reminiscent of Nazism. To Dershowitz, this attack marked the moment when the New Left turned anti-Zionist.

Moynihan and others were struggling to find the right linguistic tools to sift through the growing and competing schools of thought. Some started calling more moderate liberals the "liberal-left." *Commentary* proposed calling the radicals "Revolutionists" embracing "Revolutionism." Moynihan sometimes attacked the "authoritarian Left" or the "totalitarian left." Nathan Glazer, once a proud 1950s radical, became "deradicalized" out of disgust with 1960s radicals' "undifferentiated" dogmatism, their "style of absolute thinking, which characterized so many different things as all being in the service of 'imperialism,' 'racism,' and 'capitalism.'" These radicals seemed blinded by their fierce "hatred of the free world." Increasingly, the stance on Zionism, Blaming Israel First, helped distinguish the more moderate Left from this Far Left, with opposing Israel serving as shorthand for opposing imperialism and championing the Third World with the kind of absolutism Glazer abhorred.

Still, these harsh anti-Zionist voices remained marginal. In the African American community, Martin Luther King Jr. had repeatedly denounced anti-Zionism. Whitney Young Jr., of the National Urban League rejected "the myth of Arab-black friendship" while endorsing American military aid to Israel. Bayard Rustin of the A. Philip Randolph Institute was one of America's leading non-Jewish pro-Zionist voices. He scoffed that neither "the Arab nations" nor the Palestinians represented a "revolutionary vanguard." He toasted "Israel's democratic and egalitarian character, which stands in marked contrast to the conservatism and authoritarianism of the Arab regimes." Claims of "historic ties of brotherhood" particularly enraged Rustin, who said they required "a substantial rewriting of history" and a "disregarding" of the persisting "tensions between blacks and Arabs." Barry Levenfeld, a pro-Israel activist on the Harvard campus from 1972 through 1980, would remember the harsh anti-Israel voices there as "left-wing kooks" and black radicals. Bringing a rare sense of proportion to an issue that often invites exaggeration, Levenfeld remembers a small anti-Israel minority at the time balanced by a small pro-Israel minority, with most Harvard students and faculty—like most Americans—not engaged but basically pro-Israel.

With the Jewish sensitivity to public opinion honed over centuries, with most American Jews anxious to remain America's model minority, and with liberalism a central part of mass American Jewish ideology, the growing repudiation of the Jewish state from voices on the Left hurt. "The Israel of American Jews," Professor Jonathan Sarna explains, had long been a "mythical Zion. . . . a fantasy land," reflecting what American Jews hoped to be more than what Israel actually was. To see this ideal systematically assaulted made some unduly angry, others unduly apologetic, as concerns about Israel's reputation became a major communal obsession.

In June 1975, just weeks after Saigon fell, Betty Friedan led a large delegation of America feminists to Mexico City for an International Woman's Year World Conference hosted by the United Nations. As a feminist trailblazer whose 1963 manifesto, *The Feminine Mystique*, galvanized women across the world, Friedan traveled south "relatively naïve," she would recall, hoping "to help advance the worldwide movement of women to equality." Instead, she endured "one of the most painful experiences in my life."

Friedan was shocked by the conference's anti-Americanism, anti-Semitism, and anti-Zionism—which diverted attention from feminism. Men, political spouses, or "female flunkies" dominated so many of the official delegations. Few seemed interested in women's issues. They mocked American feminists as spoiled bourgeois elites raising marginal issues when racism, imperialism, colonialism, and poverty were far more pressing. The American women felt like vegetarians invited to a vegan restaurant, but who were served red meat.

Observing the official UN conference, Friedan saw the Israeli prime minister's wife, Leah Rabin, booed and boycotted. And she watched in horror as the "Declaration on the Equality of Women" became one of the first international documents to label Zionism racism.

When Third World and Communist delegates moved to link the Ten-Year Plan of Action for Women to the abolition of "imperialism, neocolonialism, racism, apartheid and Zionism," some feminist voices broke the silence. One European woman delegate told Friedan: "That is clear anti-Semitism, and we will have no part of it." "If Zionism is to be included in the final declaration, we cannot understand why sexism was not included," the head of the New Zealand delegation T.W.M. Tirika-tene-Sullivan shouted.

Lacking the necessary two-thirds majority, the Arab and Communist delegates forced through a procedural change requiring only a majority vote to approve a declaration. The anti-Zionist plank passed with 61 approving, 23 disapproving, and 25 abstaining. Overall, 89 countries voted for the whole declaration, 18 abstained, and only three countries voted "no"—the United States, Israel, and Denmark.

A thuggish atmosphere intimidated the American feminists, especially in the parallel NGO conference. In that hostile environment, Friedan suddenly took seriously those anonymous letters she had received before the conference warning her "not to speak 'where I was not wanted' or I would be denounced 'first as an American and then as a Jew.'" At critical moments "microphones were turned off" and speakers shouted down. Friedan recalled: "the way they were making it impossible for women to speak—on the most innocent, straightforward of women's concerns, seemed fascist—like to me, the menace of the goosestep."

Under attack, "followed by gunmen and advised to get out of town," and ultimately hustled out of the hall by three big women from Detroit concerned about her safety, Friedan had her consciousness raised in a new way. She had been criticizing American society for years. Regarding Judaism, she was ambivalent, saying her "own background was not that religious." A trip to Israel had disappointed her. Friedan sensed that Prime Minister Golda Meir dismissed her as a bra-burning radical, "this American witch of women's liberation who might possibly infect Israeli women."

Friedan now viewed these democracies' flaws in perspective. What Friedan confronted was a new phenomenon, which grew coincidentally as Friedan's feminist movement grew. America was at least acknowledging sexism as a problem. And she became suddenly dedicated to the Zionist cause, advocating Jewish self-defense in confronting vicious, obsessive lies about Israel. Friedan recognized that this was now the UN's way. "[It] is the prevention of real action on women's rights," she wrote, "for which anti-Zionism and anti-Israel is a scapegoat."

The Mexico City experience integrated Friedan's two embattled identities. She explained that the "new strength and authenticity of women as Jews, and Jews as women, which feminism has brought that enables them to combat the use of feminism itself as an anti-Semitic political tool." She linked this struggle to "part of the larger never-ending battle for human freedom and evolution. Women as Jews, Jews as women, have learned in their gut, 'if I am not for myself, who will be for me (and who can I truly be for). If I am only for myself, who am I?'"

Due in part to the upheavals of the 1960s, which put a spotlight on the colonial legacies and the struggles of developing nations, the PLO's toxic cocktail of terrorism and diplomacy found a receptive audience. A new majority emerged in the UN and other forums, appalled by the racism of the Western world, blind to the excesses of most of the West's opponents, and manipulated by the Soviets. It was a powerful combination and many Western liberals ended up crossing wires, allying with violent, illiberal forces, all under the rubric of fighting racism and advancing human rights.

The Palestinians' tactical reorientation advanced their cause on the world stage even if it did not secure them a state. United Arab armies would no longer try overrunning the Jewish state. Instead, Palestinian guerilla warfare would try subverting Israelis' security, international legitimacy, and honor, which, as Kwame Anthony Appiah teaches, involves a sense of integrity, autonomy, and history, fairly assessed. Spreading a canard libeling Zionism that Moynihan always pointed out was of Soviet manufacture, the Palestinians fought Israel with words as well as bombs. "All this has nothing whatever to do with the rights and wrongs of the Arab-Israel conflict which, despite its bitterness and complexity, is basically not a racial one," the historian Bernard Lewis would explain. "It is no service to the cause of peace or of either protagonist to inject the poison of race into the conflict now." Increasingly, Lewis and Friedan, Garment and Moynihan were in the minority in world public opinion, and certainly in the UN's corridors.

MOYNIHAN ON THE MOVE, OCTOBER 1975

We've got to stop this.

—DANIEL PATRICK MOYNIHAN TO HIS STAFF, JULY 1975

By the time the Mexico City conference ended on July 2, Moynihan was seeking opportunities to confront Third Worlders, the Soviets, and their appeasers. He had agreed to become Permanent US Representative to the United Nations shortly after meeting President Ford on April 12—nine days before Communist forces overran Xuam Loc, a city only thirty-eight miles east of Saigon. The Senate confirmed the appointment easily in early June and President Gerald Ford swore him in on June 30. The next day Moynihan visited the UN mission in New York briefly, before flying to Geneva. Despite his low expectations, Moynihan still was surprised by the Western culture of surrender he found at the UN and the State Department. The UN Economic and Social Council in Geneva, known as ECOSOC, struck him as an "exercise in EGOSAG." The United States was even more defensive than he feared; the opposition, even more ferocious.

Returning home from the International Women's Year Conference, the career diplomat who represented the United States there, Ambassador Barbara M. White, sent out a self-congratulatory cable celebrating the conference's "substantive accomplishments." White regretted the "politicization." Still, she did "not consider it of great importance to the outcome of the conference."

Moynihan received the cable while in Geneva. He fired back a reply, wondering "how, if the Declaration was so inspiring, we had voted against it, and alternatively if we had voted against it, how it could be so inspiring." When he returned to New York on July 12, Moynihan brandished the cable at a staff meeting. His colleague Leonard Garment already had warned him that the attack on Zionism from Mexico City could soon appear at the General Assembly. Banging the conference table with his fist, Moynihan exclaimed: "We've got to stop this."

Subverting all interests to the state's political objectives, in this case feminism, made the declaration a "totalitarian tract" in Moynihan's view. Yet most of his colleagues at the US mission missed the point. White praised the tribune that had traumatized Betty Friedan. Moynihan found this exasperating, as he realized that White and her colleagues believed "their job *as diplomats* was to get along with other diplomats." So they traveled around, hobnobbing and appeasing, tolerating "the most outrageous assaults on principles they should have been defending."

Within hours of being sworn in, Moynihan already had offended his nominal boss, Secretary of State Henry Kissinger. Following Kissinger's advice to respect Soviet sensibilities, President Ford snubbed the Nobel Prize–winning, virulently anti-Communist novelist Alexandr Solzhenitsyn. Even the pro-détente *New York Times* asked: "Does President Ford know the difference between détente and appeasement?" Nevertheless, Moynihan attended an AFL-CIO dinner June 30 honoring the Russian dissident, accompanying Kissinger's rival Secretary of Defense James Schlesinger. The anti-Communist union leader George Meany, when introducing Solzhenitsyn, pleaded for "echoes" of his voice . . . in the White House, the Congress, the State Department, the universities, and the media. And, Meany added, "if you please, Mr. Moynihan, in the United Nations." Meeting in Geneva on July 10, Kissinger reprimanded Moynihan. Moynihan had never seen Kissinger that angry.

Moynihan was realizing that for the United States to be in opposition at the UN, he would have to oppose many in the States as well as throughout the world. He faced the administration's ambivalence, State Department cowardice, and Far Left apologetics, along with Arab hostility, Soviet manipulation, and African acquiescence. Moynihan feared that he and his few allies were alone in Turtle Bay—without ever doubting he was right.

With the Third World and the Soviets ascendant in the United Nations, and the United States flagging, new personalities were shaping the UN's reputation. The UN of the 1950s and 1960s appeared noble and earnest, defined by Eleanor Roosevelt, Lester B. Pearson, Ralph Bunche, Dag Hammarskjöld, and other saintly figures. The UN of 1974 and 1975, on the other hand, was defined by Muammar Qaddafi, Idi Amin, and Yasir Arafat. Abba Eban, perhaps Israel's most famous diplomat, would publish a *New York Times* op-ed in August 1975, asking whether the UN wanted to solve conflicts as a diplomatic forum or wage them as some wannabe world parliament.

President Ford was sending Moynihan to the UN in part because he realized that Americans were losing faith in the organization. Moynihan's growing reputation as an aggressive American advocate was in this respect an advantage. His appointment triggered applause from those fearing the UN's transformation into what one Catholic cleric called "the Third World Congress." The *Washington Post* welcomed Ford's decision as a rare moment of diplomatic good news. The journalist Theodore White, who had known Moynihan since the Kennedy administration, advised: "Speak high and bold when you get here; speak for America; much may be saved in this melancholy year of history if you give a rallying point."

The Moynihan skeptics mostly came from the Left. The journalist Garry Wills mocked Moynihan as "a florid combination of Oxford Don and Colonel Blimp," a bloviating, posturing, imperialist snob. Professor St. Clair Drake, a Stanford University anthropologist, said that, typically, Moynihan's *Commentary* essay substituted superficial advocacy for scholarly analysis. Drake claimed Moynihan treated Third World countries in the same "white Western," "father-knows-best," ethnocentric, "patronizing" way he treated American blacks.

Rather than rising to the bait, Moynihan mastered the Washington game of appearing modest enough to invite more praise. Interviewed by the *New York Times*, Moynihan added a dash of nobility while elegantly elbowing Kissinger. Explaining that this third offer to take the UN job came in the spring, after America's Indochina humiliation and Secretary Kissinger's shuttle mission collapse, he said: "I figured this was not a time to say 'no' to the Secretary."

Privately, however, Moynihan worried, having seen his predecessors stumble. The post had attracted political celebrities such as the presidential candidate Adlai Stevenson and Supreme Court Justice Arthur Goldberg; insiders such as the former undersecretary of state George W. Ball and the former congressman George H. W. Bush; and even journalists such as the *Washington Post* editor James Russell Wiggins, who served under Johnson; as well as the ABC-TV correspondent John Scali, who served under Nixon. Yet the US mission was no longer "state department north," he observed. "I had seen Stevenson humiliated. Goldberg betrayed. Ball diminished. Wiggins patronized. Yost ignored. Bush traduced. Scali savaged." Moynihan would remember that in 1971 when reporters announced his appointment prematurely, Harry Truman's formidable secretary of state, Dean Acheson, bellowed from down the hall in Manhattan's Metropolitan Club: "Moynihan, my respect for you took a precipitous decline when I learned you even considered that ridiculous job!"

With the two racial controversies and his Nixon ties still clouding his reputation, Moynihan feared he was neither electable nor confirmable. He would never "be forgiven," he told one reporter while serving in India. He had thought the Indian ambassadorship was his public service "finale" until the *Commentary* article revived his prospects.

Nevertheless, he had been confirmed, and easily, as his drawbacks had become advantages. Moynihan's new mission was to stir enough trouble so that President Ford looked bold and Secretary Kissinger looked credible— without overstepping. Cynics, such as the *Toronto Star*'s UN correspondent, speculated that Moynihan hoped to become "the most popular UN delegate the United States has ever had at home and the most unpopular one it has ever had abroad."

With congressional concerns growing about what the *New York Times Magazine* called "The U.S. versus the UN," Moynihan's confirmation hearings had overlapped with the first Senate Committee on Foreign Relations hearings in twenty years on the subject. Reflecting the UN's fall in congressional eyes, Alabama's Senator John Sparkman, the committee chairman, launched five days of hearings echoing Abba Eban's question, wondering whether the United Nations would be a constructive diplomatic force, or become "destructive," pitting the Third World against the West. Later, Sparkman asked the legendary dove and UN booster, former Senator J. William Fulbright, about the increasingly popular slogan "get the United States out of the UN and the UN out of the United States."

Some UN boosters who testified saluted the institution's noble ideals, while all emphasized its indispensability. Senator Dick Clark recalled that when Adlai Stevenson was UN ambassador, he countered UN critics by describing Adam's marriage proposal to Eve. When she hesitated, Adam asked, "Is there somebody else?" Stevenson concluded: "There was no one else then. There is no one else now."

Predictably, those most critical of American foreign policy expressed the greatest faith in the UN. Senator Fulbright lamented the country's sore-loser image and double standards, with Americans grumbling about the UN being politicized after politicizing the institution when they had dominated it. Senator Clark, a former political science professor whose grassroots campaign in 1972 involved walking 1,300 miles across Iowa, remembered America's own revolutionary roots, asking "are we such a 'have' country, that we can no longer identify with the hopes and aspirations of the 'have nots?'"

Unsurprisingly, the American foreign policy critics were also Moynihan skeptics. Professor Richard Gardner of Columbia University worried that the "Moynihan approach" overemphasized "the UN as a rhetorical system," understating its importance as "an action system" of essential "peacekeeping and economic cooperation programs." Judge the UN by its actions not its words, Gardner argued. The Princeton political scientist Richard Falk feared Moynihan's political grandstanding would weaken the United States within the UN system.

Most experts were more disappointed with the UN than with either the United States or Moynihan. Still, they conveyed the popular consensus that Americans were not yet ready to abandon the organization, even as former UN ambassador Henry Cabot Lodge Jr. noted that faith in the UN had plummeted, with fewer Americans visiting UN headquarters in New York. The Republican senator Jacob Javits endorsed Moynihan's idea of giving them hell, as a reflection of America's historic gumption and current popular mood. Senator Clark responded: "This country's standing at the United Nations will not be enhanced by a US ambassador with a policy of storming into the General Assembly to 'give 'em hell.'"

During his confirmation hearings, Moynihan insisted that because the UN was "indispensable," Americans had to respect it by responding rather than walking away from it: "You play a part." Moynihan would seek out "engagement" not "confrontation." Because "the totalitarian powers are expansive," hoping to rule the world, America's representatives had to repudiate their "propaganda." Americans also had to be preemptive, warning governments of the consequences of defying the United States ahead of time, rather than trying to change votes once governments decided.

Moynihan rejected appeasers' tendency to say "well, after all, words don't hurt us." "Words do hurt us," he explained, his voice rising with emotion. "Words hurt....Our reputation as a free country is fundamental to us. We should not be so polite as to be misunderstood on that point, sir," Moynihan told Senator Clark.

This approach faced bureaucratic and ideological resistance, especially following the 1960s. Moynihan was fighting a culture war, especially in the State Department, where he saw traditional WASP politesse mixing with 1960s-style adversarial hypercriticism. As a result, conflict-averse, guilt-ridden, turf-oriented State Department officers in Washington usually protected their assigned country's foreign aid allocation, even when that country bashed America in the UN. Moynihan suggested asking these hostile recipients why they deigned to accept assistance from a country they so disdained? Countries "can't have it both ways," he insisted. Every nation had to know that "we take the reputation of our democracy seriously." These muscular responses made senators swoon. The Senate confirmed what *People* magazine called the "Onetime Shoeshine Boy Who Advised Three Presidents," with no debate, no objections.

Irving Kristol, Moynihan's *Public Interest* colleague, noted that Americans had to defend their "liberal values" at home before venturing aboard. But Republicans did not know "how to defend" these values, Kristol observed, while Democrats now had "very mixed feelings about the values themselves." Therefore, Kristol concluded, the only people left defending American values were conservatives or neoconservatives, so "to be a liberal today might very well mean being a neoconservative!" With his dislike for that term, Moynihan called himself a "liberal dissenter."

Swearing Moynihan in on June 30, President Ford praised this "person of high ideals and steadfast purpose...the right man for the job." Ford respected the developing nations' agenda, as long as they did not hijack the United Nations for their own petty political reasons. Playing off his reputation for garrulousness, Moynihan told the president that his new "United States representative...is just that—he says what he is instructed to say." Associating himself "wholly" with Ford's kind remarks—to warm, supportive laughter—

Moynihan concluded quickly. Privately, Moynihan the savvy bureaucratic player asked to meet Ford regularly so UN delegates would know he represented the president personally.

As anticipated, Moynihan started "raising hell," even before settling in to the US ambassador's residence in the Waldorf-Astoria Towers. Moynihan's staff of loyalists included Dr. Suzanne Weaver, a political scientist who had worked with him at Harvard, and Leonard Garment, whom Ford had chosen in 1974 to represent the United States to the UN Human Rights Commission. Every morning, Moynihan, Weaver, and Garment entered a US mission that they believed—for good reason—was crawling with State Department careerists, UN loyalists, and spies for Henry Kissinger. Most of the 125 staffers working the mission distrusted Moynihan, fearing the "liberalism is draining out of American policy," as one diplomat told a reporter. Echoing Irving Kristol, Moynihan diagnosed the State Department as a "non-ideological institution," oblivious to the importance of "words and ideas" in politics, instinctively preferring negotiation to confrontation. It was, he fretted, unprepared for the "new cold war," this ideological clash between Third World countries who considered themselves "'exploited nations' while we are a 'guilty people.'"

At his first staff briefing on Tuesday, July 1, 1975, Moynihan warned that the world's democracies were losing power, lacking influence, in eclipse. Our armies are strong but our ideology is weak, he lamented. He connected this "decline of democratic regimes in the world" with the "decline of the UN."

Ambassador Barbara White and most other diplomats rejected the pessimism and aggressiveness. White circulated a memo characterizing the State Department's mission, especially since 1969, as seeking coexistence with all countries, no matter what their ideology. Moynihan was appalled that Foreign Service officers soldiered on with this anemic worldview, despite failing abroad and frustrating Americans at home. "These were decent people," Moynihan would sigh, "utterly unprepared for their work."

Chester Finn, Moynihan's counsel in India, agreed with Liz Moynihan that Moynihan was operating in hostile territory and needed to hire his own troops. Finn recommended boosting Suzanne Weaver, appointing some loyal press secretaries, and firing some holdovers to try establishing control. Moynihan agreed. He asked Finn, crudely, for "the name of a suitable Arab" to hire, to complement the valuable contribution of Len Garment, whom Finn described as "a known Israel-phile."

Years later, Weaver, who subsequently married Leonard Garment, would remember her co-workers as "polite, deferential, civilized—but undermining." Their hypocrisy and backstabbing drove her "crazy," she recalled. Garment, a scrappy litigator who was raised as a lower-middle-class Jew in Brooklyn, played in jazz clubs in New York in the 1940s, and survived the Nixon White House, insisted that never before had he experienced such obvious anti-Semitism, an anti-Semitism of condescension and contempt, of smirks and side-comments, of camouflage and sabotage.

Throughout his ultimately brief tenure, Moynihan would be involved in a Kabuki dance with Kissinger. Considering that the US representative to the UN sat in the cabinet, Moynihan, technically, served the president directly. But the US ambassador to the UN was also subordinate to the secretary of state. In the Ford administration, the dynamics were more lopsided, considering Kissinger's power and ego. Initially, Kissinger was wary of Moynihan, eager to subdue him, yet in his own way supportive.

In one telephone conversation that summer, Kissinger mentioned to Moynihan that the influential Washington pundit Joseph Kraft had warned him that he would regret not having sent William Saxbe, the new ambassador to India, to the UN rather than Moynihan. "You told me that in Geneva," Moynihan snapped and, challenging Kissinger, asked: "He said it to you twice?" Stung, Kissinger bored in more directly, checking that Moynihan was following instructions to block Vietnam's membership bid. "Sure," Moynihan replied. Pushing further, Kissinger responded: "But I want you to carry them [the instructions] out with conviction," adding, "I don't want a drooping Irishman around there."

Part competitor, part supporter, Kissinger gave two major policy addresses in mid-July 1975 to shape the debate Moynihan had started about America's new role in a changing world. Speaking first at the University of Wisconsin in Madison, Kissinger regretted that the UN had become an arena of confrontation just as the increasingly interdependent world needed more cooperation. The UN should not become "a weapon of political warfare rather than a healer of political conflict and a promoter of human welfare," Kissinger warned. The American people were tiring of the abuse.

Kissinger adroitly balanced this combative address by endorsing the Third World's economic and social agenda. In his second speech the next afternoon, before the Upper Midwest Council in Minneapolis, Kissinger countered his reputation as an amoral Machiavellian realist by incorporating

Third World needs into America's idealistic mission. Kissinger championed human rights while encouraging Third World economies to cultivate "enterprise and industry," even as the West helped.

What *Newsweek* had termed "The World's New Cold War," pitting the wealthy developed Northern hemisphere versus the overwhelmingly poor Southern hemisphere, had now drawn in Kissinger, the man who convinced himself—prematurely—that his détente policy had ended the original Cold War. An intellectual who respected ideas but valued pragmatism, Kissinger was also an unsentimental realist who believed in diplomacy. In these speeches, as in others, he triangulated between his staffers' conciliatory instincts, Moynihan's call to arms, and the Third World's growing pains expressed through an adolescent aggressiveness against the Western mother countries. Kissinger also wanted his fellow Americans to transcend the self-loathing of the 1960s and 1970s. For "this nation to contribute truly to peace in the world it must make peace with itself," Kissinger recommended.

Although more moderate than Moynihan's riffs—he was, after all, secretary of state—Kissinger's speeches were peevish. Reflecting the Foreign Service's discomfort, Barbara White urged Moynihan to massage Kissinger's remarks so countries would not see them as "a challenge." Trying to avoid confrontation, White lapsed into the obfuscatory diplomatese Moynihan deplored. She also tried restraining Moynihan, suggesting that if reporters asked about his *Commentary* article, he should "Throw them off base a little by stressing understanding."

Moynihan mocked White and other diplomats he viewed as toadying, but he fawned on Kissinger. "Dear Henry, You made your mark on history," began one typical exchange. "Now would you like to do something truly spectacular: to make an impress on the Department of State?" Moynihan believed State Department bureaucrats failed to understand the human rights revolution taking place, just as they could not comprehend President Ford's—and Moynihan's own—demands for reciprocity. Moynihan proposed designating sixty-two "multilateral countries" expected to back America in international forums like the UN. Too often American ambassadors worried only about charming their host country without making demands. "Small countries" had to stop treating "us as if they *were* China and Russia," Moynihan argued.

The proposal was countercultural—at odds with the Foreign Service mind-set. Predictably, the State Department bureaucracy considered the initiative too confrontational, Kissinger recalled. Pressed by Moynihan, Kissinger established an Office of Multilateral Affairs but did so halfheartedly.

Preferring to seem on the outs with his State Department colleagues, Moynihan did not even acknowledge his success with Kissinger. He also blocked a Cuban effort to humiliate America. In August, in the UN's Decolonization Committee, Cuba proposed granting the separatist Puerto Rican Communist Party the same official observer status the PLO enjoyed, while designating it the Puerto Rican National Liberation Movement. Moynihan would not abide the UN branding the United States as "imperialist oppressors" in Puerto Rico: "We were not about to have dictators lecture us on democracy."

When Kissinger called about a separate matter, Moynihan pounced. He proposed, in this new spirit of multilateralism, that American ambassadors in the relevant countries inform their host governments that supporting Cuba's insult would be considered an "unfriendly act." This language echoed the phrasing Americans diplomats protecting Portugal used in 1973, designating UN assistance to Portuguese African liberation movements a "hostile act." Moynihan wondered: "Why are we so unprepared to do for ourselves what we are willing to do for others?" Kissinger agreed: "Just be brutal."

Characteristically, Kissinger then grumbled that Moynihan was being too aggressive. Brent Scowcroft and other Kissinger aides believed that Moynihan was hunting for a chance to look tough, following his *Commentary* script, but that Kissinger was restraining him. They contrasted Moynihan's "black-and-white, with us-or-against-us" approach to "the Secretary's multidimensional shades-of-grey framework."

By now, Moynihan knew his approach was unsettling Kissinger's staff and the IO, the Department's Bureau of International Organization Affairs responsible for managing America's relations with the UN. The next day, he discovered that the State Department's "fudge factory" had removed the key phrase "unfriendly act" from the cable. With time "running out," Moynihan started "hailing and shouting." Kissinger backed his UN ambassador in this multilateral initiative. As Kissinger would note decades later, "we were far closer personally than some (including Moynihan) may remember." Eventually, an Indian diplomat asked an American UN diplomat whether

America was threatening India and the other countries. Moynihan instructed the diplomat to reply: "Yes."

Unfortunately, the same day Cuba advanced its resolution in committee, the State Department eased some sanctions against Cuba. Moynihan was furious. Kissinger blamed a "bureaucratic glitch," explaining that the White House approval process for this "conciliatory gesture" began in July and ended coincidentally, that day. Still, Moynihan felt undermined—and further appalled by State Department spinelessness.

Nevertheless, the American counterattack worked. The committee voted 11 to 9 to postpone the Cuban resolution for a year. The New York Times ran a headline "U.S. WINS A UN VICTORY ON PUERTO RICO." The Times editorial rejoiced: "This victory for common sense represents an important first dividend for a tough but reasoned stance by the United States and its partners against the hollow rhetoric and mindless majorities that have brought the United Nations into disrepute and eroded its support."

Others were less buoyant. On NBC's Meet the Press in mid-September, Paul Hoffman of the New York Times confronted Moynihan about a Tanzanian editorial characterizing America's diplomatic threat on the Puerto Rico question as "rude and intimidatory." Hoffman wanted to know whether this was the new strategy. Moynihan countered, calmly, "It most assuredly is. We did not intend it as a rude act. It wasn't. We intended it to have consequences. It did." He explained that the Special Committee on Decolonization, known as the Committee of 24, which formulated the resolution, consisted of "sixteen police states, four democracies and four in between." He insisted: "We are not about to be lectured by police states on the processes of electoral democracy."

Moynihan was shocked when liberals such as the New York Post columnist James Wechsler and the Democratic Member of Congress from Harlem, Charles Rangel, criticized Moynihan's move as too aggressive. "In the name of God, what has happened to us?" Moynihan bemoaned. "Are not Puerto Ricans American?" Moynihan confessed to his friend William F. Buckley: "I shudder, and I don't shudder easily."

Despite the carping, Moynihan was starting to forge a Left-to-Right coalition of supporters. Buckley, who was now celebrating what he termed "Moynihan's Moment," was the voice of High Church conservatism. At the same time, Social Democrats like Carl Gershman were cheering Moynihan from the Left—"It was inspiring to hear an American voice say that we would not be lectured by police states on how to run our democracy."

Moynihan's assertiveness was contagious. He applauded the AFL-CIO's threat to withdraw from the International Labor Organization. Moynihan explained the significance to Kissinger, noting that the right wing, isolationist John Birch Society was no longer alone; American progressive voices were rejecting this new UN. Always happy to bash the bureaucrats, Moynihan explained the unionists' frustration by saying that unlike the Foreign Service, labor was "not used to losing." Unionists refused to endure these lopsided UN losses or "assume it must be America's fault." Still, Moynihan endorsed Secretary of Labor John Dunlop's proposal to give the necessary two years notice, providing the ILO time to reform.

Although he boasted, "we showed our teeth" at Milwaukee, Kissinger wanted to appear more conciliatory than Moynihan. At the General Assembly's special session devoted to development preceding its fall session, Kissinger articulated a generous social and economic vision to woo the Third World as dramatically as détente wowed the Soviet Union. In a 12,000-word treatise, which Moynihan read for an hour and forty-five minutes in New York while the secretary himself was shuttling between Middle East capitals, the administration offered detailed proposals to help fix the world's poorest economies, including floating a $10 billion loan fund. British Ambassador Ivor Richard led cheering delegates from the West and the Third World, comparing the speech's generous economic vision to the legendary Marshall Plan.

While Henry Kissinger was trying to transform the UN discussion—and world realities—toward nurturing a higher standard of living for all, the Soviets and Arabs continued to bash the United States and other democracies, particularly Israel. Kissinger's Middle East successes, especially Egypt's shift toward the United States, infuriated the Soviets. Both vengeful and worried, Moscow wanted to use ideology to bind the Third World together, ensuring loyalty while annoying the Americans.

The non-aligned meetings in Lima in August resulted in what Moynihan called "an interminable catalogue of accusation and demand." The document targeted the "large consumption economies," and repeatedly praised "the struggle against imperialism, colonialism, neocolonialism, racism, Zionism, apartheid and any other form of foreign domination." Meanwhile, neither the Soviet Union nor China joined America's generous economic initiative. The Soviets were too busy blaming the capitalists; the Chinese were too busy jousting with the Soviets.

Intensive multilateral negotiations followed, culminating with Moynihan and Garment undertaking a forty-hour marathon to reconcile the Lima declaration with Kissinger's proposals. A special caucus of the Non-Aligned Movement passed a resolution denouncing Moynihan for his hard bargaining, even as he and Garment produced an acceptable draft. Mischievously, the two followed the Lima format and echoed the language just enough to obscure the subtle changes they inserted to make the document more palatable to the West. To great applause from the Third World, the Special Session unanimously approved what Moynihan called "the broadest development program" in world history.

Swept up in the euphoria, the *New York Times* reflected the new American apologist ideology Moynihan abhorred. Comparing the North-South tensions to the "class struggle" in nineteenth-century early industrial societies, calling the Southern Hemisphere nations "the globe's proletariat," cast the Third World bloc as a heroic trade union, not as Moynihan's dastardly alliance of totalitarians. Such sloppy moralizing and Western self-abnegation, Moynihan believed, helped Foreign Service officers get along with their neighbors when they commuted home to "Scarsdale" nightly.

Elated by the successful negotiations, Moynihan turned to the Algerian radical presiding over the General Assembly's special session, Abdelaziz Bouteflika, saying "Mr. President. This system works." This assessment was overly optimistic. Moynihan—and others—quickly saw how dysfunctional that system had become.

The Soviet-Arab animus against Israel was so great, the desire to embarrass the United States so intense, that nearly all other agenda items became secondary. In July, in Jidda, Saudi Arabia, thirty-nine Islamic countries and the PLO demanded Israel's expulsion from the UN. In late July, the Organization of African Unity Conference held in Kampala, Uganda, divided over the Israel issue. Libya and the PLO lobbied for Israel's expulsion. Egypt proposed a milder rebuke. The heads of state debated the issue for eight hours. Before storming out, Colonel Muammar el-Qaddafi, Libya's dictator, shouted that the Egyptians and their president Anwar Sadat were betraying the Palestinian cause.

The stalemate emerged because many Black Africans, feeling American pressure, were growing nervous about expelling Israel. Universality of membership was a core UN principle. Ousting unpopular countries would set a dangerous precedent and damage the General Assembly's character as the all-country parliament. Many African leaders also appreciated Israel's help in the 1960s and early 1970s—and resented that the Arabs had not offered compensation for the oil price jump. Israelis, especially Labor Zionists like David Ben-Gurion and Golda Meir, felt a sense of "historical mission" to fulfill Theodor Herzl's dream of helping African countries. By the early 1970s, Israel had diplomatic ties with thirty-two African countries, more African embassies than any country other than the United States. Tanzania's president Julius Nyerere called Meir, Israel's prime minister from 1969 to 1974, "the mother of Africa." Many Israelis hoped for a peace payoff too, believing the popular saying: "the road to Cairo passes through Bamako," Mali's capital.

The Arab nations recognized the point. Shortly after seizing power in 1952, Egypt's Gamel Abdul Nasser vowed to run Israel out of Africa. The Arab League appealed to the new African nations in their language, calling Israel's help "a façade for neocolonialism trying to sneak through the back window after the old well-known colonialism had been driven out through the front door." Israel's 1967 triumph unsettled relations with Black Africa. Some countries succumbed to the Arab and now Soviet entreaties, too, but relations thrived with most. The rupture came with the 1973 Yom Kippur War, when Muammar Qaddafi, the Saudis, and other Arab leaders bullied and bribed twenty-one countries in October and November 1973 alone to sever diplomatic ties with Israel.

Still, two years later in 1975, many African leaders feared going too far. The OAU produced two resolutions, one supporting a media campaign against "the racist aggressive nature of the Zionist entity," one advocated cutting all ties to Israel. This resolution clumped together what the OAU now officially called "the racist regime in occupied Palestine and the racist regimes in Zimbabwe and South Africa." In a rare move, Sierra-Leone, Senegal, and Liberia expressed reservations about both resolutions, Ghana questioned one resolution, and Zaire opposed both.

Like a big brother's presence intimidating the neighborhood bully, American pushback discouraged the anti-Israel maneuvering. The non-aligned nations meeting in Lima also stopped short of advocating Israel's expulsion. Still, those who cared about America's relations with the UN worried. In early September, seven former US ambassadors to the UN, along with prominent lawyers and law professors, warned Secretary General Kurt Waldheim in a *New York Times* advertisement that expelling or suspending Israel from membership would violate the UN charter, alienate influential countries, and risk the UN's collapse. Reassuring former ambassador Arthur Goldberg and his colleagues, Waldheim said he "stressed the importance of universality" in high level meetings with key leaders.

Although pleased to see American power reasserting itself, Moynihan dismissed all this "plea bargaining." While boasting to critics how restrained he had been, he was ready to "raise hell." When His Excellency Field Marshal Al Hadji Idi Amin Dada, V.C., D.S.O., M.C., President of the Republic of Uganda and Chairman of the Organization of African Unity arrived in New York, Moynihan had his chance.

The Uganda dictator's grand reception at the United Nations further reinforced Moynihan's determination to fight the new world order. On October 1, Idi Amin, already known for feeding critics of his regime to the crocodiles, and now, midway through his eight-year tenure of terror during which he would murder as many as 300,000 Ugandans, addressed the General Assembly. Amin was visiting the UN as the president of the Organization of African Unity, a post that rotated among African heads of state. Beefy, round-faced, clutching a gold marshal's baton, wearing a dark green uniform with huge blindingly gold epaulets, and a chestful of medals extending down to his left hip—including Israeli paratroopers' wings—Amin looked cartoonish, acted fiendish.

Enjoying a warm reception and amid standing ovations, Amin urged the UN to expel Israel, while advocating the "extinction of Israel as a state." He warned his American hosts of the Zionist influence in banking, the media, and other essential American institutions. Of course, he insisted he liked Jews but only disapproved of Zionism. Finally, he insulted the African American community, blaming American blacks for their own troubles because they lacked unity.

Moynihan boycotted the dinner that the secretary general and president of the General Assembly hosted honoring Amin. When reporters asked why he would not attend, Moynihan demurred, then added mischievously that while he decided himself, had he asked his Washington bosses they would have supported his actions. Moynihan knew that *had* he asked, he would have been instructed to attend. Suzanne Weaver Garment recalls that one of her responsibilities, in those "good old days of the typewriter and the telefax," was to ensure the UN mission's facsimile machine—then a fairly new piece of technology—"broke down" conveniently, on certain occasions when it was necessary to send a sensitive speech for State Department approval.

Moynihan understood that Amin wanted to make Israel into everything the world community and Africa abhorred, then equate the United States with Israel. Amin's speech warned him that "Something was going to happen. The Non-Aligned and the Soviet bloc were reinforcing one another in a generalized assault on the democracies and a specific attack on Israel." Defending democracy, a *New York Times* editorial noted the widespread executions in Uganda and lamented the General Assembly's warm reception for the country's "President, a racist murderer."

Unfortunately, Moynihan was stuck with a State Department not only utterly incapable of dealing with ideological attacks but also addicted to "a form of good manners that is a kind of substitute for ideas." Traveling to San Francisco to address the AFL-CIO, Moynihan called Garment. Garment was drafting a speech attacking the Soviet–Third World fallback plan, which was to condemn Zionism as racism instead of expelling Israel. As Moynihan drafted his speech on the cross-continental flight, with Garment's fury feeding his, Moynihan linked Amin's anti-Zionism to all dictators' aversion to democracy.

Two days after Amin spoke, on October 3, Moynihan excoriated him—and his co-conspirators in his AFL-CIO address. Jumping off the union president George Meany's lament that "Democracy has come under increasing attack," Moynihan sighed, "I see it every day in the United Nations." Rejecting the growing numbers of those he deemed self-hating Westerners who "believe that our assailants are motivated by what is wrong about us," Moynihan retorted: "*They* are wrong. We are assailed because of what is right about us. We are assailed because we are democracy."

In attacking Amin, Moynihan slipped. He claimed it was "no accident" that Amin called for Israel's "extinction," and that it was "no accident," that "this 'racist murderer'—as one of our leading newspapers called him this morning—is head of the Organization of African Unity." Moynihan saw Amin's hostility as the hatred of all despots for all democracies, including Israel. He challenged members of the Organization of African Unity to repudiate Amin. Trying nevertheless to be diplomatic, Moynihan praised the OAU for blocking attempts to expel Israel from the UN.

Actually, it was "accidental" that Amin was heading the OAU—it simply was Uganda's turn. By claiming Amin represented the OAU accurately, Moynihan infuriated the Africans, his State Department colleagues, and Kissinger. Kissinger, apparently, at first enjoyed Moynihan's histrionics. But when both African and American diplomats complained, Kissinger "blew his stack," a "top" State Department source—which could have been Kissinger himself—told *Newsweek*.

Jews were not on Moynihan's mind. He was focused on the accusers not the accused. He used Amin's rant to critique the totalitarian apologetics sweeping the UN—and the world. He was not obsessed with Israel. He had never visited the country, and, with his modest finances, resented that he had not been invited on some professorial fact-finding mission. Moynihan understood Zionism, very simply, as defining the Jews as "a people" with the same rights to nationhood other peoples enjoyed.

Moynihan recognized that this Zionism is racism charge emanated from Moscow's suffocating totalitarian worldview. His fight for Israel's survival, therefore, did not begin with a "concern for Israel," he later explained. Rather, it was from a more "personal history... a history marked for me by Kennedy's promise to pay any price in the defense of liberty, a history now mocked by Vietnam."

While George Will and many other columnists applauded Moynihan's speech as proof that America would no longer accept "moral lectures from its moral inferiors" at the UN, Moynihan focused on the elite disdain for having behaved "undiplomatically," as *Newsweek* termed it. In two articles over two weeks, *Newsweek* would also describe Moynihan as "embattled," and "in the doghouse," for having again derailed relations between Washington and Black Africa. The *New York Times* pointedly resurrected Moynihan's earlier line about the need to "start raising hell." Moynihan particularly resented that America's supposed "newspaper of record" worked into its news rather than its editorial section the speculation of unnamed "Americans at UN headquarters" who asked "What is Pat Moynihan running for?" This charge that Moynihan was grandstanding to position himself for electoral office would become increasingly common as the controversies multiplied—and his popularity soared.

State Department colleagues were less subtle than *New York Times* reporters in trying to restrain Moynihan. The State Department's initial press statement claimed: "Ambassador Moynihan's words were his own." Seeking more distance, the department's PR machine then emphasized that no superior cleared Moynihan's remarks. Moynihan's own UN mission staff prepared an even more equivocal press release, claiming that some Amin statements before the General Assembly "earned wide approval: others were morally offensive." Moynihan yelled: "not one goddamn thing Amin had said had won my 'wide approval.'"

Clearly, American diplomats were supposed to be more diplomatic, especially in the post-Vietnam, Henry Kissinger era. The *Voice of Uganda* charged that Moynihan's speech reflected America's contempt for "international diplomacy." The executive secretary of the Organization of African Unity, Tiamiou Adjibade from Dahomey, called Moynihan's "uncivil attacks," a "deliberate act of provocation against President Amin and unfriendly towards the OAU."

Had Adjibade stopped there, he would have confirmed Kissinger's fears that the UN ambassador was alienating Black Africa. But Adjibade claimed the attack confirmed Amin's assessment of "the total control of international zionism on the USA." This attack reflected the totalitarian poison that Moynihan despised.

Moynihan wisely deferred to his colleague Clarence Mitchell Jr., a public delegate to the UN and a respected NAACP activist, to fight further. Mitchell rejected Amin's "unsolicited advice on how black Americans should conduct their affairs." With estimates that Amin had murdered at least a quarter of a million Asians and banished another 60,000 on account of their race, Mitchell said "a man is just as dead if he is killed by a black person as he is if he is killed by a white person." The civil rights leader Bayard Rustin also insisted that American blacks would "not indulge tyrants in black skins." Rustin, the national chairman of Social Democrats USA, wondered why at the UN, delegates seemed more outraged by Moynihan's calling Amin a murderer, than by Amin's murders themselves.

Rustin's colleague, the executive director of Social Democrats USA, Carl Gershman, contrasted Moynihan's bold "ideological counter-offensive" against democracy's enemies with Kissinger's perpetual fear of upsetting Moscow. Such ideological flaccidity has demoralized America and made détente a failure, Gershman argued. Noting Moynihan's equation between social democratic reform at home and confidence abroad, Gershman articulated from the Left the kind of principled self-confidence and American patriotism that was being called right wing—and which leftist radicals would reject as Reaganite and xenophobic in the 1980s.

Moynihan acted as if he were besieged in his State Department bunker. Yet in Congress, he was becoming a hero. Congressional leaders in both Houses were threatening American withdrawal from the UN if Israel was expelled or suspended. Moynihan also ignored the many African diplomats embarrassed by Amin. A number of newspapers in Africa criticized Amin's speech, ruining the impression of Africa and the Third World as one hostile, anti-Western bloc. Senegal's *Afrique Nouvelle* called Amin's appearance "the most racist act ever seen at the United Nations."

Sharing the New York intellectual's obsession with the *New York Times*, Moynihan was particularly pleased to see that the liberal columnist Anthony Lewis and his conservative colleague William Safire dominated one edition of the *Times* op-ed page praising this new confrontational approach. Lewis admitted that Moynihan's attack "inspired" him but spent much of the column blaming America as causing much "horror" in the world. Safire cheered that now, "Diplomacy is becoming a two-way street."

Watching the fracas, Kissinger seemed torn. At an impromptu party for Ford's VP Nelson Rockefeller—his former patron—Kissinger backed his UN ambassador. William F. Buckley told Moynihan that Kissinger endorsed the speech but believed that the press only applauded Moynihan's theatrics because "the proximate beneficiary was our old friend the State of Israel." In fact, since the summer Kissinger and his people had been warning the president about Moynihan acting more aggressively than the secretary of state. In the Oval Office on October 9, Kissinger complained about "This Moynihan thing," saying "We could live with his comment on Amin, but the OAU linkage is bad and your endorsement doesn't help." Kissinger asked Ford to say something at his press conference that night "to set it straight."

Kissinger had been a media darling for six years. Not since Thomas Jefferson had a secretary of state played such a starring role in a presidency. Kissinger had ranked as one of America's most admired men for many years during the Nixon administration. Now, during a tough time, after Vietnam collapsed, Moynihan was emerging as the foreign policy superstar. "I was *his* ambassador," Moynihan realized Kissinger must be wondering: "what was I doing on the front page of the *Times*?"

At some deep level, Kissinger resented that just as he was pressuring Israel's leaders, Moynihan was defending the Jewish state. In his UN memoir, quoting Nathan Glazer's observation that "Israel had become the religion of the Jews," Moynihan overreached, claiming that Kissinger's typically Jewish

Israel obsession drove his entire foreign policy vision. This distorted impression reveals Moynihan's discomfort with Kissinger—and with Jews' Zionist passions.

However, Moynihan's most important audience, the president, was pleased. At a cabinet meeting Ford declared that Moynihan and Clarence Mitchell said what needed to be said. "You seem to be surviving," Ford teased Moynihan. "If you say so," Moynihan replied, "then I am." Moreover, Ford held press conferences two nights in a row—and ignored Kissinger's advice twice, refusing to renounce Moynihan's remarks.

Moynihan claimed that the first lesson he had learned from his Idi Amin speech was: "avoid writing speeches in airplanes." The second lesson, "translated from the Gaelic," was that if you wanted to find an audience, "start a fight." In fact, Moynihan was proud of his speech and relished the fight. The State Department sabotage initially embittered him, then liberated him. Although he still felt more criticized than lionized, he delighted in the encouragement he did receive. Typical was the note from George B. Lambrakis, the deputy chief of mission at the American Embassy in Beirut, saying: "It has been a long time since a US spokesman has said many things that have needed saying, and I am sure a lot of people in the Foreign Service are cheering you on."

In defending Zionism, Moynihan was combating what he saw as an ideological assault on Western values and American power. Rejecting the hypocrisy epidemic in the international community, he feared that if human rights language could be "turned against one democracy, why not all democracies?"

Meanwhile, Communist dictatorships were bulletproof. Although Idi Amin's crimes in Uganda were horrific, Pol Pot's evils in Cambodia were worse. Alan Dershowitz and a small band of human rights activists were particularly outraged that as the Zionism is racism resolution progressed, the UN—and most of the Left—were keeping silent about the growing genocide in Cambodia. The Khmer Rouge, the Red Cambodian Communists led by Pol Pot, conquered Cambodia on April 17, 1975. On October 6, Cambodia's Prince Norodom Sihanouk addressed the General Assembly for forty-five minutes, lambasting American imperialism. Meanwhile, back home, his allies—who would depose him six months later—were depopulating Phnom Penh; "reeducating" millions; starving their own people; hunting down professionals, English-speakers, minorities, intellectuals, and scientists; raping young women; killing the old, the sick, the infirm; and ulti- mately slaughtering at least 1.7 million people over the next three years. By December 1975, Aleksandr Solzhenitsyn, among others, was denouncing the "Cambodian genocide." The UN did nothing, for years, in part because the villains were doubly protected from UN scrutiny as Third World Communists.

Moynihan and his band of idealists were both nationalists and universal- ists—true Wilsonian interventionists—trying to save the world through American democracy, demanding dignity, integrity, and consistency at home and abroad. Moynihan saw himself as an American patriot fighting for freedom. His first few weeks as US ambassador to the UN reinforced his sense that he had three sets of enemies: the world's anti-American dictators, be they Communist or postcolonialist; the "totalitarian" Left with its rela- tivist, Che Guevara rules and its anti-Zionist obsession; and those who, in Moynihan's biting, class-conscious jab, had to go home nightly to Scarsdale and indulge the new, postsixties, postpatriotic zeitgeist by enabling the America-bashing emanating from America's enemies and America's harsh homegrown critics.

The venerable Harvard government professor Samuel Beer saluted Moynihan's actions as patriotic, admitting "But then—I am an unrecon- structed nationalist." At the UN mission, Suzanne Weaver was wondering how to advance Moynihan's mission by teaching the developing countries that America's "concern with liberty" was neither parochial nor sinister but a core value to embrace as their societies matured. Henry Kissinger, charac- teristically, was more ambivalent. First, in 1974, during the negotiations leading up to the 1975 Helsinki Accords, he said the human rights provi- sions could be written "in Swahili for all I care." Eventually, he celebrated the Helsinki final act for "enshrining human rights in international law." Moynihan recognized the great potential of the human rights revolution, even as he worried, along with Irving Kristol, that in shifting from traditional liberal rhetoric about "individual rights," "human rights" was more selective, entailing trendy, collectivist groupthink.

Although many opponents caricatured Moynihan as a Zionist stooge, his primary commitment was to Americanism, not Zionism. He believed the anti-Zionist attacks reflected his foreign opponents' totalitarian impulses encouraged by his domestic opponents' unpatriotic, self-defeating, apolo- getics. Moynihan's State Department critics were at least partly correct. He was looking to prove his point about the UN, and Idi Amin's tirade provided a great opportunity. Years later Suzanne Garment, still fuming at the many State Department attempts to humiliate Moynihan, explained that the Amin fight "was the pivotal moment." In her view it was the point at which Moynihan "took control of his public life." When Moynihan said "We've got to stop this"—uncharacteristically leaving "this" undefined—he meant both the wrongdoers in the international system—and those who abetted them. He knew there was much work ahead.

OOM, SHMOOM: "WHERE ARE YOUR BLOODY JEWS?"

It took the US delegation, led by Ambassador Daniel
Moynihan, to characterize this new attack on Jewry as an
obscene act.... And yet, where were the Jewish people?
—AMBASSADOR CHAIM HERZOG TO THE CONFERENCE
OF PRESIDENTS OF MAJOR AMERICAN JEWISH
ORGANIZATIONS, OCTOBER 24, 1975.

Always sensitive to criticism, still scarred by his involvement in those two racially explosive controversies, Daniel Patrick Moynihan initially did not realize how much Americans loved his new stance. Combating the Zionism is racism resolution, as it snowballed through the UN committee structure onto the floor of the General Assembly, he did not even feel Jewish support. A number of Israeli leaders told their American Jewish colleagues simply to ignore the UN, quoting Israel's first prime minister, David Ben-Gurion, who dismissed the world body—"HaOom" in Hebrew—by saying "Oom, shmoom." At one point, frustrated by the lack of support, Moynihan barked at Israel's ambassador to the UN Chaim Herzog: "Where are your bloody Jews?"

Moynihan saw the attack on Zionism through the lens of the Cold War and America's Vietnam humiliation, fearing the Third World's rise and the

West's decline. The Israeli diplomatic establishment read the situation differently. Israelis perceived a Syrian-Libyan-Palestinian power play against Egypt. Two years after the Yom Kippur War, two years before Egyptian president Anwar Sadat's path-breaking, peace-making flight to Jerusalem, and just weeks after the latest Sinai agreement, Egypt was drifting away from Soviet patronage toward the United States. The radical Arab regimes wanted to embarrass Sadat into supporting his Arab brothers rather than his new American friends.

Although they worried about Henry Kissinger's infatuation with Sadat, the Israelis wanted Egypt to break with the Soviets and were willing to lessen Egypt's embarrassment by muting their opposition to the resolution. President Gerald Ford's springtime reassessment of relations with Israel also intimidated the Israeli leadership. Israel's prime minister Yitzhak Rabin would recall this time as "one of the worst periods in American-Israeli relations."

Another factor confused American Jews. Relations between Israel's UN mission in New York and Israel's embassy in Washington paralleled the turf wars between America's UN mission in New York and State Department headquarters in Washington. Israel's powerful ambassador to the United States, Simcha Dinitz, prizing his friendship with Kissinger, resented Israel's worldly new ambassador to the UN, Chaim Herzog. Herzog was more concerned about the Zionism is racism resolution threatening Israel's legitimacy; Dinitz more shared Jerusalem's Egypt-centered view.

Like Moynihan, Ambassador Herzog's brilliant performance in public diplomacy sometimes strained relations with quieter diplomats back home. Herzog's anger at Jewish and Israeli passivity almost caused his recall, even as he was fighting his epic battle for Zionism. Still, with his comrade Moynihan, the two went public, stoking an American public outcry against the United Nations. Nearly four decades later, the UN has yet to recover.

While Herzog and Moynihan would remain close friends until Herzog's death in 1997, their initial meeting unsettled Herzog. The two lunched together shortly after his arrival as Israel's ambassador to the UN in August 1975. He found Moynihan charming but a tad menacing. They celebrated their shared Irish heritage—Herzog was born in Ireland in 1918 and moved to Israel when he was seventeen. A year later, his father, who had been chief rabbi of Ireland, was elected chief rabbi of Palestine. Moynihan embraced Herzog as a fellow intellectual. The former head of Israeli military intelligence, a leading lawyer, a refined Israeli radio commentator and author, Herzog was one of Israel's few intellectual aristocrats at a time when the country was gruff and proletarian. Herzog's brother-in-law Abba Eban was Israel's most famous diplomat.

With his tousled hair and academic air, Moynihan appeared to Herzog like a sixties leftist who might harbor dislike of Israel. Moynihan started off by praising the smart Jewish kids in his neighborhood he had known growing up. Such "model minority" comments, objectifying Jews, can rankle a sensitive listener. Isaac Herzog, Chaim's son, recalls his father telling him that after he and Moynihan, who "both shared the love of a good drink as Irishmen," had finished two bottles of wine, Moynihan made some crack about Israel treating Palestinians harshly. That parting shot made Herzog "wary," his son recalls, "not sure that Moynihan would be a friend."

Herzog's doubts eased as the anti-Israel momentum grew, along with Moynihan's indignation. Eventually, Moynihan gave Herzog a combat veteran's highest compliment, saying "He was a man to be in a tank battle with." With their respective bosses challenging their tactics, the two freshmen diplomats bonded further.

Both Yitzhak Rabin and the foreign minister Yigal Allon felt skittish after the Kissinger-Ford browbeating. The Israelis had infuriated the Americans by refusing to cede too much territory without Egypt promising nonbelligerency. Kissinger's months of fuming about the obstructionist Israelis had resulted in Ford's springtime reassessment.

While railing against the Israelis, Kissinger extolled Egypt's president Anwar Sadat. Israelis knew Sadat as the anti-Semitic Gamel Abdul Nasser's designated successor who restored Egyptian pride by surprise-attacking Israel in October 1973. Nevertheless, they also knew that they would be safer with Egypt as an American client.

Rabin therefore wanted to encourage Sadat's transformation. "The Arabs used to talk about throwing Israel into the sea," Rabin said in late August. "But today Sadat talks of a sea of peace." Less sentimentally, Rabin also reported seeing "a mutual distaste developing between the Arabs and the Russians"—or at least this Egyptian and his Soviet patrons.

In that spirit, Rabin approved the Sinai Accords of September 1, 1975, finally ceding those kilometers around the Gidi and Mitla Passes that Kissinger had demanded for months. Israel also returned the Abu Rudeis oilfields to Egypt. Egypt, for its part, made symbolic concessions, pledging to resolve conflicts peacefully. Egypt's welcoming two hundred American civilians to operate early-warning systems monitoring compliance transformed Middle East power dynamics, boosting the United States while eclipsing the Soviet Union and the Arab rejectionists.

In late September, when Yigal Allon visited the UN, Herzog's secret briefing emphasized Israel's need to help the Egyptians befriend the Americans. When Allon met with his colleagues in New York, he framed the fight for Israel as a fight against what he called "extremist trends" in the General Assembly initiated by "uncooperative countries." Positioning Israel as peace seeking, he warned that the Soviets and radical Arabs wanted to "thwart" the Sinai Accords and unsettle—"annoy"—Egypt.

The Israelis appreciated that American pressure had blunted the push to expel Israel from the UN or suspend its membership. Over the summer Kissinger had warned that the United States would take "definite and clear action" should the UN expel Israel. The Democratic House majority leader Tip O'Neill circulated a sense of the Congress resolution paralleling a Senate effort with forty-seven sponsors urging the United States to withdraw in the event the UN either expelled or suspended Israel.

In Middle Eastern matters, the mood can shift as frequently as a desert wind. The "uncooperative countries" surprised the Israelis, just a month after the Sinai Accords, when, on October 1, Cuba, Somalia, and Dahomey, fronting for the Soviets and the Arabs, submitted an amendment to a Human Rights Committee resolution charging Zionism with being racist. This move came "out of the blue," Herzog remembered. He realized the fallback position was even worse than expulsion. Shifting the debate from expelling Israel to maligning its founding ideology assailed Israel's very legitimacy. Herzog called Moynihan and asked whether he "realized the significance of the draft resolution." Replying "I do," Moynihan vowed that the Americans would stand by Israel, even if no other country did.

The Arab rejectionist strategy was doubly diabolical. By being forced to declare Zionism racist, Egypt risked alienating the Americans, who had been pressuring Israel so intensely to make concessions. And such a worldwide attack also stirred the Israeli Right, making it even harder for Rabin's Left-center Labor Party government to compromise. "The goal of this campaign, initiated by Libya, Syria, and the Palestinians, is to sabotage the process and restart the political war against Israel," the Israeli diplomat Pinhas Elias reported. Even Kissinger acknowledged Israel's predicament,

"For Sadat, a mistake in negotiations would be a setback; for Rabin and his country, a mistake risked survival."

Despite these geopolitical dynamics, Herzog wanted to fight this resolution. He resented the UN's growing obsession with Israel. If the world organization was going to focus on the Jewish state 30 to 50 percent of the time, it should become "The United Nations Organization for the Castigation and Vilification of Israel." The issue was not Israel, but the United Nations, he insisted, believing the attack should alarm "all decent and freedom-loving people." Herzog lamented America's growing weakness in this new "era of irresponsibility," with Western society abandoning objective moral standards while appeasing "assassins and the demands of blackmailers." Like Moynihan, he understood that the "Afro-Asians and the Soviets" were filling the void that America had left. Like Moynihan, he intended to fight it.

Herzog believed he could weaken the anti-Israel coalition that had emerged. Idi Amin's rabid speech that same day endorsed the new line of attack. The Israelis started canvassing each country, claiming the proposed resolution violated the world body's mission, while seeking out those who might be willing to postpone the debate. The General Assembly's president, Gaston E. Thorn, Luxembourg's prime minister and foreign minister, encouraged Herzog. Thorn, a retiring and cosmopolitan man who had been imprisoned by the Nazis during World War II, reassured Herzog that Amin's harangue had "embarrassed" moderate Africans. Thorn nonetheless feared the growing "extremist trend amongst the Arabs." Herzog reported to Allon that Israelis needed to expect, "a severe decision with regards to the Palestinian issue," which the GA also was debating.

The Soviet-Arab approach effectively stymied Israel's lobbying efforts. The international community considered the fight against racism a holy cause. In 1973, marking the Universal Declaration of Human Rights' twenty-fifth anniversary, the 28th General Assembly passed Resolution 3057, endorsing a Decade for Action to Combat Racism and Racial Discrimination. Adding the word "Zionism" whenever the words "apartheid" and "racial discrimination" appeared in the original resolution, integrated the assault against Zionism into the broader crusade against racism. A similar tactic at the women's conference in Mexico made those defending Zionism look as if they were abandoning the fight against sexism.

The UN's passage of the generous, sweeping Universal Declaration of Human Rights reflected what the intellectual historian James Kloppenberg calls "the peak" of the "universalist mania" that swept Western and particularly American leaders following World War II. In August 1975 the Helsinki Accords provided an enforcement mechanism for this universalism. Yet by then scholars and Third World activists were abandoning their faith in the universal, burrowing deeper into the particular, the contingent, and the postmodern. Delegates representing dictatorships used universal human rights language to politicize and particularize the neutral, universal ideas this first decade against racism was supposedly celebrating. Anti-colonialist self-determination trumped intellectual consistency.

While most European countries, along with Canada, promised to oppose the entire Decade against Racism resolution and not just the anti-Zionist amendment to it, other Western countries hesitated. The Australian delegate J. B. Campbell would vote against the amendment, but Australia would only abstain from voting on the broader resolution. He feared the backlash if he appeared opposed to the anti-racist initiative. The New Zealand delegates similarly told Herzog that "they would need to vote for the general proposal given their sensitivity to charges of discrimination." Herzog "pleaded" with them. Eventually, they abstained with Australia.

The UN diplomatic ecosystem was surprisingly volatile and interdependent. Shortly after the New Zealanders and Australians agreed to abstain, some of the key Europeans—known as the "Group of 9," the European Economic Community that then included France, West Germany, Italy, Belgium, the Netherlands, Luxembourg, Denmark, Ireland, and the United Kingdom—regretted opposing the primary resolution. Israeli diplomats noted that this openness to negotiation undermined the African moderates "in their discussions with the Arabs," while radicalizing the Arabs.

The United States was resolute. As Herzog told Allon, Moynihan and the Americans "are working vigorously and we are in constant contact." Moynihan took Herzog's suggestions to threaten not to fund the conference launching the Decade against Racism that Ghana hoped to host.

As usual, Moynihan acted like a basketball superstar counting on his flamboyant success to compel his ambivalent coach to support him, even when he violated team rules. But the coach was growing testy. In August, when the Soviet-Arab bloc still hoped to expel Israel, Kissinger had tried containing Moynihan. In one phone conversation, mentioning "this Israeli thing," Kissinger warned Moynihan "not to turn it into a monumental event before it has happened." He feared that talking about it too much would "turn into a test of manhood." Moynihan replied tersely, "Well, we stopped talking." Later, Moynihan used the issue to repeat, in his macho way, that there had to be "consequences" when countries crossed the United States at the UN.

Both Herzog and Moynihan recognized the importance of mobilizing Jews, especially in the United States. By the 1970s, the "Never Again" ethos had started to transform American Jewry. Growing guilt regarding what they saw as their parents' failure to respond effectively during the Holocaust led many baby boomer Jews to work on making their community better organized, more assertive in fighting for Soviet Jewry, and more protective of Israel. Population concentration in such large Electoral College states as New York, Illinois, and Florida magnified American Jewish influence, as did the communal tradition of getting involved politically and contributing money generously. Moreover, American and Jewish values converged regarding allowing Soviet Jews freedom to emigrate, supporting Israel, and defying the UN lynch mob. Finally, lingering anti-Semitic stereotypes about Jewish power magnified whatever power Jews had by exaggerating it.

Yet, cautious leaders and a primitive political infrastructure also limited American Jewish power. Elie Wiesel was repeatedly disappointed by American Jewish leaders' cowardice, their seeming unwillingness to confront their democratically elected leaders, especially their presidents. Jewish influence on the Ford administration was particularly constrained by the noted Ford-Kissinger petulance toward Israel, in an era when few Jews voted Republican. "In a confrontation between the President and the Jewish community, the Jews will lose the battle," Kissinger warned. He was right. At the time AIPAC—the American Israel Public Affairs Committee—had fewer than four thousand members. By 1989, due to the rise of political action committees (PACs) along with growing Jewish self-confidence, AIPAC had 42,000 members, and today has more than 100,000 members. In April 1975, however, when the philanthropist and insider Max Fisher was briefing Kissinger, Fisher said: "I got a call from the AIPAC organization." Kissinger's response: "What is AIPAC?"

Still, both friendly and hostile governments followed American Jewish opinion "closely," Herzog observed. Therefore, American Jews could not afford to be passive. With his deep sense of history, Herzog cherished the opportunities afforded by the newfound responsibility, asking American Jewish audiences: "When in our history have Jews been in a position as you are today, free and loyal citizens of a great country and proud Jews, to sit and ponder how he or she is going to hit back?"

In October 1975, the "Jewish street" such as it was, was silent. Herzog worried. He heard the mutterings in the delegate lounge attributing Jewish silence to a rift between American Jews and Israel. "The Jewish public must be recruited, especially the Zionist movement, concerning their governments," Herzog told Allon on October 2. Herzog wanted "the Jewish and Zionist organizations in every locale to begin advocating and protesting," in efforts coordinated with the Foreign Ministry. But first, Herzog had to convince many Foreign Ministry colleagues that the resolution threatened Israel.

Some Jewish leaders did not need Herzog's prodding. Malcolm Hoenlein, a Soviet Jewry activist who founded the Jewish Community Relations Council in New York, was sufficiently outside the establishment at the time to mobilize against the resolution independently. He recalls that the "community as a whole was unsure" how to proceed, partially because such an "outlandish charge" as equating Zionism and racism was hard to respect. Hoenlein also recalls hearing that Rabbi Israel Miller, the chairman of the Conference of Presidents of Major American Jewish Organizations, "got a call from the Israeli officials, who said, 'look, we're not sure yet what to do.' " American Jewish leaders at the time often deferred to the Israelis, respecting the Jewish state's complicated military and diplomatic calculations.

During the summer of 1975, Israel's UN delegates had consulted with representatives from leading American Jewish organizations about fighting Israel's possible expulsion with public appeals and behind-the-scenes lobbying. In October, the Foreign Ministry's director general—its CEO— Avraham Kidron instructed Israel's representatives to mobilize Jewish communities worldwide, lobbying governments, soliciting public support, petitioning spiritual leaders, "especially non-Jews," and "staging mass demonstrations." The Ministry wanted people to "identify with Zionism, Israel and the Jewish people, as well as to denounce anti-Semitism." Kidron added, "It is important that the speeches at these demonstrations be personal from the first sentence." These instructions—although they remained dormant for three weeks—reflected three essential elements of Herzog's strategy: defining this anti-Zionist move as anti-Semitic, allying with non-Jews, and taking it personally.

On the diplomatic side, Herzog and Moynihan studied each wavering country's political calculus. The answers ranged widely. Iranian diplomats, invoking Muslim solidarity, felt compelled to support the resolution but would "nevertheless work towards toning down the Arab position." Turkish diplomats only said they expected "to either support or oppose the resolution" and would not take refuge in abstention or absence. The ambassador from Nepal promised his country would oppose the resolution, but Israeli diplomats doubted him. Others, like the Philippine diplomats, "tried to avoid giving an answer" while Burma's delegates refused to meet the Israelis.

Moynihan and Herzog worked hard to secure a "no" vote from Mexico. Mexico had its North American affinity with the United States and Canada, an influential Jewish community, and warm ties with Israel. President Luis Echeverria dithered. Israel's diplomats in Mexico reported trying to convince the Mexicans that the resolution "had no legal basis" and would risk Mexico's relations with Israel and the West pointlessly. But dreaming of becoming UN Secretary General, Echeverria suddenly decided to feel bound by the Women's Conference vote in Mexico City "and vote against Zionism again."

The diplomatic activity was most intense around the forty-six African delegations. The Africans owned the racism issue both symbolically and substantively. Some delegates resented the anti-Zionist sideshow for distracting from combating racism while diluting the moral indictment against South Africa and Rhodesia. Many delegates still appreciated Israel's development efforts and feared offending the West, particularly Moynihan's newly assertive America.

Arab delegates held what the Israeli delegation called a "surprise meeting" the night of October 10 with the African Bloc, demanding more support. Representatives from eleven African countries begged the Arabs to drop the proposal, fearing it would harm the "Decade." Although the group usually opposed the West automatically, this time it deadlocked. At Herzog's insistence, Israel's lobbying campaign intensified. Herzog requested extra funds to cover more personnel, more materials, and more security for the mission and his official residence. There were rumors that some pro-Israel delegates received occasional payments, $2,500 here, $5,000 there, possibly from pro-Israel businessmen, to help cover rent or medical expenses. These subsidies were laughable compared to the petrodollars being thrown around, especially by the Libyans and the Saudis who offered the most lavish foreign aid payoffs to the countries themselves, let alone the delegates.

During the Cold War, the UN headquarters was the setting for espionage, bribery and all kinds of chicanery taking place amid perpetual rounds paralleling *Mad Magazine*'s cartoon "Spy versus Spy" features, with the occasional delegate hitting a jackpot. Ambassador Ilan Hartuv, a veteran Israeli diplomat, recalls that while there was "no monkey business" around Security Council votes, some non-aligned UN diplomats frequently enjoyed various enticements, from call girls to cost-of-living subsidies, when it came to elections and "symbolic actions" in the General Assembly. A *Toronto Star* article in December 1975 would talk about votes being "sold and bought at the United Nations General Assembly like rugs in the bazaars of Baghdad and Damascus."

Delegates from poor Third World countries, with limited budgets in the expensive city of New York and disproportionate influence in a one-country, one-vote General Assembly were often bribed, mostly by the oil-rich Arab states. "The going market price is $6,000 to $8,000 for a vote on an important issue," the *Star* reported, although everyone agreed that "not even an oil-rich county could 'buy a resolution.'" These "blandishments," as Moynihan cynically called them, barely stirred interest—thirty years later, at a time when media scandal-mongering was more the norm, the Iraqi "oil for food" scandal would trigger more outrage about what one journalist called the UN's extensive "culture of corruption."

Israel's lobbying campaign against the resolution delayed its consideration, albeit by weeks, not a year as the Zambian delegates among others hoped. On October 13, the Third Committee delayed a vote on the resolution for the third time in ten days. "The time of the Arab steamroller tactics against the Africans is over," Herzog rejoiced, prematurely. The Soviet and Arab sponsors tinkered with the resolution, seeking the most palatable formulation. Eventually, they introduced a separate resolution denouncing Zionism, disconnected from the campaign against racism.

On October 15, the Black African countries split on three different procedural votes, heightening tensions as the actual vote approached. Many sub-Saharan delegates were beginning to resent what one called the Arabs' "petrodollar diplomacy." The desperately poor Africans needed Arab support. The Arabs insisted that the estimated $10 billion annually granted the African countries more than offset the higher oil prices. "[W]hile they want our backing in all areas, they want to say that the Middle East is an area on which they can remain neutral," an Arab diplomat complained. Critical

African delegates—speaking off the record to the *New York Times*—were skeptical. "We can understand the Arabs pushing their own priorities with their money, but no matter how poor we are, we cannot afford to trade European colonial masters [for] Arab colonial masters," one African diplomat griped.

As Herzog and the members of Israel's mission to the UN lobbied desperately against what they knew was all but inevitable, Moynihan's arm-twisting and haranguing encouraged them—and intimidated some African delegates. Indeed, the debate over whether Moynihan's confrontational style helped or hurt would intensify over the next few weeks as the push to pass Resolution 3379 gained momentum in the General Assembly. Moynihan himself would insist that more African states opposed the resolution, thanks to his lobbying and threats. His detractors said the resolution would never have hit the floor of the General Assembly without his bullying and bombast.

On Friday afternoon, October 17, the 2,134th meeting of the UN Social Humanitarian and Cultural Committee, also known as the "Third Committee," finally voted on the resolution. The debate on the innocuously named "Agenda Item 68" had been intensifying. Although many legislative bodies improvise protocols that constrict most speakers, formal debate in the UN had over time become particularly stiff. So many speakers from so many countries with similar agendas felt compelled to speak to any given resolution, making the sheer volume daunting enough. And their training as diplomats, along with the benign nature of so many UN proposals, usually made UN debates about as compelling as the finance committee report at board meetings.

Much of the debate on "Agenda Item 68" generated the usual UN blather. One delegate after another denounced racism, condemned colonialism, and "congratulated" the Committee on the Elimination of Racial Discrimination "on its hard work and valuable contributions to the work of the Decade." Many thanked the "Government of Ghana for its generous offer to host the world conference which would take place at the mid-point of the Decade in 1978."

Amid this narcotizing haze of platitudes, an unusually prickly debate about Zionism erupted. Nine Arab speakers, backed by delegates from Somalia, India, the USSR, and various Soviet satellites, articulated the case anti-Zionists had been building for decades. First, the anti-Zionists distinguished between anti-Semitism and anti-Zionism by praising Judaism and denouncing Zionism. They rejected Zionism's fundamental assumption that the Jews are a nation. Jamil Baroody, Saudi Arabia's veteran chief diplomat, insisted that "claiming Jews are a single people," let alone a "chosen people," even though they were scattered throughout the world, "was a feeling of exclusiveness very much akin to racism." Before Zionism started alienating Jews from their neighbors, for example, "a Jew from Yemen had a thousand times more in common with Christian and Moslem Yemenites than with a Jew from Belfast," the Syrian delegate Mowaffak Allaf exclaimed, a sharp reference to Herzog's Belfast origins.

These speakers and others perpetuated the myth of a golden age of Muslim-Jewish relations, in Palestine and elsewhere, ruined by the "Zionist invaders." It was a central Arab conceit that Jews had lived better under Islam than under Christianity. Nothing could compare to the Holocaust, which they would argue was the culmination of Western Christianity's eighteen-hundred-year-bloody war against Jews and Judaism; nor did Islam match medieval Christianity's brutal record of expulsions and murders. But in addition to the inferior *dhimmi* status the Koran imposed on Jews, anti-Jewish riots broke out periodically over the centuries, in Palestine and elsewhere. More recently, the mass expulsion of more than 650,000 Jews from Arab lands after 1948 also started a decades-long Arab onslaught of anti-Semitic stereotypes, cartoons, and rhetoric.

Still, the Arab ambassadors claimed that Zionism promoted anti-Semitism to advance its agenda. The only anti-Semitism they acknowledged was European anti-Semitism. They wondered why Arabs should suffer because of the European Holocaust.

Having negated Jewish peoplehood and artificially contained anti-Semitism, the Arab delegates then denied any Jewish claim to the land of Israel. They considered the Palestinians the only indigenous population, the true natives, displaced by the aggressive, expansionist, Zionist colonialists—who were as illegitimate as the Afrikaners and Rhodesians. Typically, the PLO's deputy representative, Hasan Abdel Rahman, went further, comparing Zionism to "Nazism in the sense that it was trying to exterminate the Palestinian people."

Shifting from assailing Zionism to Israel, the delegates claimed that by gathering together foreign Jews and expelling Palestinian natives, the Zionists had created what Allaf called "a huge Zionist ghetto," which now

endangered Jewish survival. The Albanian delegate Muhamet Kapllani excoriated the "reactionary Tel Aviv government" for its "racial discrimination,
persecution, imprisonment, and genocide." The critics attacked Israel's occupation of Palestinian land, Israel's "law of return," for giving immigration
privileges to Jews but not Palestinians; Israel's increasingly warm ties to
South Africa; and Israel's discrimination against its Arab-Jews, whom the
Zionists had immorally wooed to the wrong land.

The ghost of Mexico hovered over the Third Committee meetings. And
indeed one delegate after another invoked the Mexico declaration to justify
this new attack. In this UN echo chamber, the Somali delegate Fatima Isaak
Bihi would proclaim that the Mexico declaration's "single operative paragraph showed beyond question the link between Zionism and racial
discrimination."

Although the nine members of the European Economic Union all
opposed the resolution, they offered a weak rebuttal. Only Piero Vinci of
Italy spoke. Rather than defend Israel, he condemned the whole initiative
for hampering peace-making efforts and undermining the consensus against
racism.

Two Caribbean delegates fought the Arab assault on Israel directly.
Alexandre Verret of Haiti denounced racism as "a pestilence afflicting the
human race." Defining Zionism as "the expression of a religious nationalism,"
Verret said it "could in no way be equated with apartheid, which was the
exaltation of racial purity." Fostering solidarity, especially among a long-
persecuted people, was nationalist, not racist. Barbados ambassador Waldo
Waldron-Ramsey agreed, repudiating the proposal's "intellectual dishonesty." "To be born black is to understand what racism means," he said. In the
Bible, Waldron-Ramsey "found proof of the existence of Zion, of the fact
that Zionism and Judaism were the same and of the fact that Israel had
existed thousands of years ago and had not been created in 1948." Given
those facts, those who introduced the resolution in question and "diverted
attention" from the issue of racism, were "not friends of Africa and black
people in other parts of the world."

While preparing to defend his state and his people, Herzog was haunted
by thoughts of his younger brother, Jacob Herzog, who had died suddenly of
a stroke at the age of fifty-one three years before. The younger Herzog had
labored under his older brother's shadow for much of his life, except for one
magical moment in 1961 at McGill University in Montreal. There, while

serving as Israel's ambassador to Canada, Jacob Herzog confronted the great British historian Arnold Toynbee in a debate prompted by Toynbee's attacks on Israel and the Jews. Toynbee dismissed the Jewish return to Israel as being as random as India "returning" to Canada. Jacob Herzog bore in, detailing Jews' deep ties to their homeland.

Continuing his brother's argument fourteen years later, Chaim Herzog emphasized Israel, Zion, as "a vital element of the Jewish religion." Universalizing the claim, he argued that "To question the Jewish people's right to national existence and freedom was not only to deny to the Jewish people the right accorded to every other people on the globe but it was also to deny the central precepts of the United Nations."

Furious at the attacks negating the Jewish claims to the land, Herzog located the vulnerable spots in the Palestinian national argument. Herzog noted that historically, "only the Jewish people had seen the land of Israel as a distinct spiritual and political entity, as the center of its national existence, of its religion and of its civilization. The Arab inhabitants of Israel had always considered themselves to be part of the Arab nation, which had by now vindicated its rights to self-determination and independence in twenty sovereign states." And, Herzog added archly, "unlike the sponsors of the anti-Zionist draft resolution, Israel has a free and democratic society."

Leonard Garment spoke twice, first on October 3, then two weeks later before the October 17 vote. For weeks, Garment and others in the US mission had been researching the history of the UN's fight against racism. He and Moynihan had also received tutoring in Middle East history from Norman Podhoretz. Moynihan, Garment, and their aides saw the Soviet and Nazi roots in racializing Zionism. They recognized the broader attempt to demonize Israel with the trendiest and still most damning accusation. They tracked how Arab diplomats threw their new oil money around, intimidating poorer countries. Garment, revealing his trial lawyer experience, spent a long time looking "for the word that would be the most provocative," he recalls. He wanted to convey that "it's something dirty, it's obscene. It's a piece of pornography." He therefore warned that this "obscene act" would place "the work of the United Nations in jeopardy."

Garment and Moynihan predicted that the currency of human rights would be demeaned. Since World War II, through its Universal Declaration of Human Rights, the Convention on the Prevention and Punishment of the Crime of Genocide, and its moral authority, the United Nations had established an objective discourse about human rights. Now, the language of human rights was being politicized, twisted, distorted—betraying victims of human rights abuses.

This manipulation is "not only unjust but ominous, because it treated the word racism as if it were merely an epithet to be flung at whoever happened to be one's adversary," Garment explained. Thus, "an idea with vivid and obnoxious meaning" became "an ideological tool." Such sloppiness was harmful. Garment added that "To equate Zionism with racism was to distort completely the history of the Zionist movement, born of the centuries of oppression suffered by the Jewish people in the western world and designed to liberate an oppressed people by returning them to the land of their fathers."

Two weeks after his October 3 speech, Garment warned against this attempt "to commit one of the most grievous errors in the life of the United Nations." The UN was about to endorse anti-Semitism, one of the oldest and most virulent forms of racism. That, he proclaimed, "was an obscene act…it would place the work of the United Nations in jeopardy." A *Wall Street Journal* editorial one week later elaborated on Garment's position, warning that the resolution's "practical effect will be to restore respectability to the dormant irrational hatred of the Jewish people." The *Atlanta Journal* columnist George V. R. Smith agreed with the Israelis that this "attack upon Zionism is clearly an attack upon the Jewish people."

The "We're not anti-Semitic but we're anti-Zionist" approach had failed to convince Smith, the *Wall Street Journal* editors and many others. They remembered that until the 1940s anti-Semitism was respectable in the West. The fact that Jewish nationalism, meaning Zionism, was singled out in the United Nations for special opprobrium seemed anti-Jewish, not just anti-Zionist. And the special glee of the Communist and Arab nations in attacking the Jewish state seemed anti-Jewish. Most leaders and writers in 1975 had experienced World War II or grown up in its shadow. As the debate made clear, the Zionism issue was barely about Palestinian rights or Israel's boundaries. It was instead a restatement of the argument about the Jews' right to a homeland and the Jews' status as a people.

One of the last speakers that day, Chaim Herzog, scorned the many "countries whose regimes practice racism, incorporate racism in their laws and their daily practices" daring to judge his "small…free democratic country," when they themselves were so flawed. "We are a small people with a long and proud history. We have lived through much in our history," Herzog insisted. "We shall survive this shameful exhibition," he continued, although he wondered if the UN would. And as he literally shouted "We shall never forget," he knew the vote was lost but was determined that the cause would not be.

Herzog's anger shocked the delegates into silence. Then a buzz ensued with two short speeches, a few procedural votes, and the inevitable results from the vote: 70 for advancing the resolution to the General Assembly, 29 opposed, 27 abstaining. Herzog's Israeli colleagues, instructed by him to "behave with dignity," sat impassively as delegates applauded mockingly. To Herzog, the Arabs "seemed on the verge of a war dance." Moynihan, who had been silent that day, stole the show by traversing the chamber, hugging Herzog, and loudly sharing what the former sailor called "pungent words of encouragement not necessarily found in the pages of the Babylonian Talmud"—"Fuck 'em." The *New York Times* delicately reported that Moynihan "walked to" Herzog "and embraced him." Herzog recalled, "I was very moved indeed."

Addressing the opening of the Israeli Knesset's winter session three days later, Yigal Allon denounced the "shameful, benighted and arbitrary" resolution—but also sought to emphasize progress in the fight. The Arab countries failed to integrate the attack on Zionism into the broader resolution. The Soviet-Arab initiative faced repeated postponements. The "main thing," was that "the vote last Friday was the least impressive they have attained in recent years, in terms of both the scope and the composition of the various camps." Using as his standard the 1974 vote granting the PLO observer status, which passed 95 to 17 with 19 abstaining and 6 absent, Allon announced "a break in the automatic majority" that had coalesced against Israel "of 80 percent and more." The *Wall Street Journal* publicized an analysis from the US mission showing that the division in the vote was not between Left and Right, meaning socialist and capitalist, but between the free and non-free. Using Freedom House's classifications, the staffers discovered that 92 percent of the "yes" vote came from countries, which were partly free or dictatorships, while 76 percent of the "no" vote came from free liberal societies.

Back in New York, Moynihan and Herzog felt virtuous in their indignation—but also somewhat isolated. As Herzog recalled, with some drama, "We were facing the most severe attack on the Jewish people since Hitler, yet the silence of the US Jewish community was deafening, and not one voice of protest was heard in the American media." The Israelis heard "from various levels from the US government, which stressed the importance of a massive Jewish reaction." Herzog reported that Moynihan was furious at "the thundering silence of the *New York Times*" and other leading newspapers. Herzog and Moynihan may have exaggerated the silence but not their need for it to end. They needed a thunderous public outcry.

Herzog invited Moynihan to lunch to brainstorm about strategy. Moynihan was appalled by the Jewish silence, and the inability to see that the decision would legitimize every attack on Israel's existence. He and Herzog agreed to focus on the French and the African countries, hoping at least to postpone the resolution by a year. "He believes that the future of the UN is now in the balance," Herzog reported. Herzog noted that Garment said "he learned more about the Jewish problem and the severity of the situation during the eight weeks in which he has been here than in the five years he spent in the government in Washington." Even the German ambassador Rudiger von Wechmar told Herzog, "It would be helpful if the Jewish community were to react."

Still feeling burned by the Left, Moynihan feared that the overwhelmingly liberal Jewish community tolerated attacks from the Communist and anti-colonialist coalition in the still-holy UN. Moynihan's Jewish friends were recovering liberals like Podhoretz and Kristol who shared his frustration with both the liberal and Jewish blindspots when facing the faults of Communist countries, Third World Societies, or leftist intellectuals. A few years later, Ruth Wisse, a literature scholar at McGill University and a passionate defender of Israel, would ask her mentor Irving Howe, perhaps his generation's leading Jewish socialist, to oppose the Zionism is racism resolution as a man of the Left. Howe demurred. Wisse feared this great inversion: that in changing from the bloodthirsty rhetoric of Arabs and the Right— "We will destroy you!"—to the Left's self-righteous rhetoric—"the racist Zionist-Imperialists are destroying us"—Jews again were seen by a broad Left-Right coalition as a threat. Howe scoffed. Taking her arm gently he said: "Ruthie, no one pays any attention to the United Nations."

Herzog knew that UN-bashing or ignoring would not help. Addressing the Conference of Presidents of Major American Jewish Organizations, he bluntly chided American Jews' top leaders for their passivity. He was almost recalled to Jerusalem after the *New York Times* ran a story quoting him asking

"Where were the Jewish people?" and headlined "HERZOG ASSERTS JEWS DIDN'T AID ISRAELIS IN U.N. ZIONISM DEBATE." Seething, Herzog asked why "Here in this city, in the midst of the largest Jewish concentration in the world, with a small Israeli delegation fighting desperately against the heaviest possible odds to defend Jewry from a major anti-Semitic attack against Jews wherever they may be, the lead on this issue was taken to its eternal credit by the United States delegation?" Herzog ultimately attributed the passivity to American Jewish denial that such an assault could occur in the UN, and a characteristically blustery Israeli attempt to dismiss it as "*shtut*," nonsense.

The Israeli ambassador in Washington, Simcha Dinitz, secretly telegrammed Jerusalem: "I am surprised that Herzog did not correct Moynihan's remarks about the supposed Jewish indifference. More than that, I was amazed that Herzog said similar things at his appearance at the President's Conference this morning, and with the presence of the media, no less." After detailing objections to the resolution from fourteen major newspapers, 415 members of Congress, black organizations, religious organizations, and President Ford himself, Dinitz concluded archly: "Does our Ambassador in the UN really believe that all that came from him or from Jewish indifference and a lack of understanding of the potential dangers?" The Washington embassy logged many phone calls from irate Jewish leaders objecting to Herzog's tirade and detailing their efforts.

The Israeli media covered this clash, sparking rumors about Herzog's recall. Herzog insisted that he never criticized the embassy, although his defense included the more ambiguous phrasing "The activities of the embassy on this issue speak for themselves." While blaming a "small, irresponsible group of reporters" for the brouhaha, he still criticized Jewish reaction to the resolution, "This is not just any old UN resolution. It is much more significant." Herzog also objected that the cabinet had debated the issue and his behavior without checking with him. He claimed the Conference of Presidents applauded his speech enthusiastically. Zalman Abramov, the Deputy Speaker of the Knesset serving as a special adviser to the UN delegation, confirmed Herzog's account, telegraphing the Ministry to say that Herzog "wasn't criticizing the government" but was trying to stir up interest in the Jewish community.

By October 28 Dinitz felt compelled to reassure Herzog, writing: "I did not relate to anything you said as criticism of me or of the embassy." He

blamed reporters for "creating a personal rift which does not exist." Seeking
unity, Dinitz said "we all agree on the importance" of the resolution and the
need to mobilize.

At Israel's mission to the UN, the dejected diplomats now expected
Resolution 3379 to pass. A vote to postpone the Zionism discussion failed,
with sixty-nine countries voting to proceed—although forty-four countries
voted for postponement, including many African and South American
countries. Sixteen abstained and eighteen were absent. The Israelis began
planning for November 11, the day after the scheduled day for the General
Assembly vote. Their planned "immediate response" included "a sharply-
worded speech by Herzog immediately before the vote," a "demonstrative
exit out of the hall immediately following the vote"—hopefully joined by
others—and protests in Jerusalem and key capitals. Long-term, they contemplated recalling Herzog, withholding dues, boycotting key committees
or votes, and "cool[ing]" relations with some countries that approved the
resolution.

Amid this diplomatic scramble, President Sadat arrived for a state visit to
New York, Chicago, Jacksonville, Houston, and Washington, DC. The
Israelis were having trouble reading the president of Egypt, who vacillated
between talking peace and trash-talking Israel. In his youth, Sadat had been
more fanatic and ruthless than Nasser. A tough revolutionary born in 1918
in a primitive village forty miles outside Cairo, Sadat had fought against
British rule, repeatedly escaping from prison. He cooperated with the Nazis
in the 1940s and the Moslem Brotherhood in the 1950s against their
common British enemy. As Nasser's vice president, Sadat revealed a calmer,
more urbane side, a side cultivated by his elegant, half-English wife, Jehan.

When Nasser died in 1970, few expected his far less charismatic vice
president to last long. But Sadat consolidated power and even outdid Nasser
with the surprise attack against Israel in October 1973. Following his proclaiming a victory in 1973 despite Israel's effective counterattack, Sadat
quarreled with Egypt's Soviet patrons and wooed the Americans. Kissinger
saw Sadat as a "great man," the hero of Kissinger's painstaking shuttle
diplomacy, seeking peace. Meanwhile, the Israelis were the obstructionists,
sabotaging Kissinger first by saying no, then by lobbying Congress behind
Kissinger's back.

In his American tour, Sadat spoke of peace with the Jewish state while
using rhetoric justifying a war against the Jews. Addressing a rare joint

session of Congress on November 5, he quoted George Washington and Woodrow Wilson, sounding like a progressive seeker of truth, justice, and peace. Yet, earlier, when a reporter at the National Press Club in Washington asked "do you consider Zionism part of racial persecution," Sadat sounded like the peasant-turned-revolutionary he had been, rather than the statesman he was trying to become. Saying "The Jews ... dominated our economy until 1952," Sadat claimed "they" refused to sell him a radio set in 1950 because now "they were receiving their instructions from Zionism [sic] after the establishment of the state of Israel" and he was an Egyptian army officer who "had fought against Israel."

Such bigotry did not stop President Ford from fawning over his guest, even as New York's mayor and governor snubbed the Egyptian president. In one of many toasts, Ford praised the visit as symbolizing "the very close working relationship of our two countries" and hailed Sadat's "courage ... in taking the first steps toward peace in almost three decades of warfare." Meeting in the Oval Office, Ford said their previous encounters, in September "at Salzburg were personally and substantively the most constructive meetings I have had since I have been President."

Sadat hoped to build American public support for Egypt, to change American attitudes toward the PLO and the Palestinians, to secure economic aid, and to convince the Americans to push a coordinated, multidimensional agenda in the entire Middle East, not just progress with Egypt. But the Israelis protested to Kissinger. They were already miffed by seeing Ford and Sadat exchange toasts up and down the East Coast. They resented that Sadat addressed Congress although no Israeli ever had, and wondered why no American official repudiated the anti-Semitism underlying Sadat's anti-Zionism. Kissinger reassured the Israelis that the Americans had resisted Sadat's charms. Dinitz pressed, asking if he "could report to the Israeli government that during Sadat's visit, the US's stance has not changed on three issues: arms supply to Egypt, negotiations with Syria on the Golan Heights and the PLO." Kissinger agreed. Dismissing the anti-Semitic rhetoric, Kissinger said "everything depended on how Sadat would act in the future."

When Sadat left the United States, Allon, as foreign minister, instructed all Israeli diplomats there to attack Sadat's "primitive anti-Semitism." Fearing Sadat's popularity, Allon directed: "We must make an effort to undermine the image of a brave politician, a fighter for peace."

Once again in Israel's life, the fight for immediate survival trumped the search for long-term reconciliation. Yigal Allon, born in 1918—like Yitzhak Rabin, born four years later—was a practical, Israeli-born sabra, a tough former general who helped establish and unify the fledgling country. Fighting for the Palmach strike force in 1948, both men made controversial moves to encourage the Arab exodus and crush Israel's homegrown opposition. Rabin and Allon were involved in sinking the *Altalena*, the ship bringing French munitions to the Irgun, the right-wing paramilitary organization that David Ben-Gurion feared would spin off to become a rival militia. But just as Rabin would ultimately become a Nobel Prize–winning martyr for peace, Allon's first instinct after the 1967 War was to endorse an independent Palestinian state in the West Bank. Two weeks later, he unveiled the Allon Plan, proposing a string of settlements along the Israeli-Jordanian border for security but freeing the population therein, reflecting his moral commitment to avoid ruling another people. Both plans encouraged territorial compromise and represented a bold, revolutionary departure for the former Palmach commander.

Addressing the General Assembly that fall of 1975, Allon said: "it is self-evident that genuine peace in the Middle East must include a just and constructive solution for the Palestine Arab problem." It would take nearly twenty years before such specific recognition of the Palestinians became the consensus Israeli position. More typical was Herzog's vague formulation, in his maiden UN speech, that "Waging political warfare is surely irreconcilable with maintaining a process of negotiation towards ultimate peace."

Allon wanted to find a formula for peace. Most of Israel's diplomatic corps resisted plunging into the UN brawl. But the Arab enmity proved too great. The desire to delegitimize Zionism as a first step toward eradicating Israel proved so powerful it upstaged—and probably delayed—Anwar Sadat's journey from waging war to making peace.

Herzog and Moynihan understood how truly dangerous the UN threat was—that this anti-Zionist initiative was not merely words, that the UN was not a silly institution. "*Oom shmoom*" was a defense mechanism, not a policy. This worldwide pile-on against one country presented a serious strategic threat, not mere posturing. Herzog was correct to put the threat in its broadest historic context, speaking to a people scarred by anti-Semitism, warning that this resolution, too, could have lethal implications. And both Moynihan and Garment were correct to warn the United Nations that this descent into "tribalism" and into selective indignation threatened the UN's very mission.

Moynihan's anger, once again, polarized the UN delegates. In a comment to the *New York Times* published two days after the Third Committee vote, Moynihan said the twenty-nine delegates who opposed the resolution in the Third Committee represented "the decent countries." He added: "If you had to pick your company in the world, you couldn't pick better." Moynihan's enemies would harp on this implicit characterization of the rest of the United Nations as indecent.

During this delicate time, with Sadat still visiting and the fight over Zionism intensifying, President Ford was extremely distracted. The United States Senate Select Committee on Intelligence, chaired by Idaho Senator Frank Church, was, its detractors lamented, splaying out the insides of America's Cold War intelligence operations. What CIA insiders called "the family jewels" became media fodder. In this latest wallop to national morale, Americans learned about embarrassing, immoral attempts to assassinate foreign leaders, including Fidel Castro of Cuba—with some Cuban capers relying on the Mafia.

At the same time, New York City itself was at risk of bankruptcy. On October 30, 1975, midway between the Third Committee vote and the General Assembly vote, the New York *Daily News* ran its famous headline "FORD TO CITY: DROP DEAD," after the president refused to bail out New York. "The people of this country will not be stampeded," was what Ford actually said. "They will not panic when a few desperate New York officials and bankers try to scare New York's mortgage payments out of them." The New York crisis fed into the general atmosphere of chaos, concern, and indignation.

Days later, Ford shook up his foreign policy team so dramatically it became known as the "Halloween Massacre." "Détente" was not polling well with Republicans, as Ronald Reagan launched a serious challenge for the nomination. Ford wanted to show that he, not Kissinger, was in charge, and could be tough. On November 3, Ford's VP Nelson Rockefeller announced he would not run with Ford in 1976. Ford abruptly fired CIA director William Colby and Secretary of Defense James Schlesinger. And, equally abruptly, Ford demoted Kissinger, keeping him on as secretary of state but making his deputy Brent Scowcroft National Security Adviser—what had been Kissinger's power base since the start of the Nixon administration.

"Kissinger lost his title as the president's foreign policy adviser, lost his White House office, lost his hour alone with the president every day, and lost his stewardship of the NSC," the journalist Aaron Latham would note. "That old brokering magic was beginning to fail him."

Kissinger, despondent, considered resigning. His situation worsened when on November 6, the House Select Committee on Intelligence subpoenaed him, requesting documents regarding particular covert actions the US government had undertaken since 1961. The president ordered him not to comply. When he missed the November 11 deadline, the committee voted the secretary of state in contempt of Congress. Kissinger charged that the subpoena raised "serious questions all over the world of what this country is doing to itself and what the necessity is to torment ourselves like this month after month." Even though Kissinger was defending the executive branch, the contempt citation further weakened him.

With Kissinger hurt, the nation reeling, the president looking weak, Americans wanted charismatic leadership. Daniel Patrick Moynihan did not fit the mold. He was too cerebral, with a spasmodic way of speaking and an addiction to fancy language. He was too controversial, still defined to many insiders by the racial storms during the Johnson and Nixon administrations. And he was too weak, ultimately subordinate to the egotistical Kissinger. But Moynihan understood that Americans demanded moral clarity.

Moynihan wandered around Theo Kojak's New York—the New York of the detective series from 1973 to 1978 that offered a television version of Clint Eastwood's blockbuster *Dirty Harry* movies, the first three of which came out in 1971, 1973, and 1976. Every week *Kojak* depicted the nation's leading metropolis as one big gritty, grimy, terrifying crime scene slouching toward chaos, rotting from decay, reeking of fear, if not for the intervention of one ethnically idiosyncratic, hard-(and bald)-headed, sweet-talking— "Who loves ya?"—police detective defying the anarchy. As both a student of the urban scene and an American patriot, the US ambassador to the UN understood, intellectually and intuitively, what had to be done. Ironically, making his move and forging his moment guaranteed him a successful political career—even as it doomed his diplomatic one.

THE SPEECH

The United States rises to declare before the General Assembly
and before the world, that it does not acknowledge, it will not
abide by, it will never acquiesce in this infamous act.
—DANIEL PATRICK MOYNIHAN, NOVEMBER 10, 1975

Public figures, let alone public intellectuals, rarely became ambassadors to
the UN. That both Daniel Patrick Moynihan and Chaim Herzog were men
of ideas and experienced public communicators was a fluke—but one with
lasting impact. As warrior diplomats and populist intellectuals, both understood the need for melodrama, with a dash of martyrdom. Both the Irish-
American street-fighter and the Irish-Israeli aristocrat exaggerated the initial
disinterest in their fight. Each played the plucky prophet, bolder than their
gutless colleagues, be it Henry Kissinger or Simcha Dinitz, in pursuing the
real enemy. The fight over General Assembly Resolution 3379 was a grand
political battle, a colorful clash among angry Arabs, conspiring Communists,
ambivalent Africans, irritated Europeans, embittered Israelis, and avenging
Americans. Moynihan's moment did not emerge spontaneously. It was cho-
reographed by Moynihan, Herzog, and a small cadre of allies.

Without their public relations campaign, had popular interest in the
Zionism is racism resolution remained what it was in mid-October 1975, its
passage would have been a one-day story. And like Yasir Arafat's 1974 speech,

it would have been more a Jewish moment than an American moment, one of many accumulating frustrations with the United Nations. Kissinger himself hoped that the issue would pass quickly, grumbling on November 10, "We are conducting foreign policy. This is not a synagogue." But thanks in great part to Moynihan, the fight over Resolution 3379 all but demolished popular faith in the UN as it galvanized many Americans. A Harris Survey after the resolution found strong disapproval of the resolution, by margins of 49 percent to 9 percent in general and 70 percent to 8 percent among professionals. A 49 to 26 percent plurality favored cutting the US contribution to the UN.

There was also general approval of a more aggressive American stance in foreign policy. More countries than usual hesitated to support the resolution because of the three-week campaign waged by Moynihan, who intimidated them and transformed the General Assembly debate. On November 10, most delegates addressed the politics surrounding the resolution rather than Zionism itself. Others, preferring negotiation to confrontation, believed Moynihan's grandstanding failed and that confrontation marginalized the United States in the UN.

By fighting, Moynihan resurrected his political career. Accusations of political calculations confused consequence with causation. His critics assumed he grandstanded to launch a Senate run. Actually, no American chief delegate had ever launched a political run from Turtle Bay. If Moynihan's moment returned him to electoral politics, this was a consequence of the fact that the politics of patriotic indignation he helped forge were so appealing to Americans and shaped foreign policy for the next decade and a half.

Just when foreign policy idealists, Left and Right, were rejecting Kissinger's détente because his diplomatic "realism" risked becoming moral relativism, Moynihan linked anti-Zionism to the ideological assault on Western values and American power. He resented dictatorships using "human rights" against "those nations which still observe human rights, imperfect as that observance may be." Such hypocrisy would soon yield "Moynihan's Law." Moynihan observed that the volume of complaints about a country's human rights violations was inversely proportional to the actual number of violations. In other words, the more citizens can complain about human rights violations, the more human rights they enjoy.

As for Resolution 3379, Moynihan believed that only bigotry could explain singling out Zionism as illegitimate in a world political order organized around nation states. The Harris Survey showed that most Americans judged the resolution as anti-Semitic, "aimed more at Jews than at the concept of Zionism itself." "The United Nations is about to make anti-Semitism international law," Moynihan warned. This is not "merely a measure aimed at Israel. . . . It is aimed at Jews everywhere and liberal democracy everywhere."

The initiative was a bankshot worthy of a pool hustler, knocking the West for supporting Israel. Princeton University's Bernard Lewis would note in an influential *Foreign Affairs* article that Soviet propagandists had recycled Nazi canards treating Jews as a race. A nationalist movement had to be rooted in race in order to be racist, like the white Afrikaners defining themselves against the black natives, the "coloreds," and the Asians.

Justifiable disgust with South African apartheid, American racism, and European racist colonialism made this accusation particularly potent. The Arab states, following their 1973 oil embargo, deployed petropower to publicize it. The disenfranchisement of more than a million Palestinian refugees seemed to legitimize the claim. The new moral calculus favored solidarity to morality or logic. The Palestinians' identity as an oppressed people of color absolved them of responsibility for terrorism or extremism, while freeing the resolution's sponsors of the need to make a convincing case beyond the solidarity appeal.

The same day the Third Committee voted, October 17, Moynihan took his crusade to the Trilateral Commission, a network founded at David Rockefeller's initiative in 1972, uniting North American, European, and Japanese elites. The commission was not yet the obsession of conspiracy buffs, but it was the kind of WASPy establishment Moynihan loved criticizing—and conquering. He warned that the UN vote would roil American politics, not just world politics. George W. Ball, former undersecretary of state and former UN ambassador, scoffed. "Nonsense," Moynihan recalls him replying. "The campaign finance act has broken the political power of the American Jews," referring to the post-Watergate 1974 amendment of the 1971 act, placing legal limits on campaign contributions.

Moynihan viewed this sentiment as typical State Department cant—defining the issue as solely Jewish while blaming American support for Israel on Jewish lobbying. In connecting America's domestic and foreign crises of confidence, Moynihan was test-piloting a vision that would revive America ideologically. He realized that overly personalizing and politicizing the

US-Israel bond ignored common values and shared interests. This tendency to sentimentalize the narrative with colorful personalities began in 1948, when Eddie Jacobson lobbied his old haberdashery business partner Harry Truman to recognize Israel, at a point when the president was receiving conflicting advice from his cabinet. When Moynihan quoted Ball disparagingly, Kissinger agreed with Ball. According to Moynihan, Kissinger recalled that one politician offered young politicos only one piece of advice: "Be an anti-Semite."

Once again, in their perpetual chess game, Kissinger's move perplexed Moynihan. Moynihan recalled dismissing Norman Podhoretz's belief that campaign finance legislation targeted Jews' political power. Now, Moynihan considered his friend prescient rather than paranoid. Moynihan was seeing much more American anti-Semitism than he had ever acknowledged. And he was surprised to see America's first Jewish secretary of state both so fearful of it yet so ready to encourage it.

Kissinger had endured Richard Nixon's repeated anti-Semitic barbs. Now, with an Irish-American UN ambassador branding the assault on Israel anti-Semitic, Kissinger seemed both contemptuous and envious. He and his aides mocked Moynihan's Israel obsession. They wondered if he planned on converting.

With his striver's radar attuned to bosses' disapproval, Moynihan wooed Kissinger, while still confronting the anti-Zionists and fending off the Arabists. The day after the Third Committee vote, Moynihan went literary on his former Harvard colleague, beginning his long diplomatic cable by quoting James Joyce's Stephen Hero. "Its soul, its whatness, leaps to us from the vestment of its appearance . . . the object achieves its epiphany," Moynihan wrote in a telegram. "It happened yesterday to the United Nations." Characterizing the UN's move as self-destructive—and yearning to save it—Moynihan quoted the Irish ambassador Eamonn L. Kennedy, who lamented after the Third Committee vote: "The United Nations is destroying itself. This night. In this room."

Moynihan justified his confrontational strategy by noting that only 42 percent of the Black Africans voted with the "PLO-Arab-Soviet Bloc." The Africans realized that the Arabs were exploiting them and "rebelled." The Arabs lost their "automatic majority," although they swayed many South Americans, who "collapsed, nay groveled, in the face of Communist threat, Arab money, and the no doubt irresistible opportunity to be vicious." Within days Moynihan would leak to the *New York Times* word that the Arabs paid off the Chilean fascists. After years in Washington, Moynihan was a master leaker. Publicly, the idealistic UN ambassador boasted to the realist secretary of state that for twenty-nine countries "An issue of honor, of morality was put before us, and not all of us ran."

Kissinger remained skeptical. President Gerald Ford's more ideological staffers, however, saw the political benefits of confronting the Soviets and defending democracy. In late October, Robert Goldwin, whom Donald Rumsfeld considered "the Ford administration's one-man think tank, its intellectual compass," drafted a tough presidential statement. It warned that Resolution 3379 "jeopardizes" the UN's "future," and proclaimed that "a resolution connecting Zionism and racism must not pass the General Assembly."

Knowing that Goldwin had written his statement after Moynihan telephoned, National Security advisor Brent Scowcroft ordered the draft "scrubbed." Hal Horan, the UN Affairs director of the National Security Council (NSC), and William Buffum, the assistant secretary of state for International Organization Affairs, worried that when the resolution passed, a presidential statement declaring it "must not pass" would "make the President look impotent." Channeling Kissinger, they also objected to condemning the UN with such "strong" language.

Arthur A. Houghton III, "strongly" opposed any presidential statement, as did a "unanimous" State Department. Trained at Harvard University and American University in Beirut before serving in Amman and Cairo, this NSC staffer was a typical Arabist. These diplomats, whose romance with Arab culture combined with a realpolitik appreciation of Arab oil, money, and demographics, spiced with a WASPish disdain for Jews, feared jeopardizing Anwar Sadat's November visit. Nevertheless, Ford released a statement warning against weakening the UN and deploring the vote "in the strongest terms."

Staffers had to scrub even harder when Moynihan proposed a toast for Kissinger to make at the fund-raiser for the United Nations Association of the United States, shortly after the Third Committee vote. They removed Moynihan's moralisms, banning such words as "horror" and "evil." They cut Leonard Garment's accusation that the UN was "officially endorsing anti-Semitism." The NSC staffers adopted a legalistic argument the Arab delegates favored, claiming the UN's move would be anti-Semitic only if it supported "a resolution against Jews per se (and not a brand of Jewish nationalism) or all Semites, Arabs included."

In short, Foggy Bottom turned hostile. On November 10, hours before the resolution passed, Kissinger and Buffum joked about Moynihan's soft spot for Jews. Buffum, another Arabist fresh from a three-year stint as ambassador to Lebanon, told Kissinger: "We have been overdoing the defense of Zionism as a philosophy and a system." Kissinger ordered Buffum to call Moynihan "and tell him to tone it down a bit."

At 6:34 p.m. on November 10, during the General Assembly debate, Buffum told Kissinger, "Moynihan got your message and cut out the most offensive sections." "What is wrong with that guy?" Kissinger wondered. Buffum blamed Moynihan's "political ambition." Kissinger admitted that appointing Moynihan was not "one of my more brilliant moves." With Moynihan on his way to the tense General Assembly plenary, Kissinger told Buffum to make sure Moynihan cleared his statement before delivery: "You get him out and tell him I will not stand for that any more. Tell him these are direct instructions from me."

Moynihan calculated that he could justify injecting his inflammatory tough-guy language into this diplomatic duel if it resonated publicly. He would rile the American people while confronting the anti-American alliance. Moynihan had bashed the UN when addressing the Appeal of Conscience Foundation's annual dinner on October 21, 1975. He enjoyed appearing at fancy locations, in this case the Hotel Pierre on Fifth Avenue, addressing the bejeweled women with their tuxedo-clad husbands, all snug in their wealth, their power, their status. Moynihan would rise, his hair unkempt, his tie often askew but his clothes impeccable, and his height imposing. Moynihan sounded even stranger than he looked, as traces of a youthful stutter forced him to caw and pause awkwardly. Yet after just a frisson of discomfort, wherein the super-slick elites would revel for a millisecond in their relative perfection by comparison, Moynihan would start wowing them with words. The power in the room would shift from the self-satisfied hundreds to the speaker at the podium. Moynihan would turn on the charm. Alternating wit, indignation, and insight, falling just short of insulting, he seduced with his finely crafted sentences and his clear case for truth.

During October 1975, Moynihan's relationship with his audience evolved. Introductions became less necessary and more ritualistic, like warm-ups at pep rallies for a nationally ranked team. Moynihan was no longer just a personage, a Harvard professor and statesman; he was becoming a celebrity. His fame made it easier to please his listeners, as they happily anticipated dropping his name at the office water cooler or beauty parlor. But he had to work harder to impress, finding new ways to make an increasingly familiar argument.

That October night, Moynihan offered the Orwellian United Nations his own Orwellian compliment. At least the anti-Zionist resolution avoided the UN's double-speak and was simple, understandable. After again quoting Joyce, he accused the UN of championing totalitarianism, not liberal democracy. By inverting meaning and distorting truth, the resolution was "the very quintessence of the totalitarian mode." Denouncing this act as "reckless" and "obscene," he offered the evening's only good news—that the automatic majority of hatred had faltered, and that his appeal to delegates' consciences had worked. "The democracies seem to have found each other again," he exulted, contrasting America's lonely vote with Israel against totalitarian anti-Zionism in Mexico City, with the democratic coalition now saying "No to this infamous thing."

Moynihan finished by saying that he regretted the regional, religious, national, and racial tribalisms trumping the post–World War II universalist aspirations, aspirations that the US had defined and the UN had embodied. Instead of showcasing this progress, the UN became a dumping ground of anti-Western and anti-modern sentiment. He demanded that the "one-party states" not make "a one-party UN." The General Assembly should facilitate constructive international interaction, not ostracize unpopular countries.

Moynihan's frustrations about the international community reflected the frustrations he had felt in the 1960s. Now the Third World countries were the angry, immature, self-destructive student rebels, betraying the Western ideas that nurtured them, empowered them, and could liberate them. The lily-livered Western diplomats and his back-stabbing State Department colleagues were replacing the self-denigrating, impotent, hand-wringing American liberals and his cowardly academic colleagues. Once again, the immature rebels' and impotent elders' amoral blindness appalled Moynihan.

Moynihan was tapping into growing communal frustrations with both America's drift and the UN's betrayal. Shortly after the Third Committee vote, the American branch of the United Nations Association began celebrating the UN's thirtieth anniversary with an elaborate advertising campaign. Just as Moynihan was denouncing UN totalitarianism, the United Nations Association was boasting, "There's always been a 'You' in the UN." It was like having placed ads boosting the Atlantic crossing in the Sunday papers after the *Titanic* sank.

Unswayed by such boosterism, thousands of Americans began sending letters into the US mission to the UN. The secretaries opening the letters tired of counting the "bravos," reported *People* magazine. Philip and Olive Tocker of Brownsville, Texas, praised Moynihan for representing "the common people" who understand that "the art of diplomacy does not require silencing the truth." A *Los Angeles Times* columnist, Nick Thimmesch, applauded "The fine firm of Moynihan and Garment," calling Moynihan "the tonic the United States needs at the United Nations." Garment, revealing his own, poor-boy-made-good, Brooklyn-inflected humor, told the reporter: "we sometimes close for altercations." President Ford's people, fearing Ronald Reagan's threat to run for the Republican nomination, could take solace in Moynihan's loyal but self-promoting assurance that "The President gives me all the support I deserve and need."

Moynihan's scrappiness made the fight against the resolution a rumble rather than a diplomatic minuet. "The vote on anti-Zionism was as hard fought and emotional as any in recent years," Moynihan's deputy permanent representative, Ambassador Tapley Bennett Jr., would inform Senator Hubert Humphrey. In a marathon of posturing, pleading, bullying, and arm-twisting, scrambling to block the inevitable, Moynihan made many delegates squirm. Black African delegates, in particular, felt pressed by the powerful American ambassador—and swayed by his arguments. They feared for their larger initiative, the Decade against Racism. And hearing Moynihan's warnings about the UN's impending collapse, many delegates hoped the issue would disappear. Days before the vote, the NSC's Hal Horan reported that "sentiment for postponement in the United Nations is growing."

What the *New York Times* described as "anti-American pique"—but Moynihan considered more systemic—countered the growing desire to postpone. This assessment confirmed Moynihan's instincts that Israel was the lightning rod for Western democracies. One Latin American delegate admitted that "Arab propagandists have been working very hard...to sell us Latins a big cargo of anti-United States grudges under a flag of convenience, Zionism." The Cuban delegates told African delegates that "Zionism, capitalism and American imperialism are all faces of the same monster." Calling Zionists "an alien people in our midst," Saudi Arabia's ambassador Jamil Baroody attacked Jewish money and Jewish influence.

Although most proponents of the resolution claimed they loved Jews but hated Israel, their anti-Americanism was overt—which is what had first pulled Moynihan into the UN vortex. Speakers made more blatantly anti-Semitic appeals when the General Assembly debated the question of Palestine, on November 3, as mandated by its 1974 resolution. Farouk Kaddoumi, the PLO's representative, praised the delegates for listening to the "voice of the victim," a phrase capturing the new deification of Third World suffering. Playing to the Che Guevara sensibilities and celebrating "Arab-African solidarity," Kaddoumi congratulated the "Indochinese peoples of Viet Nam, Cambodia and Laos," for defeating the United States. He then insulted America's chief delegate by saying it was not surprising that Moynihan, whose "benign neglect" memo was "characterized as racist, should rally to the support of his Zionist ally."

As Kaddoumi pilloried the United States, Ambassador Baroody derided the Jews' penchant for "money changing" and their tendency to become "persona non grata" wherever they wandered. Senegal's ambassador Papa Louis Fall tried invalidating the 1917 Balfour declaration recognizing Jewish rights in Palestine by disparaging Lord Balfour for having "Jewish blood by marriage." Such rhetoric would appear more frequently in General Assembly debates, proving the continuing overlap, at the UN and elsewhere, between anti-Zionists and anti-Semites.

A week later, on a rainy November 10, 1975, the General Assembly debated Resolution 3379. That day, New York municipal and state leaders were again negotiating with federal officials to avert New York City's default. President Ford celebrated the Marines' bicentennial at the Iwo Jima memorial as reporters continued to question his firing of Secretary of Defense James Schlesinger. Patty Hearst's trial was set for December. Five hundred people mourned Lionel Trilling, the legendary Columbia University professor who coined the term "adversary culture." Early that morning the huge freighter *Edmund Fitzgerald* sank in Lake Superior, felled by what Father Richard Ingalls, eulogizing all twenty-nine crew members aboard who died, would call "contemptuous rogue waves that break hearts and crush great hulks of steel."

Belgium moved quickly to adjourn the debate. David W. Wilson of Liberia agreed, admitting that many delegates, "not too clear about what is Zionism and what is racism," awaited proper instruction from their governments. Talib El-Shibib of Iraq scoffed that amid such intense lobbying, the delegates had sufficient time, if they cared, to be instructed.

The resolution to adjourn failed, sixty-seven votes to fifty-five, with fifteen abstentions and five absent. Israel's standing in the UN had so deteriorated that Western delegates rejoiced that a majority of seventy-five resisted the Soviet-Arab orders to vote "Yes." Chaim Herzog labeled it the highest pro-Israel vote in a decade.

One African delegate who abstained said the "hard-line Arab tactics" were backfiring: "Last year, during the Palestine debate, Israel found herself almost alone with her American protector. This year all the Western developed nations rallied behind Israel"—and Black African countries dithered. Twenty-one African countries opposed deferral, but thirteen supported it. Among Latin American countries, seventeen opposed deferral, and three supported it. East Asia was split, five yes and six no. Among the Eastern European Soviet Satellites, no one voted yes, ten voted no, and Romania, protecting its strong Israel ties, was absent. Among the mostly Arab Near and Middle Eastern countries twenty-four opposed deferral, only two approved. And among the Western European and other democracies, seventeen endorsed deferral and three disagreed—Cyprus, Malta, and Turkey. The narrowed vote seemed to vindicate Moynihan's muscular strategy. He believed in making "our positions clear enough on important matters such that no one votes against us casually." His aides tracked their progress, however incremental, against the anti-Israel and anti-Western monolith. For example, Guyana's percentage of voting in agreement with the United States rather than the USSR inched up from 24.9 percent in 1973 to 27.9 percent in 1974. "So much for the 'If you were nicer...' argument," Suzanne Weaver exulted.

During this debate, many more delegates addressed the growing fears about what the UN would become rather than what Zionism was or was not. African and European delegates continued bewailing the lost "unanimity," the lost "consensus" in supporting the Decade against Racism. The UK's ambassador Ivor Richard agreed. Shifting to substance, the Oxford-trained barrister embraced the International Commission of Jurists' conclusion that stigmatizing Zionism as racism confused "racism and racial discrimination with nationalism." Richard most worried that an "atmosphere of discord and division" threatened the United Nations' future.

Semesa K. Sikivou of Fiji asked why "single out" Zionism among the many "expressions of nationalism the world over?" Reverend Benjamin Nunez from Costa Rica had a simple answer: anti-Semitism. "Is there a single representative in this Assembly," he asked in Spanish, "who, before God, can declare that the proposed anti-Semitic resolution fulfills any of the objectives of the Charter?" Other Western delegates warned that these antics placed new roadblocks on the path to peace.

The resolution's supporters resented Moynihan's tactics—and Len Garment's rhetoric. Tiamiou Adjibade of Dahomey denounced the "feverish activity by certain delegations" serving "their allies and vassals." Radha Krishna Ramphul of Mauritius claimed that the "pressure, coercion, threats, obnoxious language and the arrogant, patronizing attitude of the representatives of some big, developed countries have, for quite some time now, ceased to have much effect on the small, developing countries." And words like "obscene" and indecent precluded compromise.

The resolution's supporters rejected accusations of anti-Semitism. Jaksa Petric of Yugoslavia said it was ridiculous "to equate with anti-Semitism the just condemnation of Israel's aggression" or with supporting "the just liberation struggle of the Arab peoples." Having been "a victim of Nazism," which started with anti-Semitism, Petric reasoned, "it is absurd to impute anti-Semitism to us."

Nonetheless, the delegates who attacked Zionism now were less systematic and uniform than they had been in the Third Committee. Adjibade of Dahomey contrasted Israel's encouraging Jews to settle Palestine while refusing to Palestinians "the right to return to their homeland....As long as the Palestinian problem lasts," he thundered, "my delegation will never tire of condemning Zionism as a form of racism."

Fayez A. al-Sayegh, representing Kuwait, broadened the definition of racial discrimination beyond "race in the biological, genetic sense of the term" to repudiate any discrimination "based on descent, on national origin or on ethnic origin." Just as the heart pumps blood in and out, he claimed, "so in the heartbeat of Zionism the pumping-in of Jews and the pumping-out of non-Jews are indispensable for the fulfillment of the goal of the *Judenstaat*," using the German title of Theodor Herzl's Zionist work aimed to Nazify Zionism.

Norman Podhoretz detected the Soviet-Arab impact on the diplomats' speeches, even among the resolution's opponents. Most of the diplomats voting no nevertheless assured "the world that they yielded to no one in their dis-approval and indeed detestation of Israel's many crimes," Podhoretz wrote. Most of these no voters did not claim "the resolution was wrong but that it was politically unwise."

Wearing a gray suit with a white handkerchief stuffed in his pocket—a dandyish, Moynihan-like touch—Chaim Herzog began his rebuttal by addressing "the continued existence of the Organization, which has been dragged to its lowest point of discredit by a coalition of despotisms and rac-ists." Most of Herzog's speech, delivered calmly but pointedly, defended Zionism itself. He pointed out that the vote on this resolution occurred on the anniversary of Kristallnacht. Thirty-seven years earlier, Adolf Hitler's Nazi storm troopers attacked synagogues and Jewish businesses throughout Germany. The "film of broken glass" covering the streets of Germany, "which dissolved into millions of crystals," gave that awful night its name, Herzog explained. Kristallnacht was the nightmarish prelude to the death camps that followed.

"Zionism," Herzog proclaimed, "is to the Jewish people what the liberation movements of Africa and Asia have been to their peoples," movements of national affirmation not racist denigration. Recalling the 650,000 Jews expelled from Arab lands, he challenged: "What happened to the people, what happened to their property?" Herzog concluded, "For us, the Jewish people, this resolution, based on hatred, falsehood and arrogance, is devoid of any moral or legal value." He then replicated a gesture his father had used as chief rabbi of Palestine to protest the British "White Paper" limiting Jewish emigration to Palestine in 1939. He ripped the resolution in half.

Invoking the Holocaust was no mere rhetorical flourish for Herzog. Serving as a British officer during World War II, he helped liberate a small concentration camp outside of Bremen, then witnessed the "more apoca-lyptic" desolation at Bergen-Belsen. He bitterly remembered "the filthy huts," the "emaciated figures," the dysentery, the "indescribable" stench— and the detached denial of the German village when forced to see "the bru-talities done in their name."

Although some Israeli diplomats disliked mentioning the Holocaust or charging anti-Semitism in what they saw as a state matter, Herzog's anguished call resonated widely. The cartoon "Lurie's Opinion," seen by an estimated 32 million readers, imagined a UN official saying "ALL THOSE CONDEMNING ZIONISM RAISE THEIR HAND." An Arab terrorist, Idi Amin, Fidel Castro, and

Hitler himself voted yes by raising their arms in a collective "Sieg Heil" salute.

Elie Wiesel, whose concentration camp memoir *Night* had already introduced thousands of Americans to Nazi hell, recognized the morphology of anti-Semitic hatred in the resolution. "To prepare 'solutions' to the 'Jewish problem' the first step was to divorce the Jew from mankind," he wrote in *Le Figaro*, stimulating a massive debate in Paris. Accusing Israel, the collective Jew, of the reprehensible crime of racism started the process of ostracizing, demonizing, then dehumanizing, which in the 1940s resulted in Auschwitz. Wiesel dismissed the claim that "this is not about Jews, this is about Zionists," writing: "they try to divide us, to pit us against the other after having pitted us against the world." Instead, Jewish history teaches "Whenever one Jewish community is threatened, all others are in danger." Fearing that "hate of the Jew has once more become fashionable," the Romanian-born American immigrant admitted, "I remember and I am afraid."

Thirty years after Auschwitz's liberation, hearing the world's leaders endorse words that could isolate and ultimately destroy the Jewish state also shook most Jews. That day, B'nai B'rith took out a full-page *New York Times* ad—devoting half the page to an arresting photo of a Nazi rally with two huge swastikas. The ad charged "a number of countries" with "condoning…Nazi ideology" in the UN. "Dear Ambassadors," it pleaded, "KILL THE RESOLUTION OR DESTROY THE U.N." Remembering that Palestinians collaborated with the Nazis in the 1940s, especially Haj Amin el Husseini, the grand mufti of Jerusalem, now seeing Palestinians target vulnerable civilians regularly, Israelis could not dismiss the resolution as mere words.

The Zionism is racism resolution came amid a Palestinian terrorist typhoon, including the 1972 massacre of Israeli athletes during the Munich Olympics. These periodic bloodbaths, combined with the Yom Kippur War's lingering trauma, the growing Arab oil power, and this new ideological assault on Israel's soul, locked Israelis and Palestinians at destruction junction. In 1996 Prime Minister Shimon Peres would note that "the delegitimization of Israel made it an easy game for terrorist attacks" and made peace a hard sell. Violent denunciations discourage hopes for reconciliation. The UN was building an institutional infrastructure for this ideological assault. General Assembly Resolution 3376 (XXX) established a Committee on the Exercise of the Inalienable Rights of the Palestinian People. This committee would reflect the nihilistic Palestinian tendency to focus on denouncing Israel and Zionism, not just building a Palestinian state. A third resolution, 3375 (XXX) invited the Palestine Liberation Organization to all UN peace efforts, countering Israel's delusional policy of shunning the Palestinians and the PLO, which changed in the 1990s with the Oslo peace process.

The second resolution passed on November 10, 1975, institutionalized and ritualized the UN's condemnation of Israel. Israelis and Jews felt rejected by the world. McGill Law Professor Irwin Cotler, chairing the Canadian National Commission on Economic Coercion and Discrimination, observed that the International Labor Organization declared Israel "the enemy of the working people." UNESCO condemned Israel as "the enemy of culture." The International Women's Year declaration in Mexico declared Israel "the enemy of women." Finally, singling out Zionism as the only form of nationalism deemed to be racism, the General Assembly labeled Israel "the enemy of mankind; Israel is the pariah of humanity."

Moynihan kept silent before the Resolution 3379 vote. He did not want critics blaming his words when the resolution passed, given, he adlibbed as he began his speech, the new UN practice of "doing something outrageous," then being "outraged by those who have the temerity to point it out." Instead, he spoke after the vote, with the sense that he was addressing not just the General Assembly but the American people, the world media, and indeed the bar of history. The United States, he said, "does not acknowledge, it will not abide by, it will never acquiesce in this infamous act." The words were Podhoretz's, but Moynihan delivered them with power. Moynihan liked the line so much he concluded with it too. Moreover, by calling the resolution an "infamous act," reinforced by his charge minutes later that "this day will live in infamy," Moynihan was paralleling Herzog's instinct to invoke World War II. Even three decades later, Roosevelt's famous phrase about Pearl Harbor represented this generation's ultimate expression of repugnance.

Beyond defending Israel and Zionism, Moynihan targeted the United Nations, defying Kissinger's directives. At 11 o'clock that morning, Kissinger had told Ambassador Buffum to "call Moynihan and tell him he is so ordered not to threaten any reduction in our relationship to the Assembly any more. That is a direct order from me." Kissinger wanted Moynihan to "clear his statement" and remember his place: "As long as I am here, he is an Ambassador."

Undeterred, Moynihan directed the delegates to consider "the harm this act will have done the United Nations." Again calling the resolution "obscene,"

Moynihan charted the escalation from a furtive attack to "a shameless open-ness." Moynihan the social scientist was warning that brazen misbehavior becomes routine and thus more dangerous. This insight would lead to Moynihan's memorable *American Scholar* article in 1993—and more enduring alliterative condemnation—that, enmeshed in social pathologies, Americans were "defining deviancy down."

Ignoring the State Department Arabists, Moynihan turned moralist, pro-claiming "A great evil has been loosed upon the world." He bolstered his charge of anti-Semitism and annoyed the Soviets by quoting Andrei Sakharov. Just weeks after winning the 1975 Nobel Peace Prize, the Soviets' most prominent dissident scientist had said: "If this resolution is adopted, it can only contribute to anti-Semitic tendencies in many countries, by giving them the appearance of international legality."

Going even farther than Sakharov's warning of giving "international sanction" to Jew hatred, Moynihan accused the General Assembly of grant-ing "symbolic amnesty—and more—to the murderers of the 6 million European Jews." That phrase infuriated Henry Kissinger. "It is too much," he told Ambassador Buffum. "It is just wrong."

Moynihan made one more introductory point, addressing "historians." Saluting the many virtuous people who opposed the resolution, he said, "we fought with full knowledge of what indeed would be lost." Although Moynihan liked to win, posturing as the Patron Saint of Lost but Noble Causes was an acceptable fallback, particularly if the lost cause was a wildly popular one.

Moynihan claimed that "In all our postwar history there has not been another issue which has brought forth such unanimity of American public opinion," as the president, the Congress, American Jews, the American trade union movement mobilized. That statement, even if exaggerated, reflected a remarkable joint achievement, along with the American abhorrence of anti-Semitism. He and Herzog had publicized the issue so effectively in three weeks, that now, "one after another, the great private institutions of American life pronounced anathema on this evil thing—and most particularly, the Christian churches have done so." The Harris survey taken two weeks later suggested near unanimity among the people too, with only 9 percent sur-veyed calling Zionism racism, as support for Israel soared to a margin of 8 to 1. A higher percentage of respondents than usual opted out—answering "don't know"—because of the issue's complexity.

Having branded the resolution evil, anti-Semitic, self-destructive, and unpopular, Moynihan dissected the new big "lie" itself. In academic fashion, he made the case first by defining racism, and chiding the General Assembly for making accusations before defining the concept; second, by defining Zionism as normal, one of many nineteenth-century-based nationalist movements; and third, by examining Zionism's singular permeability, which made the racism charge particularly absurd.

On the first point, the Moynihan team's research proved useful. The night before the speech, Moynihan had worked with Norman Podhoretz, Suzanne Weaver, and his wife, Liz, at the UN ambassador's grand private quarters on the Waldorf-Astoria's forty-second floor, as a *New York Times Magazine* reporter watched. At one point Liz Moynihan asked sharply, "You took that out, didn't you?" Weaver reassured her friend, "It's out." When the reporter asked, "What part is that?" Liz Moynihan replied: "The part where Pat said that passing the resolution meant that the lunatics were taking over the asylum."

"No, we couldn't say that, even though it might be true," her husband agreed, as he mixed a drink. Instead, he argued, the resolution didn't define what racism *was*. And he credited "Suzi" Weaver with finding the "closest thing to a definition" from a 1968 debate, in which a Soviet delegate "said that racism and Nazism were the same thing! Identical!" Moynihan exclaimed. "So if Zionism is racism it means that Zionism is Nazism, and if that isn't lunacy, I don't know what is."

This concern with the specific meaning of the term "racism" began with a memorandum tracing the history of the UN discourse about race written by a young Yale political scientist named Charles H. Fairbanks Jr. Fairbanks learned from the director of the US Arms Control and Disarmament Agency, Fred Charles Iklé, to beware "semantic infiltration"—the tendency to adopt hostile foreign terms when talking politics. When Westerners echoed the rhetoric of brutal totalitarian regimes labeling themselves "liberation movements" or calling national conflicts "racist," the political frameworks became self-defeating. In what Weaver would call the fight's "Ur-document," Fairbanks concluded that "To call Zionism a form of racism makes a mockery of the struggle against racism as the emperor Caligula made a mockery of the Roman senate when he appointed to it his horse." More broadly, Fairbanks realized liberals needed to define terms more clearly to survive.

In his speech, channeling Fairbanks, Moynihan thundered: "the United Nations has declared Zionism to be racism without ever having defined racism." Then he quoted the Queen of Hearts in *Alice in Wonderland*: "Sentence first, verdict afterwards." Moynihan also quoted Gaston Thorn, the General Assembly's president, who urged delegates to wait until they achieved linguistic precision rather than rushing toward such a momentous decision.

Moynihan now entered a conceptual swampland. On October 29, the Kuwaiti ambassador asked Moynihan to lunch, along with a Palestinian activist Dr. Fayez A. al-Sayegh. When Moynihan claimed the UN never defined racism, Dr. al-Sayegh corrected him. The General Assembly had passed Resolution 2106 on December 21, 1965, defining racial discrimination as "any distinction, exclusion, restriction or preference based on race, color, descent, or national or ethnic origin which has the purpose or effect of nullifying or impairing the recognition, enjoyment or exercise, on an equal footing, of human rights and fundamental freedoms in the political, economic, social, cultural or any other field of public life." Poorly briefed and humiliated, Moynihan retreated. Now relying on his staffer Herbert Reis's research, Moynihan acknowledged that the UN had occasionally defined racial discrimination, as al-Sayegh argued. But "racial discrimination is a practice, racism is a doctrine," Moynihan noted, and that, in the "more serious charge" being leveled at Zionism no Israeli actions were ever "defined."

What seemed like Talmudic hairsplitting actually confronted the central moral question. Racially discriminatory policies could be changed; a racist ideology had to be destroyed—along with any country founded on such an evil doctrine. This sweeping essentialist charge, with its exterminationist implications, would become a staple of the anti-Israel assault for the next four decades.

Using Weaver's research, Moynihan scoffed that the one time a UN body defined "racism," on December 16, 1968, in the Third Committee, "the distinguished representative of Tunisia" and the "no less distinguished delegate of the USSR" equated "racism" with "Nazism." Such sloppiness illustrated "the intellectual precision with which the matter was being treated." The result was "a political lie" to match the most outrageous lies of the twentieth century: "The lie is that Zionism is a form of racism. The overwhelmingly clear truth is that it is not." Here Moynihan stopped short. He wanted to call it a Big Lie, using Adolf Hitler's phrase, having described it, to the *New York*

Times reporter as "a lie of Hitlerian size." Instead—perhaps edited by Kissinger but certainly influenced by his disapproval—Moynihan merely implied it.

The word "racism" was so new it did not appear in the *Oxford English Dictionary*. Moynihan defined it as based on "discredited" doctrines alleging "significant, biological differences among clearly identifiable groups, and that those differences establish in effect, different levels of humanity." He added, from *Webster's Third New International Dictionary*, that racism further involves "a belief in the inherent superiority of a particular race and its right to domination over others."

Moving to his second proposition, Moynihan proclaimed that racism, now clearly defined, was "alien to the political and religious movement known as zionism." Showing off his gleanings from his Podhoretz tutorials, reinforced in a November 6 letter Podhoretz had sent him, Moynihan described Zionism as a movement with "ancient" origins—including long-standing Christian expectations of Israel's rebirth—formally established in 1897. Moynihan normalized Zionism by noting it emerged amid a wave of nineteenth-century European nationalism that eventually overtook Africa and Asia. Challenging Africans and Asians, echoing Herzog, he defined Zionism as "a Jewish form of what today is called a national liberation movement." Challenging the Soviets, Moynihan quoted Soviet Foreign Minister Andrei Gromyko's statement at a Security Council meeting in 1948, deploring the Arab armies' attacks on Israel, aimed "at the suppression of the national liberation movement in Palestine," meaning Zionism.

Further mocking the racism claim, Moynihan found Zionism "unique," the only "national liberation movement" that defined its members not in terms of birth but of belief. Unlike other nationalities based on genes or geography, Jewish nationality accepted converts "regardless of 'race, colour, descent, or national or ethnic origin.'" This openness made Zionism among the least racist nationalisms. Consider the range of "racial stocks" among Israel's citizens: "There are black Jews, brown Jews, white Jews, Jews from the Orient and Jews from the West," most by birth, but some converts. Many non-Jews also were Israeli citizens. Zionism and racism, therefore, were mutually incompatible. "In logic, the State of Israel could be, or could become, many things, theoretically including many undesirable things, but it could not be and could not become racist unless it ceased to be Zionist."

Returning to his charge that this new, comprehensive, anti-Zionism was actually anti-Semitism, Moynihan observed that the Jews' enemies invented "the idea that Jews are a 'race,'" to find new ways to exclude them in a secular age. He scoffed that defining Jews as a race "was a contemptible idea at the beginning, and no civilized person would be associated with it. To think that it is an idea now endorsed by the United Nations is to reflect on what civilization has come to."

Invoking "civilization" returned Moynihan to his opening proposition that the UN damaged itself, humanity, and democracy. "It is precisely a concern for civilization, for civilized values that are or should be precious to all mankind, that arouses us at this moment to such special passion," he said, rebuking Kissinger and other Western voices advising restraint. This attack not only targets a fellow "Member nation," it assails "the integrity of that whole body of moral and legal precepts which we know as human rights."

"Human Rights" was not yet the popular buzzword it is today, neither internationally nor in the United States. As late as 1974, Jeri Laber, a future founder of Human Rights Watch, would not use the words "human rights" to describe her work, even while placing newspaper op-eds for Amnesty International protesting torture. And Kissinger dismissed "human rights" talk throughout his years dominating American foreign policy as "easy slogans," "empty posturing," "sentimental nonsense," and "malarkey." Still, the American and Soviet signing of the Helsinki Accords, as the Conference on Security and Co-operation in Europe ended on August 1, 1975, with its section 7 mandating "Respect for Human Rights and Fundamental Freedom," became a historic turning point. Helsinki helped make human rights sacrosanct, eventually spotlighting Soviet hypocrisy. In Congress, liberal Democrats were proposing that human rights become the benchmark for judging allies. That year, clearly in transition, the newly created State Department Bureau of Human Rights and Humanitarian Affairs' annual report would crassly claim that human rights was "no longer a bleeding heart issue presided [over] by fairies in Geneva."

As he had in the 1960s, with his controversial racial reports and Nixon-era memos, Moynihan linked a specific political moment to broader historical and ideological trends. Since his *Commentary* article, Moynihan had been primed to defend American dignity and democracy. Once again, he was pioneering in appreciating human rights' growing significance. But he also anticipated how dictators would camouflage their crimes with human rights rhetoric while targeting democracies like Israel. Yet again, Moynihan's prescience and conscience pitted him against Henry Kissinger.

All these considerations stirred Moynihan's considerable emotion when he delivered the memorable line: "The terrible lie that has been told here today will have terrible consequences." He explained: "Not only will people begin to say, as indeed they have already begun to say, that the United Nations is a place where lies are told, but far more serious, grave and perhaps irreparable harm will be done to the cause of human rights itself."

Moynihan returned to Fairbanks's indispensable memorandum, which warned that oppressors now might think that "if racism is no worse than Zionism, just how bad is it?" Similarly, Moynihan mourned "Today we have drained the word 'racism' of its meaning." He feared that "terms like 'national self-determination' and 'national honor'" soon would be "perverted."

Moynihan was not only confronting the seventy-two delegates who supported the resolution, the thirty-five delegates who abstained, and the dozens of State Department colleagues who had sabotaged him. He was targeting the media hysterics who distorted his Moynihan Report and "benign neglect" memo, the precious Ivy Leaguers who subverted democratic ideals, the spoiled student radicals who betrayed defining Western ideas, the weak-chinned European Marxists who appeased Communists yet nevertheless inspired progressive, influential Americans. Moynihan was not only opposing the Third World, he was confronting "them," as Suzanne Weaver would term it, the new nihilists, the self-hating Westerners, the adversarials, the hypercritical intellectuals, academics, journalists, students, diplomats, and politicians so blinded by Western shortcomings that they failed to see their country's own internal strengths or most external threats.

Moynihan was repudiating the Che Guevara rules that had dominated Mexico City and now Turtle Bay—while also rejecting Kissinger's amoral interest-based calculus, which discounted American ideals as defining interests. Western enlightenment, Moynihan continued, spawned the notions of "domestic and international rights." Unfortunately, most countries subordinated individual rights to the state's perceived needs. This reversal explained how these states could use human rights selectively rather than preserving them universally as a sacred trust.

Moynihan had been deriding dictators for weeks before this moment, mocking their sudden respect for human rights. The Western diplomat's code, especially at the UN, banned such direct attacks, and Henry Kissinger's breakthrough with détente involved rejecting what he called "the old extremes of world policeman and isolationism."

Making his stand, Moynihan warned: "If we destroy the words that were given to us by past centuries, we will not have words to replace them, for philosophy today has no such words. But there are those of us who have not forsaken these older words, still so new to much of the world. Not forsaken them now, not here, not anywhere, not ever." And with that, Moynihan returned to his opening line, linking through alliteration the domestic fight with the international fight: "The United States of America declares that it does not acknowledge, it will not abide by, it will never acquiesce in this infamous act."

In a lifetime of article writing and speech making, this may have been Moynihan's greatest effort. Memorable phrases became etched into the listeners' mind immediately on hearing, and the speech itself had historical and philosophical sweep. Churning with moral indignation, it had just enough sarcasm while balancing analysis and judgment, explication and exhortation.

Herzog had restated the Zionist case, eloquently, unapologetically. His speech would be studied over the decades to explain Zionism to succeeding generations. Herzog later admitted that "the event did more for Zionism than Jews getting a million speeches from Zionist functionaries." Moynihan's task was broader: he had to wrap his defense of Zionism in a defense of democracy and America—without appearing to be Israel's lackey, and he had to judge the General Assembly on the UN's terms.

As he finished in the General Assembly, spent, Moynihan treasured the presence of one American leader, who left behind his business in Washington to support the members of the US mission to the United Nations during this stressful time. Minnesota's senator Hubert Humphrey, the former vice president and presidential candidate, offered a living bridge to the optimistic liberalism of the postwar years, when American faith in the UN and liberal support for Israel were normative. Humphrey bore silent witness to the UN's fall, to the anger that Moynihan articulated. The UN had indeed endured a grievous, self-inflicted blow, from which it has yet to recover.

Irving Kristol joined hundreds of thousands of others watching Moynihan's speech on television. Kristol recognized immediately what Moynihan was articulating—and popularizing in unprecedented ways: a new, tougher take on foreign policy. Kristol embraced the label "neoconservative" for this impulse; Moynihan abhorred it. During the speech, the TV station Kristol was watching it on, WNET/Channel 13, cut away from the UN to a panel discussion about what was happening there. Cursing "those idiots" at New York's left-leaning public television station, Kristol later told Moynihan: "I would cancel my subscription to channel 13 only I don't have one."

Back in the UN, the session went very late. Jamil Baroody of Saudi Arabia demanded a right of reply. Shaping the diplomatic backlash against Moynihan, the veteran ambassador resented two words in particular, "lie" and "obscene." Where he came from, calling someone a liar could be grounds for justifiable homicide, Baroody snapped. "But we are liars, seventy-two liars?" He asked indignantly. "Do you have a monopoly of the truth?" From there, he flirted with anti-Semitism by grumbling about Jewish power: "God help any candidate in this country who is not supported by the Zionists!" A longtime New York resident, Baroody wondered why "the Federal Government does not help out this City of New York" yet finances Israel. One of the UN's most eloquent and determined Israel-bashers, Baroody also attacked Zionism as a project of European Jews, who "had nothing to do with our Jews," meaning the supposedly well-treated Jews in Arab lands. Mocking the religious Jews' belief in God's "Promised Land," Baroody barked: "Since when was God in the real estate business?"

After the session, despite the late hour, Moynihan, Leonard Garment, Clarence Mitchell, and one of the congressional delegates, Donald M. Fraser, held a press conference. The words said there were important, as Fraser, a liberal Democrat who was president of the Americans for Democratic Action, threatened congressional retaliation against the UN. But most significant was the kind of patriotic tableau Moynihan loved, with Moynihan-the-Irish-Catholic-New-Yorker, Garment-the-Brooklyn-Jew, Mitchell-the-Black-Protestant-Marylander, and Fraser-the-WASP-Minnesotan sitting together in front of the UN's world symbol—and defending American ideals. The diplomats then retired to their favorite hangout, the Palm, the legendary Second Avenue steakhouse, pleased with themselves. As Suzanne Weaver Garment would recall: "They knew they had found what we used to call a rock to stand on."

Despite this all-American image, Baroody's ripostes reinforced the impression among Moynihan's critics that his efforts were counterproductive. The debate about Moynihan's tactics divided the US mission, where some staffers were combating anti-American hostility as their colleagues claimed that aggressive responses made things worse. The State Department was futilely trying to control its own outpost. On October 31, Tap Bennett, a career Foreign Service officer whose seeming loyalty to his direct boss, Moynihan, apparently did not prevent him from leaking to his higher bosses at the State Department, circulated yet another mission-wide reminder "to clear all positions and statements for use in the General Assembly with the State Department." Dismissing the many excuses involving "written or telegraphic communication," Bennett added drily, "The telephone is usually handy and should be used."

"I will not put up with any more of Moynihan. I will not do it," Kissinger fumed the next day. The more Moynihan attacked the UN publicly, the more Kissinger fulminated against him. Moynihan is "turning into a disaster," he told the president after the Third Committee vote. "He is going wild about the Israeli issues."

Kissinger transformed his private fury into public ambivalence about America's new political superstar. Speaking in Pittsburgh after the vote, Kissinger said the United States would "pay no attention" to the Zionism resolution, but would "consider the votes on an individual basis before deciding what specific actions we will take toward various countries." Mischievously resurrecting the earlier controversy, he then suggested that Moynihan should have used "more restrained" language regarding Idi Amin.

Kissinger offered his realist reading of the UN. The original redemptive faith was "exaggerated." The current disappointment that it was not "the hope of humanity" should not blind Americans to the UN's many good works. The *New York Times* recognized that Kissinger was distancing himself from "the outspoken American envoy."

The combat sapped Moynihan, as did the criticisms. His confidantes understood that beneath the bluster, Moynihan felt "vulnerable." William F. Buckley would write "It is not easy, on the outside, to imagine the kind of pressure brought to bear, inside, on those who tell the truth—when the truth is damaging to self-esteem." Buckley described Moynihan's "heavy burden" as being "his outspoken belief in the ideals of this country."

As a frequent flyer along the Cambridge-New York-Washington corridor, Moynihan keenly felt the disapproval of the *New York Times*, Henry Kissinger, and the State Department establishment. One of the *Times'* leading liberals, Anthony Lewis, dismissed Resolution 3379 as anti-Semitic "foolishness."

Still, Lewis mocked America's self-righteousness, saying: "A superpower that drops 500,000 tons of bombs in Cambodia is in rather a doubtful position to lecture others on morality."

Still, it was the pressure from Kissinger that was the most difficult to take. *Newsweek* reported that "Kissinger raked Moynihan over the coals" for his speech at the UN when they met at a White House social event. Insisting the encounter was brief and benign, Moynihan recognized Kissinger's fingerprints on the story. Rumors fed by Kissinger began circulating that Moynihan was grandstanding to New York's Jews to run for Senate in 1976. Moynihan, who, at the time did not intend to run, first attributed the rumors to the Soviet disinformation campaign against him.

Moynihan bristled when asked about his political ambitions on CBS-TV's weekly interview show, *Face the Nation*, before the vote, on October 26. "It might please some of the people in the UN who see us as enemies…to explain positions we are taking on matters of *principle* as in fact having as their origin some squalid personal ambition." But, Moynihan proclaimed unequivocally, "I would consider it dishonorable to leave this post and run for any office." The next day, he had the US mission circulate a press release with only that question and answer.

Moynihan was furious when the *New Yorker* speculated about "using the United Nations as a forum to further himself in American politics." Moynihan described his stand as "Strong, and at times rather lonely," against "vicious anti-Semitic measures." He insisted: "It never for a moment occurred to me that in answering back—in fighting back, if you will—I might be furthering any personal ambition." Moynihan wrote to the Senate incumbent, James Buckley, his friend William F. Buckley's brother, sending him the *Face the Nation* quotation, and saying, ever so elegantly, "You were so kind to state at the Al Smith dinner that if I were to run you would resign and I genuinely regret that I can't provide you such an easy out." Moynihan never admitted exactly *when* he started planning to run for the New York Senate seat, but his newfound popularity emboldened him and reawakened his dormant political ambitions, which he had only buried reluctantly. One year and two days after writing the note, Moynihan unseated Buckley.

In his speech in early October 1975 denouncing Idi Amin, Moynihan had offered a broader overview analyzing America's "crisis of confidence." Americans were floundering, with New York City teetering fiscally and

America bumbling internationally. In his formalistic orator's manner, Moynihan said: "Less and less do we seem confident of what to do next."

Yet a month later, this same Daniel Patrick Moynihan had become a symbol of America's renewed patriotism and confidence. Moynihan's campaign against Resolution 3379 set a new template for American nationalism. Surprisingly, despite bitter partisan division, with both the Democratic and Republican parties purging their moderates and veering to the extremes, Moynihan improvised a bipartisan language of assertive idealism. Liberals, especially the post-Watergate class of '74, the young Democratic Turks who entered Congress after the Nixon-induced Republican meltdown, despised Kissinger's amorality and demanded a more principled foreign policy. Conservatives, especially the man emerging as Gerald Ford's greatest rival for the Republican nomination, Ronald Reagan, detested Kissinger's appeasement and demanded a more affirmatively patriotic foreign policy. Moynihan satisfied both.

Without using that controversial label, William Buckley praised Moynihan as a neoconservative—tough abroad but still championing liberal social policies at home. With his rococo rhetoric, Buckley said, "if it should happen, on account of the rumbling of the juggernaut, or because, finally, the Lord has cleared His throat, that the blight of totalitarianism should disappear from the face of the earth—I would find myself, in those woozy pastures, quarreling with him about some of his silly, pestiferous domestic programs. But until then, admiringly and gratefully, I am Daniel Patrick Moynihan's to command."

From the Left, Morton Weinfeld, then a Harvard sociology graduate student, would praise his former teacher "as one man of the democratic Left to another.... You stand with Sakharov, with Simone de Beauvoir, with the late Casals, with Theodorakis, all of whom have condemned by word and deed the attempts to destroy the Jewish state. With such friends, symbols of freedom, dignity, and justice, at our side, we need not doubt the moral wisdom of the cause." From Capitol Hill, Senator Frank Church, the symbol in 1975 of the hypercritical Democrats, wrote Moynihan: "You have done what you said you would do: speak out for human rights and the democratic tradition, and you have done so with great force and dignity."

Church's ideological opposite, Senator Barry Goldwater of Arizona applauded too. Goldwater had become one of Church's leading critics, as one of the minority members of the Church committee. Goldwater wrote an official dissent to the final report saying that he feared the "security and diplomatic problems" America risked by "getting into the subject of assassinations at all." Affecting an intimacy with Moynihan that he lacked, Senator Goldwater wrote a letter, which opened "Dear Dan" not "Dear Pat." The conservative Arizonan urged "Keep up the wonderful work.... It's time that somebody from the United States started talking as you have been talking...we are not going to sit back and allow a handful of countries without even the ability to govern themselves...tell us what we are going to do."

To get Barry Goldwater—Mr. National Security Establishment—and Frank Church—Senator Exposé—to agree on anything was extraordinary, especially regarding foreign policy. And after the post-Watergate election that brought in the ideological, liberal, activist Democratic Class of 1974, to be able to get 433 of 435 Members of Congress sponsoring a resolution was equally remarkable. In his three-week campaign, Moynihan had found a platform that united America's patriotic elites. But despite claiming that the American people supported him, when he spoke of America's unanimity on November 10, 1975, it was more a hope than an assessment. Moynihan and others, such as President Ford and a former California governor sitting in his Pacific Palisades home, were watching closely to see if Moynihan's message would resonate nationwide.

BACKLASH

I am a Zionist.
—POPULAR BUTTON, FALL 1975

"The vigorous reaction we are seeing throughout this country to the Zionism vote can be a healthy thing," Tap Bennett, America's deputy permanent representative to the UN since 1971, reported to Senator Hubert Humphrey on November 12, two days after the vote. Bennett believed in the United Nations. He praised the Security Council, which had just calmed conflict in the Sahara Desert, and commended the UN's peacekeeping activity in the Sinai, the Golan Heights, and Cyprus. "I hope we can be precise and selective in our response to the anti-Zionism disgrace," Bennett wrote.

Popular outrage is rarely precise or selective. But American anger against the UN was neither violent nor destructive. It was pure, passionate, idealistic. This overwhelmingly non-Jewish country recoiled against anti-Semitism instinctively, righteously, as Americans popularly reaffirmed their natural alliance with Israel, their sister democracy. At the same time, Ambassador Moynihan helped reaffirm a lesson that Professor Moynihan with his co-author Professor Nathan Glazer taught in *Beyond the Melting Pot*, that the modern vision of American citizenship now included allowing Jews to be Jews politically, and other ethnics to be ethnics politically.

Courtesy Bettmann/Corbis

Daniel Patrick Moynihan, America's ambassador to the UN from June 1975 to February 1976, was an idiosyncratic, passionate, compelling advocate for the United States during a time of national despair—and an eloquent defender of Israel and Zionism against Resolution 3379. "The lie is that Zionism is a form of racism," he would thunder. "The overwhelmingly clear truth is that it is not."

Courtesy Library of Congress 32459

Courtesy James Garrett, New York Daily News/Getty Images

In 1975 the United Nations was changing, as was the world. The repository of American hopes for a new era of peace, democracy, and justice when it was founded in 1945, the UN thirty years later was welcoming the Palestinian terrorist leader Yasir Arafat (*above*) and the Ugandan dictator Idi Amin (*below*). Many Americans were losing faith in the UN, while many American diplomats tried mollifying the new majority of angry Third World delegates, inflamed by the Soviet Union.

Both Photos Courtesy United Nations Photo Archive

America's master diplomat, Secretary of State and National Security Adviser Henry Kissinger, was more of an accommodating "realist." *Above,* Kissinger flanks President Gerald R. Ford, while meeting Israel's Prime Minister Yitzhak Rabin, flanked by his ambassador to the United States, Simcha Dinitz. Daniel Patrick Moynihan proposed a more muscular response. *Below,* Moynihan, at his farewell meeting on January 27, 1975, as ambassador to India, charms Kissinger, Chief of Staff Donald Rumsfeld, and Ford.

Five months later, Supreme Court Justice Byron (Whizzer) White, a fellow Kennedy administration alumnus, administered the oath of office to Moynihan, America's new and aggressive UN ambassador, with supporters and critics expecting him to "raise hell" at UN headquarters. Holding the Bible was Elizabeth Moynihan, Pat Moynihan's wife, best friend, and toughest critic.

Courtesy United Nations Photo Archives

Originally, the Soviet and Arab states wanted to expel Israel from the UN. Fearing America's wrath, Israel's critics settled on declaring Zionism to be a form of racism. Moynihan and Israel's new UN ambassador, Chaim Herzog, realized that this sweeping, ideological attack could prove much more damaging. Despite their efforts, the resolution passed its first big hurdle in the Third Committee on October 17, 1975 (*above*). The General Assembly endorsed Resolution 3379 on November 10, 1975, despite Herzog's eloquent defense of Zionism and plea to protect the UN's credibility (*below*). Furious, he ripped the resolution in half during the speech.

Courtesy Bettmann/Corbis

When the session adjourned, Leonard Garment, Congressman Donald Fraser, Moynihan, and Clarence Mitchell met with reporters to denounce the resolution (*above*), offering a tableau of American unity as an Eastern European Jew, a WASP, an Irish Catholic, and a black Protestant defended democracy together. More of that unity emerged the next day as an estimated 125,000 people rallied against Resolution 3379 in midtown Manhattan. Some signs—"I AM A ZIONIST," "ZIONISM IS LOVE"—were hopeful. Others were darker: "AN ANTI-ZIONIST IS AN ANTI-SEMITE" or "U.N. DEAD —DROWNED IN ARAB OIL."

Courtesy Conference of Presidents of Major American Jewish Organizations / Alexander Archer

At the rally, the aging civil rights leader Bayard Rustin (*above*) ended his speech by singing "Go Down Moses." As thousands, black and white, Jewish and non-Jewish, shouted "Let my people go," all of America seemed united in outrage. Yet Moynihan's stand alienated his colleagues at the State Department, his boss, Henry Kissinger, UN diplomats, and anti-Israel critics on the far left. At this meeting (*below*), on November 24, 1975, President Ford reassured Ambassador Moynihan. Still, Moynihan's position soon became untenable, and he surprised the president by resigning in January.

Courtesy Gerald R. Ford Presidential Library

Although Moynihan entered his UN position with limited political prospects, the fight over Resolution 3379 made him an American pop star. Moynihan and Senator Henry Jackson (*above*) became symbols of a newly assertive neoconservative approach to American foreign policy. Moynihan's defense of Israel and democracy helped him defeat a formidable lineup of Democratic primary opponents in 1976: New York City Council President Paul O'Dwyer, parking magnate Abe Hirschfeld, former U.S. Attorney General Ramsey Clark, and Congresswoman Bella Abzug (*below*).

Moynihan's politics of patriotic indignation not only inspired many Americans, it also helped shape Ronald Reagan's presidency. Reagan launched his presidential campaign against Gerald Ford in 1976, just days after Resolution 3379 passed. Reagan repeatedly quoted from Moynihan's speech on the campaign trail. After he won the presidency four years later in 1980, Reagan followed Moynihan's assertive, affirmative approach, even as the two charming American Irishmen clashed, especially regarding the importance of the welfare state, what to do in Central America, and the issue of government secrecy. Reagan and Moynihan were among the first American leaders to anticipate the fall of the Soviet Union, whose collapse helped vindicate them both.

For sixteen years, Moynihan fought to repeal Resolution 3379, even though the General Assembly had overridden only one resolution prior to that. Finally, in 1991, after the Iron Curtain lifted, the General Assembly voted down what Moynihan called "The Big Red Lie." President George H. W. Bush pushed ardently for repeal, making a special plea in his speech at the General Assembly on September 23, 1991. The final vote was lopsided, 111 for repeal and only 25 opposed, with 13 abstaining.

Both Photos Courtesy United Nations Photo Archives

Nevertheless, this attack against Zionism outlived the repeal and the Soviet Union's collapse, emerging with renewed vigor in 2001 at the UN's conference against World Racism in Durban, South Africa.

This attack's resurrection, along with the trauma of September 11, 2001, disturbed Moynihan, who had retired from the Senate after four terms in January 2001. In June 2002, Moynihan delivered the Harvard Commencement address after receiving an Honorary Doctorate. Although the warrior-statesman was suitably sober, worried about the world's many challenges, enraged by the terrorism and the demonization of Israel, he nevertheless retained his wit, charm, and clear understanding of the values Americans had to be fighting for, not just the evils they had to fight against. Moynihan died nine months later, on March 26, 2003, ten days after turning seventy-six.

Regarding the UN, Moynihan wanted to teach Americans that the correct reaction "should not be to walk out of this place but to stay and fight." Mastering the politics of patriotic indignation, Moynihan channeled the moralistic anger to boost American morale. This act of political alchemy would be repeated—and perfected—by an actor-turned-politician Ronald Reagan, following Moynihan, the scholar-turned-diplomat.

In the fall of 1975, most Americans, Left and Right, repudiated the UN, not Zionism. Following Moynihan's lead in rallying around Israel, they rallied around America too. Here was the Brandeisian synthesis renewed and popularly ratified, the notion developed by the Progressive Supreme Court Justice Louis Brandeis that being a good Zionist was a way to be a good American and a good liberal. Moynihan had touched a national nerve, proving that seventies culture was not as defeatist as many historians believe and that the patriotism of the eighties evolved more gradually than many triumphalist Reaganites suggest. While the 1980s economic boom was aborning, thanks to the baby boomers who were busy mastering skills and perfecting inventions, the patriotic politics of the 1980s was also developing, thanks to Moynihan and his allies. Moynihan's moment belongs to a sequence of often underappreciated events, including the 1976 Bicentennial "tall ships celebration" and the 1980 US Olympic hockey "Miracle on Ice" upset of Russia, all of which propelled Americans out of their post-Vietnam despair even before Ronald Reagan's presidency.

Americans from across the political spectrum rejected Resolution 3379 by wearing a button in protest. Inverting the Israeli flag's color scheme, bold white letters jumped out from against a blue background proclaiming: "I AM A ZIONIST." Israel's former prime minister Golda Meir, who along with the silver-tongued diplomat Abba Eban and the one-eyed war hero Moshe Dayan, embodied the new Jewish spirit flourishing in Israel, urged all of Israel's supporters to wear the button. In New York especially, Jews and non-Jews alike sported the button in the days following the vote. A *Washington Post* editorial explained that "Zionism in its most fundamental sense is Jewish nationalism, the doctrine that holds that Jews, like a hundred and more other groups—including twenty or more Arab groups—have a right to political self-determination in a territorial homeland of their own." This particular group seeking national liberation, the *Post* added, had a "spiritual and cultural heritage reaching back more than 3,000 years on the same ground."

Liberals anxious for a Middle East compromise understood that any victory for extremism hurt Middle East peace prospects. The *New York Times*, which ran hot and cold in covering Moynihan and Israel, published an editorial blasting the vote "in condemnation of one member-state's national movement," calling it "offensive, spiteful and futile—and stupid as well." The paper warned "This is not the diplomacy of conciliation; it will give comfort only to extremist ideologues on all sides, and tragically so since the first signs of moderation among the belligerents seemed to be coming to fruition" with the Sinai agreement.

At the time, thirty years after the Holocaust, most Americans could not see how to affix the word "racism" to Zionism or Judaism. From his jail cell, the former "Minister of Information" for the Black Panthers, Eldridge Cleaver, wrote that "of all people in the world, the Jews have not only suffered particularly from racist persecution, they have done more than any other people in history to expose and condemn racism."

Proposals to leave the UN, or at least suspend paying dues, abounded. Members of an older generation feared the UN was degenerating as the League of Nations had. Those from a younger generation more defined by World War II felt that the UN had abandoned its founding vision during its thirtieth anniversary year.

The day after Resolution 3379 passed, the Conference of Presidents of Major American Jewish Organizations, the coalition of thirty-two leading Jewish groups, organized a noontime "rally against racism and anti-Semitism" at the Brotherhood-in-Action plaza in Manhattan's Garment District. Formed in 1956 at the Eisenhower administration's request, the Conference of Presidents addressed Franklin Roosevelt's frustration that the Jews lacked a pope. The American Jewish community's alphabet soup of organizations generated a cacophony of seemingly authoritative voices representing self-proclaimed "major" Jewish organizations. Even most Jews, for example could not distinguish the influential AJC—the American Jewish Committee—from the influential AJC—the American Jewish Congress. The conference coordinated consensus positions, especially on Israel.

Malcolm Hoenlein, a young Soviet Jewry activist from Philadelphia who in 1986 would become the conference's powerful executive vice chairman, recalled feeling nervous before the rally regarding the turnout. The conference had not built a popular case against the UN, even among the major Jewish organizations. No one yet knew whether Moynihan's appeal was resonating beyond committed Zionists. Ed Prince, at the time a Yeshiva University student, who as the nineteen-year-old president of the North American Jewish Youth Council was the youngest Jewish chief executive, remembers that the leaders initially called it a "youth rally," to provide cover in case they failed to mobilize the 100,000 people they felt they needed to make the rally respectable.

Hoenlein and other grassroots campaigners had mastered community organizing and public relations in fighting for Soviet Jewry. In this case—but not always—the activists cooperated effectively with some established organizations such as the American Jewish Committee. Founded in 1906 by anti-Zionist German Jewish elites, the AJC in the 1970s was becoming more populist, more Zionist, more proactive. On October 21, Zalman Abramov from the Israel mission had conveyed an "urgent message" to AJC leaders from Chaim Herzog. Moynihan's staffers had approached the Israelis, requesting more American Jewish pressure. This meeting triggered intensive lobbying in Congress, a library of information booklets, meetings with editors, clerics, and other opinion leaders. By November 10 the organized community was alarmed, but it was not yet clear how the masses were responding—be they Jewish or not.

One indication of popular passion emerged on October 26, when the conference ran a full-page advertisement in the Sunday New York Times, with five bold super-sized words: "...this is an obscene act." Calling October 17—the day the Third Committee approved advancing Resolution 3379 to the General Assembly—"a day of shame in the history of nations," the ad blasted this "horrifying reminder of the Nazi campaign." If the daily New York Times was the bulletin board of the East Coast intellectual elite and the wannabes, setting the daily conversational agenda for hundreds of thousands, the Sunday Times was their Bible. By the 1970s, in New York, there were many more People of the Book—am haSefer—scrutinizing the Times's many sections over coffee on Sunday than reading Holy Scripture in synagogue on Saturday. Full-page ads were clarion calls—including the all-important coupon at the bottom appealing for money—and this one resonated. The money flowing in financed similar ads in Washington and elsewhere.

Hoenlein and other rally organizers soon discovered that American Jews lacked the ambivalence initially found among Jewish and Israeli leaders. The UN's actions and Moynihan's reaction had alarmed America's Jewish community. The UN-blessed rejection of Israel reawakened fears of Nazi persecution while threatening the two most positive postwar achievements: establishing the United Nations to assure no Hitler would ever return, and establishing the State of Israel in 1948.

That all this occurred in New York, the city with the largest Jewish population in the world, intensified the trauma. From Flatbush and Flushing, from Forest Hills and Kew Gardens Hills, from Great Neck and Syosset, Glickmans, Rosenbergs, Salzburgs, Goldsteins, Cohens, and Kahns all praised Moynihan—and cursed the UN. Most of these people were the success stories of the great Eastern European Jewish immigration, writing from the gritty old neighborhoods in the Bronx, the awkward, aspiring middle-class neighborhoods of Queens, and the fancy suburbs of Long Island, united in fear and gratitude. Others chimed in from the new centers of suburban Jewish life beyond New York, from Houston and Chicago, from Shaker Heights, Ohio, and Deerfield Beach, Florida.

More than three hundred chartered buses brought thousands of protesters from Washington, Baltimore, Philadelphia, Boston, as far west as Pittsburgh. Others flew in from Chicago, Montreal, Atlanta, and Toronto. Parallel events—rallies or press conferences—took place in Miami, Chicago, Los Angeles, Detroit, Cleveland, Denver, and Baltimore. Tens of thousands streamed toward Midtown from throughout the metropolitan area, jamming Seventh Avenue from Thirty-ninth Street to Forty-first Street, spilling over into the side streets.

Looking at this "sea of people," Ed Prince felt an "extraordinary shared sense of solidarity—and a sense of danger, a feeling that this was a personal attack on them." For once, "politics didn't matter" in the famously fractured American Jewish community. Fear solidified the solidarity. "There was some mumbling that this is a beginning of a new anti-Semitism, that we had to be careful in America too," Prince recalls. "Gas prices were again in the news. There were fears of Jews being too prominent, and blamed if things went wrong."

Traffic backed up for more than three hours, choking the downtown core. Volunteer parade marshals from the Jewish War Veterans, B'nai B'rith, and the Shomrim Society, the organization of New York's Jewish police officers, worked crowd control with officers from the Midtown South precinct. The veterans reflected the American Jewish community's proud patriotism. With more than half a million American Jewish soldiers having fought in World

War II—and having earned 52,000 citations, including the Congressional Medal of Honor—the November 11 date, Veterans Day, added patriotic poignancy to the protest. B'nai B'rith epitomized the robust community spirit among secular Jews who expressed their identity by belonging to Jewish charitable or fraternal organizations. The Shomrim represented the Jewish masses, the *New York Post* Jews, proof that not every Jew read the *New York Times* or worshiped Woody Allen. Tens of thousands of first-generation working-class American Jews, like these Jewish cops, helped New York work by policing its streets, fixing its pipes, teaching its students, running its bureaucracies.

Rabbi Israel Miller, as chairman of the Conference of Presidents, the rally's emcee, periodically announced larger and larger crowd estimates, with greater and greater excitement—and relief. Eventually, officials estimated 125,000 attended. Called "outspoken yet softspoken" by the *New York Times*, most appreciated as a community diplomat, Rabbi Miller was a passionate Zionist, Malcolm Hoenlein recalls. But Miller deferred when Israeli ambassador Simcha Dinitz first counseled silence. Now, set free, Miller was indignant and eloquent. "The voices of hate are raised against Zionism, but are directed at all free people," Miller said at the rally, following Moynihan's approach, which argued that the resolution universalized the attack against the Jews: "The Arab and Communist totalitarian dictatorships and their cohorts are again using the big lie" against "the civilized world." In tethering 3379 to Adolf Hitler, Nazism, fascism, Soviet Communism, and Arab totalitarianism, Miller, like Moynihan, linked this fight with World War II and the Cold War.

Miller understood that seeing the once-sacred UN denounce Zionism as racism was a modern Jewish nightmare, a pogrom against the Jewish soul; Idi Amin and Yasir Arafat loomed as the "new" Hitlers. Rabbi Marc Tanenbaum, the director of interreligious affairs for the American Jewish Committee and one of America's best-known rabbis, thanks to his weekly syndicated radio show, would later explain the escalator toward violence Miller and the Jewish masses intuited. In his classic 1954 work *The Nature of Prejudice*, Harvard's leading social psychologist, Gordon Allport showed how anti-black bias ballooned, from "verbal violence" to lynching. His five-point scale built from Antilocution—talking—to Avoidance—snubbing—to Discrimination—shunning—to Physical Attack—wounding—to Extermination—killing.

Referring to Professor Allport, Rabbi Tanenbaum emphasized that dehumanization escalated the ugliness. The Nazis first dehumanized Jews before slaughtering them. Now, the radical Arabs' "anti-Zionist propaganda campaign" appeared to be "an effort to replicate the mass dehumanization of Israel and the Jewish people...to liquidate Israel."

Amid such a threat, Moynihan had defended these newly fearful Jews and simultaneously reaffirmed America's ideals. Natalie Kahn of Woodbury, Long Island, began her letter to Moynihan, which was typical of thousands of others, praising him, identifying herself "as an American"—emphasizing the universal welcome she and her parents received. Others, like Irwin Guber of Stewart Manor, New York, acknowledged their two complementary heritages, as he wrote: "As a natural born American and a Jew I would like to thank you on your determined and American way you took your stand against our enemies at the United Nations." Many mentioned Hitler, justified Zionism, asserted their Americanism, and decried the Arabs' new oil power. Many begged Moynihan to stay in office, or run for higher office, including the White House. One elderly woman, perhaps reflecting the post-sixties' sensibility, called the professor-turned-diplomat "sexy." For all his academic work on ethnicity, much of this was an education to Moynihan. He wrote to his friend Stephen Hess a month after the resolution passed, "I'm becoming specially sensitive to the various ramifications of The Jewish Question."

"They must not triumph," Miller shouted—uncharacteristically—at the rally. "They will not triumph! Liberty and justice will live. The Jewish people will live! Israel will live!" With his last two slogans, Miller echoed in English the Hebrew phrase *Am Yisrael Chai*, which had become the defiant post-Holocaust slogan, sung in a rousing, cascading melody affirming that the Jews are a people (*am*) and that they live (*chai*). The song was so ubiquitous most Jews assumed it was an ancient melody. Actually, the charismatic "Singing Rabbi" Shlomo Carlebach, the hippie Hasid who bridged the world of prayer shawls, sidelocks, and fringes with the Greenwich Village coffee-houses hosting Pete Seeger and Bob Dylan, wrote the melody, honoring Soviet Jewry, in the mid-1960s.

"We are not merely rallying against racism and anti-Semitism," Miller continued. "We are rallying *for* international justice, decency and morality, *for* liberal democracy, *for* the values which gave birth to the United Nations, *for* the Jewish people and *for* Israel." Here too, Miller's words stitched together a quilt of comforting concepts, interweaving Jewish and American values.

More than a dozen other speakers slammed the UN and defended Zionism. Although the order of speeches was haphazard, taken together the speakers represented the major constituencies most distressed by the resolution—and most ready to respond. Faye Schenk of the American Zionist Federation and Hadassah, the formidable 300,000-strong, women's Zionist organization; David M. Blumberg, an insurance agent and president of the 500,000-person national service organization and fraternal order, B'nai B'rith; Ed Prince of the North American Jewish Youth Council; and Rabbi Arthur Hertzberg, the president of the American Jewish Congress, represented the organized Jewish community. A leading liberal Zionist who endorsed Israel's withdrawal from the territories shortly after the 1967 war, Rabbi Hertzberg particularly resented seeing the UN violate its charter commitment to resolve disputes peacefully and fairly.

Hertzberg and his fellow American Jewish leaders also worried about Soviet Jews. By requiring countries to report on their attempts to combat racism, which now included Zionism, the UN had given the Soviet authorities an internationally sanctioned license to harass Jews wanting to emigrate to Israel for being racist, which was a crime. Three years later, Soviet state prosecutors would claim that by calling himself a Zionist, the Soviet dissident Anatoly Scharansky implicitly admitted guilt to the crime and that, Scharansky (now Natan Sharansky) recalls, "not only the Soviet Union but the whole world was condemning Zionism as racism," as seen in Resolution 3379. "It became legitimate for the Soviets to say they were against anti-Semitism and against Zionism, because both were forms of racism."

David Blumberg riled the crowd by exclaiming: "Zionism is beautiful!" The affirming phrase echoed the "Black is beautiful" racial self-esteem movement of the 1970s. Many shouted back—appropriately—"Right On!" Three weeks later, the American Jewish Congress would run a big, bold advertisement in the *New York Times*, "PROUD TO BE JEWS. PROUD TO BE ZIONISTS." Ed Prince perceived desperation in all the pride talk. The central post-Holocaust Zionist idea of "Israel as the ultimate safety net, had been turned on its ear," he recalls. Activists both left and right were perplexed, realizing that "Zionism may not save the Jews, it may endanger them." His peers now sought "a response, an affirmation that Zionism is good and that Israel is fundamentally good, to validate our faith in it."

In addition to sloganeering, many Jews dusted off books written about Israel and Zionism in the 1940s and 1950s, and were eager for new works like Hertzberg's impressive collection of original Zionist texts, *The Zionist Idea*. This Jewish backlash became a consciousness-raising moment. Rabbi Fabian Schonfeld, leader of the orthodox Rabbinical Council of America, endorsed a "crash program of lectures, publications," to "stress the relationship of 'Zionism and the land of Israel and the Jewish people.'" New York's Board of Jewish Education distributed a booklet explaining Zionist history to the 120,000 students in the region, grades K through 12, who attended Jewish day schools or afternoon Hebrew schools.

Capturing the crowd's defiant exuberance, Leah Rabin, the wife of Israel's prime minister Yitzhak Rabin, declared "our history will not go backwards; there will be Jewish extermination no more; there is an independent state of Israel." Rabin reflected the two moods witnessed in the posters scattered throughout the crowd, some printed, others scrawled. Some slogans, such as, "I AM A ZIONIST," "ZIONISM FOREVER," "ZIONISM IS LOVE," were hopeful; others broadcast a darker mood: "THOSE WHO CONDEMN ZIONISM, CONDONE HITLER," "ANTI-ZIONISM—CODE WORD FOR ANTI-SEMITISM," "U.N. DEAD—DROWNED IN ARAB OIL," "YOU ARE INVITED TO BE AN AMBASSADOR TO THE UN—JUST SAY SIEG HEIL!"

Ambassador Herzog, luxuriating in the crowd's cheers, invoked his UN speech by remembering how he felt while ripping the resolution. "I somehow sensed at that moment the feeling of the Jewish heart beating as one throughout the world," he said. "I knew that the thoughts of every Jew—whether he be in Eilat or New York, in London or Buenos Aires, in Jerusalem or Mexico City, in Sao Paulo or Paris, in Moscow or Casablanca—w[ere] with me."

Herzog told the crowd that, facing the hostile General Assembly, he knew that not only was he not alone, "but that we as a people were one as we have never been before." This sense of solidarity, this glue of peoplehood, was the national—not religious—adhesive cementing Jews to Israel.

Because their leaders initially minimized it, Resolution 3379's passage shocked most Israelis. Their incredulity that anyone would believe such nonsense reflected the unsentimental, unapologetic, insular confidence of the Sabra, the native-born Israeli, so unlike the stereotypical, perpetually worried, Diaspora Jew. From England, Baronness Gaitskell, the widow of the former leader of the British Labour Party, Hugh Gaitskell, exclaimed that Israelis were "bone stupid" in public relations. "Why don't they get professionals?" she sniffed.

Suddenly, with Zionism formally labeled racism, Israelis were traumatized. Moshe Dayan, the great hero of the 1967 war, tried shrugging it off, claiming November tenth was not a "black day" because "The future of Israel will be decided on the farm, fields, and if necessary, on the battlefields of Israel." This time, this Sabra bravado sounded feeble. The world's abandonment stung. The betrayal was scary. The inversion that labeled the victims of both Nazi racism and Arab racism as racist, was unnerving, even if absurd. The state of the Jews, the great Israeli historian J. L. Talmon mourned, became the Jew of the states.

Still recovering from the 1973 Yom Kippur war, Israelis reacted strongly. Municipalities changed "United Nations Street" to "Zionism Street." The government debated withdrawing from the UN and suspending diplomatic relations with 3379's supporters, while inviting Zionist leaders worldwide for a special consultation in early December. Thousands of schoolchildren protested in Jerusalem and elsewhere, with 10,000 high school pupils listening to Golda Meir explain Zionism in Tel Aviv's municipal plaza. Students also distributed half a million of those "I AM A ZIONIST" badges.

Shocked by 3379, many Israelis began redefining Zionism for a new generation. Speaking to a packed and emotional Jerusalem crowd a month after the resolution passed, the Brooklyn-born philosopher Rabbi David Hartman, a recent Israeli immigrant, said: "Zionism gave expression to a people's capacity to transcend their given plight in history, through their own effort." Comparing Athens and Jerusalem, Hartman grounded this Zionist "world of radical possibility" in the traditional Jewish "theology of creation." For Nathan Laufer, an 18-year-old American yeshiva student, Hartman's oration proved "that Zionism wasn't a Johnny-come-lately, late nineteenth-twentieth century movement that emerged out of the proximity with the Holocaust; but rather a movement that emerged out of the deepest, most fundamental axioms of Judaism held by the Jewish People and embedded in Jewish civilization." This fusion of his "Jewish passion" and "Zionist passion" ultimately drew Rabbi Laufer to move to Israel 28 years later, after leading the Wexner Heritage Foundation for nearly a decade.

Yitzhak Rabin charged that the UN lost all moral authority. Addressing a special Knesset session on November 11, the prime minister said that Israel was not the victim of the resolution; by violating its universal ideals, the UN was the victim. Rabin linked the three resolutions passed on November 10—not just 3379—branding all as supporting the enemies of "the Jewish people and Israel" in presaging an "Arafatian State."

Rabin and subsequent speakers at that session contrasted the destructive UN resolutions with the recent, constructive Sinai agreement. Rabin criticized Egypt's vote, gingerly, mourning that it "contradicts the positive trend of events." Zalman Abramov of the opposition Likud party recognized the resolutions' aim to sabotage the new relations with Egypt. Nevertheless, he and others questioned what Meir Talmi of the ruling Labor party called Egypt's "double game."

Rabin used the enmity against his people to unite them. "Zionism, Judaism, the State of Israel and the Jewish people are one," he said. Articulating standard Zionist doctrine, Rabin located the pull to the land of Israel and longing to return to Zion at Judaism's core.

Had they tried, the Arabs and Soviets could not have designed an initiative more likely to send Israelis scurrying into their psychological bunkers. Israel's foreign minister Yigal Allon sent a telegram to Israel's major diplomatic missions the day of the vote: "The United Nations Versus Zionism." He accused the UN of "reneging on its vote to 'establish a Jewish State'" in favor of the terrorist Palestine Liberation Organization, "purporting to represent the Palestinians," which "violated every principle of the United Nations charter." Attacking the Arab sponsors' "racist record," Allon noted that the resolution pitted the totalitarian and dictatorial regimes against the world's democracies. Openly evoking the Holocaust, Allon claimed that just as "the Nazis sought to make the Jew an 'untermensch' [a sub-human], the Arabs are trying to render Israel an 'unterstaat' [a sub-, or pariah-, state]." Compromise, self-criticism, malleability, trust, were all impossible, considering that the "United Nations had now officially sanctioned anti-Semitism, and on a global scale."

At 7:10 p.m. on Thursday evening, November 13, three days after the resolution passed, a bomb exploded in the center of Jerusalem, near Zion Square on Jaffa Street. Bodies were catapulted into the air. "Another one, another one," a woman wailed again and again, meaning another terrorist attack. Three young couples, ranging from fifteen to seventeen years old, three boys, three girls, strolling along, were killed, with more than forty people wounded. As the Popular Democratic Front for the Liberation of

Palestine celebrated the slaughter, Wafa, the Palestinian press service, spread the terrorist communiqué boasting of "a heroic and daring operation... resulting in a large number of casualties among the settlers." The term "settler" was not yet used broadly as a pejorative among most Westerners, but for Palestinians it referred to all Israelis. Encouraged by the UN, a PLO spokesman at Turtle Bay responded to the bombing: "This assembly confirmed the legality of the Palestinians to the use [*sic*] of armed struggle in order to liberate their country and to combat domination."

Further proving the expression, in both Hebrew and Arabic, that knives sharpen knives, Resolution 3379 broke the Labor government's resistance to the burgeoning settler movement. Left-wingers seeking concessions felt abandoned, while right-wingers felt persecuted, that the world was against them. Yisrael Galili, a minister without portfolio, sought a "fitting response" to the UN in the settlement committee he chaired. The committee authorized more settlements, as many as thirty in the next year and a half.

The neo-Messianic Gush Emunim—"Bloc of the Faithful"—movement, hoping to expand the thin band of security settlements Israel established in the West Bank, had tried repeatedly to settle Sebastia, ancient Israel's capital in Samaria. Since 1967 no Israelis had settled there, in the Northern West Bank. On November 25, 150 activists tried again, brandishing signs proclaiming: THE PROPER ANSWER TO THE UN AND ALL ISRAEL HATERS IS SETTLING IN ALL PARTS OF THE WHOLE LAND OF ISRAEL. Soldiers removed them yet again.

On November 30, during the Hanukkah holiday, hundreds of Israelis marched on the ancient site. "You who see how the people of Israel is abandoned in the UN," read one newspaper advertisement inviting more joiners, "you who feel the pain and humiliation of parts of the land of Israel emptied of Jews.... join the great movement of the people of Israel returning home." They were led by Naomi Shemer, whose classic song "Jerusalem of Gold," had captured Israel's mood in 1967. A young attorney and Likud Knesset member, Ehud Olmert, called settling Sebastia the Zionist response to the UN. In the center of what passed for a road in the primitive settlement, someone hung a homemade sign, "Zionism Avenue."

On this, Gush Emunim's eighth try to settle Sebastia, Rabin capitulated, fearing a confrontation during the worldwide solidarity conference in Jerusalem responding to Resolution 3379. Defense Minister Shimon Peres, whose own government was being defied, proclaimed: "This is the Zionist and Israeli answer to the recent UN resolutions." Sebastia became the first of many ideological settlements, and the first in Samaria. The resolution changed Israeli history. The author Yossi Klein Halevi explains. "Gush Emunim's greatest triumph coincided with the precise moment when most Israelis felt that the world had once again become a hostile place." "The mood of the country is hysterical," the Republican power broker Max Fisher told President Ford. "I have never seen it so bad."

That week in America, and at the rally, Jews felt the love of their fellow citizens, from the man on the street to the president. The fury against the UN revealed an abiding consensus about core American values during an era of seeming chaos. Jonathan Sarna, then a Yale graduate student and now a chaired professor in Jewish history at Brandeis as well as chief historian of the National Museum of American Jewish History, remembers being one of the few skullcap-wearing, obviously Orthodox, Jews on campus in autumn 1975. "Many people approached me, seeking me out as a visibly Jewish person, saying how outraged they were, offering support." David Lehrer, a Zionist activist at University of North Carolina–Chapel Hill, could not believe how angry many non-Jewish students were, on a campus with few Jews. Over 1,500 UNC and Duke students signed a petition opposing the resolution, conveying, Lehrer said, "the gut reaction of the American people." Lehrer presented the petition to President Ford when he visited North Carolina on November 14.

At Harvard seventy-six professors and more than seven hundred students signed a petition opposing Resolution 3379, published as a full-page ad in the *Harvard Crimson*. The petition honored the value of national "self-determination" for Jews, like all other people. Diplomats from Israel's Boston consulate tried blocking the petition, not wanting to encourage self-determination for the Palestinians even while complaining that 3379 tried depriving Jews of theirs.

Mexico became a particular focus of grassroots Jewish anger for its support of the resolution. "We had nothing to do with it," an Israeli diplomat told the *New York Times*. Will Maslow of the American Jewish Congress agreed. "This was an instance where the organizations—the leadership had to follow the members." Within weeks, more than 60,000 tourists cancelled flights to Mexico. These flights, which had been solidly booked as of November 10, now had rows of empty seats. Mexican officials tabulated 100,000 cancelled room nights in Acapulco alone—a loss of at least ten million dollars.

Ignoring Gaston Thorn's sage advice that the Zionism is racism issue was too important to dodge, the president of Mexico Luis Echeverria Alvarez insisted he "in no way" identified Zionism with racism. Echeverria hosted delegations of Jewish leaders, hearing their complaints, embracing them warmly. But Mexico voted in the General Assembly in December to adopt the Women's Conference declaration, so the drought of Jewish tourist dollars in his country continued. Feeling pressed and trying to mollify, in early 1976 Mexico granted landing rights to Israel's national airline El Al, initiated new cultural exchange programs, and supplied Israel with oil along with increased trade.

After weeks of delay, the New York rally had galvanized opinion into action. Jacob Javits, the veteran New York senator, had long been a UN enthusiast, having served as a US delegate to the United Nations Conference on Trade and Employment in 1947. Nevertheless, at the rally he described Americans' "moral loathing" for the resolution and admitted he was rethinking his support for the UN. "It is time to speak out and call a halt to this vicious brand of name-calling which brings back echoes of the propaganda machine of Goebbels and his Nazi-party colleagues in the 1930s," the New York Republican said.

Considering that Javits was a Jewish politician who regularly attended such rallies, his anger was not surprising. President Ford's vehement statement, which "deplored the resolution," on the other hand, was. Ford's warning about the UN's jeopardized credibility more than offset Henry Kissinger's growing exasperation with Moynihan. Naturally, this crowd adored Moynihan. Ford's statement, tailored to fit the way the crowd wanted to see itself, proclaimed, "Your gathering today is a reaffirmation of the American belief in justice and basic human values."

Ford was articulating the consensus. Liberal church groups and chapters of UN associations protested. City councils and state legislatures passed resolutions condemning the resolution, as did both houses of Congress. The Senate voted unanimously by voice vote for S. Con. Res 73 criticizing the resolution, boycotting the Decade for Action to Combat Racism and Racial Discrimination, and calling for congressional hearings to reassess America's relations with the UN. A leading liberal, the Massachusetts congressman Tip O'Neill agreed, demanding hearings. "I consider the resolution a moral blot," he said. The House of Representatives measure, H. Res 855, used the same language as the Senate to denounce this new expression of anti-Semitism—but did not call for hearings. The measure passed 384 to zero.

Three years earlier, Congress had reduced America's share of the regular UN budget from 31.5 percent to 25 percent to punish the UN for expelling Taiwan. Now, legislators debated imposing new financial penalties. Alabama senator James B. Allen even wanted the US to leave the General Assembly, while other colleagues echoed Moynihan's idea of cutting off funding to the countries that supported the resolution.

The backlash remained bipartisan. "Wherever Hitler may be I am sure he drank a toast to the devil last night and rattled the cage," Oregon's Senator Bob Packwood declared. "The United Nations has shown it doesn't take itself seriously as a body designed to keep world peace, let alone world morality." Packwood wondered whether America should leave the UN, as did Alabama's governor George Wallace, perhaps the leading conservative Democrat. Wallace charged that "the UN is in the hands of the enemies of the United States." George Wallace and Bob Packwood generally were even less likely to agree than Barry Goldwater and Frank Church.

Joining Javits on the podium were two other New York leaders, the City Council president Paul O'Dwyer and Harry Van Arsdale, the president of the Central Labor Council. At the rally, the heavy "New Yawk" accents resounded loudly. The rally benefited from the noontime scheduling, as many non-Jews and Jews who worked nearby attended. The pictures on the front page of the *Daily News* and other newspapers showed an all-American crowd with a New York edge, a tribute to the diversity, openness, passion, and sense of justice churning in the city, at a moment when many were busy eulogizing New York.

Paul O'Dwyer epitomized the tough New York pol whose liberalism was as inbred as his ethnic identity. Born in 1907 in Ireland, O'Dwyer was the eleventh surviving child in a family that had made it to America. A progressive lawyer who defended Zionists in the forties, southern blacks and Communists in the fifties, antiwar protesters and striking union activists in the sixties, O'Dwyer would say: "If I thought at the end of the year that all I did was make a living, I'd regard it as a pretty incomplete year." Now, he was enjoying a rare stretch in electoral office—having won only two elections in twelve tries for various positions, losing twice to Jacob Javits. O'Dwyer expressed New Yorkers' sense of betrayal, having hosted the UN, believed in the UN, championed the UN, only to see the UN turn on New York's largest ethnic group—and all New Yorkers' values. "One more act like they did yesterday and we can do without the United Nations!" O'Dwyer shouted.

Harry Van Arsdale Jr., days short of his seventieth birthday, a true son of Hell's Kitchen, now leading the 1.2 million member Labor Council, expressed the anger of working-class New York. The *United Teacher*, the periodical of the heavily Jewish United Federation of Teachers, had run a front-page call advertising the rally. The local SCME—State, County and Municipal Employees Union—also mobilized its membership. Thousands of members from the ILGWU (International Ladies Garment Workers Union) and the ACWU (Amalgamated Clothing Workers Union)—both traditionally Jewish and gradually becoming more ethnically diverse—walked over from their respective Garment Center factories. "When Pat Moynihan rose on October 17 after the anti-Zionism vote to embrace the Israeli Ambassador," Van Arsdale growled, "his arms were the arms of all of us Americans: black and white, Christian and Jew, immigrant and native-born, worker and employer."

Beyond the ethnic affinity, union members tended to be, like Moynihan, socially progressive, sympathetic toward the oppressed, open to government redistribution of power and prosperity but fiercely anti-Communist and anti-totalitarian. Union leaders were already so disturbed by the International Labor Organization's embrace of the PLO that they demanded that America withdraw from that organization. Solidarity had its limits. In a lengthy telegram before the vote, the crusty AFL-CIO president George Meany warned the General Assembly that approving the "ludicrous" resolution risked triggering "a massive alienation of American support." A Cold Warrior, Meany did not want "despots" overrunning the UN.

In that spirit, the International Conference of Free Trade Unions, the world's largest grouping of non-Communist unions deemed the decision "morally and historically unthinkable and wrong." From California, Cesar Chavez, president of United Farm Workers, asserting his people's special sensitivity to the oppressed, branded Resolution 3379 anti-Semitic, while affirming the union's belief that "a national home for the Jewish people is a natural and legitimate aspiration of one of history's most oppressed minorities."

Many in the black civil rights community resented the Arabs hijacking their language and sloppily misapplying it to the Middle East. The Manhattan borough president Percy Sutton, a crusading lawyer who had represented Malcolm X and once been arrested with the Black Panther Stokely Carmichael, spoke. So did Clarence Mitchell, the only individual associated with the US mission to the UN, or the executive branch itself, to attend the rally. Moynihan's deputy, Mitchell was best known as the NAACP Washington Bureau's director, hailed as the "101st US Senator" for helping to pass the defining civil rights laws of the 1960s and 1970s.

"Smearing the 'racist' label on Zionism is an insult to intelligence," wrote Vernon Jordan, the president of the National Urban League. "Black people, who recognize code words since we've been victimized by code words like 'forced busing,' 'law and order,' and others, can easily smell out the fact that 'Zionism' in this context is a code word for anti-Semitism." Jordan, a southern-born lawyer, based his case against the General Assembly for saying "that national self-determination is for everyone except Jews." And he detailed Arab discrimination, against Christian Copts, Kurds, Sudanese Blacks and Jews—especially dark-skinned Sephardic Jews.

While Clarence Mitchell and Percy Sutton became political insiders, the third African American speaker, Bayard Rustin, had embraced the role of outsider. Born in 1912, a Communist during the Great Depression, a Quaker pacifist and draft resister during World War II, a gay activist long before it was safe to be one, a labor union organizer, Rustin coached his friend Martin Luther King Jr., in Mahatma Gandhi's ethos of nonviolence. Rustin believed in "social dislocation and creative trouble." Called "Mr. March" by the venerable black labor leader A. Philip Randolph, Rustin helped organize the 1963 March on Washington for Jobs and Freedom, meeting Moynihan shortly thereafter on the civil rights circuit. Rustin worked closely with Jews, championing Israel as a democratic sentry surrounded by Middle East dictatorships. Rustin knew how much Jews craved black support for Zionism in refuting the UN's racism charge, and he happily provided it.

Rustin considered the resolution "an insult to the generations of blacks who have struggled against real racism." In his syndicated column, he described the "incalculable damage" done to the fight against racism, when the word simply becomes a political weapon rather than a moral standard. Rooting anti-Zionism in the ugly intersection between traditional anti-Semitism and the Arab desire to eradicate Israel, Rustin quoted Martin Luther King Jr., a strong supporter of Israel, who said: "when people criticize Zionists, they mean Jews, you are talking anti-Semitism."

Rustin and others also feared a distraction from the anti-apartheid fight. Before the vote on Resolution 3379, twenty-eight African American intellectuals appealed to the General Assembly to bury this "extraneous issue."

The scholars warned that a taint of anti-Semitism around the broader mission "will heavily compromise African hopes of expunging apartheid from the world."

Given his roots in the labor movement—and his role heading the A. Philip Randolph Institute—Rustin resented the Arabs' hypocrisy, considering their traditional contempt for black laborers. At the rally, Rustin noted Arabs' historic involvement in the African slave trade. "Shame on them!" he shouted. "[They] are the same people who enslaved my people."

Tall and handsome, with his Afro sticking up and looming over his high forehead, Rustin ended his speech by bursting into song, singing "Go Down, Moses." As thousands of New Yorkers, black and white, Jewish and non-Jewish, joined in shouting "Let my people go," the black and Jewish experiences reached a harmonic convergence, increasingly rare in the 1970s, and which would appear obsolete by the 1980s.

Rustin's support was more than simply rhetorical. Earlier in the year, as the fight intensified over Zionism in the UN, he had established BASIC—Black Americans to Support Israel Committee—with A. Philip Randolph to leverage the credibility of civil rights and anti-apartheid activists to support the Jewish state. He wrote to black African ambassadors, urging the resolution's defeat to avoid distracting from the anti-racism fight. Rustin also mobilized 135 national civil rights organizations as the Executive Committee Chairman of the Leadership Conference on Civil Rights. On November 4, the executive committee unanimously adopted a statement calling the resolution an "appalling" idea that "threatens to make a mockery of a noble idea." Zionism itself, the civil rights leaders argued, "was part of the long fight against racism."

Similarly, America's clerical leaders condemned Resolution 3379. Christians demonstrated their post-Holocaust protectiveness of Jews. An American Jewish Committee analysis noted the "near unanimity of criticism from Christian spokesmen," even from those "not normally politically supportive of Israel." Dr. Philip Potter, general secretary of the World Council of Churches, a black Jamaican and Third World liberation advocate, had often criticized Israel. He issued a bland, nonjudgmental call for peace after Egypt and Syria attacked Israel in October 1973. Now, two years later, Potter demanded the General Assembly rescind the resolution. He acknowledged that supporters may have objected to "some concrete Israeli policies" but he and his group stated "our unequivocal opposition" based on what racism really means. Rabbi Marc Tanenbaum, who had lobbied his Christian colleagues to denounce the resolution, proclaimed on his weekly radio commentary on New York's WINS, that in twenty-five years he had not seen an issue that so united Christians with Jews.

The theologians in this coalition of outrage did not read the resolution in the context of the Israeli-Palestinian struggle but as a breach of core UN values reeking of anti-Semitism. They were rejecting what Moynihan called the "totalitarian" nature of the critique while reserving the right to criticize Israeli actions. "Christian concern for Palestinians can and does go hand in hand with sympathy for Israel and with a forceful and deeply felt abhorrence of anti-Semitism," an American Jewish Committee analysis noted. Over the ensuing decades, this nuance would turn into a wedge for pro-Palestinian forces, using sympathy for the Palestinians to blot out concerns among some about the blurring of anti-Semitism with anti-Zionism.

For now, the National Catholic Conference for Interracial Justice put it bluntly in what read almost like a Haiku: "We recognize racism when we see it. We recognize anti-Semitism when we see it. Zionism is not and never was racism. This resolution is anti-Semitism at its worst."

At the rally, Monsignor James F. Rigney, the rector of New York's flagship St. Patrick's Cathedral, read a message from Cardinal Terence Cooke of New York. Invoking the Vatican Council declaration, which barely a decade before had denounced anti-Semitism, Cooke's statement declared: "We must reject anti-Semitism just as much when clothed with seeming legality at the United Nations as when crudely exhibited on a neighborhood street corner."

In addition to joining in the broad yet still relatively new Christian and specifically Catholic renunciation of anti-Semitism, Cardinal Cooke's message caught the Roman Catholic dimensions of Moynihan's moment. A proud Catholic, Moynihan felt Catholics' praise and criticism extra keenly. He was particularly grateful when his friend, the popular priest and pundit Andrew Greeley, would say that his "blunt honesty at the UN" captured "the imagination and support of the country" while helping recapture "self-confidence among the American people." Similarly, Moynihan took particular offense as a Catholic when, for example, the Reverend Theodore Hesburgh, the president of the University of Notre Dame, would attack Moynihan's insistence on letting "The Tanzanians" and other dissenters "get their aid from the same capitals from which they got their politics."

Responding to Hesburgh's *New York Times* op-ed calling such diplomatic bullying "immoral and counterproductive," Moynihan would sidestep the ethical critique. Instead, Moynihan claimed the essay revealed American Catholics' insecurity and cluelessness. More significant than the disagreement, however, was the broad agreement that Resolution 3379 was in Hesburgh's words "silly and stupid," and that Americans remained committed to what he called "the well-being of humanity," even after Vietnam.

Speaking to the crowd on November 11, the Episcopal bishop Paul Moore concurred with the critique of 3379, expressing the American ecumenical consensus. Moore celebrated Jews' role in the civil rights movement, invoking the holy sixties trinity of Andrew Goodman, Michael Schwerner, and James Chaney, two Jews and a black murdered by Ku Klux Klansmen. "My strongest fellow workers in the fight against racism have been Jewish; how can anyone call these people racist?" Moore wondered.

Similarly in Western Europe, the widespread disgust with the resolution emphasized Jewish suffering during the Holocaust and insulated the discussion from the Palestinian question. Leading intellectuals such as Jean-Paul Sartre, Pierre Mendes-France, and Simone de Beauvoir, the Socialist leader François Mitterrand, and Nobel Peace Prize–winners including René Cassin, the French jurist who helped draft the Universal Declaration of Human Rights, called the vote "a forgery of historical truth" that "forgets the genocide of six million victims." The Dutch foreign minister Max van der Stoel said the Dutch government would not cooperate with the anti-racism program at all, in protest. Weeks later, a left-wing Israeli parliamentarian, Dov Zakin, would find the Communist Party leaders of Italy, Denmark, and France condemning what they recognized as a Soviet-Arab attack, an obstacle to peace efforts.

Many of these European thinkers also feared a resurgence of anti-Semitism. Seven years later, the French philosopher Bernard-Henri Lévy would confirm those fears, saying subtly, gradually, "through tiny slips of meaning within these drifts of language and words, the taboo is being broken." Demonizing Israel, especially by calling Zionism racism, helped paint "a portrait" of Jews as "a shameful people, a satanic people…this abominable people, universally loathed"—and deservedly so.

In Midtown Manhattan, while their messages resonated more popularly than usual, most of the speakers were familiar figures at such rallies. The trek to the Garment Center or Dag Hammarskjöld Plaza near the UN headquarters for a rally—to free Soviet Jews, to condemn Yasir Arafat's UN appearance, to mourn an act of Palestinian terror—was a common Jewish ritual in the 1970s. The intelligent outreach formula mixed Jewish and non-Jewish speakers, established leaders with fresh faces.

Betty Friedan was the one unexpected speaker. After she returned to New York from Mexico City, Friedan had mobilized to "save the UN." She signed petitions, noting that having risen from the "ashes of the Holocaust," the UN was now sacrificing its credibility in targeting one country. At the rally against 3379, identifying herself "as a woman, as an American, and as a Jew," Friedan proclaimed: "All my life I have fought for justice, but I have never been a Zionist until today."

The events of 1975 had raised Friedan's Jewish consciousness and brought her into Jewish organizational life. She remembered Mexico City as "among the most painful experiences in my life." She alternated between "shame" and anger when thinking about this attempt to use women "as a ploy by male-dominated powers to deny the legitimacy of Israeli statehood."

When she heard that the UN was considering expelling Israel, Friedan started lobbying against the move. Her Ad Hoc Committee of Women for Human Rights, believing "all human rights are indivisible," objected to the racist label being "applied solely to the national self-determination of the Jewish people." Politicians including Bella Abzug, Helen Gahagan Douglas, Margaret Heckler, Elizabeth Holzman, and Pat Schroeder; celebrities including Lauren Bacall, Beverly Sills, Shelley Winters, and Joanne Woodward; writers including Nora Ephron, Margaret Mead, Adrienne Rich, and Barbara Tuchman; Joan Ganz Cooney, the inspiration behind *Sesame Street*; La Donna Harris, the American Indian activist; and the feminist Gloria Steinem, among others, joined Friedan's committee.

Subsequently in an American Jewish Congress Symposium called "Woman as Jew, Jew as Woman," Friedan would root her feminism in her Judaism. As the movement took off she often wondered, "Why me?"—what prompted her to confront sexism? Eventually, she traced "this passion against injustice" to the values she absorbed and the mild anti-Semitism she experienced "as a Jew growing up in Peoria, Illinois."

Friedan's Jewish transformation was mostly public and political. Letty Cottin Pogrebin, who traveled to Mexico City with Friedan, experienced a more personal awakening. Pogrebin said that although Israelis were the targets of the hatred in Mexico City, "I knew the arrow also was meant for me."

She realized: "to feminists who hate Israel, I was not a woman, I was a *Jewish woman.*" Launching a deeper Jewish journey, Pogrebin wondered "Why be a Jew for them if I am not a Jew for myself."

While hard to quantify, many Jews reported experiencing an identity reawakening following the Zionism is racism trauma. Like Pogrebin, and modern Zionism's founder Theodor Herzl, many discovered that anti-Semitism can make the Jew, but that it is more satisfying for the Jew to make the Jew. As the huge crowd in New York on November 11, dispersed, as the clean-up crews swooped in to sweep, the rally's impact continued resonating. Nationwide, Jewish communities large and small gathered to pray, to weep, to shout, and to hope. On Thursday night, Jews gathered at Congregation Etz Chaim in Toledo, Ohio, to protest. On Friday night, Toledo's Reform rabbi Alan Sokobin, leading "a service of concern," urged his congregants to send messages of support to the embattled UN ambassador.

Blurring a political response with a religious one, 3,000 delegates to the 53rd biennial assembly of the Union of American Hebrew Congregations, representing 715 Reform Jewish congregations, recited the Kaddish, the traditional prayer for the dead, mourning the "moral collapse of the United Nations." The delegates then got political, signing their names to a one-hundred-foot-long petition addressed to Secretary General Waldheim. As the conference began in Dallas, Rabbi Alexander Schindler, the Union's president, said: "We are all of us Jews and whether we use a small 'z' or a large 'Z,' we are all of us Zionists." Schindler's rhetoric and his "triple covenant" between the land of Israel, meaning Zion, the children of Israel, and the God of Israel, changed a movement that fought Zionism officially until 1937, and still included many skeptics.

Even as Moynihan fretted about the *New York Times*'s and the State Department's disapproval, he was becoming a national icon. "As a sort of ambassadorial fighting Irishman, Pat Moynihan has become an American pop hero," *Time* magazine gushed. Bags of mail cascaded into the US mission to the UN, totaling more than 26,000 letters in a matter of weeks. Barely two hundred were critical. The first week alone 7,308 letters arrived, only 94 critical.

Generally speaking, people were showering Moynihan with the kinds of compliments reserved for their greatest political heroes—a "give 'em hell Harry" type or a "profile in courage" type. Cab drivers honked their approval, shouting "attaboy Pat," as he walked around New York. The entire audience at Carnegie Hall rose to applaud when Moynihan attended a concert there. A postcard from Gabriel Hague, a speechwriter and special assistant for Domestic and International Affairs for Dwight Eisenhower, urged: "Pat, Hang in there! We need your voice at the UN." "I'm still hanging," Moynihan replied, sensitive both to the accolades and the brickbats.

Polls showed most Americans approved Moynihan's move. One assessment found that all of America's fifty leading newspapers ran editorials condemning the UN. The denunciations were "vigorous—not gentle." Of those, 34, or 68 percent, deemed Resolution 3379 anti-Semitic. Fourteen called for the US to reassess its membership, although none endorsed withdrawing, and 20 editorials warned against overreacting. Moynihan's defense of Israel also improved Israel's standing after the tense "reassessment." The Harris poll found the margin of support for Israel over the Arabs, which dipped to 5 to 1 during the summer, now 8 to 1 pro-Israel.

Moynihan stirred a politics of patriotic indignation which went beyond the traditional know-nothing populism that often repulsed intellectuals like Moynihan. This anger was more sophisticated, more moderate, more centrist—and more easily channeled. It stemmed from an altruistic American sense of justice and fair play rather than from personal grievance or class resentment. And it was focused on action, hoping to be proactive not reactive. Ronald Reagan would build on this politics of patriotic indignation, offering both action plans and a lighter touch.

For decades, American Jews had blurred the argument for Israel's survival with the need to remember Adolf Hitler's evil. Incorporating Holocaust references into so many public messages and political arguments, they had treated Israel as the survivors' refuge and the world's payoff for the mass murder of six million European Jews—even though Zionism and the state-building project predated the Holocaust. In May, 1967, the aggressive Arab build-up to the Six Day further intertwined Israel's story with the narrative of post-Holocaust Jewry, as many Jews feared "it" was going to happen again. The publication that year of Arthur Morse's *While Six Million Died: A Chronicle of American Apathy*, added a new dimension of American—and American Jewish—guilt for not doing enough in the 1940s to prevent the Holocaust.

The shared burden of communal guilt made the Zionism is racism charge particularly inflammatory. Jews and non-Jews thought about 1939 to 1945 while experiencing the events of 1975. Many non-Jews wanted to demonstrate they had learned from the Holocaust to combat anti-Semitism. The resolution that passed both the House and Senate contained a clause saying the "campaign against Zionism brings the United Nations to a point of encouraging anti-Semitism, one of the oldest and most virulent forms of racism known to human history." The *Seattle Times* made the link more explicit when it editorialized: "Who would have thought that only a generation after the death of Hitler and the end of his racist war, the UN itself would officially endorse anti-Semitism?" The *Detroit News* speculated about a future Holocaust, predicting that "Jewish communities in Africa and South America will be sleepless for a long time."

"Christians seem to know anti-Semitism when they smell it," Rabbi Marc Tanenbaum observed, "and are moving in dramatic ways to clobber it when it surfaces." He added that "these manifestations of Christian solidarity with a victimized American and world Jewry will be as much needed tomorrow as they are welcomed today."

Resolution 3379 would help trigger such a jump in Holocaust consciousness that a myth developed exaggerating American Jewish silence about the Holocaust from the late 1940s through the 1960s. By the end of the 1970s, the survivor Elie Wiesel was on his way to becoming a Nobel Peace Prize–winner and his Holocaust memoir *Night* a perennial best seller. Gerald Green's novel *Holocaust* had become a blockbuster television mini-series. The American Jewish community was doing collective penance over the sins of silence during the 1940s by championing Soviet Jewry and the State of Israel. American Jews now acknowledged how central the Holocaust had become to their collective worldviews yet considered this focus a relatively recent phenomenon.

The shadow of the Holocaust clearly amplified the outrage in 1975 among both Christians and Jews. The shock of the racism charge, which seemed to defy logic, also gave American Zionism a popular standing and ideological clarity it had not always enjoyed. Even many American Jews—especially in the Reform movement—had long doubted an ideology that seemed to value the Jews' Promised Land over America's. After Resolution 3379, Jews and non-Jews supported Israel enthusiastically. Under attack and in solidarity with Moynihan popularizing, democratizing, and Americanizing the public discussion about Zionism, the doubts disappeared.

Still, it is an oversimplification to claim that American Zionism at this moment only became about "perpetual victimhood," as Peter Beinart and other

Jewish critics of Israel contend. A more triumphalist American Jewish narrative balanced out the Jewish entry into "the victimization Olympics" that the historian Peter Novick condemns. The New York rally and its many offshoots celebrated Israel, while demonstrating modern Jewish pride and power. Moynihan's gift to American Jews included helping them feel empowered to act politically as Jews and to build a rich inner Jewish life while still being "good" Americans. Letty Cottin Pogrebin and many other American Jews who pursued richer Jewish journeys were acting affirmatively, not living defensively.

This broad American revulsion at the UN's action reinforced the narrative of American philosemitism, making the United States the historic antithesis to Nazi Germany and the Soviet Union. The Israeli government formally recognizes the many "righteous Gentiles" who risked their lives to save Jews during the Holocaust. For all the beauty behind this historic thank you, the term is objectifying. The American reaction, spearheaded by Moynihan, did not involve "righteous Gentiles" but true friends. Thanks to Moynihan, along with Gerald Ford, most of the Congress and Senate, thousands of opinion leaders, civil rights activists, church leaders, and editorialists, as well as millions of Americans, American Jews felt embraced. Never before in history had there been such a popular, widespread, grassroots repudiation of anti-Semitism by the citizens of such a powerful country. This redemptive story of American success, convergence, and brotherhood was imprinted into the American Zionist narrative along with the sense of victimhood, thanks to Moynihan's moment.

Memories, public and private, individual and collective, are malleable. Just as American Jews would forget how conscious they were of the Holocaust in that earlier period, the fall of the UN in collective American esteem would be so complete, and lasting, that it dulled American memories regarding how much faith so many of them once had in the UN before the 1970s. As a result, few would remember just how intense the November 1975 firestorm was. Nevertheless, Ronald Reagan, finely attuned to American popular opinion, would build on this politics of patriotic indignation, offering both action plans and a lighter touch. He would declare a decade later on November 12, 1985, that the American people were deeply affronted by the Zionism is racism resolution; it "was as if all America stood to affirm the response of our chief delegate, Daniel Patrick Moynihan." Millions cheered Moynihan—yet many colleagues closest to him and most significant to his immediate future in the UN—were stomping in fury rather than standing in solidarity.

BACKLASH AGAINST MOYNIHAN

I spend a lot of time preventing rows at the UN—not looking
for them. Whatever else this place is, it is not the OK Corral
and I am hardly Wyatt Earp.
—BRITISH AMBASSADOR TO THE UN, IVOR RICHARD,
NOVEMBER 17, 1975

The fury against UN hypocrisy, Third World ingratitude, Arab aggression, Soviet manipulation, and American impotence had been building for years. Daniel Patrick Moynihan stoked these fires expertly, bringing to diplomatic life the cinematic role of the plain-speaking American mastered by Henry Fonda and Jimmy Stewart: the lone sane man speaking truth to power in a corrupt institution. Decades after the comparatively more innocent Fonda-Stewart years, one movie blockbuster that autumn of 1975 would be Milos Forman's manic masterpiece, *One Flew over the Cuckoo's Nest*. Jack Nicholson starred as Randle Patrick McMurphy, who resists Nurse Ratched's abusive lunatic asylum. The movie ends tragically, with McMurphy lobotomized, then killed by a friend who cannot bear to see him tamed. But most Americans responded to McMurphy's exuberant rebelliousness captured in his Moynihanesque expression after a failed escape attempt: "But I tried, didn't I? Goddamnit, at least I did that." Similarly, many Americans hailed Moynihan—including his slightly lunatic, impulsive, unpredictable side— for defending their country, even though the resolution passed. "As we were certain to lose the vote," he would say, explaining his approach, "it was essential that we win the argument."

Immediately after an accident, people instinctively take a moment to see what hurts, what has been damaged. The day after the Resolution 3379 confrontation, UN delegates attempted a quick institutional damage assessment. Moynihan was already planning his next fight. Many Western delegates were dejected. Johan Kaufmann of the Netherlands said that, as "an attack on the existence of a people," the resolution's "adoption tarnished the United Nations." The British ambassador Ivor Richard considered the resolution "an appalling thing." But he rejected the gloomy predictions. "The United Nations is not about to crumble into the East River—yet," he told reporters.

The Thursday after the resolution passed, Henry Kissinger spoke by telephone to the Swedish prime minister Olof Palme, who was visiting the United States. A social democrat, Palme had slammed America's involvement in Vietnam, combated apartheid, and cheered Third World liberation movements. Nevertheless, both Kissinger and Palme disliked the resolution. Palme was lunching with some UN ambassadors from the Third World and said he was "criticizing them heavily on the Zionism issue." Kissinger, grateful, added: "They have made our domestic situation very much more difficult for no purpose I can see."

Mediating, Palme reported that the ambassadors "feel somewhat bad about it." Kissinger made the bizarre point that "No one knows what Zionism is. It raises many profound moral issues." For his part, Palme focused on the resolution's "terrible mistake" of targeting "the Jewish community of the world instead of speaking of the proper role of the State of Israel." Worried about his shuttle diplomacy, Kissinger agreed: "To attach a stigma to the State of Israel on Jewish grounds makes the problem insolvable." Palme and Kissinger objected to branding Jewish nationalism racist, rather than criticizing particular Israeli policies. The surprising harmony between Kissinger and Palme marked the State Department and European consensus on 3379. All agreed the resolution foolishly endangered the UN. And all agreed that Moynihan's overreaction backfired, despite the evidence.

A few weeks after the vote, the Iranian embassy hosted a diplomatic banquet. Liz Moynihan sat next to the French ambassador, Louis de Guiringaud, suitably distinguished and haughty but friendly. Mrs. Moynihan mentioned that "awful" resolution. The ambassador responded: "Well, you know, we never would have lost that vote if it hadn't been for your husband's speech.... [I]t was so intemperate." "I'd like to remind you that he gave it after the vote was taken," she responded, drily. Pat Moynihan, who told the story frequently, noted that Europeans loved saying: "Well, the Americans blew it. It wouldn't have happened except...."

The resolution's potential impact particularly worried UN loyalists. Popular reaction, especially in the host city of New York, was hostile. In an unprecedented move, the US Committee for UNICEF denounced the anti-Zionism resolution and many American branches of the United Nations Association were thrown into turmoil. Still, many longtime supporters refused to send UNICEF cards in December 1975 because, they told officials, "it would embarrass them" following the General Assembly vote.

In the landmark glass tower, the rancor unsettled the United Nations' two leaders, Secretary General Kurt Waldheim and the General Assembly president Gaston Thorn. Waldheim, the elegant but oleaginous Austrian, was exceedingly cautious, perhaps because the Soviets were at the time blackmailing him to keep secret his participation in the Nazi war machine as a young man. In his public statement, Waldheim blandly warned, "we may lose the future through discord and confrontation."

Gaston Thorn of Luxembourg, who actually resisted the Nazis, offered a more passionate response, condemning this "unnecessary" power play by those trying to "impose a point of view which is historically and philosophically false." Thorn also wondered how on such an important "moral" question, which threatened the institution's future, thirty-two countries abdicated their responsibilities by abstaining. No one could recall a General Assembly president repudiating a vote, let alone chiding abstainers.

In the charged atmosphere of Moynihan's UN, Arab delegates reacted furiously. Waldheim, characteristically, retreated. Thorn also apologized, claiming he spoke only as his country's prime minister. Having bullied both men, the Arab League delegates accepted their apologies.

The Arab ambassadors felt triumphant. Dr. Saadoon Hammadi, Iraq's foreign minister, praised the "wise and sound resolution" as adding "a glittering page to the annals of the United Nations" in leading "the unremitting struggle of the people" for "freedom and independence." Hammadi's anti-colonial rhetoric, contrasting with American rhetoric about democracy and decency, highlighted the great shift that Moynihan's "U.S. in Opposition" essay charted. The Vietnam War and Soviet propaganda cast the United States, the original anti-colonial nation, as the leading colonialist nation.

Still, many of the resolution's supporters remained offended by the American accusations of indecency and obscenity. Muslim delegates particularly resented having their solidarity with Palestinians labeled anti-Semitic. Beyond playing the word game that as Semites themselves they could not be anti-Semitic, Arab propagandists continued insisting that they only hated Zionists.

The Arab League's information center, a $600,000-per-year, New York-based operation led by Egypt's ambassador Amin Hilmy II, financed a major advertising campaign to condemn Zionism, not Judaism. One Arab League statement declared: "The Arabs have a deep and natural respect for Judaism as a universal religious faith and as spiritual values." The statement again defined Judaism as just a religion, implying the Jews were not also a people.

This campaign was part of a broader initiative to change the Arab image in America. Major oil companies had donated at least $9 million toward this effort since 1967. After 1973, the Arab Lobby intensified its effort against what Hilmy called "the picture that was painted of us—as mentally retarded cowards who couldn't handle modern machinery and would not stand and fight."

The Arab League used Resolution 3379 to restate objections to Zionism, speaking the language of Western reason and democracy, with an anti-colonial twist. Zionism was "settler colonialism" displacing "the indigenous majority" with "Europe's unwanted surplus." The *New York Times* ran an op-ed on November 13 by A. M. El-Messiri, an adviser to the Arab League's UN office. El-Messiri insisted that the Asian and African states were not bullied, bribed, or blackmailed but expressed their long-standing opposition to Zionism, an offshoot of European imperialism. The Arab League sponsored full-page advertisements denouncing Zionism in major metropolitan newspapers nationwide, including some New York dailies. The papers also ran ads with public letters to Ambassador Hilmy from Rabbi Elmer Berger, formerly executive director of the American Council for Judaism.

The American Council for Judaism represented what once had been American Jewry's majority position. Founded in 1942 by Reform rabbis protesting their movement's turning Zionist, the ACJ considered Judaism "a universal religious faith, rather than an ethnic or nationalist identity."

Awkwardly uniting universalistic Jewish socialists with aristocratic German Jews, these "Jews against Zionism" became increasingly marginal. After the Six-Day War, its executive director Elmer Berger became so aligned with anti-Israel voices that the board forced him to resign. Berger hoped that 3379 could offer a new platform. Mainstream Jewry rejected Berger, Alfred Lilienthal, and their small clique of Jewish anti-Zionists as "useful tools for Arab propaganda."

Some mainstream media voices dissented from the national consensus, without accepting Berger's or the Arabs' rejection of Zionism. The *Los Angeles Times* rejected the "overreaction" equating anti-Zionism with anti-Semitism. Some Jews dismissed Jewish nationalism on principle, the editorial argued, while speculating that "many" nations "probably supported" 3379 only because Israel was occupying "Arab territories and Arab populations taken in the 1967 war."

The Arab League arguments swayed American radicals, black and white. Some Black Power advocates favoring Third World solidarity viewed Palestinians as the "niggers of the Middle East." The African American Committee of Black Organizations burned Bayard Rustin and Clarence Mitchell in effigy to show support for Idi Amin and intimidate pro-Israel blacks. Harlem's fiery Black Nationalist, James R. Lawson, denounced Rustin's pro-Israel organization "BASIC," as "Black turncoats" and Uncle Toms, charging: "We smell Zionist money, handed over to Black dupes to perpetuate Israeli racist tactics."

African American radicals were angrier about Moynihan's contempt for Idi Amin, which they generalized to all of Africa, than his pro-Israel stand. The popular show *Positively Black* convened a pro-Palestinian panel, which saw an "element of truth" in calling Zionism racist but focused most on repudiating Moynihan's undiplomatic histrionics. Mal Goode, who had become the first black television news correspondent, for ABC in 1962, believed Moynihan targeted only one dictator, Idi Amin, because Amin was a Black African. In Moynihan's condemnation of the African countries for electing Amin, Goode saw America's patronizing approach to minorities. The *Cleveland Press* columnist George Anthony Moore agreed, criticizing Moynihan's "neo-colonialist mentality" that treated Africa as "Jungles with natives still walking around in loincloths."

These dissident voices agreed with more establishment voices offended by Moynihan's belligerence. Diplomacy to them was an elegant art, not a loud contact sport. Dwight Dickinson, a retired Foreign Service officer who had served in the US mission to the UN, dismissed Moynihan's shock therapy approach. He asked Moynihan if dividing the world into "decent countries" and "police states" was "likely to improve our relations with those countries?" Dickinson blamed the problem on America being on the wrong side of the Third World's two biggest concerns, fighting apartheid and helping Palestinians. Moynihan saw the letter, read it, but ignored it. Doug Marlette, the biting syndicated editorial cartoonist for the *Charlotte Observer* depicted Moynihan and another middle-aged white diplomat sitting in the General Assembly. The diplomat whispers, "PERHAPS THE THIRD WORLD NATIONS WOULD BE MORE COOPERATIVE, MR. MOYNIHAN, IF YOU DIDN'T INSIST ON REFERRING TO THE U.N. AS 'THE WHITE MAN'S BURDEN.'"

The debate about Moynihan and about anti-Zionism persisted for weeks. In mid-December, Moynihan's friend, Harvard colleague, and co-author of *Beyond the Melting Pot,* Nathan Glazer, addressed the anti-Zionism–anti-Semitism confusion in a *New York Times* op-ed. Glazer began with the iconoclastic but true statement that "The Arabs are right: Zionism is not Judaism." He also said Zionism, as the idea and the movement, differs from Israel, the actual nation-state, just as American nationalism differs from the United States. Therefore, "one is not condemning the Jewish people if one condemns Zionism." Nevertheless, tempering his philosophical parsing with historical context, American common sense, and New York street smarts, Glazer recognized the "Jew-hatred" underlying anti-Zionism, especially among Arabs and Soviet Communists.

Glazer's distinctions remain relevant. Not all criticism of Israel or even Zionism is anti-Semitic. Critics claim supporters see every criticism of Israel as anti-Semitic; supporters claim critics never acknowledge any anti-Semitism.

The popular acclaim and the intense debate emboldened Moynihan. Right after the vote on Resolution 3379 Moynihan opposed establishing a UN press office. He did not believe the UN's 130 dictators deserved help in dealing with a free press when they denied their own citizens a free press. "We have a long-term problem now with Moynihan," Kissinger told President Ford the morning after Moynihan's triumphal speech. "It's not just the Zionism resolution. He has carried on more violently than the Israeli ambassador" and is now "starting a brawl" with 130 other countries, referring to the proposed press office. Ignoring Kissinger, the president answered a different question, saying he would recycle his statement from October for the New York rally. Kissinger, meanwhile, was now actively trying to contain his UN ambassador. William Buffum had already told Moynihan that attacking the public information office was "totally unacceptable."

Moynihan was undeterred. He wanted revenge for 3379. On the morning of November 12 he told Barbara Walters on NBC's *Today Show* that the United States should punish countries that oppose American interests in the UN. Later that day, Moynihan introduced a new resolution proposing that the nations of the world mark "this moment rare in history, when no nation-state anywhere in the world is at war with another" by freeing all political prisoners. Moynihan first demanded amnesty in two unpopular, right-wing dictatorships, South Africa and Chile. Then, fighting against selective morality and for universal human rights standards, he added, "if some governments, then all governments."

Continuing his argument from November 10, Moynihan complained that, even while being "distorted and perverted," the language of human rights was being deployed only against democracies, which took it seriously, while dictatorships were indulged. Moynihan was repeating his warning that singling out Israel heralded a broader assault targeting democracies. Just as the Helsinki Accords in 1975 would launch the modern, universalized concern with human rights, this Soviet-Arab alliance pushing the Zionism-racism link in 1975 would launch the particularized approach to human rights, as Third World dictators harassed Western democracies and most especially Israel with selective indignation. Moynihan sensed that he was positioned at the pivot of these two nascent and opposing forces. He would make the most of it. Moynihan was "at his brilliant best," the *Detroit News* exulted, calling the speech "a classic defense of the values America stands for," deserving popular acclaim.

Kissinger and his aides quickly tired of Moynihan's grandstanding. Moynihan had not coordinated with the State Department or with America's nine major European allies. An unnamed Western diplomat told reporters that Moynihan doomed his amnesty resolution by linking it to the Zionism fight, which "alienated the Arabs." Opposing delegates adroitly burdened the resolution with fifteen additional amendments, including demanding the release of persons jailed for attacking racism, colonialism, and racial discrimination—UN code words for Israel, South Africa, and Rhodesia. Outmaneuvered, both Garment and Moynihan retreated.

In withdrawing the resolution, however, Garment again defended democracy and civil society. Refuting the hallway trash talk against Moynihan, Garment said that America did not fear being in a minority, in "an open political system." But, now, delegates were violating the universality of "the rule of law," and therefore "the central idea of the United Nations itself."

This perversion had serious consequences, Garment concluded. Innocents would continue languishing in prison, many despairing of ever being freed, and many now robbed of hope by the UN itself. Brilliantly exposing the new UN's lynch-mob mentality—a mentality that would still dominate four decades later—Garment noted, "We spoke of universality; we are given parochialism. We sought consistency and were presented with a radically inconsistent treatment of peoples and circumstances. We asked for precision and are answered with slogans."

Still, the Moynihan-Garment resolution, though withdrawn, unnerved the opposition and won them friends worldwide. After hearing Moynihan propose mass amnesty, one German woman approached him and said: "I expect you don't think you've done very much tonight, but I'll tell you this. By tomorrow night, they will be whispering this news from cell to cell in prisons in East Germany. I know; I spent four years in one, and it is such things that keep us alive." Moments like that sustained him.

Some independent voices amid the generally hostile establishment defended Moynihan. C. Robert Zelnick, the manager of national news for NPR—who would soon help produce David Frost's Richard Nixon interviews—regretted that Moynihan's approach "has been badly misunderstood both by many of my journalistic colleagues and others in the foreign affairs community. It is refreshing these days to encounter a public official who insists that words retain their plain meaning."

Meanwhile, the bureaucratic and diplomatic backlash against Moynihan intensified. Two days after 3379 passed, Moynihan flew down to Washington for a White House dinner. When Ford saw him, he said: "Pat, keep on fighting." At one point, Kissinger hosted Moynihan in a White House back office. Moynihan asked for a drink, but all Kissinger's secretary could find, to Moynihan's horror, was a Mai Tai, the "awful Chinese drink," as he called it—and in a plastic mug. Moynihan would remember a pleasant exchange, among two "very old and close friends." Yet, somehow, *Newsweek*, relying on "highly placed" anonymous sources, claimed that Kissinger "raked Moynihan over the coals."

Moynihan suspected the usual Kissinger double cross, charming in person then posturing to staffers and pet reporters. Such backbiting made Moynihan even more defensive, ever more vigilant in countering any criticism. Fighting to prove his positive impact and control the elites' gossip, Moynihan contacted his old mentor, Averill Harriman. Moynihan boasted that when the women's conference condemned Zionism, only two countries voted no; when the Third Committee condemned Zionism, there were four no votes; yet his actions secured fifty-five nays when the General Assembly voted. For the first time, the "combined vote" of nos and abstentions favored Israel, Moynihan bragged, noting, "we won a majority of the Black Africans."

Although Moynihan's count was accurate, few diplomats shared his calculus, either moral or political. Barely a week after 3379 passed, the British ambassador to the UN, Ivor Richard, skewered Moynihan—without mentioning any names, of course. Addressing the United Nations Association on Sunday, November 17, Richard affirmed Britain's faith in the world organization, even as he deemed Resolution 3379 "absurd." More of a professional politician who served in Parliament for a decade than a career diplomat, Richard nevertheless said he did not see the UN "as a confrontational arena" for dueling with competing ideologies or boosting one form of government over another. "I spend a lot of time preventing rows at the UN—not looking for them." Then he added, "Whatever else this place is, it is not the OK Corral and I am hardly Wyatt Earp." Richard's slam—echoed in headlines around the world—resonated with decades of English contempt for American bluster.

Subsequently, Richard explained that his job became harder the more aggressive Moynihan became. "I'm haggling in corridors, trying to get Britain back on good terms with its former colonies. . . . When we can't agree we can say no quite firmly. Pat says no but so firmly, so bluntly, so comprehensively, that it is difficult to come to accommodation on other issues." To Moynihan, this rationale raised appeasement of former colonists into a guiding principle.

Richard took public a "whispering campaign" that had been building against Moynihan, the *New York Times* reported. "The Nine" European Economic Commission ambassadors resented his "cowboy" independence for excluding them and alienating others. "If he is in trouble he richly deserves it," one African remarked. "He can always go into American politics; he has built a constituency for himself." Another African delegate blamed

Moynihan, not the Arabs, for turning September's optimism into November's acrimony. As proof, he mentioned Moynihan's line about the "decent" countries, which still rankled. An Asian delegate considered Moynihan friendlier than his predecessors but blamed his media grandstanding.

Moynihan's defenders viewed Richard as the direct heir of the British appeasers who apologized their way into World War II. Showing that Jews were not the only ones hearing the echoes of World War II thirty years later, the conservative columnist William F. Buckley observed: "the United States in these days is doing the lion's share of the work in keeping the Hitlers of the world at bay," and therefore "must from time to time, roar like a lion." In England, Paul Johnson of the *New Statesman* called Moynihan's speech "the one thing that redeemed an otherwise squalid occasion." Embarrassed by Richard, Johnson also recalled the 1930s "when British diplomats in Berlin kept insisting that if only Germany were to be treated more tactfully it could be counted on to behave more reasonably."

Hypersensitive to criticism, and always ready to play the lonely prophet defying conventional wisdom, Moynihan felt the attacks keenly. Yet his popularity intimidated UN diplomats. Living in New York, feeling New York's "vibe," as hipsters called it in the 1970s, many feared punitive American budget cuts. When *Newsweek* profiled Moynihan, he focused on the barbs in the article labeling him the "undiplomatic diplomat." By contrast, anxious UN delegates worried about *Newsweek*'s gushing finale, hailing "Moynihan's brainy Irish emotionalism," making him "a fascinating and unpredictable character in an age of cardboard and plastic."

Ivor Richard's attack, on the other hand, was a multilevel assault on diplomatic precedent, as the British ambassador assailed his American colleague to Americans in America. William Safire, the *New York Times*'s house conservative who served in the Nixon White House with both Kissinger and Moynihan, wrote: "Ivor took advantage of the kick-me sign that Henry pinned on Pat." By Friday morning, the *Times* was reporting "MOYNIHAN'S STYLE IN U.N. NOW AN OPEN ISSUE"—and Moynihan had offered his resignation to President Ford.

Coincidentally, earlier in the week, Kissinger attended an economic summit in France with the British foreign secretary James Callaghan. Moynihan and his loyalists believed Kissinger fed these lines to Ivor Richard through Callaghan; they were sure such remarks required high-level approval. Moynihan's supporters assumed that the foreign secretary or the prime minister Harold Wilson would have at least informed Washington first, perhaps getting a wink and a nod of encouragement. A State Department spokesman dismissed the charge as "utterly preposterous." Moynihan insisted to supporters that it was plausible, given Kissinger's mendacity—even while only vaguely sensing how much Kissinger was ranting against him.

When no leading administration official responded to this unprecedented attack from an ally, Moynihan felt humiliated—and even more suspicious that Ivor Richard was Kissinger's mouthpiece. Washington's silence, Moynihan believed, conveyed tacit approval, neutralizing him at the UN. Once again, Moynihan felt betrayed by his colleagues and his boss. He had already noticed that none of the diplomats in the New York mission would comment to reporters about his tenure—meaning defend him—when interviewed, although one complained anonymously that his staff meetings felt like college classes with a hectoring professor. "You could almost feel the gleeful chuckles" when Richard attacked, one of Moynihan's few friends at the UN told a reporter. "And you could almost see the smiles down in Washington from up here in Turtle Bay."

Moynihan complained, without publicly identifying Kissinger, saying "that's no way to treat a guy. You say, 'ok, he's a son of a bitch, but he's our son of a bitch.'" Moynihan emphasized that President Ford understood, as an old football star, that you never abandon your teammate in the field. In fact, Ford kept encouraging Moynihan's approach of hit-him-again, harder and harder. Ford and Moynihan frequently riled each other up using Moynihanesque tough talk. At one meeting, Ford would complain about Congress, "There is a lot of talk but no guts." Moynihan would respond "You want to attack some congressmen—I want to attack the Soviet Union."

Nevertheless, Moynihan felt compelled to resign—or at least make a show of it. He told colleagues, one reported, that if he did not quit, or get some public backing, by Monday morning he would be "about 4 feet 2 inches tall." Despite his mastery of bureaucratic gamesmanship, as a poor-boy-done-good with a pocketful of resentments, Moynihan remained sensitive to slights. His rhetoric showed how viscerally he experienced the attack. He was proud of his height, which he used to dominate a room, just as the slightly shorter, 6-foot-3-inch Lyndon Johnson had done.

Moynihan's office scheduled a press conference for 12:30 on Friday, November 21. Moynihan let reporters know that his wife would be joining him, usually a sign in Washington of promotion or demotion. Minutes before the conference, as Moynihan drank at the UN's delegate lounge, the president and Kissinger called, begging him to stay. The White House released a clipped, formal statement saying, "The President fully approves of what the ambassador is doing at the United Nations." Kissinger told a *Newsweek* reporter, "There is no unhappiness with him on any level that matters. The President is pleased with him, and I am pleased with him." But then, unable to resist, Kissinger added that Moynihan was doing what he had been hired to do—"give or take an adjective."

At 12:20—with ten minutes to go—Moynihan cancelled the press conference. Instead, he claimed the day's big news was the appointment of the legendary African American singer Pearl Bailey to the UN delegation. He purred, innocently: "Here I am in my blue suit, waiting to take Pearl Bailey to lunch." When reporters asked if he enjoyed Ford's and Kissinger's support, Moynihan said he had "no reason to think I don't." Then he added, "What time is it? Ten minutes to one?"—implying the support might be fleeting.

Now, both Moynihan and Kissinger were feeling wronged. Friendly reporters, briefed by "Persons familiar with Moynihan's thinking"—probably Moynihan himself off the record—detailed four instances of State Department sabotage: Kissinger's overture to Cuba when Moynihan fought the Cuban-led move against Puerto Rico in the anti-Colonialism committee, Kissinger's discomfort with the Idi Amin brouhaha, the State Department's unwillingness to lobby in world capitals against resolution 3379, and State Department resistance to Moynihan's amnesty call for political prisoners.

Meanwhile, Kissinger brooded over the false Ivor Richard rumor and Moynihan's mock martyrdom. Kissinger's press aide Robert Anderson explained that Moynihan's hastily canceled press conference fed suspicions. Kissinger wanted reporters to know that he "pleaded" with Moynihan not to resign, "there has not been any dispute between him and me. It is a God-damned outrage." Anderson tried calming his boss, noting that the press viewed this conflict as pitting Moynihan against Richard.

Moynihan later admitted that he was wrong. This time, Kissinger had not undermined him. On November 22, the UK mission to the United Nations issued a rare statement dismissing as "nonsense" the rumor that Richard's speech received "prior American approval." And of course the British diplomat insisted, Ambassador Richard "wishes to maintain the closest working relationship" with Ambassador Moynihan.

Nonetheless, the two master bureaucrats and compulsive leakers remained at war. Moynihan seems to have been leaking his side of the story. Having lost two major media battles, first under Johnson, then under Nixon, he wanted to win this one. Kissinger felt particularly betrayed because he was now vulnerable. And the fact that this Irish-American ambassador was out-flanking the first Jewish secretary of state on the Israel issue, further infuriated Kissinger.

At the UN, Moynihan—and the United States—suffered another blow that Friday, November 21, when the General Assembly's Fourth Committee on Decolonization voted 103 to 1 to condemn American military bases on Guam. Moynihan moaned "*Nobody* in my mission even bothered to tell me." The State Department did not want him issuing even the most basic statement expressing opposition. Moynihan dismissed this delusion that if America ignored the affront, no one else would notice. "On the contrary," he explained, "they say, 'You see, you can do something to the U.S. you wouldn't *dare* to do to the Soviet Union or the Chinese.'" American passivity invited more bullying.

The next day, Dean Rusk, secretary of state under presidents Kennedy and Johnson, called Kissinger, dismayed by America's isolation on the Guam vote. "It seems that this is personal against Pat," Rusk said, reporting that he was hearing rumors that he is "fouling" his own nest and alienating supporters. Kissinger, in turn, complained about Moynihan's cancelled press conference antics, plays for Ford's affection, and false accusations of secretarial sabotage.

Rusk acknowledged that their ambiguous relationship with the Secretary of State frustrates all US ambassadors to the UN, "but the usual channel is from the President through the Secretary." Kissinger complained that Moynihan was "on a tremendous trip up there," meaning that Moynihan had taken the Zionism issue at the UN beyond what was in America's best interests. "We could have won it if he had not used the adjectives obscene etc." Rusk agreed that Moynihan was undisciplined and erred by attacking the Africans about Idi Amin: "That cost God knows how many votes."

In this frank private exchange with Rusk, Kissinger was now calling Moynihan's "impact" really "disastrous for us." Raising the Ivor Richard affair, Kissinger said, "When the British ambassador attacks an American ambassador publicly you know they must have been goaded beyond endurance." Moynihan's accusation that he and Callaghan "cooked" the whole thing up still infuriated Kissinger. "There is nothing so low now that it won't get printed." Kissinger guessed that Moynihan had to leave the UN job before he ran for Senate because of his comments that it would be "dishonorable" to go from the US Mission to a campaign.

"If he would make one slight move toward resignation I would grease the pan," advised Rusk. Kissinger responded that his own aides were urging reconciliation, but "My own instinct is that if I do, he will come after me in two months again." Kissinger added that President Ford would want to retain Moynihan, for political purposes, "at least through the New Hampshire primaries." Rusk ended by reminding Kissinger he was filling Thomas Jefferson's chair—meaning Kissinger should be strong—and offering to write Ford a "personal note." "It would be terribly helpful," Kissinger agreed.

A few hours later, ABC News' diplomatic correspondent, Ted Koppel, called. Koppel, himself the son of German-Jewish refugees, was close to Kissinger. After reassuring the secretary that "the kids still love you," Koppel warned that ABC News was doing a story on Moynihan that night. "Jesus Christ," replied Kissinger. Koppel said that Moynihan wanted to quit and felt pressured by "the State Department," meaning Kissinger. "Well, it is nauseating," Kissinger said, confirming Moynihan's threat but denying any collusion with Ivor Richard. Kissinger fumed about the "paranoia" and the unfair rumors: "Moynihan is a friend of mine. Let him cite one God-damn pressure. He has had the run of the bloody place up there."

Koppel asked Kissinger whether he approved of Moynihan's tactics. Ever diplomatic, even though he was offering "guidance" not for "quotation," Kissinger replied, "Sometimes he is a little exuberant in his expressions. But the basic direction I approve of." He added, truthfully, that he had no dispute with Moynihan "of any consequence"—meaning they agreed on all votes. Kissinger admitted that they occasionally had to remove some sentences in speeches, but that Moynihan's words always remained "aggressive enough even with the deletions." When pressed if every Moynihan speech was State Department–approved, Kissinger singled out the "OAU part" although not "the Amin part" of the San Francisco speech, but dismissed that as "minor league stuff."

Moynihan spent the weekend in New Haven, fortified with a trunk full of Guinness, enjoying the Ivy League hijinks of the traditional, departmental, informal Yale Political Science versus Harvard Government football scrimmage during the Harvard-Yale weekend. A tradition stretching back to

1875, "The Game" enables members of two of America's most exclusive clubs to luxuriate in their special status while indulging the intellectuals' conceit that they are "just folks" nevertheless. Hobnobbing that weekend undoubtedly reassured Moynihan, as he received repeated confirmation of his newfound fame, from all the heads he turned as a celebrity and the compliments he received as a hero.

Moynihan's friend and Harvard colleague, the late James Q. Wilson, pointed to this adulation as proof that Americans had not been so inspired regarding foreign policy in a decade, perhaps a generation. Moynihan would claim that only then did he realize how profoundly he had touched "the national spirit." America "had had enough of defeat, enough of evasion, enough of worldly acceptance of decline."

Starring in "The Game" weekend must have been especially satisfying, having endured the pointed fingers, whispered asides, and studied looks askance during the Nixon years and his two controversies. As the liquor flowed to celebrate Harvard's narrow 10–7 victory, Moynihan knew that on Monday, November 24, he would be in Washington meeting the president. He was increasingly confident of finding a welcoming White House. Representative Peter Peyser, a New York Republican, telegrammed Ford, "SINCE WHEN DOES... FIGHT[ING] INJUSTICE CONSTITUTE A REASON FOR RECALL?" Peyser and many Republicans canvassed by party leaders that weekend wanted the president to abandon the UN, not Moynihan.

Suzanne Weaver prepared a dossier for the White House meeting detailing eleven incidents of State Department failure to support Moynihan. Weaver painted a picture of the Washington bureaucracy sabotaging the UN ambassador—withholding clearances on speeches, countering his actions, refusing to lobby vigorously, leaving him exposed. Hoping Moynihan would keep his job, Weaver offered a wish list, which included a presidential statement supporting Moynihan, a formal protest against Ivor Richard's attack, and "personnel changes" at the UN mission. Weaver understood that these "organization" men and women only cared about "organizational... consequences." Reflecting the animosity between Moynihan's small band of supporters and most of their colleagues at the State Department, Weaver pleaded: "Your leaving mustn't be their victory."

Some insiders were quietly cheering Moynihan. John St. Denis, a mid-career Foreign Service veteran, lamented what he called the State Department's "patterns of appeasement," habits that now were "so profound

as to seem wholly normal." St. Denis saw delegations to international conferences "return from devastating defeats proclaiming victory." A "don't-make-
waves" ethos had developed, draining the department of "intellectual
ferment and creativity." No critics have refuted Moynihan's statements of
fact, St. Denis noted. His crime was being undiplomatically frank.

That Monday meeting between Moynihan and Ford humiliated Kissinger.
Kissinger, who had lost his White House office with his National Security
adviser post, waited in the hall for forty minutes while the president hosted
the ambassador in the Oval Office. The secretary of state joined for the last
ten minutes. President Ford rejected Moynihan's resignation. The White
House statement proclaimed: "The President wants it clearly understood
that Ambassador Moynihan has his complete confidence." "His complete
confidence" had been written in over a crossout of "been speaking on his
behalf and on behalf of the Administration," a line which Kissinger had
vetoed. But the statement added that the "President and Secretary Kissinger
encouraged Moynihan to continue to speak out candidly and forcefully on
major issues coming before the United Nations." *Newsweek* reported that
"Kissinger had to eat crow by issuing his own statement in support of
Moynihan." Daniel Schorr on CBS Newsradio declared Moynihan "on top
of the world, a man of the hour, the intrepid American."

The truth was that President Ford could not afford to lose Moynihan just
then. Moynihan was electrifying Americans, providing a rare source of good
news for the embattled president. "FORD LIKES MOYNIHAN'S DIPLO-
MOUTHY," ran the New York *Daily News* headline, The *Washington Star*
praised him as "A Warrior among Diplomats." Kissinger added: "I very much
want him to stay. I consider him a good personal friend."

Moynihan, having won the day, was philosophical. "Everyone leaves
eventually. I serve at the pleasure of the President." He was also unapologetic. The "United Nations has become an ideological forum where most of
the actors seek confrontation actively," he explained. Defending American
values blunted the attacks from within the organization as well as the
American calls to withdraw. "Because we have been tough, we no longer
hear: 'Let's get out of the United Nations,'" he insisted: "We can hold
our own."

Moynihan blamed the backlash against him on the new Western defeatism. Western elites were exhausted, defensive. "Guilt is a weapon which our
adversaries contrive to have us use against ourselves," he argued. Amending

the truism that if Communists took over the Sahara desert they would soon run out of sand, he added that some Westerners would attribute the shortage to building "swimming pools for the rich—in the West."

On cue, the liberal columnist Clayton Fritchey, once Adlai Stevenson's UN spokesman, thought the United States *should* feel guilty, claiming that the world had little patience for the American ambassador's "sanctimonious" lectures "on government morality," just as Frank Church's Senate Committee on Intelligence was exposing America's sins. The *New York Times* ran a particularly uncharitable editorial, suggesting Moynihan could not resign because it would have seemed to be an American "retreat" in opposing such UN "follies" as Resolution 3379. Having implied that Moynihan was a coward for almost leaving, the *Times* criticized Moynihan's "oratorical excesses," suggesting they backfired, prompting some African delegates to approve the resolution to punish Moynihan. Moreover, "It surely required great provocation for an old and trusted friend of the United States as British Ambassador Ivor Richard to ridicule" his colleague's "verbal gymnastics." The *Times* warned that "overstatement, overpressure and overkill" would usually "backfire."

The accusation that he had failed always prompted Moynihan to mobilize the statistics and reiterate Chaim Herzog's quotation insisting that the opposite was true. Moynihan understood how hard it was to fight general impressions with specifics. When debating a political opponent in 1994 he would say "Everyone is entitled to his own opinion, but not his own facts." To him, the attacks reflected the appeasement approach of the establishment adversarials, modern day Neville Chamberlains futilely trying to placate opponents.

Moynihan also realized that he was turning into a symbol, making arguments on the factual plane all the more tenuous. Indeed, as his grip on his position loosened, his popularity continued rising. Moynihan enjoyed collecting the trophies of a celebrity culture—a *People* magazine profile here, a *Time* magazine cover story there. A North American Newspaper Alliance poll would find him exceedingly popular among all American demographic groups. Seventy percent of Americans polled endorsed Moynihan's approach. Only 16 percent preferred a softer touch. At a celebration of anti-Communists—Left and Right, proving that not every advocate of a strong American foreign policy became a neoconservative—Lane Kirkland of the AFL-CIO used Richard's attack to compare Moynihan to the movie star Gary Cooper. "I am sure that you have discovered how the sheriff of *High Noon* felt," Kirkland said. In Kirkland's rendering, the song in the background was not "Do Not Forsake Me O My Darlin'," but "Do Not Forsake Me, Ivor Richard." Kirkland praised Moynihan "for what he is, and for what he stands for, for his courage, for his class, and for the enemies he has made."

Among those enemies was in his way, Kissinger. All this popular acclaim could not protect Moynihan from the secretary of state's machinations. Kissinger had an ambiguous relationship to popular politics. He was one of the most popular cabinet members ever—consistently more popular than the two presidents he served. In 1973 and 1974, Gallup's annual poll ranked this German-born refugee academic-turned-statesman as the world's most admired man. Kissinger cherished his popular standing and envied Moynihan's surge in popularity. But, never quite the crowd pleaser, Kissinger frequently was politically tone-deaf. His jealousy of Moynihan reflected the contempt of academic elites and government insiders who disdain mass appeals while yearning for mass acclaim.

Kissinger increasingly either ignored Moynihan—who technically was not his subordinate—or humiliated him, most dramatically by demanding silent acquiescence when Indonesia brutally invaded East Timor in early December 1975, ultimately resulting in an estimated 200,000 deaths over the next fourteen years. On this human rights issue, Moynihan, to his discredit, deferred to Kissinger, and later regretted his "shameless" behavior. Over the winter, Moynihan faced a difficult decision. If he stayed in government after February 1, 1976, he would have to resign his Harvard professorship, which represented both financial security and social status to someone who grew up with neither.

As Moynihan's frustration at the UN mission grew, the critique of Moynihan became sharper although not appreciably louder. Some of the most stinging attacks from what Moynihan sometimes called "the elites," but were more broadly the adversarials, the hypercritical Westerners who challenged Moynihan's character, motivation, and ideology rather than his tactics or Zionism's legitimacy. In December, the leftist *Nation* magazine savaged Moynihan as "the wrong man, in the wrong place, at the wrong time" to handle this delicate racial issue, because of his supposedly racist past. Accusing Moynihan of "intellectual know-nothingism," the journalist Paul Good called him the "bombastic spokesman for the new, Mr. Clean image of America that Washington is trying to project," following the

Vietnam humiliation. Gone is any complexity, guilt, or self-doubt. Hiding behind what Good called "The Mask of Liberalism," Moynihan brought an imperial ego to foreign relations, making him as insensitive in this realm as he was domestically, further proving he is "particularly unfitted to deal with people of color."

The Pulitzer Prize–winning journalist Frances Fitzgerald also saw Moynihan as trying to exorcise Vietnam. Fitzgerald's essay, "The Warrior Intellectuals," published in *Harper's* May 1976 issue, targeted Moynihan, whom she called "Kissinger's Agnew"—a reference to Richard Nixon's disgraced, hatchet man-cum-vice president, Spiro Agnew. While acknowledging that Moynihan had been antiwar, she accused him of now championing the same mind-set that enmeshed America in Vietnam: "paranoia about communism, cultural chauvinism, manifest-destiny mythology and the go-it-alone, tough-it-out syndrome." Fitzgerald recoiled at Moynihan's roguish nostalgia for the simple days of JFK, and his deeper yearnings, supposedly informed by the philosopher Leo Strauss, for the delusional Western triumphalism of pre-1960s America. A *Harvard Crimson* article echoing Fitzgerald's—without attribution—would mock Moynihan's "gung-ho junior officer's rhetoric couched in references to Yeats and Locke" calling the Harvard professor on leave "possibly the most hated man in the underdeveloped world," but "the most admired man here."

According to Fitzgerald, reeling from the loss of Vietnam, yearning for the moral clarity of yesteryear, Moynihan scapegoated young radicals, crusading journalists, America's elites, State Department bureaucrats, and the new anti-colonial voices emerging from the Third World. Moynihan became America's sheriff, fighting "the decline of authority," "liberal guilt," "the failure of nerve." Irish-Catholic herself, Fitzgerald understood the class dynamics behind Moynihan's tendency to treat his domestic adversaries as Patty Hearsts—the California heiress kidnapped in 1974, who turned radical and was arrested in September 1975. In fact, leftist critics like Fitzgerald feared Moynihan's cachet as a rising intellectual and political superstar with working-class roots—who related better to working-class concerns than did most intellectuals—or radicals.

Mixing New Left character assassination techniques by comparing him to the anti-Communist Joe McCarthy, with New Class 1970s psycho-babble, Fitzgerald diagnosed Moynihan's pathological yet popular demagoguery. "With so much repressed anger involved," she wrote, "the transference of blame must lead to violence. Moynihan's abuse of the Africans and the Arabs in the United Nations stirred enthusiasm among some people in the same way as did President Ford's decision to send in the marines and bomb a Cambodian town instead of negotiating for the return of the *Mayaguez*"—the *Mayaguez* being the merchant ship seized by Khmer Rouge guerillas in May 1975, rescued three days later at the cost of eighteen American lives.

Claiming, without evidence, that his aggressive tactics backfired, Fitzgerald dismissed Moynihan's approach as "Death Wish politics." This reference to one of the decade's surprise cinematic hits linked the fear of weakness abroad with the fear of crime at home. In *Death Wish*, released on July 24, 1974, Charles Bronson starred as an architect and a Korean War C.O.—conscientious objector—turned gun-toting vigilante when New York City hoodlums rape his daughter and murder his wife in a home invasion. The movie, capturing the perceived apocalyptic chaos of the 1970s—and the cry for a return to law and order—was so popular it inspired four sequels. The *New York Times* film critic, Vincent Canby, detested the movie's comic book "far right-wing" politics. He called it "bird-brained" and "despicable," raising "complex questions in order to offer bigoted, frivolous, oversimplified answers." Moynihan was more like Al Pacino's honest cop whose corrupt colleagues betray him in Sidney Lumet's 1973 movie *Serpico*, or Jack Nicholson's straight-talking private eye navigating the bizarre rituals of *Chinatown*, Roman Polanski's 1974 classic.

Although he often approached his diplomatic post as a forum for staging performance art, Moynihan nonetheless believed he was fighting a civilizational conflict. The first lengthy essay he would write after completing his UN service in the spring of 1976, would examine "Three Structural Problems in American Foreign Policy": that "the long-term trend of world affairs is against liberal government," that "détente has become a form of disguised retreat," and that American politics was not likely to reverse this retreat anytime soon. Moynihan was bemoaning, 1970s style, America's decline, at home and abroad. He blamed the Vietnam defeat for causing a "failure of nerve with the American elites." He blamed Kissinger's doctrine of defeatism, hatched in a State Department where "It is not that appeasement is desired: appeasement is expected." Traumatized by loss, Foreign Service officers "now won't say boo to Botswana and are prepared to depict anyone who does as an incipient war criminal."

The bankruptcy of New York, the lack of leadership, the stagflation, the crime wave, the immorality, the loss of American pride—all made it worse. Every day as Ambassador Moynihan wafted through a magical Woody Allen New York of the Waldorf Towers, the *New York Times*, power breakfasts, Park Avenue dinners, and the UN's genteel façade, he nevertheless witnessed the noisy, dirty, grimy, crime-ridden New York of murder, drugs, graffiti, trash, urine-soaked subway corridors, and broken lives suggesting civilization in crisis.

Beyond these political and diplomatic traumas, Moynihan rejected the post-1960s culture of reverse priorities and self-abnegation. The rise of crusading investigative journalists, encouraged by leakers, reflected the new, "antigovernment" ethos. Media arrogance combined with the bureaucrat's "absence of loyalty" and pride, terrified him. Reporters so believed in their mission that they would go to jail to protect a source. By contrast, Moynihan added, "Imagine a deputy assistant secretary of state being prepared to go to jail rather than reveal the contents of a cable on ominous goings on in Chile." Such ambition and commitment now resided among America's critics not America's leaders, he lamented.

Equally disturbing, in his mind, was the obsession with America's shortcomings and an inability to see America as a force for good, especially abroad. Moynihan would resent hearing Senator Birch Bayh, while running for the 1976 Democratic nomination, complain about America in Angola, saying, "just once I'd like to see my country on the side of the freedom fighters." Bayh erred. The United States supported one of the Angolan groups resisting Portuguese rule, just not the Soviet puppets. That is why Moynihan fought so hard against Resolution 3379, he admitted, fearing that America's liberal elites would again succumb to Soviet agitprop and "acquiesce in the defamation of foreign regimes friendly to the United States." Moynihan feared "that the fight has gone out of us," although "us" really meant the appeasers, the elites, those who seemed seized with what the journalist Malcolm Muggeridge called "the Great Liberal Death Wish."

Worrying about liberalism did not make you neoconservative, though. Michael Walzer, a Harvard colleague of Moynihan's, and a leading social democrat, shared Moynihan's fears about liberalism's "failure of nerve" and "moral confusion." While Moynihan fought Resolution 3379, Walzer dueled with young radicals in the *New Republic* and *Dissent* magazine about the new phenomenon of terrorism that the General Assembly had implicitly endorsed a year earlier in embracing Yasir Arafat. A philosopher working on what would become the classic text *Just and Unjust War*, Walzer rejected the commitment to "total war" expressed in terrorists' mass targeting of civilians as the "ultimate lawlessness." Walzer advocated a return to a "minimal standard of political decency," which would stop justifying mass murder.

In response, Roger Morris, a former State Department employee who resigned in protest from Kissinger's staff in 1970 after America bombed Cambodia—with a PhD from Walzer's Harvard Department of Government— acknowledged the "conceivable rationality of terrorism." Morris romanticized Patty Hearst's maturation from spoiled socialite to freedom fighter, downplaying her kidnapping and sexual abuse to paint her as an American suburban version of Che Guevara. Looking abroad, Morris equated terrorism's supporters with "our own day-to-day lives" which implicitly enable acts of war to take place in our name.

Walzer, indignant, argued that modern terrorism, meaning the "random murder of innocent people" rather than targeted killings of controversial actors, was a new and particularly ugly phenomenon. Morris, by purporting to be "'sensitive' to oppression," was actually romanticizing terrorism as the weapon of the weak, justifying "anything they do." This increasingly popular stance actually patronized these "oppressed" peoples by holding them "to no standards." Individuals like Morris, seeking to assuage their own guilt feelings by rationalizing murder, ultimately reflected the same "loss of moral confidence" that Moynihan was combating. The "record this past decade for liberal democratic values is not holding up very well," Moynihan wrote Walzer.

Throughout December 1975, Moynihan continued seeing signs of American weakness. Leading senators and President Ford's people quarreled over which faction to support in the chaotic Angolan civil war, as Portugal lost control of its southwestern African colony. Moynihan warned that if the Soviet-backed Popular Movement for the Liberation of Angola helped the Communists conquer Angola, Soviet control of so many oil lanes and so much of Africa would weaken America. Graham Hovey, a *New York Times* editorial writer, found that both the warring senators and administration officials "rejected the apocalyptic scenario envisioned by Daniel Patrick Moynihan, the free-wheeling ambassador to the United Nations."

This kind of legislative-executive power struggle confirmed Moynihan's doubts about Congress's post-Vietnam empowerment. "Power is the basis of foreign policy," Moynihan believed, as did Kissinger. "Only a country with power can have a moral foreign policy, because only such a country has choices." And the executive had to wield the foreign policy power. By contrast, with America broadcasting weakness, petty dictators like Syria's Hafez Assad were telling the Americans, Kissinger reported, "you sold out Vietnam, Cambodia, Chile—why should we not suppose you will not sell out Israel?" For that reason, Kissinger and Moynihan both noted, the "Jewish intellectuals" who disliked executive power but favored Israel were mistaken. Israel needed strong American presidents.

In mid-December, Moynihan pronounced the Thirtieth General Assembly session a "profound, even alarming disappointment." Remembering the hopes regarding economic cooperation back in September embittered him more. Moynihan rehearsed by-now-familiar themes, that the General Assembly was pretending to be a parliament although its recommendations were not binding, and that only 28, maybe 29, of the 144 member countries were democratic. In one of its final actions, the General Assembly, implementing the more substantive, less conceptual, anti-Israel resolutions of November 10, appointed twenty countries to the Committee on the Exercise of the Inalienable Rights of the Palestinian People. No Western European delegates joined the committee, an unannounced boycott for which Moynihan took credit.

Still, his final denunciation was greeted coolly. Your speech was "too much," Homer A. Jack, secretary general of the World Conference on Religion and Peace, wrote Moynihan, accusing him of "appealing to the worst instincts of the American people regarding the UN. It is not only the Arabs which are doing damage to the UN, but also Daniel Patrick Moynihan by your hyperbole." Moynihan responded legalistically, saying he attacked the General Assembly's factionalism, not the UN itself. But pointing to the polls, Moynihan rejoiced: "the American public seems to have little difficulty making up its mind about what is happening at the United Nations when it hears some straight talk."

On January 27, 1976, in a meeting with President Ford, the National Security adviser Brent Scowcroft, and then Chief of Staff Dick Cheney— significantly not Kissinger—Moynihan agreed to remain at the UN. Ford was already fighting for the Republican nomination with Ronald Reagan, the former governor of California who had declared his candidacy on November 20, 1975. Moynihan told the president that "it may or may not be true as the *Wall Street Journal* put it that I was the most popular member of the administration, but I certainly did not want to give any ammunition to Reagan who was constantly invoking my name." Moynihan emphasized that this would entail sacrificing his Harvard professorship, which "meant more to me than anything save my family and my dog." Having demonstrated his loyalty, Moynihan then complained, "I was completely cut out of policy."

When Moynihan left the meeting, he answered a pressing message from a *New York Times* reporter, Leslie Gelb, who was writing about a cable Moynihan had sent to all American embassies and State Department personnel. The leaked cable explained that Moynihan's tactics only "appeared confrontational…because the United Nations General Assembly had become the setting of sustained, daily attacks on the United States such that our counterattacks made it look like all hell was breaking loose up here." More pointedly, the cable complained about a "large faction" in the State Department that considered Moynihan a failure. Moynihan suggested that with America's few, remaining allies "slipping into" appeasement because they perceived American power "irreversibly declining," perhaps "some brave spirits" in the Foreign Service would reexamine the evidence and start celebrating America's successes when representing America.

The headline suggested a bureaucratic turf war: "MOYNIHAN SAYS STATE DEPARTMENT FAILS TO BACK POLICY AGAINST U.S. FOES IN U.N." In addition, the leaked document revealed some sources of Moynihan's information within the UN secretariat. Writing such a document and circulating it widely was inflammatory. It was bound to be leaked. Moynihan himself may even have leaked it. Still, President Ford called to reassure Moynihan. Both the president and the secretary of state supported Moynihan.

Three days later, however, the *New York Times'* influential columnist James Reston, a Washington insider close to Kissinger, delivered the killer blow. Describing "Pat" as "an Irishman, a brilliant teacher, a vivid writer, and a non-stop talker: in short, a 'character,'" Reston described the Moynihan-Kissinger clash as inevitable. Reston—and it seemed much of the establishment—felt Moynihan had overstepped, that he had "turned his appointment and his principle into a crusade, and has lately been challenging not only the anti-American bloc in the United Nations but his own Government and colleagues in the State Department." Reston said Moynihan at the UN ignored his own advice, that some problems sometimes needed some "benign neglect"—referring of course to Moynihan's infamous Nixon-administration-era race memo.

Reston was speaking for Kissinger. At the time, this act of ventriloquism was only lightly camouflaged; six months later Reston confirmed as much to Moynihan. "Mr. Kissinger agrees with Moynihan's defense of American interests," reported Reston, "but not with his style, his provocative rhetoric, his rambling off-the-cuff debating tactics, his self-concerning appeals to the rest of the U.S. Foreign service, or his vicious attacks on the State Department bureaucracy." "Now," Reston wrote, "Messrs. Ford and Kissinger support him in public and deplore him in private. Having put him in the job, they can neither tame him nor repudiate him."

Moynihan immediately understood that the column ruined him. He resigned in time to preserve his Harvard professorship. "I have been most falsely accused!" Moynihan wrote Reston. "Time to go." Writing to Cheney, Moynihan elegantly blamed Reston and implicitly Kissinger while absolving the president. Moynihan insisted: "we did not do badly. The American public is altogether supportive of the President's policy at the United Nations, and I shall waste no opportunity in the months ahead to make clear that it was indeed the *President*'s policy, and that it continues." Nevertheless, Moynihan emphasized he was being muscled out. "I am scarcely without fault in this," he admitted to Cheney, "but mine is not the preponderance of fault."

To Kissinger, Moynihan was more subtle, simply saying: "After an agonizing reappraisal (!) I have decided to return to teaching....We've had a good run here. With something to show for it." To the president, Moynihan was cryptic. He simply wrote: "Today is the last of my leave from the University." Moynihan appeared to leave to preserve his professorship.

Moynihan claimed that even with the insult from Kissinger via Reston, he still dithered over the decision. "I made up my mind thirty times," he said. "It's like Mark Twain said: 'Giving up smoking is easy. I've done it a thousand times.'"

Hearing the news, Ford frowned and asked, "Why?" "Pat was doing precisely what the President wanted him to do," said a White House aide. The president ignored the leaked cable. Ford appreciated that Moynihan had mollified the party's rebellious right wing. Moynihan, as he put it, had "asserted our position forcefully, cogently and honestly."

Returning to teaching was a Crimson-colored fig leaf, as Moynihan's friend David Riesman confirmed to *Time* magazine. Harvard demands "institutional loyalty," the sociologist said. Others recalled that when Richard Nixon was recruiting cabinet members in late 1968, he asked Harvard's president Nathan Pusey to grant Kissinger a leave. Pusey agreed, but only for two years. Nixon asked for more time, noting that, unlike during the Kennedy and Johnson administrations, "We will not be taking so many" from Harvard "this time."

"It is hard to leave the United Nations," Moynihan told friends, "but I have spent thirteen of the past nineteen years in government—one Governor, four Presidents!—and it really is time to get back to teaching." Although he confessed to having regrets, Moynihan felt vindicated. "[W]e had changed the language of American foreign policy. Human rights emerged as one of the organizing principles that define our interests and help us to inform our conduct in world affairs."

Moreover, Moynihan now had a national platform—and the standing among America's elites he always craved. "In a very short time you made a very great impression," the retired senator and ambassador Henry Cabot Lodge wrote him, "because you think straight, know the English language and are a solid debater. You have rendered a great service and I am sure you will render many more."

Although Moynihan's UN tenure was abbreviated, it was a turning point nevertheless. He had enjoyed his ascent to popular stardom—and the public exoneration for his previous rhetorical sins. When Kissinger and others first accused him of grandstanding to woo the Jewish vote in anticipation of a run for the New York Senate, Moynihan was sincerely indignant, insisting it was not his intention. But as the public excitement built, and the diplomatic backlash intensified, Moynihan, reading the polls and enjoying the adulation, began positioning himself for the run his critics originally suspected had tempted him from the start.

THE POLITICS OF PATRIOTIC
INDIGNATION

I'm as mad as hell and I'm not going to take this anymore.
—THE CHARACTER HOWARD BEALE
IN THE MOVIE *NETWORK*, 1976

Daniel Patrick Moynihan's edgy UN stand resonated nationwide, even in the mellow capital of "the new consciousness" in the 1970s, Southern California. George Putnam, the legendary Los Angeles news anchor whose booming voice and tailored appearance inspired the actor Ted Knight in creating the *Mary Tyler Moore Show*'s buffoonish Ted Baxter, echoed Moynihan's fury. Putnam began one of his nightly broadcasts, *Putnam at Ten*, with a rant. "Pat Moynihan is *tired* and angry, as I am, at being lectured on democracy by totalitarian dictatorships, and third world 'pseudo' countries—*tired* of their attempts to link Zionism and racism—*tired* of their snake dances before the UN rostrum—*tired* of Yasser Arafat's swaggering through the UN assembly, with a pistol on each of his hips."

Putnam ended by declaring that he had found a hero: "I think it is refreshing—mighty refreshing—to have a man like Moynihan stand on his two feet, as a citizen of the United States—and a citizen of the free word—and tell it like it is."

In 1976, a year after Resolution 3379, there were more echoes of Moynihan's approach in the Academy Award–winning movie *Network*, starring Peter Finch. "I don't have to tell you things are bad," Finch begins in his role as Howard Beale, a network news anchor. In one of the most famous tirades in recent American history, where the 1960s' edginess lingered but the idealism soured, he says: "I want you to get mad. I don't want you to protest. I don't want you to riot. I don't want you to write to your congressman because I wouldn't know what to tell you to write.…All I know is first you've got to get mad." Beale commands his viewers to stand up, open the window, "stick your head out, and yell, 'I'm as mad as hell, and I'm not going to take this anymore!'"

The screenwriter Paddy Chayefsky recognized a growing public anger, particularly among many American Jews. He wrote a *New York Times* advertisement run by the Jewish Anti-Defamation League, protesting the UN's embrace of the PLO in autumn, 1974. A year later, Chayefsky denounced the UN as "an utterly corrupt, vicious lynch mob," calling Resolution 3379 "a plain and unmitigated pogrom." Americans "don't want jolly, happy family-type shows like *Eye Witness News*," Chayefsky scribbled in an early *Network* script treatment; "they want angry shows."

Moynihan's UN performance occurred just as Chayefsky was both writing *Network* and fighting the UN, and it seems likely Chayefsky modeled Finch's famous tirade on Moynihan's moment. Chayefsky's slogan captured the 1970s' Zeitgeist. On campuses nationwide fliers announcing "IMAHAINGTTIAM Midnight" had students screaming the slogan out of their dormitory windows when the clock struck twelve. The American people seemed fed up; the elites were defeated and defeatist. Not coincidentally, in *Network*, a Middle East–related news item about "Oil ministers of the OPEC nations" boosting prices triggers Finch's rant.

Many of the 1970s' most successful politicians understood that many Americans were indeed mad as hell. Big city Democratic mayors such as New York's Ed Koch, elected in 1977, and Philadelphia's Frank Rizzo, perfected an aggressive in-your-face leadership style. In 1975 Mayor Rizzo coarsely promised in his victorious reelection campaign that if he won in November he would be so tough he would make "Attila the Hun look like a faggot." In the South, what the historian Bruce Schulman calls the "redneck revival" symbolized a new culture of resistance that went national.

On the state level, California's anti-tax crusader Howard Jarvis epitomized the angry white man, proclaiming "We have a new revolution. We are telling the government, 'Screw you.'" When Jarvis's Proposition 13 limiting property taxes passed in June 1978, *Time* announced a "middle-class tax revolt." To Jarvis, Proposition 13 taught that "People *can* collectively effect change in the public interest if only they get mad enough, and if their anger is rational and justified." He called his 1979 memoir *I'm Mad as Hell.*

Even in the era of the smiley face and the "Have a Nice Day" mantra, even amid America's characteristic stability and widespread liberty, there was a surliness to seventies culture. The fall 1975 television season's top show— for the sixth consecutive year—was *All in the Family*, with Archie Bunker. This iconic working-class American detested the same hypercritical elites who frustrated Moynihan, calling them "commie pinko fags." Viewers knew whom he meant. Other popular shows, including *Maude, Sanford and Son, The Jeffersons*, and *Chico and the Man*, had grouchy stars, as did the pioneering children's television show, *Sesame Street*, with Oscar the Grouch. The popular sitcom that ran from 1998 to 2006, *That '70s Show*, which relived the period from May 1976 to December 1979, featured Red Forman, Eric's misanthropic father, as yet another ornery World War II veteran annoyed by the new decadent America festering in his own home.

Many American WASPs and rationalist American historians have long been ambivalent about anger. Modern Americans frequently tried repressing this emotion rather than channeling it. The most famous historical analysis of anger stigmatized it. "American politics has often been an arena for angry minds," Richard Hofstadter wrote in "The Paranoid Style in American History," in *Harper's* in 1964. He chose the word "paranoid" to evoke "heated exaggeration, suspiciousness, and conspiratorial fantasy." Five decades later, left-wingers still scorn conservative anger as bullying, demagogic, and irrational, while right-wingers deem liberal anger socialist, self-righteous, and irrational.

Anger has shaped America foreign policy too. Part of the American sense of mission, of idealism regarding the world, stemmed from indignation against injustice in the world, not just self-protective or vengeful rage against actual attacks. Franklin Roosevelt and Winston Churchill stoked anger against the Nazis and the Japanese during World War II, intelligently, effectively, and righteously. Americans also expressed a perfectly reasonable, justifiable wrath against Soviet oppression during the Cold War.

During the 1960s and the fight over Vietnam, Moynihan worried that, as he put it, "the educated elite of the American middle class have come to *detest* their society." He sought to restore Americans' sense of mission by getting Americans angry again at the world's bad guys—the totalitarian thugs whose representatives he encountered in the UN. His efforts helped shape what came to be known as the Reagan Revolution, found sweet vindication with the collapse of Communism, and echoed through other, subsequent, presidencies as well.

By 1975 America had been steeped in two decades of political fury. In the 1950s, the anti-Communist Right expressed the defining political passion, with Senator Joe McCarthy embodying the unhinged, angry extremist during a relatively placid time. In the 1960s the defining political passion came from the antiwar Left, and the other counterculture movements demanding social change. While Martin Luther King Jr. epitomized the American ideal of channeled anger, tempering his righteous anger with the pacifist discipline of Mohatma Gandhi and Henry David Thoreau, the avenging Black Panthers, furious feminists, and raging anti-Vietnam warriors set the political tone.

The angry backlash against this New Left anger propelled into the White House Richard Nixon, the grouchiest president since Herbert Hoover or possibly even Andrew Jackson. When he won in 1968, despite all his campaign speeches about seeking harmony, Nixon told staffers it was time to "get down to the nut-cutting." Accepting the Republican nomination that year, Nixon regretted that "We see Americans hating each other; fighting each other; killing each other at home." He vowed to listen to the "Silent Majority"—which was becoming louder. In 1970, the country singer Ernest Tubb, lamenting the disrespect for the law and "the steppin' on the flag," would sing: "It's America: Love It or Leave It."

By the mid-1970s, a paralyzing despair mingled with the popular fury, thanks partly to Nixon's own revenge-seeking corruption. The Vietnam debacle had not only created moral confusion in Indochina, with many Americans fearing they were the *real* "bad guys," it had also blunted anger against genuine Soviet oppression. In this new world, Hollywood had moviegoers feeling like survivors, not heroes, after cinematically enduring a cruise ship sinking in *The Poseidon Adventure* (1972), a 140-story building burning in *The Towering Inferno* (1974), and a great white shark's stalking in the blockbuster *Jaws* (1975)—which ends with one of the three hunters, Quint, the grizzled fisherman, eaten alive.

This epidemic of relativism and self-criticism spawned the "age of non-heroes," the *U.S. News and World Report* lamented in July 1975—a

Tinseltown *Superman* returned just three years later. America's number-one song for three weeks beginning October 11, 1975, had Neil Sedaka, who made his career crooning ditties like "Happy Birthday, Sweet Sixteen," singing "Ba-a-ad...blo-o-od..., Brother, you've been deceived. It's bound to change your mind. About all you believe." The following three weeks Elton John's incongruous "Island Girl," topped the charts, an up-tempo song with bleak lyrics about a young Jamaican girl "turning tricks" in a decadent mid-Manhattan. No wonder a *Time* cover story in 1974 speculated that if an alien landed from outer space, demanding "take me to your leader," there would have been nowhere to take him—or her or it.

Moynihan's politics of patriotic indignation offered a welcome alternative to popular resignation, while alienating his diplomatic colleagues, making him, by his own admission, an embarrassment to the State Department. As what the journalist Jonathan Rauch calls "the Howard Jarvis of U.S. Diplomacy," Moynihan responded to Americans' despair. Recalling his reaction to Moynihan as a fifteen-year-old Arizonan in 1975, Rauch says: "It was like a jolt of electricity when we realized we could push back and tell the truth." This inspired, principled, political response to the blows of the 1960s and 1970s would help shape the 1980s.

Like most of his allies, from Nathan Glazer to George Meany, Moynihan was a liberal anti-Communist. He was not anti-Communist in the sneering "Are-you-now-or-have-you-ever-been-a-Communist" McCarthyite way. His progressivism tempered the Nixonian backlash anger against the angry sixties rebels. Moynihan's fight against totalitarianism and his commitment to human rights were, if anything, Wilsonian. After Woodrow Wilson's presidency, "governments became legitimate only as they could show that they were democratic," Moynihan would write admiringly. "This was a religious vision."

The defense of democracy was also exuberant. He and Len Garment wanted "to generate excitement," to be "theatrical," to "dramatize the ideology of the West." And, even in the glum 1970s, their vigorous, up-with-America rhetoric found "a surprisingly warm response," Garment reported—although many resisted Moynihan's claim that the Soviets, not the Arabs, orchestrated Resolution 3379.

Moynihan's indignation was ideological but not personal. Other than confronting Idi Amin, Moynihan directed his populist emotion against an institution, an idea, a worldview. His approach did what a good political tantrum does—releasing mass emotion while empowering once-frustrated citizens. Both Gerald Ford and Jimmy Carter, the two presidential nominees in 1976, failed to connect with the mounting feelings of frustration. Ronald Reagan, the Republican runner-up in the 1976 nomination battle, and the eventual winner in 1980, outdid Moynihan by rejecting the UN ambassador's pessimistic prognosis. Reagan took Moynihan's already compelling message and popularized it even farther, telling an optimistic, redemptive tale, culminating in patriotism and uplift.

While Moynihan fought to free America's polity from self-defeating policies, Bruce Springsteen sought to free American individuals from feeling defeated. The working-class rocker from New Jersey's breakthrough album, *Born to Run*, debuted in the same summer that the working-class diplomat's tenure at the UN began. Both Moynihan and Springsteen brought a gritty but hopeful touch to the 1970s' bleak landscape. Springsteen appeared on *Time* and *Newsweek* covers in October 1975, just as Moynihan became a celebrity. Both remained famous for decades thereafter.

If Moynihan was the poet responding to America's political, diplomatic despair—and providing catharsis, Springsteen was the poet responding to America's existential despair—and providing catharsis. "Bruce" as he was lovingly called, sang about breaking free from "a town full of losers" toward "the promised land" in "Thunder Road," the first song on the *Born to Run* album, whose title expressed the promise of liberation from dead-end, working class, Rust-belt communities.

Michael Novak, the author of 1972's instant classic, *The Rise of the Unmeltable Ethnics*, praised Moynihan for changing America's "climate of discussion." Novak was a Slovak Catholic who began on Moynihan's left and ended on Moynihan's right. His book, identifying white ethnics as "the new political force of the seventies," was his "declaration of independence from the cultural Left." Repelled by the narrow bigotry of the nation's cultural "gatekeepers," Novak appreciated Moynihan's broad, liberating impact on public discourse. "I now find it possible to make in public many points that just a few months ago I would have had to defend at length," he reported. "Now, many heads in the audience nod affirmatively, because they heard these points from Ambassador Moynihan."

Novak appreciated that Moynihan did not just resist the Third World's self-righteous rhetoric but the Communists' détente deceit as well. "Pat tried to reawaken the will of our people, especially of its leadership, and not least of its elites," Novak wrote. "I think he showed the strength in the people, and the soft corruption in the elites." Moynihan, pleased with Novak's praise, said, in late February 1976, "I think you are right about our having challenged the proposition that we have lost our nerve." This fear of decline drove Moynihan's politics of patriotic indignation.

Fed up, especially after Moynihan's bleak doomsday warnings fearing the fall of Angola, Kissinger publicly denied he wanted to force out Moynihan. They were old friends, the secretary insisted, and he had advocated sending Moynihan first to India and then to the UN. But when reporters pressed, Kissinger's annoyance showed, as he grumbled: "The ambassador makes so many remarks in the course of a day that it's not easy to keep up with him." Privately, Kissinger was telling Ford that they had "a Moynihan problem," accusing the ambassador of leaks, of intrigues, and of being very pro-Israel—all true.

When Moynihan did resign, the PLO's chief delegate, Naim Khader, led the Third World cheers, welcoming the "very good news." Moynihan's successor, said Kissinger, would continue confronting America's critics, though in a more restrained way. "There are no two Pat Moynihans in America," Kissinger said trying to sound complimentary. Reporters detected "relief" in that statement.

Moynihan's departure gave Kissinger a rare victory that winter. Yaacov Kirschen, the *Jerusalem Post*'s "Dry Bones" cartoonist, had one of his characters say: "OK, so Henry was hoodwinked in South Vietnam.... So he was tricked by the Russians.... So he hasn't come out exactly on top in the Mid-East.... But you can't say he's lost every battle. He just beat Pat Moynihan."

Moynihan's successor was the colorless former Republican governor of Pennsylvania, William Scranton, who in 1968 first proposed America's taking an "evenhanded" approach to the Middle East. One State Department insider joked: "We're not going to give another Democrat a platform to run for the Senate." Moynihan now responded to the political rumors by saying he was "leaving the door open, without in any way trying to open it myself." The new caution revealed growing ambition, which Moynihan himself never fully acknowledged. Secretly, he had already shifted his voting registration from his Cambridge address to his upstate New York farmhouse.

Having denied interest in the Senate seat so emphatically, his friend Chester Finn advised that he had to be drafted. The cynics and critics remained dubious—while supporters were begging Moynihan to run for president. Remembering Moynihan's race-related scars and noting Harlem's congressman Charles Rangel's recent accusation that Moynihan engaged in "insulting behavior" toward the Third World, Finn warned of "more trouble with the blacks. Though if Clarence Mitchell and Eldridge Cleaver [!]—stay in your camp, and say so, it'll surely help," with Mitchell from the NAACP and Moynihan's UN mission representing the black establishment and Cleaver representing the angry radicals.

On Monday morning, February 2, Moynihan called Harvard's dean Henry Rosovsky from New York, saying, "on Saturday I sent my letter of resignation to the president." "I'm terribly disappointed," Rosovsky replied. "So am I in a way," Moynihan agreed. "But it has become impossible for me to stay here." "Oh!" Rosovsky interjected, from Cambridge, an alternate universe where "the College" was Harvard, "the president" was Derek Bok, and few tenured professors walked away voluntarily. "You mean *that* president!"

As Ford himself had feared, Moynihan's resignation gave Ronald Reagan a new campaign issue. "Isn't it too bad," Reagan told an audience in Florida, "that the Administration could not keep such a good man? He was the first ambassador saying a lot of things to those jokers up there that should be said." Reagan's California buddy, the actor-turned-senator George Murphy, empathized with Moynihan. "I know something of the harassment and other problems which can be organized against an individual by a small segment in our Department of State," Senator Murphy wrote. He reassured Moynihan that "the general reaction is extremely strong not only in Washington but in many areas across the country."

Murphy was correct. Just as more than 26,000 letters, with all but a few dozen supportive, reached Moynihan after 3379, Moynihan's resignation triggered another wave. Michael Samuels, America's ambassador to Sierra Leone wrote: "Your telling it like it is has provided a backbone absent for many years from U.S. policy." The *St. Louis Globe-Democrat* proclaimed "MOYNIHAN WILL BE MISSED," counting him "the latest victim" of Henry Kissinger, détente, and Kissinger's double dealing State Department culture. Back at Harvard, Michael Segal, the student chairman of the newly formed Harvard Committee on American Foreign Policy, looked forward to welcoming this new hero home—and advancing a proud, values-based foreign policy.

Though officially returning to Harvard to teach, Moynihan left the UN still pumped with adrenaline, still wanting to shape history. He claimed he had only one hero in his life—the Yankee first baseman Lou Gehrig—although others dazzled him, including John F. Kennedy and Aleksandr Solzhenitsyn. And like a veteran character actor finally catapulted to star status with a hit movie, Moynihan enjoyed the newfound adulation. Celebrities like the "Yankee Clipper," Joe DiMaggio, now recognized him when they crossed paths at La Scala, a Midtown Italian restaurant. Moynihan understood that he now had political capital to spend.

Yet acquiring that capital had been costly. The end of the "Moynihan Affair"—as the New York Times was calling it—had been messy, diminishing everyone involved. To some, Moynihan had appeared thin-skinned and fickle. Kissinger looked like an insecure boss who undermined a valuable if strong-willed subordinate. And Ford, still wounded by the resignation of Labor Secretary John Dunlop and the mishandled firings of Defense Secretary James Schlesinger and CIA Chief William Colby, mocked weekly by comedians as a klutz, seemed to lack control of his own administration.

All the tension and drama had drained Moynihan. "You look positively haggard," Chester Finn warned. Knowing Moynihan as "a very sensitive and vulnerable person," Michael Novak wrote Suzanne Weaver, "sometimes I feel myself almost every blow I see delivered against him, often so stupidly.... I have never felt more esteem for Pat. I have never felt he did more brilliantly."

Moynihan had become as much a "case" as a "cause." The New York Times's columnist Russell Baker described "The Case of the Outspoken Ambassador" as Washington's latest mystery. "At its center is Daniel Patrick Moynihan, an egghead of Irish extraction, unorthodox mind and articulate tongue.... A convivial imbiber of spirit and grape." He "outraged all humanity" by speaking English, eloquently, directly, in the UN. Yet who could fire him? "What President, what Secretary of State, dares fire an Irishman who has raised his shillelagh in the cause sacred to the heart of the Jewish vote? And with an election year approaching!"

More seriously, Baker wondered who leaked Moynihan's controversial cable attacking the State Department. Chiding his own colleagues, Baker believed that "government manipulators" were playing the press. The New York Times received the leaked memo yet was covering the story of the search for said leaker. When Moynihan read a Times column asking "who leaked the cable," he sent a letter to the editor, noting, "Clearly, the New York Times knows." He wondered, "Why does it not say?"

Nonetheless, on balance, Moynihan's moment had been a turning point. His brilliant rhetoric as ambassador had exonerated him for his previous rhetorical sins. Moynihan now recognized his new political opportunity. "This was in New York after all," George Will notes, "Ground Zero for American anxiety about Israel, Zionism, and all the rest."

Within weeks of returning to Cambridge, Moynihan became a New York delegate for Washington State's senator Henry "Scoop" Jackson's campaign for the 1976 Democratic nomination. "I'm not a hawk or a dove," Jackson liked to proclaim. "I just don't want my country to be a pigeon." Jackson and Moynihan had become the leading Democratic critics of détente. Each had most dramatized his opposition to the status quo by championing a Jewish community concern. Jackson fought to link America's granting Most Favored Nation (MFN) trading status to the Soviets to looser Soviet emigration policies, especially to free Soviet Jews.

Many American Jews loved Moynihan and Jackson—one the florid Irishman, and the other the stolid Norwegian. Their stands brought them national acclaim and reflected a surprising centrality for Jewish issues in a power struggle, which would reconfigure American foreign policy and ideology. American Jews in the 1970s were not like Jews today; then they had less political clout, were more poorly organized, and felt less comfortably American. The movement to free Soviet Jews, following the surge of confidence after the Six-Day War, brought a new generation of activism and leaders to American Jewry. In the 1970s, Jackson and Moynihan both stumbled into issues that simultaneously reflected their respective political perspectives and also happened to address deep Jewish concerns. This convergence was coincidental—but consequential.

Both Jackson's and Moynihan's missions helped the community mature, giving it greater success in freeing Soviet Jewry, defending Israel, and fighting Soviet totalitarianism. Kissinger believed both politicians were counterproductive. He complained that Jackson's tenacity made it harder to free Soviet Jews, just as he claimed that Moynihan's histrionics helped pass the Zionism is racism resolution.

Many New York Democrats anxious to unseat the Conservative incumbent James Buckley pressured Moynihan to run for the Senate. Moynihan agonized, having earlier pronounced that it would be "dishonorable" to catapult from the UN into politics. He had also initially offered to remain at the UN, which proved, he felt, his disinterest in running for public office. By returning to Harvard, albeit briefly, he was not entering New York politics by the front door, or from the UN directly.

While dithering, Moynihan was like a teenage boy preparing to ask a popular girl he has not yet dated to the prom: ambition and uncertainty, confidence and insecurity all churned together uncomfortably. The week before the deadline to file, Moynihan told Len Garment that he would not run. On the last day on which to file for candidacy, Liz Moynihan asked him one last time. Rather than "taking a nap"—as he put it, trying to affect just the right Franklin-Roosevelt-style insouciance—and by "an internal vote of 51 to 49," Moynihan flew to New York and announced for the Senate.

"Mr. Moynihan wore a navy-blue pinstripe suit, a blue-and-white polka-dot bow tie and white shirt with a button-down collar as he read in a sing-song voice, the first four pages of his announcement text," the *New York Times* reported when he entered the race just five days before the state convention. The speech "was one of the few in recent political history that included semicolons among the punctuation marks." Not yet attuned to modern campaigning realities, this Democratic diplomatic dandy offended the most important people in the room—the television and radio crews— by asking them not to block others, saying, "get out of the way because there are some journalists here."

Moynihan emphasized his deliberations to justify his earlier demurrals. "This is not a decision I have come to easily and, as some of you know, much less have I come to it quickly." Predictably, one reporter challenged him. Moynihan, as usual, was convinced of his own sincerity. "I said what I said then and I meant it entirely," he replied. "The simple fact is I did not leave the United Nations to run for political office." He also emphasized the many different people urging him to run.

Ultimately, Moynihan was swayed by his fury at the party's "McGovernite" wing and his fears that reelecting James Buckley would doom New York City's chance of the loan guarantees it needed. Moynihan was the sixth candidate entering the 1976 Democratic primary for the Senate. Most were equally ardent defenders of Israel, including City Council president Paul O'Dwyer, assemblyman Andrew J. Stein, and the parking magnate and former pre-state Palestine fighter, Abe Hirschfeld. The frontrunner, Rep. Bella Abzug, had deep ties to the Jewish community. She defended Zionism with other American feminists in Mexico City and could answer an Israeli television reporter who asked "Why do you think you are going to win?" by retorting, in Hebrew, "Because I'm good and I'm beautiful." But Abzug was despised by New York's Orthodox Jewish community along with a growing number of pro-Israel hawks, especially for her attacks on the ballooning defense budget. The sixth candidate, the former attorney general Ramsey Clark, had turned radical and hostile to Israel.

It was a robust primary campaign. Abzug called Moynihan "Nixon's man in New York, with a record of defending the gang who gave us Watergate." Appealing to Jews, Catholics, and upstate New Yorkers, Moynihan, according to the *New York Times*, "presented the image of the fighter for America in the United Nations who now was prepared to fight for New York and America in the Senate." Moynihan's two main Democratic rivals, Abzug and Clark, were leading voices on what he considered the defeatist, elitist, self-hating foreign policy Left. Running to their right, he appeared to be a moderate supporting strong families and a strong military.

By the time the candidates met for an awkward, choppy debate, Stein had dropped out and the name-calling had escalated. Amid charges of McCarthyism and mudslinging, Moynihan described his attempt to fuse his earlier domestic-oriented persona with his new muscular foreign policy persona. Calling himself a Kennedy Democrat, Moynihan wanted to resurrect the "older, central traditional" Democratic party, remembering it as a "party of coalitions," which appealed to "the working masses of the state, and their moral concerns and their patriotism, their feeling that this is not a country which is somehow a disease the rest of the world might catch and have to be isolated from."

Both Abzug and Clark denounced Moynihan's "confrontational" foreign policy. Clark proposed going back to 1939 instead of 1964 as a baseline for the defense budget, predating massive American military involvement in overseas conflicts. Happy to paint Clark as an appeaser and repudiate the McGovernite leftists, Moynihan retorted: "You may want to go back to 1939; I do not."

Many attributed Moynihan's narrow primary victory over Abzug, by just over seven thousand votes amid nearly a million cast, to the *New York Times*'s last-minute endorsement. This was still a moment when the *Times* could sway elections. The paper's publisher, Arthur Ochs "Punch" Sulzberger, circumvented his cousin John Oakes, the editorial director and a longtime Moynihan nemesis, who was vacationing. Sulzberger made his unprecedented move because he felt the *Times* had to start changing with the times by becoming less reflexively liberal.

The editorial expected that Moynihan could win and would represent New York effectively. Sulzberger praised Moynihan as "that rambunctious child of the sidewalks of New York, profound student and teacher of social affairs, aggressive debater, outrageous flatterer, shrewd adviser—indeed manipulator—of Presidents, accomplished diplomat and heartfelt friend of the poor—poor people, poor cities, poor regions such as ours." Evoking the *Times*'s wariness at other points of Moynihan's career—which always wounded Moynihan—the editorial chided him for flattering Nixon excessively and defending "Israel against hypocrisy at the United Nations with such zeal that he was forced to demonstrate sincerity by vowing not to seek the nomination that he is seeking." Still, "Moynihan for the Senate" concluded, "These were excesses of a passionate public servant whose motive and intellect we nonetheless admire."

Ethnic politics helped Moynihan the ethnic expert win. Moynihan edged Abzug among Jewish voters, enjoyed a three-to-two lead among Catholics, but suffered with black voters. One Liberal Party critic called Moynihan a "bigot in a bowtie." Voters generally perceived Moynihan as the most moderate, and Abzug as the most liberal. Two-thirds of those who voted for Henry Jackson in the 1976 New York presidential primary chose Moynihan.

Senator Buckley was a low-key patrician who had won his Senate seat by a fluke six years earlier as a Conservative third-party candidate in a Democratic citadel. Domestically, Moynihan took standard liberal positions, endorsing big government, while vowing to defend New York ferociously during its fiscal crisis. The two candidates mostly agreed on foreign policy. "The Professor," as Senator Buckley dismissively called him, continued combating the Abzug-Clark Democratic apologists, defending the more muscular, John-Kennedy-to-Scoop-Jackson tradition.

The disciplined Buckley assumed that Moynihan would self-destruct. Moynihan frequently fraternized with reporters, ending marathon campaign days with a few beers. Once, he asked some journalists how he was doing. The reporters, squirming, responded he was doing fine, "unless...." Moynihan completed the thought, "Unless I step on myself."

On Election Day, November 2, Moynihan ran ahead of his fellow Democrat Jimmy Carter in Catholic and Jewish neighborhoods, but, unsurprisingly, far behind in African American districts. He won with 54.2 percent of the vote. Moynihan would serve in the Senate from 1977 to 2000—four Senate terms—winning commanding majorities despite relatively modest campaigns, frequently managed by Liz Moynihan.

Sulzberger's primary switch heralded a political transformation. Even though later in his first term Senator Moynihan became one of Reagan's leading critics, Moynihan's moment in the fall of 1975 helped pave the way for the Reagan Revolution. Rather than just being a lone frontiersman wandering the foreboding wilderness of the 1970s, Moynihan served in the UN as the scout leading a landing party, demonstrating that many Americans wanted more aggressive and rejuvenating leadership. When the perception grew that Jimmy Carter failed to deliver it, Reagan arrived, promising to revive America.

Initially, Carter appeared comfortable in Moynihan's ideological zone, as a conservative southern Democrat and navy veteran. Carter had condemned Resolution 3379 in 1975 as "a ghastly and reprehensible mistake," which "may cause a loss of faith and support for the United Nations by many who have been its staunchest supporters." As a candidate, Carter repudiated the Ford-Kissinger realpolitik. Accepting the Democratic nomination in July 1976, Carter promised to deliver security and peace. But, he added, "peace is not the mere absence of war. Peace is action to stamp out international terrorism. Peace is the unceasing effort to preserve human rights."

Those stipulations could have been the twin pillars of a Carter-Moynihan doctrine. Targeting international terrorism, if done effectively, could have shown grit while framing support for Israel as support for democracy, civilization, and humanity. Championing human rights tapped Helsinki's potential and the growing appreciation for a new cosmopolitan idealism.

Moynihan's faith in Carter's candidacy soared when Carter's people entrusted Moynihan to write most of the Democrats' foreign policy platform. Moynihan expected Carter's centrism to reunite the two competing Democratic Parties in foreign affairs that essentially emerged during the Nixon-Ford years. The Third World–oriented, leftist "McGovernites" combated the tough anti-Communist labor unionists, the neoconservative intellectuals, and the Henry Jackson supporters belonging to his CDM, Coalition for a Democratic Majority, who doubted the Soviet Union but believed in the welfare state. This mix could also attract liberals like Michael Walzer, who condemned what he saw as his peers' failure of nerve and moral confusion.

If Kissinger was too much the cynical realist, however, Carter was too much the naïve idealist. As the challenger, Carter had to highlight American mistakes. But in 1976 many Americans did not want to hear too much about the government's "dubious tactics" in Vietnam, Cambodia, Chile, and Cyprus, or indeed on "the limits on our power." Repudiating Kissinger, Carter suggested a president "must be *just as* sensitive to the need for morality in our foreign policies as he is realistic about the need for a strong national defense."

On the campaign trail, these sentiments provoked applause, appearing problematic only in retrospect. Carter's earnestness hurt him politically when he praised the UN to the largest Jewish fraternal order, B'nai B'rith, as the "conscience of the world community" deserving "far more support than our government has given...in recent years." That statement uttered to the same organization four years earlier would have garnered applause. Now, it disturbed the audience—and many Americans who read about it the next day. The syndicated columnist Tom Braden, a former CIA operative and World War II hero who had just published his charming family memoir *Eight Is Enough*, criticized Carter's "boner" for overlooking most Jews' new rejection of the UN. President Ford told B'nai B'rith "I am proud that my ambassadors at the United Nations have stood up and spoken out for the elementary principle of fairness that Americans believe in." The crowd cheered.

Ultimately, in 1976 both nominees' upbeat messages misread America's gloomy mood. With Gerald "time to heal" Ford confronting Jimmy "why not the best" Carter, there was no "mad as hell" candidate, once Ronald Reagan lost. The *New York Times* columnist William Safire noticed a new "center-right" consensus emerging, with talk of cutting taxes, balancing the budget, boosting defense, and postponing social spending.

Then, Moynihan recalled, Carter's triumph produced "our great shock." President Carter governed as a Georgian McGovern, promising a new foreign policy based on "justice, equity, and human rights," free from the "inordinate fear of communism." Carter and his secretary of state Cyrus Vance populated the State Department with "persons of the opposite camp from us," Moynihan complained, who "regarded us as their enemies." The only posting a Jackson ally from CDM received "was to Micronesia."

Carter brokered a significant foreign policy breakthrough, as Egypt and Israel signed the Camp David peace treaty. But he also presided amid double-digit inflation, a new energy crisis, the shah of Iran's catastrophic collapse, Nicaragua's fall, Soviet expansionism, Islamist Iran's holding

American diplomats hostage, and a fear that neither he nor the nation could face the late 1970s' challenges. Carter's America was "weak," Moynihan mourned. It was an "utter bankruptcy of policy. Utter failure." Even Kissinger wondered, "Could it be that there is no penalty for opposing the United States and no reward for friendship to the United States?"

Carter was too much the preacher-convinced-his-flock-had-sinned to blame the kind of enemies Moynihan targeted so effectively at home and abroad. Carter as the national scold became increasingly unpopular and ineffectual. Even while rehearsing for a major address in mid-July 1979, Carter resisted doing what came so naturally to Moynihan. During a desultory speech rehearsal, with Carter's advisers begging for more edge, the speechwriter Gordon Stewart, hired from Broadway, momentarily forgot the proprieties. Playing the highhanded director, Stewart announced he was leaving because he was bored. Offended, Carter became animated, waving his hands to emphasize his points. Stewart replied: "Now you've got it." It wasn't enough. By March 1980, *Time* found only 14 percent of Americans "optimistic...an alltime low," down from a Carter-administration high of 47 percent.

At the UN, Carter repudiated Moynihan's legacy. Carter's UN ambassador was the former congressman Andrew Young, a forty-four-year-old pastor and civil rights activist who had been with Martin Luther King Jr. when he was murdered. In 1970 Young defended the Black Panthers, saying: "it may take the destruction of Western civilization to allow the rest of the world to really emerge as a free and brotherly society."

Young pitched himself as the un-Moynihan—humble and warmhearted toward the Third World in solidarity as an African American. When first interviewed on NBC's Sunday morning talk show *Meet the Press*, Young insulted Moynihan by resurrecting the Idi Amin controversy. Promising not to "express any opinions about national leaders," Young regretted that "my predecessor"—meaning Moynihan not William Scranton—talked "about the Organization of African Unity, and by so-doing demeaned an entire continent's leadership, which certainly doesn't fall into the category of being racist murderers."

Moynihan could have snapped that his successor's discretion should extend to "national leaders" in his own country. Instead, feeling magnanimous, the forty-nine-year-old rookie senator said of the new ambassador, five years his junior, "He's young"—pun intended. "Give him a chance."

In the fall of 1978, Moynihan, with Suzanne Weaver as his co-author, published his UN memoir, *A Dangerous Place*. Reviewers rehashed their feelings about Moynihan's ambassadorship. *Kirkus Reviews* characterized his foreign policy approach as "individualistic Manicheanism," now described "with characteristic wit and equally characteristic immodesty." The *New York Review of Books* mocked Moynihan's particular form of politicized Irishness: "the brutal sentimentality, the gift for lyric nonsense, the bashful charm that can turn vicious in a moment, the cultivation of injured sensibility, a kind of self-pity for the world's ills." And the *New York Times* ran a review by Yale's diplomatic historian Gaddis Smith praising Moynihan as "the bugler in chief of a red, white and blue ideological offensive," but ultimately deeming him a jingoist "appealing to the nation's worst emotions."

Moynihan's admittedly self-congratulatory memoir was particularly unwelcome in a Carter administration which had Ambassador Young boasting, "We've ended the politics of confrontation and started an era of cooperation." Young mediated between Black Africa and the racist white regimes in South Africa and Rhodesia, with the United States and Europe squirming in the middle. In August 1979, Young's tenure ended abruptly when he violated American policy by meeting secretly with Zehdi Labib Terzi, the PLO's UN observer—then lied about the encounter.

Young's successor, Donald McHenry, was also African American. A soft-spoken career diplomat, not a firebrand, McHenry disavowed "confrontation politics" and "name-calling." Years later he would claim that Moynihan left such a mess at the UN that his successor Bill Scranton "didn't need a wheelbarrow behind him. He needed a dump truck to clean up after him." McHenry bought the State Department consensus that Moynihan lost votes for the United States explaining that it was counterproductive "going in with a chip on your shoulder," acting "as if the United States is holier than thou."

Four days before Israel and Egypt signed their peace treaty on March 26, 1979, the Security Council passed the first in what would be seven harsh condemnations of Israel through mid-December 1980. The United States abstained on that one, Resolution 446, along with three others, vetoed one, and endorsed two. To Moynihan, each resolution's particular complaint was unimportant; each one reflected the Soviet-Arab attempt to undermine "Carter's single greatest achievement," the Camp David Peace Accords, by treating Israel as an "outlaw state." Failing to secure UN approval for the Israel-Egypt peace treaty, Carter and his people instead cooperated in an escalating campaign of what Moynihan called "viciously anti-Israel" resolutions, many of which routinely indicted "Israel for Hitlerian crimes" by invoking the Fourth Geneva Convention.

In March 1980, two weeks before Carter faced Sen. Ted Kennedy, his Democratic challenger for the nomination in the New York primary, McHenry actually voted *for* Security Council Resolution 465, condemning Israeli settlement as a "flagrant violation of the Fourth Geneva Convention." The language implicitly compared Israel's policies, Moynihan complained, "to the Nazi practice of deporting or murdering vast numbers of persons in Western Poland—as at Auschwitz—and plans for settling the territory with Germans." The Israeli case differed in many ways, especially because Jewish rights to settle in this disputed territory remained in force from the British Mandate days. The false comparison, Moynihan noted, played "perfectly into the Soviet propaganda position that 'Zionism is present-day fascism.' "

Fearing the political damage, Carter claimed miscommunication and eventually had McHenry veto the next attack on April 30. But American policy at the UN toward Israel had shifted. Carter's tense relations with Israel's prime minister Menachem Begin stemmed partly from the surge in new Jewish settlements in the West Bank and Gaza since 1975.

When Carter lost the New York primary to Kennedy, by 59 percent to 41 percent, his campaign chairman, lieutenant governor Mario Cuomo, called to apologize. "No," Carter answered, knowing that Jews abandoned him by nearly 4 to 1, "it was the United Nations vote." New York helped Kennedy last long enough to cripple Carter's fall campaign. "New York was our chance to knock Kennedy out of the box early," the campaign chair Robert S. Strauss griped. "We blew it with that vote."

Moynihan hated that the self-hating American appeasers had arisen –with his naïve assent. Andrew Young, Donald McHenry, and their State Department liaison, William Maynes, the assistant secretary of state for International Organizations, were guilty, Moynihan charged, of "psychological arrogance," for believing the Third World–Soviet bloc would change simply because America avoided "confrontation politics." Moynihan was throwing back at his rivals the phrase they used earlier to criticize him.

Moynihan shared the "liberal internationalism" shaping this faith in the UN, but it became self-destructive when mixed with adversarials' self-critical, self-abnegating, 1960s-style breast-beating. These people, Moynihan sniffed, foolishly attributed the Third World's hostility to America's sins. By overlooking the rank anti-American bigotry, they exaggerated America's ability to mollify the Third World. As a result, Carter's people surrendered at the UN too often to the persistent America-bashing and meekly abstained on most of the anti-Israel attacks. Nevertheless, the Carterites deluded themselves, boasting as Maynes did to Congress, that "the UN has become the crossroad[s] of global diplomacy" and is now less "dangerous a place than some have led us to believe." Moynihan was those "some," considering the title of his ambassadorial memoirs *A Dangerous Place*—although he meant the world, not the UN.

"American failure was total. And it was squalid," Moynihan proclaimed. "These men, in New York and Washington, helped to destroy the President... deeply injured the President's party, hurt the United States, and hurt nations that have stood with the United States in seeking something like peace in the Middle East." Once again the fight over Israel occurred on competing planes. Moynihan was addressing sweeping language and a strategy that defamed Israel and Zionism's basic character. Carter's men addressed particular, controversial Israeli policies.

In December 1980, when the United States again approved a Security Council resolution invoking the Fourth Geneva Convention against Israel, the *Washington Post* accused the Carter administration of "Joining the Jackals." The resolution passed just days after the General Assembly denounced the Camp David Accords without even an American rebuttal. The editorial called the Security Council vote "the essential Carter," unnecessary as a policy matter, naïve in futilely flattering the "virtuous souls of the Third World," harder on America's friends than America's enemies, unduly trusting of the UN, diplomatically destructive as well as politically self-destructive.

Carter's opponent in 1980, Ronald Reagan, like Moynihan, did not need coaching to show indignation. Despite coming from different sides of the political aisle, Reagan and Moynihan shared a genial Irish background, some overlapping childhood traumas from drunken, inadequate fathers, and, most important of all, a common devotion to Franklin D. Roosevelt. Roosevelt was both Reagan's and Moynihan's first political role model and their ideal president. Growing up under Roosevelt, Reagan and Moynihan each felt protected, inspired, and redeemed personally by the president. They also absorbed Roosevelt's proud patriotism, aversion to totalitarianism, and daring leadership strategy—all three proved willing to be judged by the enemies they made, as FDR put it.

Like Moynihan, post-Vietnam, Reagan recognized the political benefits of channeling Americans' anger outward rather than inward. Back in 1975, during the UN fight, he called Resolution 3379 "outrageous," "hypocritical," "stupid," "vicious." He proposed reevaluating America's relationship to the United Nations and challenging the Third World. "We should say to them that if you are going to play the game that way, we're going to go home and sit for awhile," he said. Reagan attributed the Zionism is racism debacle to America's fear of confronting the Soviets and the Third World.

Even in states with few Jews, such as New Hampshire, Reagan's patriotic, anti-UN rhetoric wowed crowds, during his failed campaign against Gerald Ford for the 1976 Republican nomination. That year, Reagan's stump speech quoted Moynihan's UN speech. The ensuing cheers confirmed Reagan's instincts that Americans wanted more assertive and idealistic leadership.

Reagan denounced Ford's feeble foreign policy. Quoting Kissinger's claim that "The day of the U.S. is past and today is the day of the Soviet Union," Reagan insisted that "peace does not come from weakness or from retreat. It comes from the restoration of American military superiority."

With his storyteller's ability to illustrate abstractions, Reagan focused on the proposed ownership transfer of the Panama Canal to Panama. "When it comes to the canal, we built it, we paid for it, it's ours, and we are going to keep it." As with the UN, the Panama Canal issue invited this kind of tele-graphic, patriotic, popularizing that stirred many Americans still frustrated with post-Vietnam pessimism. American politicians—and reporters—were learning the power of single-issue politics, as occasional media hurricanes about abortion, busing, gun control, gay rights, and euthanasia would grab public attention and transform the political terrain.

Both Reagan and Moynihan were more idealists than realists, more con-frontational than accommodating. It is easier to fit candidates—and UN ambassadors—into these either-or-boxes than presidents or secretaries of state. Even Henry Kissinger, whose détente policy epitomized realism, acknowledged the need to consider human rights, morality, and other American values. Still, Americans most identified Reagan, Moynihan, and Jackson with a principled, pugnacious, and public approach to post-Vietnam foreign policy. Moynihan, with his Harvardian erudition, called it Wilsonian; the humbler Reagan called it all-American common sense.

Reagan had lost narrowly to Gerald Ford in 1976—then watched Ford lose and Carter flounder as many Americans seethed. When the California conservative launched his 1980 campaign, he was a stronger candidate running in a nation increasingly disillusioned with its commander in chief. Reagan's announcement speech demonstrated his distinct leadership blend—mixing Moynihan-like indignation with FDR-like inspiration. "Negotiations with the Soviet Union must never become appeasement," Reagan proclaimed, fearful that "too often in recent times we have just drifted along with events, responding as if we thought of ourselves as a nation in decline."

Sounding epigrammatic, even rabbinic, Reagan asked: "if we do not accept the responsibilities of leadership, who will? And if no one will, how will we survive?" Typically, Reagan looked to America's glorious past and noble ideals to fight despair and defeat totalitarianism. His historical homilies reassured Americans they could again perform political, economic, and cultural miracles. Kissinger would admit that "Reagan proved to have a better instinct for America's emotions by justifying his course in the name of American idealism."

Like Moynihan, Reagan loved melodrama, understanding that in the television age great theater made for good politics. Reagan thrilled Americans on February 23, 1980, by shouting at a New Hampshire candidate forum marred by a procedural dispute: "I am paying for this microphone." Three days later, Reagan defeated George H. W. Bush in the New Hampshire primary—and soon won the nomination.

The Iranian hostage crisis, which began nine days before Reagan's campaign announcement in November 1979, haunted the 1980 campaign. The Islamist takeover of the American embassy in Tehran stirred all the anxieties Moynihan addressed in 1975: Third World impunity, the breakdown of international civility, the adversarials' apologias, American impotence. Accepting the Republican nomination, Reagan complained "we are given weakness when we need strength; vacillation when the times demand firmness." A few weeks later, addressing the Veterans of Foreign Wars, Reagan denounced "Vietnam Syndrome," challenging Americans to stop feeling guilty and considering themselves the imperialist aggressors. He deemed the war "a noble cause."

Still, 1980 was an "ABC election"—Anybody but Carter—with exit polls showing that more voters were disgusted with Carter than committed to Reagan or Reaganism. After the election Moynihan exploded in *Commentary*'s February 1981 issue, after four frustrating years of party loyalty to

Carter. His article resurrected the title of the *Washington Post* editorial condemning Carter, "Joining the Jackals." Moynihan pronounced Carter's UN policy disastrous, undermining America's allies, sabotaging the Democratic Party, and, ultimately, losing Carter the presidency.

Moynihan admired President Reagan's achievement in making the Republican Party "the party of ideas," a shocking reversal from the Great Society Days. Reagan hired many of Moynihan's neoconservative friends—and ex-friends. Kissinger, their bête noire, rejected the neoconservative yearning for a "return to a militant, muscular Wilsonianism." While this characterization described Moynihan, he still resisted the label. Defining a neoconservative as "a liberal who votes for the defense budget," Moynihan would ask "Punch" Sulzberger of the *New York Times* to have reporters call him a liberal patriot whenever they considered calling him neoconservative.

Whatever the label, Moynihan's stand against Soviet and Third World bullying in the United Nations helped inspire Reagan's more aggressive approach there. Reagan liked quoting Moynihan's slam against totalitarian governments, that "countries which have papers filled with good news usually have jails filled with good people." Reagan's UN ambassador Jeane Kirkpatrick, a lapsed Hubert Humphrey Democrat, also hired after impressing the president with a fiery *Commentary* article, frequently chastised the UN for its "infamous" Zionism is racism resolution and demanded its repeal. Running for reelection in 1984, Reagan once again invoked Moynihan's "forthright and courageous" words at "that moment of shame" in 1975, while boasting about his administration's opposition to the UN becoming "a forum for the defamation of Israel." Reagan withheld $466.9 million in dues from the United Nations to force reforms and pushed the world organization to restore its original character.

Reagan fought hard against the UN, ideologically and politically. He explained Americans' disappointment by saying "Governments got in the way of the dreams of the people." This analysis welded his anti-government philosophy to his contempt for UN antics. Reagan also used the kind of quick-witted, patriotic repartee Americans enjoyed from him. When some delegates complained about America's lack of hospitality after one Cold War flashpoint—the Soviet downing of a South Korean jetliner KAL 007, killing all 269 abroad—Reagan suggested the critics convene in Moscow instead of New York. He emphasized that the US was not expelling anyone, "but if they chose to leave, goodbye."

Soviet power persisted, as did the demonization of Israel, but Moynihan, then Reagan, helped inspire many Americans not to take it anymore. In March 1982 the Ad Hoc Group on U.S. Policy toward the UN issued a twenty-two-page report bemoaning the "selective morality" that "seriously compromised" the UN. Dwight Eisenhower's UN ambassador Henry Cabot Lodge, along with former Democratic secretaries of state Dean Rusk, Edmund S. Muskie, and Cyrus Vance were the most prominent signers. They condemned the UN's anti-Israel obsession, including its "strange failure" to endorse the Camp David Accords between Israel and Egypt. The group proposed a "gentlemen's agreement" between Western and African countries in the UN to join in fighting apartheid as well as any resolutions labeling Zionism racism.

This surprising statement, coming during divisive debates over Reagan's economic cutbacks and aggressive anti-Communism, reflected broad, bipartisan, and establishment frustration with the United Nations. It resulted directly from the campaign Moynihan initiated seven years earlier while also demonstrating Reagan's restoration of American audacity, even among his critics. This kind of new, proud defiance, in the UN and in other international arenas, would help Americans claim victory when the Soviet empire collapsed, rather than simply blaming internal rot.

Reagan set the tone of the times. His 1984 reelection slogan, "Morning in America," offered the happy ending to the traumas of the 1960s and 1970s—which he was always primed to run against. This was the Reagan narrative of Democratic decay then Republican renaissance, using the students, the elites, and the adversarials as foils, just as Moynihan did. Showing more edge, Jeane Kirkpatrick savaged her fellow Democrats, whom she called "San Francisco Democrats," in the 1984 Republican Convention keynote address, as "the blame America first" crowd.

While agreeing with Reagan that the Soviet Union was an evil, decaying empire, Senator Moynihan was too much the FDR liberal, the New York Democratic politician, and the contrarian to support Reagan's Revolution. Domestically, he defended the "great idea" at the heart of the Democratic Party, "that an elected government can be the instrument of the common purpose of a free people; that government can embrace great causes and do great things." Moynihan also criticized Reagan harshly for bankrupting the country, building a national security state, encouraging a culture of secrecy, supporting oppression in Central America, neglecting the anti-apartheid struggle in South Africa, and becoming too obsessed, in his first term, with fighting Communism.

Unruffled by Moynihan and other Democratic critics, Reagan framed the national conversation to his benefit, converting patriotic indignation against Americans' adversaries into political support for their president. Meanwhile, American politics increasingly was buffeted by periodic media hurricanes, especially skirmishes in the "Culture Wars." Various politicians, preachers, or community activists whipped Americans into occasional frenzies, sometimes fighting familiar battles over an issue like abortion, and sometimes galvanizing around a one-time issue, such as allegations of pornographic rock music lyrics, unpatriotic educational reforms, or obscene art. Moynihan's handling of the Zionism-racism issue showed how to parlay these passing media hurricanes into sustained fame and influence.

Communism's collapse vindicated both Senator Moynihan and President Reagan. Since 1979 Moynihan had anticipated that Communism "could blow up" and, unlike most Americans, had proclaimed that the "Soviet idea is spent." Both Moynihan and Reagan knew this victory was not inevitable. While both had long thought the Soviet Union was defeatable, both had also warned repeatedly in the 1970s of America's vulnerabilities. Still, the speed with which the world changed both astonished and delighted Moynihan. "The age of totalitarianism is ending," he rejoiced in 1989. "Freedom prevailed."

Assigning historical causation, like understanding weather systems, is complicated. Just as the National Weather Service makes more than one million observations to shape daily weather forecasts, an overwhelming number of factors shape any particular historical event. While it is impossible, when assessing a phenomenon like the end of the Cold War to quantify just how much impact any one individual or event had, it is easier to justify inserting an overlooked actor or event into the narrative. On the American side, as the president who dominated the 1980s, Ronald Reagan deserves much of the glory. But America's winning Cold War narrative is broad and bipartisan, stretching back to the wise, bold decisions of Harry Truman and Dean Acheson in the 1940s. It should include Moynihan's eloquent, courageous, indignant charge against Resolution 3379 in the 1970s—a noteworthy event in American history and a cataclysmic event for the Middle East—and the Jewish people.

"WORDS MATTER"

The general assembly decides to revoke the determination
contained in its resolution 3379 (XXX) of 10 November 1975.
—GENERAL ASSEMBLY, 46/86, DECEMBER 16, 1991

When first nominated by President Gerald Ford and Secretary of State Henry Kissinger to be America's ambassador to the United Nations, Daniel Patrick Moynihan told them, "words matter." When politicians, including Israeli officials, dismissed the Zionism is racism resolution as "just words," he told them "words matter," quoting the Talmudic dictum his friend Chaim Herzog taught: that "life and death can be shaped by words." His protégé Tim Russert recalled Senator Moynihan frequently proclaiming: "Ideas are important and words matter." And when, retiring as senator, he made a farewell tour thanking New York publishers including Arthur O. Sulzberger of the *New York Times*, Liz Moynihan boycotted this gracious charade. She was protesting a critical *New York Times Magazine* portrait describing her husband as "our era's most magnificent failure," and, she explained, Pat had taught her that "words matter."

For years, insisting that "words matter," Moynihan lobbied to rescind Resolution 3379. The General Assembly had only ever reversed one resolution. In 1950 the UN admitted Spain, overriding a 1946 resolution banning this former wartime Axis ally. In the late 1980s, Allan Gerson, the former counsel to Ronald Reagan's UN ambassador Jeane Kirkpatrick, considered talk of a campaign to repeal 3379 "ridiculous because it will never happen."

The now-free Eastern European leaders repudiated what the Ukrainian president Leonid Kravchuk called "a resolution born out of bitter ideological confrontation among the nations of the world." An independent Ukraine would never have supported such a resolution. Such apologies treated this "Big Red Lie," as Moynihan called it in a *Washington Post* column in September 1991, emphasizing its Soviet pedigree, as a Cold War relic. The repeal symbolized George H. W. Bush's post-Communist New World Order.

But Bush's new world was not that orderly. Moynihan's prediction about tribalism and ethnic conflict spreading was proved true repeatedly. The Zionism is racism story proceeded on two divergent tracks. Momentum built for repeal in the UN even as the once-shocking accusation became axiomatic in anti-Israel circles, especially among what Moynihan had called "totalitarian" leftists. Days before the repeal, the General Assembly approved four resolutions criticizing Israel, reflecting the continuing anti-Israel obsession. UN delegates still spent between 30 and 50 percent of their time scrutinizing tiny Israel.

Anti-Zionism has flourished for many reasons. The Zionism is racism charge, however, still provides an essential intellectual foundation for anti-Zionism and remains a major cause of Israel's continuing isolation. Outlasting the Soviet Union's collapse, and the UN resolution's repeal, the claim slandered Israel, slowing progress toward peace. It effectively kept the Jewish state on probation, shifting debate from Israel's policies to its very existence. It linked anti-Zionism with anti-Americanism, while obscuring the new anti-Semitism with self-righteous rhetoric. Totalitarian anti-Zionism helped many blacks, feminists, leftists, and intellectuals overlook the Palestinian national movement's excesses, particularly its tendencies toward violence, Islamism, sexism, and homophobia. Providing the cement for what critics called the Red-Green alliance uniting leftists with Islamists, the "Big Red Lie" became the "Big Red-Green Lie" that refuses to die.

The Soviet propagandists chose well. Reading the Israeli-Palestinian national conflict as a racial struggle both demonized Israel and idealized Palestinians. Racism was the great modern ideological sin. Knowing that the UN had developed an elaborate infrastructure for combating it, the PLO counted on member-states confusing territorial struggle with racism. One of the overlooked but significant resolutions passed on November 10, 1975, established the "Committee on the Inalienable Rights of the Palestinian People." Especially with the General Assembly's launching of the Division for Palestinian Rights in 1977, separate, well-funded UN bureaucracies were now devoted to promoting the Palestinian cause—and propagandizing against Zionism.

Opponents of Israel now linked "Zionist Racism" to the twentieth century's other two "perfect racisms": "Nazi Racism" and "Apartheid Racism." Saddam Hussein celebrated Resolution 3379's first anniversary by convening the University of Baghdad's International Symposium on Zionism. There, Fayez A. al-Sayegh, a Georgetown philosophy PhD and Palestinian activist serving in Kuwait's UN delegation, linked Nazism's "biological determination," and apartheid's white supremacy with Zionism's grounding in "the biblical concept of the 'chosen people.'" Anti-Zionists frequently incorporated traditional Christian anti-Semitic tropes like this one. Sayegh and his colleagues spread their attack on an international circuit, speaking at conferences from Libya to Canada, appearing on television throughout the West.

The logic proceeded like a geometric proof: If Zionism is racism and racism is evil, therefore Israelis are bad, Palestinians are good. Such framing internationalized this local conflict, Jeane Kirkpatrick noted, deploying "the world's colored peoples" in "one more battle against white exploiters." Lumping Israel together with the racist regimes in South Africa and Rhodesia united Arabs and Africans. Israeli rejoinders that the Arabs and Africans traded more with South Africa than Israel did, failed to mollify what the *New Republic* called "the world's underdog-lovers." Western elites who romanticized Third Worlders cast Palestinians as noble, oppressed, disenfranchised people of color and Israelis as ignoble, oppressive racist whites— though there were light-skinned Palestinians and dark-skinned Israelis.

The labeling was not just libelous but incendiary, perpetuating the Middle East conflict. Palestinians seized on this designation because it resonated with their culture of victimization and their anger at Israel's existence. Understanding and resisting their genuine suffering through the lens of racism made compromise more difficult. Emphasizing the ontological (Palestinians' and Israelis' identity) rather than the transactional (their actions) justified Palestinian terrorism too. As Kirkpatrick explained, designating Israel a racist state was "tantamount to formal designation as a target."

Anyone fighting racists could fight dirty. By 1979, the UN's International Convention against the Taking of Hostages exempted any act committed "against colonial domination and alien occupation and against racist regimes." In rationalizing Palestinian terrorism and reinforcing anti-Americanism with anti-Zionism, the UN enabled the spread of Islamist terrorism.

After Resolution 3379 passed, the UN—and other international forums—became more welcoming to random anti-Israel outbursts and nearly Hitlerian invective. When the Security Council denounced the South Africans' Soweto Massacre in 1976, the PLO delegate gratuitously condemned "These policies, whether practiced in southern Africa or in Palestine." One day the Jordanian ambassador would spread lies about "Mr. Rothschild" and his price-fixing cabal. Another day, the Saudi representative would claim Jews are commanded "to drink a Gentile's blood." Updating the Jew-as-Christ-killer libel, diplomats with access to government power, university podiums, and media platforms repeatedly accused the collective Jew—Israel or as they called it "the Zionist entity"—of slaying innocent Palestinians.

As an unintended Soviet propaganda bonanza, the racism charge linked the United States, with its appalling Jim Crow past, and the Jewish state in a kind of international original sin. In UN rhetoric—and elsewhere worldwide—anti-Zionism and anti-Americanism increasingly intersected. The Six-Day War first merged anti-Zionism with anti-Americanism in the minds of many European leftists. "Israel made a big mistake in succeeding in 1967," George Will quips. "This was when the Left decided it liked victims; it still does." The language of 3379 rationalized that newfound disdain and popularized it in the Third World. The world's new twin bogeymen—America and Israel—modernist upstarts increasingly disdained by Europeans and Third Worlders—were placed in the perpetual international docket. The righteous rhetoric against racism and for human rights tried masking the underlying anti-American and anti-Zionist bigotry. The Third World's verdict that Zionism is racism helped alienate many African Americans from Israel, as the clashes over affirmative action, busing, and crime strained the 1960s' black-Jewish coalition. Many blacks blamed "the Jews" when President Carter ousted Ambassador Andrew Young in August 1979 for lying about that unauthorized meeting with a PLO representative, Zehdi

Labib Terzi. Tensions then worsened when the next ambassador, Donald McHenry, voted against Israel in the Security Council.

After Young resigned, the African American foreign policy lobby, TransAfrica, endorsed Palestinian statehood, while the Reverend Joseph E. Lowery, Martin Luther King Jr.'s successor at the Southern Christian Leadership Conference, pointedly met with Ambassador Terzi. Other African Americans expressed a cruder anti-Semitism. Sherry Brown, an Anacostia community leader, called the Jews "our true enemies," having "historically profited as slumlords and merchants from the suffering of black people." Paralleling the growth of an elite, left-wing anti-Semitism among some Progressives, African American anti-Semitism increased with income, status, and education.

In September 1979, weeks after Young's resignation, Jesse Jackson visited Israel. Jackson compared the Palestinian refugee camp Kalandia with the Chicago ghetto "stench" of his youth. Just as Jews did not need the UN to dream about a Jewish state, Jackson did not need the UN to cry "racism." Still, just as the UN 1947 Partition plan amplified Jewish cries for a Jewish state, Jackson's charges of Zionist racism resonated more broadly after 1975.

Three years later, on July 1, 1982, President Reagan sent Jeane Kirkpatrick to Bujumbura to celebrate Burundi's twentieth anniversary of independence. In the six-hour-long parade, revelers carried a six-foot-wide banner, proclaiming LE SIONISME EST LE RACISME. Back in December 1973, Burundi had amended a resolution condemning South Africa by denouncing Zionism too, anticipating Resolution 3379. Kirkpatrick understood how rich Arab states and the Soviet empire exploited genuine postcolonial anger against previous injustices. And every good deed the UN did—delivering food, providing medicine, spreading literacy—further legitimized the organization, including its resolutions. Standing 2,403 miles away from Israel in that poor, landlocked African country, Kirkpatrick was amazed by the Burundi conundrum, "how hate-filled acts like that spread around the world."

As a political scientist, Kirkpatrick had long wondered how the Holocaust could have occurred and how few leaders responded to it. Witnessing the "comprehensive, intense, incessant and vicious" UN campaign against Israel, she told a colleague she feared another Holocaust: "I'm in a cesspool of anti-Semitism here. They think that because my name is Kirkpatrick they can talk freely to me."

While delighting radicals, the PLO, the Soviets, and their allies, these attacks further diminished the UN in the eyes of mainstream American liberals. Allard K. Lowenstein, the peace activist Jimmy Carter dispatched to the UN Commission on Human Rights, revered the UN. In college, Lowenstein had rejected Zionism as segregationist, Jewish "Jim Crowism." He nevertheless abhorred that "stinking little resolution" 3379 and resigned his UN post in 1978 to protest its continuing potency. It encouraged anti-Semitism, diminished America, made racism a divisive issue, and "multiplied the number of people who dismiss the U.N. as a kind of radicalized Lewis Carroll contraption filled with leftist mad hatters who might next announce that slavery is freedom, or that Jews are Nazis."

By the end of the 1970s, despite such liberal complaints, anti-Semitism, anti-Americanism, Third Worldism, anti-racism, pro-Palestinianism, and legitimate concerns about Israel's actions converged in the kaleidoscopic attacks against Israel and Zionism. As Israel's defenders counterattacked, opponents nimbly readjusted the lens to suit their argument, defending the legitimacy of Third World prerogatives, fighting racism, or criticizing Israel's approach to Palestinians, without acknowledging any uglier motives or echoes. At Harvard Law School, in February 1979, when Jewish students protested that a conference on "Third World Communities and Human Rights" was honoring a UN delegate from Libya's repressive regime, the sponsoring Asian, Black, and Chicano Law Students Associations accused the Jewish students of trying to "censor" and "thwart" people of color. Predictably, the conference ignored Libyan and Arab human rights abuses while alleging that Israelis placed Palestinians in concentration camps.

Reflecting the totalitarian impulse of sacrificing core values to serve a political aim, some lawyers even abandoned their commitment to applying the law universally. In 1978 Alan Dershowitz challenged the National Lawyers' Guild to explain why the organization censured Israel yet refused to observe the Soviet trial of the dissident Anatoly Scharansky or even scrutinize any Eastern European Socialist countries. Guild officials admitted they did not approach matters "purely from a human rights perspective." They weighed "the importance" of highlighting abuses in a particular country. Besides, too many pro-Soviet members would never criticize a Soviet court.

While remaining popular among Americans by margins ranging from 5 to 1 to 9 to 1, Israel endured special condemnation from some elites. As Jews individually enjoyed a golden age on American campuses, radicals also thrived there. Elite colleges in particular had an adversarial, politically correct public culture, which left many Jewish activists feeling besieged. The 1960s sensibility ripened into a growing intolerance for intolerance, which seemingly only tolerated intolerance toward Zionists. At the University of Maryland, the Black Student Union publicized a "seminar" on Zionism with a flyer alleging "Zionism Supports the Murder of Black People." On that campus and elsewhere, the Black Power activist Kwame Toure, aka Stokely Carmichael, proclaimed during his popular speaking tours in the mid-1980s that "the only good Zionist is a dead Zionist." More subtly, American radicals and Jewish radicals showed that Americans could nevertheless be "anti-American," and Jews could perpetuate the "new anti-Semitism." These ideologues, the philosopher Michael Walzer explained, luxuriated in the "moral purism of blaming America"—or their own people—"first."

On British campuses, the National Union of Students' (NUS) policy of "No Platform" for racists and fascists triggered numerous attempts to ban Jewish Student Societies after Resolution 3379 passed. Over Easter vacation in 1986, an NUS conference pitted one leftist faction demanding "no platform for Zionists" against opponents demanding "no platform for idiot anti-Zionists." Robin Shepherd, a British journalist and political commentator who attended the University of London and the London School of Economics in the late 1980s and early '90s, remembers watching these attempts to ban Jewish student societies using the "justification" that "Zionism was racism." He recalls: "It was a charge that would put anyone with even mildly pro-Israeli leanings right on the back foot. It was a verbal jab to the chin. It was a way of telling you to conform to the anti-Israel orthodoxy or be vilified."

In the classroom, radicals from the 1960s "decolonized" Middle East studies with a new Third-World oriented orthodoxy. The 1978 publication of Edward Said's *Orientalism* provided these scholar-activists with a popular, professorial Palestinian champion combating Western racism, American imperialism, and Zionism. Said constructed the dominant intellectual edifice blaming Westerners automatically, as his "postcolonial" revolution opposed the "Eurocentric" prejudice against Arabs and Islam. By the 1990s, even a leading Middle Eastern historian from that dominant school, UCLA's Nikki Keddie, would complain that "Orientalism" had become "a generalized swearword" demonizing scholars deemed too pro-Israel or too conservative.

As "Orientalism" mainstreamed anti-Zionism intellectually, the network of UN organizations and conferences worked diplomatically to "add Zionism to all the nasty 'isms' " the world wanted "eliminated," lamented the Israeli diplomat Tamar Eshel. Eshel represented Israel at the United Nations' International Women's Conference, which convened in Copenhagen in July 1980. In May, Moynihan warned the State Department it remained "unprepared" for "the ritualistic assault upon our democratic ally Israel." And Moynihan co-sponsored Senate Resolution 473 "deploring" the conference's "politicization."

Moynihan was right. The attacks on Israel, Jews, and the United States were uglier in Denmark than they had been in Mexico City five years earlier. After presiding over the conference, Denmark's culture minister Lise Ostegaard, marveled how in this theater of the absurd "a simple majority could turn black into white and white into black." A huge portrait of Ayatollah Khomeini, Iran's Islamist anti-feminist leader, decorated the conference headquarters. Gangs of young women muscled into the parallel "Forum" sessions, shouting down Zionism and imperialism, bullying American feminists. Most Third World delegates insisted that sexism was exclusively a Western problem, because only Western women complained about it. On day five, Peg Downey, a young American, ran out of the conference in tears. "I cried," she recalled, "because the more than 8,000 women from 187 countries in attendance at this UN conference were not unified in a feminist approach to their universal oppression," and very "little real sisterhood appeared."

Ann Robinson, of the National Council of Jewish Women, felt doubly oppressed as an American and a Jew, amid what the feminist psychologist Dr. Phyllis Chesler called a "psychological pogrom." Sonia Johnson, a Mormon, heard delegates pronounce: "The only way to rid the world of Zionism is to kill all the Jews" and "The only good Jew is a dead Jew."

Many Jewish feminists were discovering that, as the lesbian record promoter Judy Dlugacz realized, "It's just not cool to be a Zionist. It makes you a pariah in radical feminist circles." During one American delegation meeting, an African American woman asked why Zionism was *not* racism; she was cheered. The Jewish feminists sat flabbergasted. "I'll tell you what Zionism is," Bella Abzug exclaimed. "It is a liberation movement for a people who have been persecuted all their lives and throughout human history."

Sarah Weddington, co-chairing the American delegation, had her Moynihan moment by demanding that the women's conference address women's needs. A special assistant to President Carter, the winning lawyer in the landmark Supreme Court abortion case *Roe v. Wade* when she was twenty-six, Weddington objected that "To equate Zionism with colonialism and imperialism is in a sense to state that the destruction of Israel is a prerequisite for peace."

Anti-Zionism was not just emerging as a piece of a broader puzzle but as the identity marker, the glue keeping a broad, diverse, often contradictory left-wing movement together. This time, in 1980, the PLO delegates succeeded in condemning Zionism in the Action Program, not just the Declaration. In 1975 feminists at least could endorse Mexico City's Action Plan. "The real test of our fabled 'Jewish power' is how powerless Jews were in Copenhagen," the radical writer Ellen Willis of the *Village Voice* glumly reported. A liberal "Diaspora Jew" uninterested in Jewish nationalism, Willis opposed Israel's occupation. Still, she slammed radical leftists' collective blindspot regarding the anti-Semitic impulses triggering their anti-Israel obsession. Eventually, she proclaimed: "I'm an anti-anti-Zionist."

Amid growing anti-Zionism and anti-Americanism, the United States began threatening to boycott hostile conferences, including withholding its 25 percent budget share. After his January 1981 inauguration, Reagan approached the UN aggressively. Kirkpatrick, like Moynihan, emphasized that she fought the UN because she respected its power to shape the world agenda.

A series of congressional resolutions, many Moynihan-initiated, encouraged the administration. By 1984 the United States had withdrawn from UNESCO. Jean Gerard, the American delegate, explained that UNESCO had become "so skewed, so radical-political, that it is not serving the purpose it is supposed to be serving, which is development." The United States returned to UNESCO only in September 2003. Still, some bloated UN bureaucracies, including UNESCO, began implementing some administrative reforms as many Western countries backed American demands.

As the United States tried reforming the UN, Chaim Herzog launched a campaign to repeal the hated resolution. In 1983 Herzog became Israel's sixth president—partially due to his eloquent defense of Zionism. Moynihan, always partial to melodrama, would proclaim that Herzog summoned him a second time—the first being in 1975—to join "his campaign to enable the democratic world, to *make* the democratic world, understand the portent of this monstrous lie, not only for Israel but for Israel as a symbol of democracy."

Moynihan continued going "door to door" to fight the resolution, ultimately delivering over 750 speeches refuting the Zionism-racism slander, his Senate aide, Dr. David Luchins, estimated. Once again, Herzog had to rouse reluctant Israelis. Some still dismissed the resolution as mere words, while others dismissed Herzog's quest as quixotic. On November 11, 1984, Herzog hosted a conference at the President's House in Jerusalem "Refuting the Zionist-Racism Equation." Moynihan flew to Jerusalem to plan the repeal. Still feeling abandoned, Moynihan complained that no Israeli university hosted the conference.

Herzog was again defying Israel's skittish foreign ministry. Foreign Minister Yitzhak Shamir shocked his bureaucrats by championing repeal, explaining "the wording has, like poison, filtered into the minds of many people." David Harris, a Soviet Jewry activist now leading the American Jewish Committee, repeatedly debated Israeli diplomats who feared that attacking the resolution "reminded the world again and again that Zionism is racism according to the UN." Cynical about the UN—"*oom shmoom*"— they believed that, without the fuss, the resolution "would collect dust with every other UN resolution." Many believed their "thin-skinned" Diaspora brethren were too worried about what non-Jews said.

Yet Harris and other American Jews felt the impact of this new Big Lie regularly. Malcolm Hoenlein of the Conference of Presidents of Major Jewish Organizations witnessed the "cover" this devastating indictment provided "for everyone who wanted to legitimize their anti-Israel agenda." The resolution "generated a life of its own," Harris agreed. "It resurfaced in a thousand ways, in a hundred places: on placards, on signs, in demonstrations, in other resolutions, in the media."

Still, most believed—as Kirkpatrick had during the Reagan years—that repealing any UN resolution was what one activist called "Mission Impossible." Frequently, when American Jewish Committee representatives worldwide lobbied for repeal, their diplomatic hosts explained that "no resolution" had ever been rescinded. They "basically were rolling their eyes," Harris recalls, wondering: "How quickly can I get these folks out of my office without being calling an anti-Semite?" Eventually, the AJC held well over one hundred meetings, swaying diplomats as distanced from the conflict as those from South Korea and Japan. The World Jewish Congress, B'nai B'rith, and others joined the campaign. The Conference of Presidents of Major American Jewish Organizations organized at least seventy meetings between its organizations and foreign diplomats in New York. Harris calls this "nudnik diplomacy"—after the Yiddish word for pest. But, "lo and behold, the nudniks prevailed."

Meanwhile, American feminists tried liberating the international women's movement from its Zionist obsession. Some activists, disgusted by the Mexico City and Copenhagen attacks, spent years preparing for the July 1985 International Women's Conference, in Nairobi, Kenya. Applying feminist methods, Letty Cottin Pogrebin and Bella Abzug convened Black-Jewish Women's dialogue groups and tried establishing some Palestinian-Jewish dialogues. Emerging from what she called "virtual feminist retirement," Betty Friedan mobilized Jewish women worldwide to tap the "strength that comes from authentic assertion of one's own identity, as Jew or woman." Abzug and the others emphasized "our deep commitment to feminist issues," fighting anti-Zionism because it distracted from feminism's agenda.

The mostly Democratic Jewish feminists allied with their ideological enemies, the Reagan Republicans. Republican Senator Nancy Kassebaum sponsored an amendment demanding the president prevent "political issues extraneous to the goals of the 1985 women's conference" from dominating—which basically meant limiting the anti-Israel obsession. The "business of the conference is women, not propaganda," President Reagan declared, resisting what Moynihan called *the* totalitarian tack. Reagan appointed his daughter Maureen to head America's twenty-nine-person delegation, instructing her to walk out if the conference demonized Zionism.

Finally, at this conference, women wanted to avoid the sideshow about Zionism, and talk, Betty Friedan noted, "as feminists about their common women's problems." Even Egypt's ambassador tired of the PLO agitation, asking after one marathon session: "Will they never stop?" "This is an insult to women," one elderly African woman complained. Amid another dreary debate about Zionism and racism, a French woman began chanting "The women of the world are watching and waiting." Others joined in, until the PLO and the Iranian delegates relented. Representatives of 157 countries, many teary-eyed, many singing the conference's unofficial theme song "We are the World, We are the Women," unanimously adopted the final document with, Betty Friedan exulted, "every reference to Zionism gone."

That November, Israeli diplomats and Jewish activists used the tenth anniversary of 3379's passing to demand repeal. Hundreds crowded into a UN conference room, reserved by the chief Israeli delegate Benjamin Netanyahu. Delegates cheered Reagan's call for "removal of this blot from the United Nations record." Jeane Kirkpatrick, back teaching at Georgetown University, said that passing 3379 "symbolized the death of the dream of the United Nations as an institution dedicated to reason, democracy and peace." Netanyahu explained the resolution's potency, noting "there is no worse epithet in today's lexicon than 'racist,'" the word is "the modern version of 'Christ killers,' 'traitors,' 'usurers,' and 'international conspirators.'" The resolution therefore was a "license to kill," comparable to the Nazi libels. Netanyahu's conference succeeded, and it did so by highlighting the UN's role in fomenting a new anti-Semitism and in enraging the Arab delegates for addressing these issues at UN headquarters. Nonetheless, repeal remained a distant goal.

Moynihan worried about a permanent American rupture with the UN. Word in 1985 that Kurt Waldheim, the UN Secretary-General from 1972 to 1981, had hidden his Nazi past further blackened the UN's reputation. Moynihan insisted that anyone who cared about the UN had to criticize it, because the institution needed a revolution to be saved. Most UN boosters missed that point. Moynihan was America's first UN ambassador not granted an honorary chairmanship by the United Nations Association upon retirement.

In 1986 the Australian parliament welcomed President Herzog's visit by passing a short, pointed resolution endorsing repeal. The resolution declared that Resolution 3379 impeded the peace process, violated the UN Charter, misrepresented Zionism, and helped "incite anti-Semitism." A year later, when Herzog made an Israeli president's first state visit to the United States, Moynihan introduced the exact resolution in the Congress, to make the call universal.

President Herzog addressed a joint session of Congress on November 10, 1987, twelve years after ripping up Resolution 3379. Understanding his audience, Herzog exulted: "Never in history has a nation given to mankind in so unselfish a manner what the American people have made available to the world." The *Los Angeles Times* noted how a Congress wearied "by anti-American rhetoric" welcomed these words. Similarly charmed, Reagan signed the resolution. "Finally, there was an American policy," Moynihan rejoiced. Feeling optimistic, Martin Raffel, the Israel Task Force director of the National Jewish Community Relations Advisory Council, targeted "key countries" in seeking repeal: Mexico, Nigeria, Brazil, Kenya, Peru, Thailand—and the Soviet Union, which was beginning to reform under Mikhail Gorbachev.

The push for repeal grew beyond the Herzog-Moynihan circle of offended Zionists and outraged Americans. Those protective of the UN, including Secretary-General Javier Perez de Cuellar of Peru, wanted "to see this blemish erased"—although he cautioned "there is no tradition" of repeal. Sir Brian Urquhart, the veteran UN undersecretary-general who had proposed the blue helmets for UN peacekeeping forces, called the resolution "the stupidest thing anybody ever did at the UN...an absolutely mindless piece of provocation," which "did nothing for the Palestinians." And Andrew Young, sensitive to Third World dynamics, wanted the repeal to restore "the moral authority of the United Nations and the partnership of the United States in the continuing search for peace."

Reagan's successor was less ideological, less confrontational, and less pro-Israel. As president, George H. W. Bush, along with his secretary of state James Baker III, clashed periodically with Israel—and Israel's supporters. In a dramatic September 1991 press conference, Bush said he was "one lonely little guy" facing "powerful political forces," after 1,200 Israel activists lobbied Congress seeking loan guarantees to help Israel resettle emigrating Soviet Jews. The Bush administration feared the money would help build settlements.

Malcolm Hoenlein, the veteran executive director of the Conference of Presidents of Major American Jewish Organizations, disagreed that Bush and Baker were "anti-Israel." Hoenlein recalls that after Bush's controversial press conference, Shoshana Cardin, chairing the Conference of Presidents, met the president privately. Cardin explained that talk of Jewish lobbyists outmuscling the president echoed traditionally bigoted exaggerations about Jewish power. "Mr. President, I think you need to understand how deeply American Jewry was hurt by your statement," she said. "Because of your statement, you drew blood and the sharks came swimming." Bush pointed out that he "didn't use the word 'Jews.'" Cardin explained he did not have to. "Everyone understood that the people you were referring to were Jewish. That's why the White House switchboard lit up with so many messages of support from anti-Semites." "I never intended to hurt anyone," Bush said, teary-eyed, "Or give encouragement to anti-Semitism." He then apologized to the American Jewish leaders gathered to meet him.

Although Moynihan believed individuals make history, history had to catch up with his sensibility. The revolutions of 1989 ended Soviet domination of Eastern Europe. That spring, Secretary Baker, understanding that delegitimizing Israel discouraged peacemaking, asked the Arab states to "repudiate the odious line that Zionism is racism." Yasir Arafat continued opposing the "Zionist state," insisting: "Zionism is a racist movement, according to a UN resolution." Vice President Dan Quayle, speaking at a Yeshiva University dinner that December, said Resolution 3379 "undermines the UN's moral authority and credibility." Quayle then made the first formal call from an American administration for repeal.

For Eastern Europe's leaders, repudiating the resolution affirmed their new freedom. Czechoslovakia's president Vaclav Havel rejoiced in February 1990: "We are in a position to decide for ourselves." His position was: "I didn't approve of it then; I don't approve of it now." A month later the new Polish prime minister, Tadeusz Mazowiecki, called 3379, "an attempt to foster hatred of Jews."

John Bolton, assistant secretary of state for International Organization Affairs, wanted to mark Resolution 3379's fifteenth anniversary by repealing it. A Reagan administration lawyer and diplomat, Bolton believed the resolution violated "basic UN principles." At a Senate hearing to advance legislation endorsing the repeal, Moynihan challenged Bolton—and his bosses—to be more aggressive, asking "Did we ever tell one country, just one country, that you are getting American money, and you are not getting any more until you change your mind?" Moynihan detailed the "message" he wanted Bolton to send, that 3379 is "a residue of a Stalinist, totalitarian Soviet Union...and they lost."

Yosef Abramowitz, a leading Soviet Jewry and anti-apartheid activist, along with Elie Wurtman, a Columbia University senior and vice president of the North American Jewish Student Network, mobilized students to urge repeal. A November 10 rally outside the UN attracted more than 1,400 students from as far away as Michigan and Illinois. Dismaying some of his more courteous elders, Wurtman tore the UN's flag as students chanted: "Shame on you, United Nations."

Ultimately, the Israelis and the Americans hesitated. The Israelis wanted to wait until they secured a lopsided vote providing a "moral victory." Both

Bush and Baker feared distractions as they assembled a fragile coalition against Saddam Hussein's invasion of Kuwait.

By autumn 1991, however, world conditions favored repeal. The Soviet Union was imploding. The United States had won the Gulf War. Bush's "New World Order" included a redeemed UN, which had authorized the US invasion with Security Council Resolution 678.

UN Secretary-General Javier Perez de Cuellar called 3379 "a wrong and unfair interpretation of what Zionism is"—subtly condemning the resolution without endorsing repeal. The resolution offended the Secretary-General's sense of fairness: "You cannot say that trying and get[ing] a state for your nation is racism, [as] for instance the Kurds or the Basques in Spain are not racist. These are two different things that should not be mixed up." Privately, he had told Bush officials that 3379 was "actually dead but the Israelis have kept it alive." He agreed, however, that the repeal required a decisive majority.

In mid-September, five years after winning the Nobel Peace Prize, Elie Wiesel led a delegation to the Ukraine, marking fifty years since the Babi Yar massacre. On September 29/30th, 1941, just outside Kiev, the Nazis had gunned down 33,771 Jews, the Holocaust's largest one-time mass killing. Moynihan considered the Soviet lie blaming Babi Yar on the Gestapo collaborating with "the Zionists" the opening propaganda falsehood that culminated in the "Big Red Lie" branding Zionism as racism.

Meeting the Ukrainian president Leonid Kravchuk, Wiesel described the scene from 1941, with thousands of Jews being marched down Kiev's streets to their deaths. "Tell me, was there one door that opened to pull in a Jewish child?" Wiesel asked. "One? Not even one. Why did no one take one Jewish child in and say to that child 'You will not die?'" Kravchuk reddened visibly and sputtered in response. But he promised to endorse a repeal of 3379. Briefing Bush, Senator Moynihan insisted, "This is the moment." Get the repeal, "get a treaty on tactical nuclear weapons, and you will have pretty much wrapped up the twentieth century!"

When President Bush addressed the General Assembly on September 23, he welcomed a "new era." Bush justified the repeal substantively, explaining "Zionism is not a policy" but the idea of a Jewish homeland. And he made the institutional argument that the UN needed to "enhance its credibility and serve the cause of peace." The story dominated the front pages and nightly news shows. The *New York Times* noted, "Zionism-is-racism remains code language for bigotry," now expressed by the world's greatest villain, Saddam Hussein. Most surprising, the Soviet foreign minister Boris D. Pankin called Resolution 3379 "obnoxious," "a legacy of the Ice Age" and "an obstacle" to peace.

Once again Bush and Baker tried leveraging America's power surge to make peace in the Middle East. Their pressure caused the mid-September conflict with Israel over loan guarantees but also yielded the three-day Madrid Peace Conference, which convened October 30 in Spain's magnificent royal palace. Israel demanded reversing Resolution 3379 as a condition for granting the UN observer status at the conference, which, significantly, included Syria, Jordan, Lebanon, and the Palestinians, in Israel's first bilateral talks with neighbors other than Egypt. While Arab leaders feared repeal might make Israel more intransigent, American diplomats assured them it would bolster Israeli confidence and engagement. European diplomatic sources reported that the Bush people kept saying: "You're not doing this for Israel. You're doing this to help George Bush make peace."

The American Jewish leadership was pushing for a "simple *unconditional* resolution." Conservative Evangelical Protestants who in the 1980s emerged as ardent Israel supporters cooperated with the liberal National Council of Churches and the National Conference of Catholic Bishops. Jewish activists asked influential Congressional Black Caucus members to lobby African countries. The enthusiastic participation of John Lewis, Donald Payne, Kwiesi Mfume and other members of Congress illustrated the Black-Jewish alliance's continuing resilience despite its being eulogized so frequently. By contrast, Egypt opposed the repeal, providing a rare disappointment during this final phase.

Then, suddenly, the White House went passive. Bolton worried, knowing that political strategy can shift as quickly as the stock market. Brent Scowcroft, Bush's National Security Adviser, viewed the whole issue as an "irritant" and hoped the repeal could proceed "quietly," without "much fanfare." Chief of Staff John Sununu, an Arab American who was the only governor in 1987 to vote against a collective gubernatorial statement urging repeal, tried sabotaging the efforts by not forwarding Bush's directives on the subject to subordinates.

The White House inaction frustrated Edgar Bronfman, the World Jewish Congress president, a Bush fundraiser, and an heir to the Seagram beverage fortune. Coincidentally, Bush demanded Sununu's resignation on December 3, a day which brought the president to Seagram's Tropicana plant in Brandenton, Florida, promoting its drug-free workplace. Hoping to break the logjam by speaking directly to Bush, Bronfman decided to host the presidential visit. While escorting Bush, Bronfman requested permission to raise a different issue. He asked why UN ambassador Thomas Pickering had received "no instructions" to bring the repeal to a vote, when the World Jewish Congress and the State Department had secured the necessary support. Bush was flabbergasted. According to Stephen Herbits, a Bronfman confidante with Republican ties who was there, the president stopped abruptly and said he had authorized the vote. When the tour ended, Bush excused himself and entered the temporary presidential holding room. He emerged a few minutes later, furious that Sununu had defied his orders, saying, "I'm sorry, my now-former-Chief-of-Staff held things up." The order then went from Bush to Pickering and to Baker, who ordered a "full-court press" from the State Department.

Unlike in 1975, the president, secretary of state, and their ambassadors, lobbied aggressively. Both Bush and Baker were "mad dialers," Bolton recalled, recruiting co-sponsors, not just supporters. The president directed America's ambassadors to warn their hosts that any country that deviated on this issue risked jeopardizing ties with the United States. On December 12, at Baker's direction, the United States submitted a one-line, eighteen-word resolution that respected UN protocols by not actually proposing repeal. Instead, Resolution 46/86 proclaimed: "The general assembly decides to revoke the determination contained in its Resolution 3379 (XXX) of November 10, 1975."

The resolution now had eighty-five sponsors, more than half the member states—including the Soviet Union. Achieving this magic number prevented any possible Arab procedural blocks. Addressing the General Assembly, the deputy secretary of state Lawrence Eagleburger remembered how the Cold War's "Ideological conflict eroded the UN's most precious asset—its claim to impartiality and moral honesty." Recalling "the era which produced Resolution 3379," Eagleburger insisted: "it is not Israel which needs this action; it is the United Nations which requires it." Repeal would "redeem" the UN and help "efforts currently under way" to bring peace. Sixteen years after Moynihan accused the UN of betraying its core identity, Eagleburger toasted the organization's second chance.

Ultimately, on December 16, 1991, 111 countries voted to repeal the resolution—eleven more than the US mission expected. The countries that switched their vote included Brazil, India, Nigeria, the Soviet Union, its freed Eastern European satellites, Yugoslavia, and Mexico, which had paid dearly for its 1975 vote. Twenty-five countries opposed 46/86, including many Arab and Muslim countries, with Afghanistan, Algeria, Cuba, Indonesia, Iran, Iraq, Jordan, Lebanon, North Korea, Pakistan, Sudan, Saudi Arabia, Syria, and Yemen now having voted twice to declare Zionism racism. Thirteen countries abstained, including Turkey and Uganda, with China, Egypt, Kuwait, Morocco, South Africa, and Tunisia among the seventeen countries that did not vote. Bolton enjoyed watching the issue split the non-aligned caucus. The General Assembly's president, Saudi Arabia's Samir S. Shihabi, a Palestinian, walked out.

When the resolution passed, the delegates cheered. Lawrence Eagleburger called the repeal his most "satisfying moment" in "a diplomatic career spanning more than thirty years." Eagleburger believed the new resolution strengthened "Israel's international standing" and showed "those who hate Israel" to be "anti-Semites, terrorists, international gangsters, gangster states, and other such despicable trash." Edgar Bronfman assured Bush that the vote would make the Israeli people "feel less isolated, and therefore more ready to make some sacrifices for peace."

Herzog called December 16 the happiest day of his life. Nine days after the resolution passed, the Soviet Union collapsed. Moynihan—who had initiated yet another Senate resolution demanding repeal that passed 97 to 0 with an unprecedented 97 co-sponsors in 1990 demanding repeal—was in the General Assembly chamber during the vote. He toasted this "moment of truth and deliverance," which exorcised, he said dramatically, "the last great horror of the Hitler-Stalin era."

Bipartisan support for Israel, uniting a Republican president with a Democratic Congress, backed by a galvanized Jewish leadership, finally blessed by the right historical winds, succeeded. More Americans demonstrated interest in the repeal than in almost any UN measure since 1975. American perceptions that the UN was doing "a good job" almost doubled from the mid-1980s, from 28 percent to 54 percent. Still, the original passage had stirred much more mass emotion. World support for Zionism proved as difficult to restore as Americans' faith in the UN. Americans were so disillusioned that, like divorcees rewriting their romantic pasts, many simply forgot their initial ardor. The repeal was a necessary first step in redeeming the institution, but it was not enough.

Many Arabs, especially Palestinians, now resented the UN. Faisal Husseini, a leading Palestinian deemed a "pragmatist" by the *New York Times*, proclaimed: "Israeli repression of the Palestinian people and (Israel's) denial of their national rights, foremost that of self-determination, is racist in essence." The UN fight encouraged the Society of Arab Students (SAS) at Harvard— and sister groups at universities worldwide—to resume campaigning against Zionism as racism. On December 15, 1991, on the eve of the vote, SAS members blanketed the Cambridge campus with anti-Zionist fliers— "a door-drop" in Harvard-speak. One senior, Richard Primus, confronted members of the group in the Lowell House courtyard. "I'm a Zionist," he said, "and I'm not a racist. So I have a problem with the claim that Zionism is racism." "The United Nations says it is," one Arab student replied.

Primus invited the students to begin a dialogue, but they refused. "Naïve student that I am," he would write in the *Harvard Crimson*, "I thought that all other students on this campus, no matter what their disagreements, would concur on the importance of productive discourse." Four days later, as the conflict continued in the student newspaper, the SAS members insisted they were defending "truth, morality, and justice," not "a mere piece of paper passed by the UN," while charging that the revocation was muscled through by a "political bully...the US."

This Harvard duel indicated the tenacity of the Zionism is racism conception. It had penetrated too deep to be revoked by vote or, many feared, eradicated by even dramatic peace gestures. The Harvard students refused to engage because this notion was not just a tenet of faith but an identity marker. It was not debatable. The radical Left on campuses and elsewhere, more so in Europe than in North America, simply saw Israel as illegitimate, and Zionism as evil, guilty of racism and "ethnic cleansing." This new phrase would become popular after 1992 as the old Yugoslavia collapsed, with the concept rapidly applied by Zionism's enemies to Israel.

Nevertheless, Resolution 3379's revocation was a strong link in a chain of good news that promised to transform the Middle East in the 1990s. Just as 3379 had emboldened the rejectionist front and the settlement movement, the repeal made Israelis feel less embattled and confident enough to compromise. By 1993, the world witnessed the unexpected scene of Yitzhak Rabin and Yasir Arafat shaking hands awkwardly at a White House ceremony launching the Oslo Peace Process. The repeal "paved the way for a clear cut rejection of terrorism by the international community" and encouraged the "peace makers," said Shimon Peres, the Oslo Accords' architect. Academic experts subsequently called the repeal the noteworthy step in reaching "Oslo via Madrid."

At Turtle Bay, Cold War power politics had disappeared along with the Soviet Union. In March 1996 Chaim Herzog, now retired, gave a speech rejoicing that "our delegation...enjoys open and cordial relations with many Arab delegations." Moynihan was less giddy, dismayed at the ethno-national conflicts now haunting the world, and furious that the American government still trusted the same intelligence analysts who, unlike him, never anticipated the Soviet collapse.

Still, the libel lived. Resolution 3379 "has never quite gone away," David Malone, a veteran Canadian diplomat and president of the International Peace Academy from 1998 to 2004 would say a decade after the repeal. Assuming that Zionism was racism consistently interpreted Israeli policy toward the Palestinians malignantly, especially during times of tension. Malone also noted that the Arab masses' "sense of powerlessness" to influence events was so great, that many took refuge in doing "what they can...at the rhetorical level." Malone's analysis helps explain the intense anti-Semitic imagery and verbal violence in Arab anti-Zionism.

Ironically, the collapse of South Africa's apartheid regime in the early 1990s sullied Israel's image. Radicals now identified Israel as the world's worst racist. Accusations calling Israel an apartheid state spread, even with Israel trying to disentangle from the Palestinians, at the Palestinians' insistence, with most demanding that their territory be free of Jews. Lecturing in 1997, Elaine Hagopian, a Simmons College sociologist, articulated the "Soweto on the Jordan" strategy. If Israeli policies toward the Palestinians could be compared "to the policies of the pre-1994 South African apartheid government, then American policy toward Israel would be forced to change under public pressure, and the Palestinian cause would be warmly embraced by Uncle Sam."

Within the UN, the anti-Israel infrastructure mapped out in the accompanying resolution on November 10, 1975, remained—and was renewed by the same General Assembly that repealed 3379. "The State Department had simply not focused on that operation," the assistant secretary of state for human rights and humanitarian affairs at the time, Richard Schifter, now recalls. Only two General Assembly committees targeted a single state, with both aiming at Israel, mounting conferences and campaigns to demonize the Jewish state. Israel was institutionally ostracized too, barred from the Asian regional group by the Arab states. Only through the regional blocs could a state function fully within the UN. The Third World still dominated. UN institutions, from UNWRA to UNESCO, repeatedly censured Israeli actions, rarely acknowledging Israel's violent neighbors or difficult dilemmas.

In December 1999, addressing the American Jewish Committee, Secretary-General Kofi Annan acknowledged the "regrettable impression of bias and one-sidedness" in the UN against Israel. In 2000 Israel joined the Western Europe and Others (WEOG) regional group temporarily, but indefinitely.

Despite the growing prosperity and hopes for peace during Israel's fiftieth anniversary year in 1998, many radical Jews internalized the harsh critiques. Our traditional Zionist images "have all been tarnished," a leading anti-Zionist Judaic Studies professor, Marc Ellis, alleged. Overstating the communal shame, Ellis claimed that Jews now responded to criticism against Israel guiltily, with "little attempt to assert or shore up a narrative of Israel as innocent and redemptive." In fact, polls in 1998 showed that 69 percent of Jews still felt "very close" or "fairly close" to Israel, with 74 percent in 1998 deeming their connection to Israel "very important" to them as Jews. Jews in the 1990s were also better organized and more effective Israel advocates than they had been during the Nixon-Ford days.

Curiously, despite the resolution's repeal, some radical Israelis also began internalizing the Zionism is racism critique, especially the outspoken group of intellectuals who distanced themselves from their country's founding ideology by calling themselves "post-Zionists." In the mid-1990s Shulamit Aloni, a left-wing politician who served as Israel's minister of education from 1992 to 1993, called the idea of Israel as a Jewish state "anti-democratic, if not racist." Zionists had debated for decades how to balance Israel's Jewish and democratic traditions, so the dilemma was not new. Using the language of race was so outrageous that the post-Zionists received disproportionate attention.

That so many of these shifts coalesced in the 1990s during the Oslo Peace Process sandwiched between two Palestinian uprisings, suggests the attitudes had more to do with Western ideological trends than particular Israeli actions regarding the Palestinians, be they positive or negative. The French philosopher Bernard-Henri Lévy observed that after Marxism collapsed, radicals lacked an organizing framework. Anti-Zionism became their organizing principle, with the Zionism is racism charge as their central reference point. In fact, in many left-wing circles, anti-Zionism took on disproportionate importance, serving as ideological glue, while raising suspicions that the anti-Semitic obsessions of yesteryear were now being updated as anti-Israel passions.

In September 2000, when Yasir Arafat led the Palestinians away from the Oslo Peace Process's negotiating table back toward terrorism, the global campaign against Israel became a potent propaganda force. Many on the Far Left targeted Israel along with the United States as the modern world's great colonialists and racists. Blinded by anti-Americanism and anti-Zionism, refusing to criticize those they deemed "oppressed," radicals now romanticized the Palestinian cause and excused Islamist extremist excesses. This phenomenon was more widespread in Europe than in the United States, where a small but vocal anti-Zionist minority clustered on certain campuses and particular intellectual ghettoes. The sincere concerns of many other onlookers for the genuine suffering the dispossessed Palestinians endured, amplified the extremists' voices. Both friends and foes had difficulty distinguishing between those most motivated by a pro-Palestinian impulse and those with an anti-Zionist animus.

The word "Zionist" had become a pejorative term to many. Arab diplomats called Israel the "Zionist entity" or "Zionist presence," still insisting they were not anti-Semitic, which was not legitimate, but anti-Zionist, which now was. At the political extremes, both the Far Left and the Far Right spit out the word "Zionist" or "Zionism" telegraphing contempt for Israel, Jews, and the American government, and serving as what the journalist Jeffrey Goldberg calls "a dog whistle," a silent signal to insiders. Chic, radical celebrities like the Academy Award–winning actress Vanessa Redgrave would say "Zionism is a brutal, racist ideology." White-Supremacist, Far Right militants would attack their own American polity as ZOG—a Zionist Occupied Government. That three-word libel launched decades ago, Zionism is racism, proved surprisingly resilient.

In the fall of 2000, Moynihan's endorsement helped the First Lady, Hillary Rodham Clinton, win his Senate seat. Moynihan retired in a "melancholic" mood. He saw the festering anti-Zionism. He worried about the culture of secrecy and the national security state that continued growing even after the fall of Communism. He mourned his prescience in predicting the decline of the American family and the broader moral crisis he captured with his trenchant phrase "Defining Deviancy Down." And he feared the proliferation of ethnic conflict in the United States and especially abroad. These were the subjects of the nine major books he had produced since leaving the UN. Moynihan's output would prompt the columnist George Will's quip that New York's senator "wrote more books than some of his colleagues read."

Especially surprising for a man hailed as the nation's greatest scholar-statesman since Professor Woodrow Wilson became President Wilson, Moynihan was very much the warrior-statesman too. He liked the image—which he provided to his beloved *New York Times* in 1966—of first taking his college entrance exams with a longshoreman's loading hook in his back pocket to show he was no "sissy kid." Even though he now sported an Irish tweed walking cap, tailored suits, the occasional bowtie, and his distinctly eccentric air for his battles, he frequently wielded words as aggressively as some longshoremen wielded their loading hooks in barroom brawls. Moynihan was tough and he wanted people to know that he meant what he said, that words mattered.

CONCLUSION
"What We're Fighting For"

In the 1990s, as politicians squabbled over allocating the "peace dividend" they hoped to extract from bloated Cold War defense budgets, Daniel Patrick Moynihan was one of those credited, along with Margaret Thatcher and Dan Quayle, with saying, "the peace dividend is peace." Moynihan worried that splintered tribal wars would proliferate after the Cold War. The horrors of September 2001 threatened his life's work, bringing his nightmare home to New York City.

Moynihan acknowledged the lure of the irrational, the conspiratorial, and the destructive, at home and abroad. When bidding New York's citizens farewell, Senator Moynihan recalled the historian Richard Hofstadter's lecture, the "Paranoid Style in American Politics," delivered at Oxford, on what turned out to be the day before John Kennedy's assassination. Moynihan warned: "the paranoid style still persists, and we have got to take care." He had titled his 1993 book on ethnicity in international politics, *Pandaemonium*, which, in John Milton's *Paradise Lost*, is the capital of hell.

Moynihan nevertheless believed leaders should use emotion, fostering a politics that was, when necessary, angry, idealistic, and redemptive. Appreciating the power of patriotic indignation in a world of relativisms, compromises, and Faustian bargains, he cultivated what Ronald Reagan called "clean hatred" for totalitarians, especially Communists, then terrorists.

Even as a senator, Moynihan was more interested in shaping the national conversation than building his power base. And his activist credo as warrior diplomat and scholarly statesman built on the insight he scribbled in his notes: "if you define world as rich and poor—we are guilty; if you define world as liberal and illiberal *they* are guilty."

Moynihan feared that "they" were menacing liberalism yet again as hopes from the 1991 repeal evaporated from the rage preceding the United Nations World Conference against Racism, Racial Discrimination, Xenophobia, and Related Intolerance, held in Durban, South Africa, from August 31 through September 7, 2001. "Any equation of Zionism with racism would be catastrophic," warned former Canadian UN ambassador David Malone, the president of the International Peace Academy think tank in New York. "No single measure adopted by the UN... has done the institution more damage than Zionism is racism."

Against the backdrop of renewed Palestinian terror that triggered Israeli army crackdowns, the conference showcased the Red-Green alliance's global reach and anti-Zionist obsession. The main UN conference asserted "green" Islamist power, with the Arab states bullying others to denounce "the racist practices of Zionism" and Israel's treatment of Palestinians as "a new kind of apartheid." Although the official Durban Declaration ignored Zionism while condemning both anti-Semitism and Islamophobia, the anti-Zionist rhetoric in the hall—backed by anti-Semitic hooliganism on the street—popularized the Zionism is racism charge. The parallel NGO forum celebrated "red" values, with leftist human rights organizations condemning racism, colonialism, and imperialism—selectively, especially in the West, most especially in Israel.

Durban essentially repealed the repeal. The final NGO declaration launched the forum's "Durban Strategy," which endorsed reinstating Resolution 3379, accused the "Israeli racist system" of "acts of genocide," and demanded boycotting "Israel as an apartheid state." The Palestinian legislator and academic Hanan Ashrawi stirred these Third World leftist passions. Casting the conflict as the virtuous victim versus the violent victimizer, Ashrawi avowed: "in the struggle against oppression, injustice, racism, intolerance, colonialism, and exclusion, there can be *no* neutrality."

Treating Zionism as the world's worst form of racism created what Congressman Tom Lantos called "an anti-American, anti-Israeli circus," often expressed in anti-Semitic terms. A Hungarian Holocaust refugee who became Congress's human rights conscience, Lantos experienced "the most

258 • MOYNIHAN'S MOMENT

sickening and unabashed display of hate for Jews I have seen since the Nazi period." Some Durban delegates distributed a booklet caricaturing Jews with hook noses and fangs dripping blood. Seventeen thousand anti-Zionist protesters rallied, with some waving a banner reading "HITLER WAS RIGHT!" Other posters wished Hitler had "finished the job."

The racism accusation and lynch-mob atmosphere encouraged the more perverse inversion, comparing Israelis to Nazis. There were no similarities in ideology, intention, tone, or, violence, in terms of treatment of civilians and combatants, severity of occupation, numbers in jail, or body count. But if all racists were alike, there was no difference between a Nazi SS mass murderer, a South African secret policeman, an American redneck, and an Israeli settler. The British MP Denis MacShane would call this increasingly trendy Nazi-Israeli comparison "a grotesque, anti-Jewish and therefore anti-Semitic act."

President George W. Bush rejected this overt racism at an anti-racism conference. Colin Powell, the first African American secretary of state, wanted to attend the conference to celebrate South Africa's purging its racist past. Yet Powell, with Bush's backing, boycotted the event, sending a mid-level representative instead. Eventually, the American and Israeli delegates walked out in disgust.

"Oh, no," Moynihan, now retired, said, when he heard about the Arab resolutions. "Not again." He added: "To say that the Jews, who have been subject to the most hideous racial oppression of this century, are racist, well, then you're in an Orwellian world and you better snap out of it." In the summer, Moynihan warned the conference would be "a disaster," grumbling: "As usual, the State Department is very slow."

As American liberals such as David Greenberg in *Slate* unhappily noted a new generation now "Lyin' about Zion" by calling Zionism racism, many quoted Moynihan's words from 1975. New York's new senator, Hillary Rodham Clinton, echoed Moynihan, saying Resolution 3379 "was criminal then, and it's still criminal today." Just as Zionism is racism provided the central ideological cover to the new attack on Israel, Moynihan's words provided essential weapons for defense.

The totalitarian anti-Zionism Moynihan had long opposed, subordinating all other goals to the anti-Israel impulse, again upended a UN conference, as "Durban became the tipping point for the coalescence of a new, virulent, globalizing anti-Jewishness," according to the Canadian parliamentarian and human rights activist Irwin Cotler. The rhetoric at Durban, and the conference's coincidental juxtaposition with the September 11 terrorist attacks days later, further linked anti-Zionism with anti-Americanism, "laundered" through opposition to racism, as Cotler noted.

Driving the new anti-Semitism, Zionism is racism updated many traditional anti-Semitic memes, meaning "something imitated," an idea or impression popularized through repetition. Christian Europe traditionally viewed Jews as the ultimate villains; now Zionism is racism cast Israel, the collective Jew, as today's ultimate villain. Christian theology warned that Jews, the people of Israel, were particularly punitive and vengeful in the image of the Old Testament God; Zionism is racism helped caricature the State of Israel as particularly punitive and vengeful in its actions, even when defending itself. The Roman Catholic Church traditionally labeled Jews as "Christ killers"; Zionism is racism cast Israel, the collective Jew, as colonialists slaying innocent Palestinians. Medieval Europeans feared the Jews, despite their weakness, treating the perpetual victim as potential victimizer; Zionism is racism made Israel, the collective Jew, the greatest racist today rather than the greatest victim of Hitlerian racial mass murder. Anti-Semites traditionally used the Jewish concept of "chosenness" to accuse Jews of being clannish and arrogant; Zionism is racism claimed Israel, the collective Jew, used the Holocaust's unique horror to justify being tribal and superior. Jews living in a Christian world traditionally stood out, with their foreignness justifying European Christians' obsessions with them; Zionism is racism in an anti-racist world singled out Israel, the collective Jew, for obsessive scrutiny. And just as yesterday's anti-Semitism was a rallying point, uniting against the common Jewish enemy, Zionism is racism cast enmity against Israel, the collective Jew, and against Zionism, Jewish nationalism, as a rallying point, uniting Islamic fundamentalists and cosmopolitan liberals, while offering unity to an often divided Europe and fragmented Left. "Today Jew-haters try to avoid using the term 'Jew' or 'Jewish' and instead reach for the word 'Zionist' or 'Zionism,'" Denis MacShane explained.

Thrown into the Middle East pyre, the Zionism-racism charge has been an accelerant, angering, alienating, polarizing both sides. The accusation integrated every tension into a monolithic narrative of racism and delegitimization, which the intensifying Israeli-Palestinian violence exacerbated. By viewing Zionism as racism, many Palestinians saw Israelis harshly as cruel brutes. The severe denunciations, the low expectations, alienated many

Israelis from the Palestinians and from their traditional concern with maintaining a reputation for ethical conduct. Just as a sense of honor can help society stretch and reform, accusations of dishonor can alienate adversaries while blocking impulses to trust, transcend, or transform.

What the British attorney and author Anthony Julius calls yesterday's "earned anti-Semitism"—those Jews deserve it!—became today's "earned" anti-Zionism—see what Israel did! Yet the Left's anti-racist anti-Semites proclaimed their innocence. Such protestations, denying the overlap with traditional anti-Semitic apparitions, were the rhetorical equivalent of the surgeon general's warning against smoking printed on cigarette packs. The posture failed to make the act less toxic.

By maligning the Jewish state's essential character and making the conflict zero-sum, the Zionism is racism charge helped anti-Israeli sentiment degenerate into Jew hatred masked by high-minded human rights rhetoric. It also upstaged the valid criticisms that the complex Israeli-Palestinian conflict required. The leftist Nobel Prize–winning novelist Jose Saramago of Portugal called Israel "a racist state by virtue of Judaism's monstrous doctrines—racist not just against the Palestinians, but against the entire world, which it seeks to manipulate and abuse." Few European leftists dissented. Signs saying "ZIONISM = RACISM" and "JEWS = NAZIS" proliferated at anti-Israel protests after Durban, even appearing on liberal, cosmopolitan US campuses, such as San Francisco State University.

After the al-Qaeda terrorist attacks of September 11, 2001, and the worldwide protests against America's invasion of Iraq in March 2003, the Zionism is racism charge further enmeshed the United States with Israel, "Big Satan" with "Little Satan." This perpetually hostile feedback loop had hatred for one feeding hatred for the other. Exploiting Israel's unpopularity to justify his mass murders in his first post-9/11 message, Osama Bin Laden suddenly emphasized Palestinian concerns, trying to visit "the wrath of God upon the United States and Israel." Before the Iraq War, "peace marchers" ignored Saddam Hussein's crimes while demonizing America's President George W. Bush and Israel's Prime Minister Ariel Sharon. Signs charging "HITLER HAD TWO SONS: BUSH AND SHARON," treated anti-Americanism and anti-Zionism as ideological twins. This hatred was more bitter fruit from the lies nurtured in the 1970s that Moynihan combated but could not kill.

Both anti-Semitism and "Yankee-phobia" had venerable European pedigrees. America had long functioned as European political thinkers'

Schreckbild, their image of horror. Soviets linked distaste for Americanism and Zionism under the rubrics "imperialism," then "racism." Among Western radicals, prejudice against Israel and the United States seemed to be the last legitimate bigotry, one of the few hatreds acceptable in polite circles.

Anti-Americanism and anti-Zionism have proven particularly resilient. Attacking each country's character transcended anger at specific, changeable policies. The French philosopher Jean-François Revel noted that the same critics attacked the United States as "imperialist" when it intervened internationally, but "isolationist" when it didn't. Such "wonderful illogicality" revealed "obsession."

Sensitive as he was to Soviet propagandists' role in anti-Zionism and anti-Americanism, Moynihan abhorred such absolutism, sacrificing facts, consistency, and integrity, to serve the authoritarian agenda. Nearly three-and-a-half decades after Moynihan's UN tenure, the British leftist Nick Cohen, for one, wondered: "Why is it that apologies for a militant Islam which stands for everything the liberal-left is against, come from the liberal-left?....Why is Palestine a cause for the liberal-left, but not China, Sudan, Zimbabwe, the Congo or North Korea?" Moynihan attributed such consistent inconsistency to totalitarian capriciousness. Many American radicals also treated racism as an ideological genetic marker linking Israel with the United States. Malik Z. Shabazz of the New Black Panthers Party, frequently hosted on television and campus, appeared at the National Press Club shortly after 9/11 to label America and Israel the world's "No. 1 and No. 2 terrorists." He proclaimed: "Zionism is racism. Zionism is terrorism. Zionism is colonialism. Zionism is imperialism, and support for Zionism is the root of why so many were killed on September 11." After he became widely reviled for calling those murdered in the World Trade Center on 9/11 "Little Eichmanns," and the University of Colorado–Boulder fired him for research misconduct, Ward Churchill traveled to campuses lecturing about "Zionism, Manifest Destiny, and Nazi Lebensraumpolitik," linking Zionism and Americanism with Nazism. The Reverend Jeremiah Wright, the charismatic preacher of Trinity United Church of Christ, an African American megachurch in Chicago, attacked Zionist racism and "ethnic cleansing," while complaining about the "all-controlling Jewish vote" which he spelled "A-I-P-A-C."

Most of these blatant expressions of anti-Semitism remained on the fringe and garnered outraged headlines when exposed. In 2008, public fury forced

Barack Obama to repudiate Rev. Wright, his former mentor and pastor. In 2011, eleven Muslim activists were prosecuted for disrupting Israeli ambassador Michael Oren when he spoke at UC Irvine.

Still, it became common on many campuses to call Zionists "racists" and to demonize Israel disproportionately, using human rights rhetoric. The cumulative effect on Israel's "reputation" was "devastating," the British political pundit Robin Shepherd concluded: "consider the words and images with which Israel has in recent years been associated: 'shitty,' 'Nazi,' 'racist,' 'apartheid,' 'ethnic cleanser,' 'occupier,' 'war criminal,' 'violator of international law,' 'user of disproportionate force,' 'liability'.... No other state in the world is talked about in such terms." Moynihan had predicted after Resolution 3379, that increasingly, "Whether Israel was responsible," for particular world problems, "Israel surely would be blamed: openly by some, privately by most. Israel would be *regretted*."

Of all the libels, the Israel-as-South-Africa analogy increasingly was mainstreamed. The apartheid rhetoric was subtler, allowing many to camouflage harsher demonizing sentiments behind sincere objections to Israel's occupation. The apartness dictated by security needs in the West Bank, Israeli settler ideology, and Palestinians' own desires, could easily blur in the public mind to link with apartheid, despite the term's historic connotation of color-based separation. Decades of propagandizing claiming Zionism was racism reduced the great leap required to transform the Israeli-Palestinian national conflict over territory into a racial struggle, even though Israel lacked any formal infrastructure, language, or ideology of racial characterization.

In 2005 radical University of Toronto students launched Israeli Apartheid Week, which soon became the annual focus for anti-Israel activities in dozens of campuses and cities. In 2006 Jimmy Carter made his latest Middle East policy tract a best seller by titling it: *Palestine: Peace Not Apartheid*. Carter mentions the term "apartheid" only four times in the course of the book, using it as a synonym for "apartness" rather than what it meant—a legislated racial classification system. Still, the words "Israel" and "apartheid" increasingly became intertwined, just as since 1975 the word "Zionism" often evoked "racism."

Given the prophetic and Talmudic traditions of Jewish self-criticism, sprinkled sometimes with dashes of self-loathing as a shortcut to achieving popularity among non-Jewish critics of Jews, leftist Jewish critics of Israel increasingly embraced the "racism" and "apartheid" rhetoric. In his 2012 book, *The Crisis of Zionism*, Peter Beinart—the enfant terrible of American Zionism—used the two terms repeatedly and loosely. Perpetuating the nearly four-decades-old fashion, he viewed the mutually fraught relations between two competing national groups, Arabs and Jews, through the distorting lens of "anti-Arab racism." And invoking his South African roots to sharpen the moral condemnation, he equated "occupation" with "apartheid," despite being unable to find in Israel any of the formal racial distinctions that defined South African apartheid.

As Zionism-racism inflamed Israel's enemies, it also broadened the circle of Israel's defenders. Following 9/11, the Palestinian assault on Israel was so extreme, and so bloody, some leftists who abhorred Israel's occupation nevertheless defended the Jewish state's right to exist. The academics rationalizing Palestinian suicide bombings confirmed the liberal French philosopher Raymond Aron's 1955 warning that ideologues can tolerate "the worst crimes as long as they are committed in the name of the proper doctrines." "Even the oppressed have obligations, and surely the first among these is not to murder innocent people," Michael Walzer argued. Continuing his decades-long fight against Palestinian terrorism and leftist fellow-traveling, Walzer sought "a decent (intelligent, responsible, morally nuanced) politics," including a "Decent Left."

"What is the nerve that Israel hits?" Ellen Willis of the *Village Voice* wondered in an article published in 2007. Without justifying Israeli settlements or Israel's counterterrorism, yet dismayed by the "one-sided view of the conflict," and the "intense and consistent outrage" only Israel attracted, Willis concluded that "left animus toward Israel is not a simple, self-evident product of the facts." "It would be foolish to suggest that all criticism of Israel is motivated by anti-Semitism," said Steven Lubet, a law professor, as Palestinian terrorism, Israeli crackdowns, campus protests, and anti-Semitic rhetoric peaked in 2002, "but it would be irresponsible to believe that none of it is."

The sociologist Todd Gitlin, a leading 1960s activist, mourned this return of "wicked anti-Semitism," as many anti-Zionists started complaining about "the Jews." Such self-righteous stereotyping represents the "recrudescence of everything that costs the Left its moral edge," Gitlin fumed. A major factor motivating the Left was indeed the Big Red Lie that Zionism is racism.

In June 2002 Harvard awarded Moynihan an honorary doctorate of laws and the opportunity to deliver the commencement address. This would be one of his final public appearances. Harvard praised him as "A quintessential scholar-statesman whose capacious learning and independence of mind have shaped our national conversation; to complex questions of consequence his answers are never pat"—pun intended.

Harvard's honor was gracious, nostalgic, and suitably self-reverential, with Moynihan having become one of America's senior statesman and one of Harvard's most famous affiliates. Now, decades after "the Moynihan Report" and the stain of "benign neglect," the 2002 Harvard undergraduate English orator, Zayed Yasin, not Moynihan, proved controversial. Yasin, a Bangladeshi-Irish-American who once headed the Harvard Islamic Society, spoke "Of Faith and Citizenship: My American Jihad." After intense protests, he modified the title using only the first phrase, but he did not change the speech. Acknowledging the tensions between his American national identity and his Muslim religious faith, Yasin defined "Jihad" in personal terms as an ongoing struggle for virtue, not holy war. His framing played to Harvard's "the best and the brightest" crowd as a call for excellence and goodness, and he received a standing ovation.

In a fitting metaphor for his never-quite-perfect fit with the place, a thunderstorm washed out much of the audience for Moynihan's speech, which was delivered after lunch. He spoke from under a huge white canopy drooping from the downpour to an estimated three hundred drenched, chilled, devoted souls rather than the usual twenty thousand happy graduates and their families.

The former senator's speech was suitably sobering—culminating an academic year that began with the September 11, 2001, terrorist attacks. He endorsed his colleague Samuel Huntington's view that a clash of civilizations menaced the modern world. Moynihan warned that these terrorist attacks "were not nuclear, but they will be." And, anticipating the Democratic backlash against George W. Bush, he continued warning against a too-powerful state, saying, "there is police work to be done. But so many forms of secrecy are self-defeating."

The Jihad brouhaha nicely anticipated Moynihan's speech, which noted that Americans now boasted "sixty-eight separate ancestries." Since the 1960s Moynihan had been deviating from the modernists who assumed the world would evolve beyond ethnic, racial, religious and other tribal divisions; now, sadly, he was vindicated yet again. While welcoming everyone who wanted to build the New World, Moynihan feared those who imported "the clashes they left behind." Indicative of this "ominous trend" was the pro-Palestinian march that spring in Washington, filled with signs proclaiming "Zionism equals Racism" and placards "with a swastika alongside a Star of David." Seeing "this hateful equation" in America's capital chilled Moynihan, this "murderous attack on the right of the State of Israel to exist—the right of Jews to exist!" Despite all his efforts and the efforts of so many others, he still lived in "a world in which a hateful Soviet lie has mutated into a new and vicious anti-Semitism."

Moynihan looked his seventy-five years, his tall frame beginning to sag, his mouth sunken with age, his hair white. But the hair still flew wildly, with the eyebrows as thick as ever, his smile still welcoming, and his eyes—behind owlishly large glasses—still inviting any potential audience to come enjoy his wit. He was still fighting totalitarianism with the well-crafted quip and the well-chosen quote. He now articulated a fallback position: "Democracy may not prove to be a universal norm," he acknowledged. "But decency would do." Violations of that, he still could not abide and would never acquiesce to.

In that same spirit, Moynihan had signed "A Letter from America" in February 2002 with fifty-nine other leading thinkers, ranging from Left to Right, explaining "What We're Fighting For." The University of Chicago philosopher Jean Bethke Elshtain admitted that the authors wanted to confront the widespread academic assumption "that the American use of force always represents an imperial or nefarious purpose."

The lengthy humanistic missive affirmed four core "American values," beginning with the "founding ideals" that "universal moral truths" exist, including the "conviction that all persons possess innate human dignity." Because human "access to truth is imperfect," discourse should be civil and open, with everyone enjoying "freedom of conscience and freedom of religion."

Moynihan hoped these four freedom-oriented principles—echoing FDR's speech that helped inspire the UN's founding—would trump the three words about Zionism that proved so potent over the decades, along with the broader totalitarian evils America still fought. The manifesto trusted in "reason and careful moral reflection," as Moynihan did, affirming "that there are times when the first and most important reply to evil is to stop it." Moynihan never doubted such assertive moral leadership reflected his liberal ideals and America's democratic sensibilities.

The Moynihan model of warrior leadership and crusading foreign policy idealism remained popular following the Reagan years, as many Americans continued seeking Reagan's clarity and conviction. George H. W. Bush lacked Reagan's intuitive feel for popular sensibilities, though. Bush effectively balanced realism and idealism in managing the ultimate collapse of the Soviet Union and the first Gulf War against Saddam Hussein, but when the economy flagged he seemed out of touch.

In the 1992 election, Bill Clinton outflanked Bush emotionally, indignantly defending middle-class Americans and telegraphing a toughness from his "war room" that many Americans sought in their leaders. As president, Clinton appreciated the power of indignation—even when caught sinning. He survived the Monica Lewinsky adultery scandal with more rage than shame, blasting the Republican witch-hunters and the media. Unfortunately, Clinton dithered amid two great moral challenges overseas. When Bosnian Serbs slaughtered Bosnian Muslims, and when Hutus mass-murdered Tutsis in Rwanda, he demonstrated what the *Atlantic*'s Robert D. Kaplan called the "fatalism of the appeasers." Clinton's prolonged passivity irritated Moynihan, who took a dangerous trip to the former Yugoslavia in late autumn 1992 but was never invited to brief the new president personally.

George W. Bush drifted along as president until the mass murders of September 11, 2001. Bush then flashed an anguished, vengeful "Bring it on" rage, a fighter's fury, different from Moynihan's or Reagan's. Still, this rage powered his presidency, while inducing a powerful backlash. Proud neoconservatives, seeking the moral purity Moynihan found in the Resolution 3379 fight, ignored Moynihan's many subsequent warnings during the Reagan administration against overconfidence abroad and an overzealous national security state at home. They overstepped—and were blamed for Bush's extremism and incompetence.

Like Moynihan, Barack Obama was an eloquent professorial type who used wordsmithing and celebrity to fast-track up the political food chain. Obama's 2004 Democratic National Convention debut speech denounced those pundits who slice and dice America into polarized "red" and "blue" sectors. As president, Obama ended up tagged by harsher labels. The conservative radio host Rush Limbaugh and other right-wingers called Obama a socialist, a Muslim, a traitor—making some Democrats yearn for the time when they were only defined by the nontoxic color "blue."

In 2008 Obama emerged as the hipster healer, countering the anger and the chaos. This posture reassured Americans after the Bush tumult and as the economy crashed. With his natural reserve reinforced by the calculation to avoid any racial stereotypes of the angry black man, Obama deployed bursts of Reaganesque lyrical, patriotic, "Yes We Can" idealism, rather than the occasional squall.

With Obama's retreat into a "Mr. Spock" persona during a devastating recession, the balance of anger after 2008 shifted back toward the Republicans. During the 2010 congressional campaign, the Tea Party activists became raging Republicans, declaring cultural, economic, political, and ideological war against the president. Obama was not temperamentally suited to a politics of indignation or demagoguery. Even when a terrorist struck Fort Hood or when Obama confronted Wall Street tycoons, he seemed restrained. By contrast, many Republicans, forgetting their cries for reason, civility, respect for the presidency during the Bush years, indulged their anger. The "Boiling Mad" Tea Party activists exceeded Moynihan's politics of indignation, which targeted foreigners, but only landing indirect blows against domestic adversarials.

Obama's foreign policy blurred the seemingly rigid categories of Moynihan-Reagan idealism versus Nixon-Kissinger realism. George W. Bush's Iraq overreach soured many Americans on any kind of Woodrow Wilson–John Kennedy interventionist democratic crusading. Obama surprised conservatives by appearing tough and realist in hunting down terrorists and helping to depose Libya's Muammar Gaddafi. But Obama eschewed Moynihan's moral clarity and unapologetic Americanism. Obama frequently expressed his idealism in ways that critics compared to Jimmy Carter, demonstrating an accommodating, apologetic streak toward some American adversaries that infuriated Reaganite Republicans and already-demoralized neoconservatives.

In fall 2011 "Occupy Wall Street" (OWS) forces rallied in cities across the United States. The protesters' slogan, claiming to represent the "other 99 percent," brilliantly captured the us-versus-them populism that frequently surged during economic crises. But the OWS demands were too vague, the "flat" leadership too chaotic and anonymous, to match Moynihan's or Reagan's focused indignation. The 2012 presidential campaign revealed an unfortunate, unhealthy disconnect between Americans' genuine, justified, anger and the cautious, bloodless, major party nominees who emerged.

Moynihan died in March 2003 with the Zionism is racism resolution repealed but the libel still living and the new Islamist totalitarian threat still raging. Many who fought the proposition—to ensure that Zionism never became racism, to repudiate anti-Semitism, to argue that Israel, while not perfect, deserved a fair hearing, and to defend America as well as democracy on this hostile planet—continued relying on his words. And the leadership lesson Professor Moynihan mastered in 1975 and taught by example, particularly to Reagan, still held.

Politics has an emotional dimension that can be harnessed constructively. In 1970 Moynihan advised Richard Nixon that "the pragmatic mind in politics tends to underestimate, even to be unaware of, the importance of moral authority. In a nation such as ours... moral authority is a form of political power." The resulting struggle for moral authority "can assume surpassingly complex and involute forms, but it is at bottom pretty much an affair of tooth and claw. Those who ignore it do so at their own peril."

Five years later, shortly after the Zionism is racism vote, a Cornell University historian, Gerd Korman, wrote a letter to Ambassador Moynihan congratulating him on his "unique ability to register moral outrage when events require it. No one speaks with your voice. Upon hearing it I suddenly realized what I had never heard in public life." Amid thousands of fan letters, Korman's accurately summed up one of Moynihan's signal contributions. Many Americans shared that same "eureka" sensation Korman articulated when they watched Moynihan in action, delighted to rediscover the proud, powerful, authentically American voice that had been temporarily muffled by the strains of the 1960s and 1970s. That is why they "attaboyed" Moynihan on the streets of New York. That is why they bombarded the US mission with letters from across the nation proclaiming "bravo." That is why they resoundingly approved his actions in public opinion polls. Just as Bill Gates, Steve Jobs, and other techies were incubating the 1980s revival in the 1970s, Moynihan in 1975 helped invent the 1980s patriotic revival.

Moynihan's politics of patriotic indignation achieved political power by asserting moral authority. It worked for him: he became a four-term senator. It worked for Ronald Reagan: he became a two-term president. And it worked for the American people as so many celebrated "Morning in America" in the 1980s.

Moynihan's was the rage of the zealot, appalled at the desecration of liberal ideals in his temples, be they the United Nations, the academy, or the world itself. But he never let the rage consume him or destroy his optimism. He tempered that sacred rage with a positive life force that combined the lilt of his idealized ancestral home in Ireland with the grit of New York City, helping him persevere through the racial controversies and other setbacks that would have ended most people's careers.

Even though his biography was a little more complicated than the Hell's-Kitchen-to-Harvard tale he—and others—liked spinning, Moynihan always remembered his humble origins and took pride in rising from shoeshine boy to statesman. His greatest traits, especially his wit and his iconoclasm, were the sparks generated by his internal clashes, between feeling at home and feeling estranged, infuriated by the world yet delighting in it.

In 1976, shortly before leaving the UN, Moynihan told Thomas Gleason, the president of the International Longshoreman's Association, "My journey from the North River"—insider's lingo for the Hudson—"to the East River took many turns. But I carried with me the idea that a man ought to stand for something and beyond that an idea of what some of those things ought to be and what can be done about them." Weeks earlier, during one of his long telegrams to Kissinger, Moynihan summed up his mission—and his accomplishment—saying: "AN ISSUE OF HONOR, OF MORALITY, WAS PUT BEFORE US, AND NOT ALL OF US RAN."

Twenty-seven years later, Moynihan ended his Harvard commencement address by saying, "History summons us once more in different ways, but with even greater urgency. Civilization need not die. At this moment, only the United States can save it. As we fight the war against evil, we must also wage peace, guided by the lesson of the Marshall Plan—vision and generosity can help make the world a safer place." On the evening of November 10, 1975, Moynihan had made his moment, reminding Americans that only the United States could save civilization by defying evil. Yet, despite his anger, with all the anxiety, amid the infighting, Moynihan remained affirmative, visionary, generous, resisting despair. In 2002 as in 1975, Moynihan still knew what he was fighting against, and never allowed that to obscure what he—and we—should be fighting for as well, making Moynihan's moment resonant, resplendent, and remarkably relevant today.

ACKNOWLEDGMENTS

I met Daniel Patrick Moynihan once—and corresponded with him one other time. During his 1976 run for Senate, I volunteered to canvass my neighborhood for him and ended up shaking hands with the great—and very tall—man, at the Queens Democratic headquarters on Main Street. To my chagrin, the Queens political hacks gave me Jimmy Carter leaflets to distribute, thereby teaching me what Moynihan would have considered an important lesson about the limits to freedom in democratic politics, at least for lowly teenage volunteers.

Twelve years later, while writing my doctoral dissertation at Harvard, I sent Senator Moynihan a letter correcting a statement he made about the history of campaigning while campaigning for re-election in Syracuse. To my surprise, Moynihan responded personally, acknowledging his error, and recalling Franklin Roosevelt's embarrassment in 1936 about having promised to balance the budget in his famous Pittsburgh speech four years earlier. Roosevelt's speechwriter advised: "Deny you ever were in Pittsburgh." I will now follow that advice, Moynihan wrote graciously, and deny ever having been in Syracuse.

As a student of political history, I have long been fascinated with Moynihan the scholar-politician, the activist intellectual, the Thomas Jefferson of the late twentieth century. But having built my academic career studying the presidency, I did not expect to write a monograph about Moynihan. Yet, after his death in 2003, as I saw the slogan he had fought so hard to defeat—claiming Zionism is racism—spread around the world with renewed virulence, I started thinking about Moynihan and his moment.

In 2009 I had my modest eureka breakthrough. I noticed that Saigon fell in April 1975—just months before Moynihan denounced Resolution 3379 as America's ambassador to the UN. Suddenly, I understood the long-overlooked significance of Moynihan's fight through my perspective as an American historian. In confronting the Soviet–Third World coalition in the UN in 1975, Moynihan was being countercultural—fighting the defeatism that gripped America in the 1970s. Having written two books on the Reagan Revolution and working on a third, I also understood that Moynihan's mode of patriotic indignation anticipated Reagan's assertive and affirmative Americanism, which proved so popular. Watching America in its post–George W. Bush doldrums, struggling with a devastating downturn, hearing many voices in the world again pillorying the United States and Israel, I decided that we could use a dose of Moynihanism; I wanted to explore the impact of his stand in the UN in November, 1975, on American politics, democracy, human rights, the Cold War, the UN itself, the continuing conflict around Israel's existence, and the enduring friendship between the US and Israel.

Like most authors who stumble upon an idea, I assumed it was such a great topic others must have done it before. That summer I interviewed Suzanne and Leonard Garment, both of whom worked so closely with Moynihan at the UN. I asked them if they knew of any authors working on the topic. Their "no" made me feel relieved and encouraged; their enthusiastic support for this project has been a great inspiration ever since.

I am grateful to all those listed under the Oral Histories who made the time to meet with me and educate me about Moynihan and the 1975 Zionism is Racism resolution. They were all great talkers—and teachers. Each in his or her own way helped bring alive that extraordinary phenomenon who was Pat Moynihan. But I would be remiss if I did not single out Senator Moynihan's widow, Elizabeth Moynihan, Liz, for her candor, her insight, her encouragement, and her generosity. She was particularly gracious in greeting me and my escort that day—my nine-year-old son—and I thank her for that and many other kindnesses.

In addition to the Oral History subjects, I am deeply grateful, in the research phrase, to a strike force of extraordinary research assistants, who have assisted me again and again. Zachary Honoroff and Theodoric Meyer got the project rolling, with very thorough, creative research, and were then followed by Sébastien Alexander, Zachary Javitt, Gabriel Mitchell, Emma Quail, Shoshanna Silberman, and Gadi Weber, each of whom brought so much to this project. I also thank Oren Abelman for help in the Israeli

Foreign Ministry Archives; Ayelet Rose Brinn who covered the Betty Friedan and Tip O'Neill archives; Rachel Goldstein, who hit the Gerald Ford Library; Michal Loving, who explored the American Jewish Archives; Harris Shain for his roundup of 1970s popular culture; Byron Tau, who helped me with the voluminous Moynihan papers at the Library of Congress; and Aaron Wenner, who did a great job answering one specific, offbeat research question after another.

I also thank the following for various kindnesses in research, in sharing insights or introducing me to potential interview subjects or lines of inquiry: Tamar Abraham, Yosef Abramowitz, Julian Adams, Danna Azrieli, Sandy Cardin, Steven M. Cohen, Irwin Cotler, L. M. Figura, Rachel Fish, Vera Golovensky, Steve Greenberg, David Hartman, Stephen Hess, Isaac Herzog, Howard Liebman, Brice Long, Gidi Mark, Michael Miller, Cokie Roberts, Jonathan Sarna, Bruce Schulman, Michael Siegel, Saul Singer, Keith Urbahn, Sarah M. Walton, and Morton Weinfeld. I remain grateful to the many archivists at the institutions listed above who helped—they remain the unsung heroes of the history world—with particular gratitude to Veena Manchanda of the United Nations Photo Library, Nancy Mirshah of the Gerald R. Ford Library, Michael Pinckney of the Ronald Reagan Library, Ellen M. Shea of the Schlesinger Library, Radcliffe Institute, at Harvard University, and Leah Goldberg and her special team at the Chaim Herzog Institute.

In February 2010 my friend and teacher Donniel Hartman of the Shalom Hartman Institute invited me to join a team he was assembling at his extraordinary think tank. His invitation to this Engaging Israel Research Team launched me on a tremendously exciting intellectual journey and bonded me to a family of scholarly brothers and sisters who have contributed greatly to this project and to my intellectual development. I thank the extended Hartman family and broader EI team but am particularly grateful to the core group, consisting of Tal Becker, Donniel Hartman, Yossi Klein Halevi, Rachel Sabath Beit-Halachmi, and Noam Zion—each of whom read all or part of the manuscript and provided invaluable comments. Noam Zion's encyclopedic knowledge, deep insights, and tremendous intellectual energy, encouraged me, broadened the project and saved me from countless errors. Yossi Klein Halevi has embraced me as a friend and has mentored me on this project in numerous ways, including sharing insights from his monumental forthcoming work *Like Dreamers: The Israeli Paratroopers Who Reunited Jerusalem and Divided a Nation,* which explained the way Resolution 3379 encouraged the settlement movement. I also thank Alan Abbey, Ronit Dukofsky, Laura Gilinski, Sharon Laufer, and Yonatan Zlotogorski for various kindnesses.

I very much appreciated the two anonymous reviewers for Oxford University Press who read the proposal carefully and critically. I particularly thank one of them who outed himself, Professor James Patterson, who then provided detailed and thoughtful feedback on various chapters of the first draft. Jim's generosity with his time and great skill in critiquing represents a scholarly camaraderie and classiness we see all too rarely these days.

In a more familiar but no less appreciated act of friendship, my good friend the novelist and journalist Ray Beauchemain also read the manuscript and provided helpful comments, as did my two brothers Tevi Troy and Daniel Troy, who continue to stretch me and support me in so many ways. McGill University continues to be a most welcoming academic home. I owe particular thanks to Principal and Vice-Chancellor Heather Munroe-Blum, Dean of Arts Christopher Manfredi, Chair of the History Department Professor John Zucchi, along with the friendly and efficient departmental support staff and colleagues.

Warm thanks to my agent, Brettne Bloom of Kneerim and Williams who helped find this book such a congenial home at Oxford University Press, where I have been blessed with a superb editor, Timothy Bent. Tim is an old-fashioned editor in the best way: someone who loves books, loves the written word, and takes time to edit carefully, thoroughly, creatively. I also thank the first-class team at OUP including production editor Joellyn Ausanka and my copy editor, Mary Sutherland.

Finally, as I take full responsibility for all the book's mistakes and short-comings, I am pleased, once again, to thank my family—I am lucky to have friends who are like family—and family who are like friends, most especially my parents, my father-in-law, my wife, and my four children, all of whom hope to see me liberated from this Moynihan obsession and find peace, beauty, and perpetual sunshine as I spring back from the 1970s to the twenty-first century.

APPENDIX

RESOLUTION 3379

3379 (XXX). Elimination of all forms of racial discrimination.

The General Assembly,

Recalling its resolution 1904 (XVIII) of November 20, 1963, proclaiming the United Nations Declaration on the Elimination of All Forms of Racial Discrimination, and in particular its affirmation that "any doctrine of racial differentiation or superiority is scientifically false, morally condemnable, socially unjust and dangerous" and its expression of alarm at "the manifestations of racial discrimination still in evidence in some areas in the world, some of which are imposed by certain Governments by means of legislative, administrative or other measures,"

Recalling also that, in its resolution 3151 G (XXVIII) of December 14, 1973, the General Assembly condemned, *inter alia*, the unholy alliance between South African racism and zionism,

Taking note of the Declaration of Mexico on the Equality of Women and Their Contribution to Development and Peace 1975, proclaimed by the World Conference of the International Women's Year, held at Mexico City from June 19 to July 2, 1975, which promulgated the principle that "international co-operation and peace require the achievement of national liberation and independence, the elimination of colonialism and neo-colonialism, foreign occupation, zionism, *apartheid* and racial discrimination in all its forms, as well as the recognition of the dignity of peoples and their right to self-determination,"

Taking note also of resolution 77 (XII) adopted by the Assembly of Heads of State and Government of the Organization of African Unity at its twelfth ordinary session, held at Kampala from July 28 to August 1, 1975, which considered "that the racist regime in occupied Palestine and the racist regime in Zimbabwe and South Africa have a common imperialist origin, forming a whole and having the same racist structure and being organically linked in their policy aimed at repression of the dignity and integrity of the human being,"

Taking note also of the Political Declaration and Strategy to Strengthen International Peace and Security and to Intensify Solidarity and Mutual Assistance among Non-Aligned Countries, adopted at the Conference of Ministers for Foreign Affairs of Non-Aligned Countries held at Lima from 25 to August 30, 1975, which most severely condemned zionism as a threat to world peace and security and called upon all countries to oppose this racist and imperialist ideology,

Determines that Zionism is a form of racism and racial discrimination.

UNGA Resolution 3379 Voting Record (November 10, 1975)

Sponsored by: (25) Afghanistan, Algeria, Bahrain, Cuba, Dahomey, Egypt, Guinea, Iraq, Jordan, Kuwait, Lebanon, Libyan Arab Republic, Mauritania, Morocco, North Yemen, Oman, Qatar, Saudi Arabia, Somalia, South Yemen, Sudan, Syrian Arab Republic, Tunisia, and United Arab Emirates.

Voted yes: (72) The 25 sponsoring nations above, and additionally 47 nations: Albania, Bangladesh, Brazil, Bulgaria, Burundi, Byelorussian Soviet Socialist Republic, Cambodia (formally known as Democratic Kampuchea), Cameroon, Cape Verde, Chad, People's Republic of China, Congo, Cyprus, Czechoslovakia, Equatorial Guinea, Gambia, German Democratic Republic, Grenada, Guinea-Bissau, Guyana, Hungary, India, Indonesia, Iran, Laos, Madagascar, Malaysia, Maldives, Mali, Malta, Mexico, Mongolia, Mozambique, Niger, Nigeria, Pakistan, Poland, Portugal, Rwanda, São Tomé and Príncipe, Senegal, Sri Lanka, Tanzania, Turkey, Uganda, Ukrainian Soviet Socialist Republic, and the Union of Soviet Socialist Republics.

Voted no: (35) Australia, Austria, Bahamas, Barbados, Belgium, Canada, Central African Republic, Costa Rica, Denmark, Dominican Republic, El Salvador, Fiji, Finland, France, Federal Republic of Germany, Haiti, Honduras, Iceland, Ireland, Israel, Italy, Ivory Coast, Liberia, Luxembourg, Malawi, Netherlands, New Zealand, Nicaragua, Norway, Panama, Swaziland, Sweden, United Kingdom of Great Britain and Northern Ireland, United States of America, Uruguay.

Abstaining: (32) Argentina, Bhutan, Bolivia, Botswana, Burma, Chile, Colombia, Ecuador, Ethiopia, Gabon, Ghana, Greece, Guatemala, Jamaica, Japan, Kenya, Lesotho, Mauritius, Nepal, Papua New Guinea, Paraguay, Peru, Philippines, Sierra Leone, Singapore, Thailand, Togo, Trinidad and Tobago, Upper Volta, Venezuela, Zaire, Zambia.

Speech to the United Nations General Assembly, by US Ambassador to the UN Daniel Patrick Moynihan, November 10, 1975

There appears to have developed in the United Nations the practice for a number of countries to combine for the purpose of doing something outrageous, and thereafter, the outrageous thing having been done, to profess themselves outraged by those who have the temerity to point it out, and subsequently to declare themselves innocent of any wrong-doing in consequence of its having been brought about wholly in reaction to the "insufferable" acts of those who pointed the wrong-doing out in the first place.

Out of deference to these curious sensibilities, the United States chose not to speak in advance of this vote: we speak in its aftermath and in tones of the utmost concern.

The United States rises to declare before the General Assembly and before the world, that it does not acknowledge, it will not abide by, it will never acquiesce in this infamous act.

Not three weeks ago, the United States Representative in the "Social, Humanitarian and Cultural Committee"—and with what irony those terms ring on our ears today—pleaded in measured and fully considered terms for the United Nations not to do this thing. It was, he said, "obscene." It is something more today, for the furtiveness with which this obscenity first appeared among us has been replaced by a shameless openness.

There will be time enough to contemplate the harm this act will have done the United Nations. Historians will do that for us, and it is sufficient for the moment only to note the foreboding fact: a great evil has been loosed upon the world.

The abomination of anti-Semitism—as this year's Nobel Peace Laureate Andrei Sakharov observed in Moscow just a few days ago—has been given the appearance of international sanction. The General Assembly today grants symbolic amnesty—and more—to the murderers of the six million European Jews. Evil enough in itself, but more ominous by far is the realization that now presses upon us: the realization that if there were no General Assembly, this could never have happened.

As this day will live in infamy, it behooves those who sought to avert it to declare their thoughts so that historians will know that we fought here, that we were not small in number—not this time—and that while we lost, we fought with full knowledge of what indeed would be lost.

Nor should any historian of the event, nor yet any who have participated in it, suppose that we have fought only as Governments, as chancelleries, and on an issue well removed from the concerns of our respective peoples. Others will speak for their nations as others have: I will speak for mine.

In all our postwar history there has not been another issue which has brought forth such unanimity of American public opinion. The President of the United States has from the first been explicit: This must not happen. The Congress of the United States in a measure unanimously adopted in the Senate and sponsored by 436 of 437 [sic] Representatives in our House, declared its utter opposition. Following only American Jews themselves, the American trade union movements was first to the fore in denouncing this infamous undertaking. Next, one after another, the great private institutions of American life pronounced anathema on this evil thing—and most particularly, the Christian churches have done so. Reminded that the United Nations was born in struggle against just such abominations as we are committing today—the wartime alliance of the United Nations dates from 1942—the United Nations Association of the United States has for the first time in its history appealed directly to each of the 141 other delegations in New York not to do this unspeakable thing.

The proposition to be sanctioned by a resolution of the General Assembly is that "Zionism is a form of racism and racial discrimination." Now that is a lie, but as it is a lie which the United Nations has now declared to be a truth, the actual truth must be restated.

The very first point to be made—and here I must respectfully take issue with my colleague from Kuwait, a man genuinely distinguished for his scholarship but who none the less on this matter is simply wrong—is that the United Nations has declared zionism to be racism without ever having defined racism: "Sentence first, verdict afterwards," as the Queen of Hearts said. But this is not Wonderland. It is a real world where there are real consequences to folly and venality.

It was only on 7 November that the President of the General Assembly, speaking on behalf of Luxembourg, warned not only of the trouble which would follow from the adoption of this resolution but of its essential irresponsibility, for, he noted, members have wholly different ideas as to what they are condemning. "It seems to me," he said—and to his lasting honor, he said it when there was still time—"that before a body like this takes a decision they should agree very clearly on what it is approving or condemning, and it takes more time."

Lest I be unclear, the United Nations has, in fact, on several occasions defined "racial discrimination." The definitions have been loose but recognizable. It is "racism," incomparably the more serious charge—racial discrimination is a practice, racism is a doctrine—it is racism that has never been defined. Indeed, the term has only recently appeared in the General Assembly documents.

The one occasion that we have been able to find on which we know it to have been discussed was the 1644th meeting of the Third Committee on 16 December 1968, in connection with the report of the Secretary-General on the status of the International Convention on the Elimination of All Forms of Racial Discrimination. On that occasion—to give some feeling for the intellectual precision with which the matter was being treated—the question arose as to what should be the relative positioning of the terms "racism" and "nazism" in a number of the preambular paragraphs. The distinguished representative of Tunisia argued that "racism" should go first because, he said, Nazism was a form of racism. Not so, said the no less distinguished delegate of the USSR, for, he explained, nazism contained the main elements of racism within its ambit and should be mentioned first. That is to say that racism was merely a form of nazism. The discussion wound to its weary and inconclusive end, and we are left with nothing to guide us, for even this one discussion of "racism" confined itself to word orders in preambular paragraphs and did not at all touch on the meaning of the words as such.

Still, one cannot but ponder the situation we have made for ourselves in the context of the Soviet statement on that not-so-distant occasion. If, as the distinguished representative declared, racism is a form of nazism, and if, as this resolution declares, zionism is a form of racism, then we have step to step taken ourselves to the point of proclaiming—the United Nations is solemnly proclaiming—that Zionism is a form of nazism.

What we have here is a lie, a political lie of a variety well known to the twentieth century and scarcely exceeded in all that annal of untruth and outrage. The lie is that Zionism is a form of racism. The overwhelmingly clear truth is that is it not.

The word "racism" is a creation of the English language, and relatively new to it. It is not, for instance, to be found in the Oxford English dictionary (appears in 1982 supplement to Oxford Dictionary). The term derives from relatively new doctrines, all of them discredited, concerning the human population of the world, to the effect that there are significant, biological differences among clearly identifiable groups, and that those differences establish in effect, different levels of humanity. Racism, as defined by Webster's Third New International Dictionary, is "the assumption that...traits and capacities are determined by biological race and that races differ decisively from one another." It further involves "a belief in the inherent superiority of a particular race and its right to domination over others."

This meaning is clear. It is equally clear that that assumption, that belief, has always been altogether alien to the political and religious movement known as zionism. As a strictly political movement, zionism was established only in 1897, although there is a clearly legitimate sense in which its origins are indeed ancient. For example, many branches of Christianity have always held that from the standpoint of the Biblical prophets Israel would be reborn one day. But the modern zionist movement arose in Europe in the context of a general upsurge of national consciousness and aspiration that overtook most other peoples of Central and Eastern Europe after 1848 and that in time spread to all of Africa and Asia. It was to those persons of the Jewish religion a Jewish form of what today is called a national liberation movement. Probably a majority of those persons who became active Zionists and sought to emigrate to Palestine were born within the confines of Czarist Russia and it was only natural for Soviet Foreign Minister Andrei Gromyko to deplore, as he did in 1948, in the 299th meeting of the Security Council, the act by Israel's neighbors of "sending their troops into Palestine and carrying out military operations aimed"—in Mr. Gromyko's words—"at the suppression of the national liberation movement in Palestine."

Now it was the singular nature—if I am not mistaken it was the unique nature—of that national liberation movement that, in contrast with the movements that preceded it, those of that time and those that have come since, it defined its members not in terms of birth but of belief. That is to say, it was not a movement of the Irish to free Ireland or of the Polish to free Poland; not a movement of the Algerians to free Algeria or of Indians to free India,

Mr. Alarcón (Cuba), Vice-President, took the Chair.

It was not a movement of persons connected by historical membership in a genetic pool of the kind that enables us to speak loosely but not meaninglessly of, say the Chinese people, nor yet of diverse groups occupying the same territory which enables us to speak of the American people with no greater indignity to truth. To the contrary, Zionists defined themselves merely as Jews, and declared to be Jewish anyone born of a Jewish mother or—and this is the absolutely crucial fact—anyone who converted to Judaism. Which is to say, in terms of the International Convention on the Elimination of All Forms of Racial Discrimination, adopted by the General Assembly at its twentieth session, anyone—regardless of "race, colour, descent, or national or ethnic origin...."

The State of Israel, which in time was the creation of the Zionist movement, has been extraordinary in nothing so much as the range of what I call sometimes "racial stocks" from which it has drawn its citizenry. There are black Jews, brown Jews, white Jews, Jews from the Orient and Jews from the West. Most such persons could be said to have been "born" Jews, just as most Presbyterians and most Hindus are "born" to their faith, but there are many Jews who are converts. And with a consistency in the matter which surely attests to the importance of this issue to that religions and political culture, Israeli courts have held that a Jew who converts to another religion is no longer a Jew. In the meantime the population of Israel also includes large numbers of non-Jews, among them Arabs both of the Muslim and Christian religions and Christians of other national origins. Many of those persons are citizens of Israel, and those who are not can become citizens by legal procedures very much like those which obtain in a typical nation of Western Europe.

Now I wish it to be understood that I am here making one point, and one point only, which is that whatever else zionism may be, it is not and cannot be "a form of racism." In logic, the State of Israel could be, or could become, many things, theoretically including many undesirable things, but it could not be and could not become racist unless it ceased to be Zionist.

Indeed, the idea that Jews are a "race" was invented not by Jews but by those who hated Jews. The idea of Jews as a race was invented by nineteenth century anti-Semites such as Houston Steward Chamberlain and Edouard Drumont, who saw that in an increasingly secular age, which is to say an age which made for fewer distinctions between people based on religion, the old religious grounds for anti-Semitism were losing force. New justifications were needed for excluding and persecuting Jews, and so the idea of Jews as a race—rather than as adherents of a religion—was born. It was a contemptible idea at the beginning, and no civilized person would be associated with it. To think that it is an idea now endorsed by the United Nations is to reflect on what civilization has come to.

It is precisely concern for civilization, for civilized values that are or should be precious to all mankind, that arouses us at this moment to such special passion. What we have at stake here is not merely the honor and the legitimacy of the State of Israel— although a challenge to the legitimacy of any Member nation ought always to arouse the vigilance of all Members of the United Nations; a yet more important matter is at issue, which is the integrity of that whole body of moral and legal precepts which we know as human rights.

The terrible lie that has been told here today will have terrible consequences. Not only will people begin to say, as indeed they have already begun to say, that the United Nations is a place where lies are told but, far more serious, grave and perhaps irreparable harm will be done to the cause of human rights. The harm will arise first because it will strip from racism the precise and abhorrent meaning that it still precariously holds today. How will peoples of the world feel about racism, and the need to struggle against it, when they are told that it is an idea so broad as to include the Jewish national liberation movement?

As the lie spreads, it will do harm in a second way. Many of the Members of the United Nations owe their independence in no small part to the notion of human rights, as it has spread from the domestic sphere to the international sphere and exercised its influence over the old colonial Powers. We are now coming into a time when that independence is likely to be threatened again. There will be new forces, some of them arising and visible now, new prophets and new despots, who will justify their actions with the help of just such distortions of words as we have sanctioned here today. Today we have drained the word "racism" of its meaning. Tomorrow, terms like "national self-determination" and "national honor" will be perverted in the same way to serve the purposes of conquest and exploitation. And when these claims begin to be made, as they already have begun to be made, it is the small nations of the world whose integrity will suffer. And how will the small nations of the world defend themselves, and on what grounds will others be moved to defend and protect them, when the language of human rights, the only language by which the small can be defended, is no longer believed and no longer has a power of its own?

There is this danger, and then a final danger, which is the most serious of all. Which is that the damage we now do to the idea of human rights and the language of human rights could well be irreversible. The idea of human rights as we know it today is not an idea which has always existed in human affairs. It is an idea which appeared at a specific time in the world, and under very special circumstances. It appeared when European philosophers of the seventeenth century began to argue that man was a being whose existence was independent from that of the State and that he need join a political community only if he did not lose by that association more than he gained. From this very specific political philosophy stemmed the idea of political rights, of claims that the individual could justly make against the state; it was because the individual was seen as so separate from the State that he could make legitimate demands upon it.

That was the philosophy from which the idea of domestic and international rights sprang. But most of the world does not hold with that philosophy now. Most of the world believes in newer modes of political thought, in philosophies that do not accept the individual as distinct from and prior to the State, in philosophies that therefore do not provide any justification for the idea of human rights and philosophies that have no words by which to explain their value. If we destroy the words that were given to us by past centuries, we will not have words to replace them, for philosophy today has no such words.

But there are those of us who have not forsaken these older words, still so new to much of the world. Not forsaken them now, not here, not anywhere, not ever.

The United States of America declares that it does not acknowledge, it will not abide by, it will never acquiesce in this infamous act.

RESOLUTION 46/80

"The general assembly decides to revoke the determination contained in its resolution 3379 (XXX) of November 10, 1975."

UNGA Resolution 46/86 Voting Record (December 16, 1991)

Sponsored by: Albania, Antigua and Barbuda, Argentina, Australia, Austria, Bahamas, Barbados, Belarus, Belgium, Belize, Bolivia, Brazil, Bulgaria, Burundi, Canada, Central African Republic, Chile, Colombia, Costa Rica, Cyprus, Czechoslovakia, Denmark, Dominica, Dominican Republic, Ecuador, El Salvador, Estonia, Federal States of Micronesia, Finland, France, Gambia, Germany, Greece, Grenada, Guatemala, Guyana, Honduras, Hungary, Iceland, Republic of Ireland, Israel, Italy, Jamaica, Japan, Latvia, Liberia, Liechtenstein, Lithuania, Luxembourg, Madagascar, Malta, Marshall Islands, Malawi, Mexico, Mongolia, Mozambique, Netherlands, New Zealand, Nicaragua, Norway, Panama, Papua New Guinea, Paraguay, Peru, Poland, Portugal, Republic of Korea (South Korea), Romania, Rwanda, Saint Lucia, Saint Kitts and Nevis, Saint Vincent and the Grenadines, Samoa, Sierra Leone, Singapore, Solomon Islands, Spain, Suriname, Swaziland, Sweden, Ukraine, Union of Soviet Socialist Republics, United Kingdom of Great Britain and Northern Ireland, United States of America, Uruguay, Venezuela, Yugoslavia, Zaire, Zambia.

Voted yes: (111) The sponsoring nations listed above, and additionally: Benin, Bhutan, Botswana, Cambodia, Cameroon, Cape Verde, Congo, Côte d'Ivoire, Fiji, Gabon, Haiti, India, Kenya, Lesotho, Madagascar, Namibia, Nepal, Nigeria, Philippines, São Tomé and Príncipe, Seychelles, Thailand, Togo.

Voted no: (25) Afghanistan, Algeria, Bangladesh, Brunei Darussalam, Cuba, Democratic People's Republic of Korea (North Korea), Indonesia, Iran, Iraq, Jordan, Lebanon, Libya, Malaysia, Mali, Mauritania, Pakistan, Qatar, Saudi Arabia, Somalia, Sri Lanka, Sudan, Syria, United Arab Emirates, Vietnam, Yemen.

Abstaining: (13) Angola, Burkina Faso, Ethiopia, Ghana, Lao People's Democratic Republic, Maldives, Mauritius, Myanmar, Trinidad and Tobago, Turkey, Uganda, United Republic of Tanzania, Zimbabwe.

Absent: (15) Bahrain, Chad, People's Republic of China, Comoros, Djibouti, Egypt, Guinea, Guinea-Bissau, Kuwait, Morocco, Niger, Oman, Senegal, Tunisia, Vanuatu.

CHRONOLOGY

March 16, 1927	Daniel Patrick Moynihan born in Tulsa, Oklahoma
April 25, 1945	The United Nations is established
November 29, 1947	UN General Assembly Resolution 181 passes 33 to 13 with 10 abstentions, recognizing a Jewish state, and partitioning Palestine
May 14, 1948	The State of Israel is established
May 1955	Moynihan marries Elizabeth Brennan
July 1961	Moynihan arrives with his wife and three children in Washington as a special assistant to the secretary of labor, Arthur Goldberg
November 22, 1963	President Kennedy is assassinated
July 28, 1965	Moynihan resigns from the Johnson administration to run for New York City Council president, but he loses
August 18, 1965	The Moynihan Report controversy erupts
1965–1966	Moynihan is a Fellow at the Center of Advanced Studies, Wesleyan University
1966–1969	Moynihan is director of the Harvard-MIT Joint Center for Urban Studies
June 1967	Six-Day War
1969	Moynihan becomes a professor in the Harvard School of Education
1969	Moynihan joins Richard Nixon's administration as counselor to the president and assistant to the president for Urban Affairs
March 1, 1970	Moynihan's "benign neglect" memo leaked
1971	Moynihan returns to Harvard
1971	Moynihan serves as a Public Delegate to the United Nations, part of the ceremonial five-person delegation
September 5–6, 1972	Massacre of 11 Israeli athletes and coaches at the 1972 Munich Olympics

February 20, 1973	Moynihan begins serving as ambassador to India
October 6, 1973	Yom Kippur War breaks out
October 17, 1973	OPEC begins an "oil embargo," which lasts until March 17, 1974
October 22, 1973	Middle East cease-fire
November 9, 1973	Henry Kissinger's Shuttle Diplomacy succeeds. Israel exchanges prisoners with Egypt but balks on further territorial withdrawals
December 17, 1973	PLO attacks Leonardo da Vinci Airport in Rome, as predicted by the Egyptian ambassador who warned Moynihan of a PLO hit squad going to New Delhi
January 18, 1974	Israel and Egypt sign a disengagement agreement
May 1, 1974	The General Assembly passes its Declaration on the Establishment of a New International Economic Order
May 15, 1974	Palestinian terrorists attack Ma'alot, killing 16 Israeli teenagers
May 29, 1974	Israel and Syria sign a disengagement agreement
June 3, 1974	Yitzhak Rabin begins serving his first term as prime minister of Israel
August 8, 1974	Nixon resigns. Gerald Ford sworn in as president
October 15, 1974	UN General Assembly grants the PLO a voice in the UN
October 30, 1974	Arab summit in Rabat designates the PLO as the "sole legitimate representative of the Palestinian people"
November 13, 1974	Yasir Arafat addresses the UN
December 6, 1974	US ambassador John Scali warns against seeking "paper triumphs" that reflect the "tyranny of the majority"
January 6, 1975	Moynihan resigns as ambassador to India to return to Harvard
March 1975	*Commentary* publishes Moynihan's essay "The U.S. in Opposition"
March 23, 1975	Failing to reach a Middle East agreement, Kissinger announces "a period of reassessment is needed." President Ford agrees
April 30, 1975	Saigon falls. America defeated in the Vietnam War
May 12–15, 1975	Mayaguez merchant ship seized by Khmer Rouge guerillas, rescued three days later at the cost of 18 American lives
June 19–July 2, 1975	International Woman's Year World Conference hosted by the UN in Mexico City, which turns anti-American and anti-Zionist
June 30, 1975	President Gerald Ford swears in Moynihan as US ambassador to the UN
July 16, 1975	In Jidda, Saudi Arabia, 39 Islamic countries and the PLO demand Israel's expulsion from the UN

July 18–25, 1975	The Organization of African Unity Conference held in Kampala, Uganda, which divides over the Israel issue
August 1, 1975	The Helsinki Accords signed, a landmark in the history of human rights
August 19, 1975	Chaim Herzog presents his credentials as Israeli ambassador to the UN
August 20, 1975	Moynihan postpones Cuba's proposal in the UN's Decolonization Committee to recognize the separatist Puerto Rican Communist Party
August 25–30, 1975	The Conference of Non-Aligned countries, meeting in Lima, Peru, "severely condemns" Zionism
September 1, 1975	Israel and Egypt sign the Sinai Accords
September 1, 1975	Moynihan reads Kissinger's 12,500 word speech, generously offering economic development to the Third World on its own terms
October 1, 1975	Idi Amin of Uganda addresses the General Assembly
October 1, 1975	Cuba, Somalia, and Dahomey, submit an amendment to the Third Committee characterizing Zionism as a form of racism
October 3, 1975	Moynihan in San Francisco blasts Amin as a "racist murderer"
October 15, 1975	The Black African countries split on three different procedural votes on the Zionism is racism issue, heightening tensions as the actual vote approaches
Afternoon of October 17, 1975	The vote to postpone the Zionism discussion fails in the Third Committee with 68 voting to proceed—although 45 countries vote for postponement, 16 abstain, and 18 are absent
Evening of October 17, 1975	The Third Committee passes Draft Resolution A/C.3/L2159 labeling Zionism as a form of racism with 70 in favor, 29 against, 27 abstaining, 16 absent
October 24, 1975	Herzog chides the Conference of Presidents of Major American Jewish Organizations for Jewish passivity
October 26–November 4, 1975	The president of Egypt, Anwar el Sadat, arrives for a state visit to New York, Chicago, Jacksonville, Houston, and Washington, DC
October 30, 1975	The New York *Daily News* runs its headline "FORD TO CITY: DROP DEAD"

November 3, 1975	Vice president Nelson Rockefeller announces he will not run with Ford in 1976
November 4, 1975	Halloween massacre—Ford abruptly fires CIA director William Colby and Secretary of Defense James Schlesinger, while demoting Kissinger
November 10, 1975	The United Nations General Assembly passes Resolution 3379 (XXX), 72 votes for, 35 against, 32 abstentions, 3 absent
November 10, 1975	General Assembly resolution 3525 establishes the "Committee on the Inalienable Rights of the Palestinian People"
November 11, 1975	Moynihan opposes establishing a UN press office so the 130 dictators represented in the UN do not pretend to have a free press
November 11, 1975	Massive rally against the General Assembly decision in New York
November 11, 1975	Kissinger misses deadline to provide documents for congressional inquiry, which results in contempt of Congress charges
November 12, 1975	Moynihan proposes freeing all political prisoners worldwide
November 13, 1975	Bomb explodes in Zion Square, Jerusalem, killing 6 teenagers
November 17, 1975	British Ambassador Ivor Richard proclaims the UN "is not the OK Corral and I am hardly Wyatt Earp"
November 20, 1975	Former California governor Ronald Reagan declares his presidential candidacy
November 21, 1975	Moynihan abruptly cancels his 12:30 press conference when Ford and Kissinger urge him not to resign
November 21, 1975	The General Assembly's Fourth Committee on Decolonization votes 103 to 1 to condemn American military bases on Guam
November 22, 1975	The United Kingdom Mission to the United Nations denies that Ivor Richard's speech received "prior American approval"
November 22, 1975	Harvard-Yale game, Harvard wins 10–7
November 23, 1975	"Black Americans to Support Israel Committee" takes out full page *New York Times* ad against Resolution 3379
November 24, 1975	Moynihan meets President Ford, who expresses "his complete confidence"
November 30, 1975	On Gush Emunim's eighth try to settle Sebastia, this first settlement in Samaria is established
January 27, 1976	Moynihan meets the president, agrees to remain at the UN
January 30, 1976	James Reston column in *New York Times* undermines Moynihan
January 31, 1976	Moynihan sends in his letter of resignation
November 2, 1976	Moynihan elected US Senator from New York

1978	Publication of Edward Said's *Orientalism*
July 14–30, 1980	Mid-decade International Women's Conference held in Copenhagen
January 20, 1981	Reagan inaugurated as president
March 22, 1983	Chaim Herzog becomes Israel's sixth president
December 31, 1984	The United States withdraws from UNESCO
November 11, 1984	Herzog hosts a conference "Refuting the Zionist-Racism Equation"
July 15–26, 1985	International Women's Conference, held in Nairobi, Kenya
November 10, 1987	President Herzog addresses a joint session of Congress
December 10, 1989	Vice president Dan Quayle endorses repeal of Resolution 3379
1989	Soviet domination of Eastern Europe ends
November 10, 1990	Rally outside the UN demanding repeal attracts more than 1,400 students
December 16, 1991	The General Assembly votes 111 to 25, with 13 abstaining and 17 no-votes or absences, to revoke Resolution 3379
January 2001	Moynihan retires from the Senate after four terms
August 31–September 7, 2001	United Nations World Conference against Racism, Racial Discrimination, Xenophobia, and Related Intolerance, held in Durban, South Africa
September 11, 2001	Islamist terrorists murder nearly 3,000 people in an attack on the United States
March 26, 2003	Moynihan dies at the age of 76

ABBREVIATIONS

2400th GA	Nov. 10, 1975, 2400th Plenary Meeting of the United Nations General Assembly, *Official Records*
AJC MSS	American Jewish Committee Archives, New York
BS	Brent Scowcroft
DPM	Daniel Patrick Moynihan
DPM For Rel	Hearings before the Committee on Foreign Relations, United States Senate, Ninety-Fourth Congress, First Session on the United States and the United Nations and the Nomination of Daniel Patrick Moynihan to be US Representative to the United Nations with the Rank of Ambassador, 1975
DPM Letters	Steven R. Weisman, ed., *Daniel Patrick Moynihan: A Portrait in Letters of an American Visionary* (New York, 2010)
DPM MSS	Daniel Patrick Moynihan Papers, Library of Congress, Washington, DC
Friedan MSS	Betty Friedan Papers, Schlesinger Library, Radcliffe Institute, Harvard University, Cambridge, MA
GHWB MSS	George H. W. Bush Papers, George Bush Presidential Library and Museum, College Station, TX
GRF	Gerald R. Ford
GRF Lib	Gerald R. Ford Presidential Library, Ann Arbor, MI
GRF NSA	National Security Adviser's Memoranda of Conversation Collection at the Gerald R. Ford Presidential Library, Ann Arbor, MI
HAK	Henry A. Kissinger

HAK TelCon	*The Kissinger Transcripts: A Verbatim Record of U.S. Diplomacy, 1969–1977,* Digital National Security Archives, http://nsarchive.chadwyck.com/marketing/index.jsp
Herzog MSS	Chaim Herzog Archives, Herzliya, Israel
JTA	Jewish Telegraph Agency
Miller MSS	Israel Miller Archives, Yeshiva University, New York
MemCon	Memorandum of Conversation
MFA	Ministry of Foreign Affairs, Jerusalem, Israel
MFA MSS	Ministry of Foreign Affairs Papers, Israel State Archives, Jerusalem, Israel
NSC	National Security Council
NYT	*New York Times*
NYTM	*New York Times Magazine*
OH	Oral History
Tap MSS	William Tapley Bennett Jr. Papers, Richard B. Russell Library for Political Research and Studies, University of Georgia Libraries, Athens, GA
TelCon	Telephone Conversation
ThirdCom	Verbatim Record of the Third Committee of the United Nations General Assembly, Thirtieth Session, New York
TNR	*The New Republic*
UN GA	United Nations General Assembly, Thirtieth Session, New York
UN MSS	United Nations Archive, New York
UN NY	Israel Mission to the United Nations

NOTES

INTRODUCTION: "JUST A MATTER OF DECENCY"

5   made Zionism palatable: Melvin I. Urofsky, *American Zionism from Herzl to the Holocaust* (New York, 1975), 2.

"Pat was colorful": Donald Rumsfeld OH.

"It was good": DPM to Richard Funkhouser, Sept. 2, 1975, Folder 5, Box 327, DPM MSS.

"Israel was not": DPM, *A Dangerous Place* (Boston, 1978), 166.

"The accused": DPM, *Dangerous Place*, 168.

"spend an evening": *Washington Post*, May 18, 1975, 33.

"Pat couldn't": Elizabeth Moynihan OH.

6   "lived in": *The Robert MacNeil Report* transcript, on Channel 13, Dec. 15, 1975, Folder 10, Box 340, DPM MSS.

"an abbreviated posting": DPM, *Pandaemonium: Ethnicity in International Politics* (New York, 1993, 1994), 36.

"just a matter": Leonard Garment OH.

"It was the beginning": George Will OH.

"Did I make": DPM, *Dangerous Place*, 209.

"It struck one": Will OH.

7   "The United Nations": *Saturday Night Live* transcript, season 1, episode 5: aired Nov. 15, 1975, NBC.

"With 3379": Leonard Cole to author, Dec. 4, 2011. See also Leonard Cole, *Blacks in Power: A Comparative Study of Black and White Elected Officials* (1977).

"scorecard": Stephen Solarz, House of Representatives *Congressional Record*, Nov. 9, 1987, 179:133, Records of the American Jewish Congress, "Zionism is Racism"-U.N. Resolution 3379. 1975–1986, 1991, I-77, Folders 28–29, Box 715, American Jewish Historical Society, New York.

"anybody on the": Michael Walzer OH.

"It was the turning": Alan Dershowitz OH.

"to condemn the": Eldridge Cleaver, "The Myth of Zionist Racism," *New America*, Feb. 1976, 5.

"More than two hundred": *Washington Afro-American Red Star*, Sept. 16, 1975.

7 "If one preposterously": Michael Harrington, "UN Zionism Vote: Blow to New Economic Order," *Newsletter of the Democratic Left*, Dec. 1975.

8 "Approximately half": C. L. Sulzberger, *NYT*, Oct. 26, 1975.

"More than 70": *Boston Globe*, Jan. 13, 1976.

"A FIGHTING": *People*, Dec. 29, 1975–Jan. 5, 1974, 27.

"A deplorable": *NYT*, Nov. 12, 1975, 17.

"outrageous": Rumsfeld OH.

"UNICEF": *NYT*, Jan. 6, 1976, 2.

"The country is simply": Eric Sevareid, "Commentary," *CBS Evening News with Walter Cronkite*, Jan. 13, 1976, 6:30 p.m.–7:00 p.m., EST, Tap MSS.

"the most celebrated": James T. Patterson, *Freedom Is Not Enough: The Moynihan Report and America's Struggle over Black Family Life—from LBJ to Obama* (New York, 2010), xv.

"most sought-after": Don Walker to author, Feb. 5, 2012.

"Few events have": "Reagan Pledges His Support for Removal from UN Record of the 'Blot' of the Zionism-Racism Resolution," JTA, Nov. 12, 1975.

9 "total inversion of": Address by Ronald Reagan to the General Assembly, Oct. 24, 1985, available at http://www.reagan.utexas.edu/archives/speeches/1985/102485a.htm.

"nadir": *NYT*, Aug. 7, 1988.

"wave of nationalist": Max Lerner, "A Nationalist Wave," *New York Post*, Dec. 6, 1975, Tap MSS.

"You have voiced": Lewis F. Powell to DPM, Nov. 26, 1975, Folder 7, Box 330, DPM MSS.

10 72 percent of: Opinion Research Corp, Polls Jan. 2–4, 1976, in North American Newspaper Alliance, "Public Solidly Behind Moynihan," Jan. 12, 1976, Folder 8, Box 343, DPM MSS.

Historians are recognizing: Laura Kalman, *Right Star Rising: A New Politics, 1974–1980* (New York, 2010).

"standing up and": Ed Koch OH.

11 On Syria see: http://www.unwatch.org/site/apps/nlnet/content2.aspx?c=bdKKISNqEmG&b=1316871&ct=11551461.

"unfair treatment": Remarks by Ambassador Susan E. Rice, U.S. Permanent Representative to the United Nations, at the Leaders' Recognition Reception for the Conference of Presidents of Major American Jewish Organizations, Dec. 14, 2011, available at http://usun.state.gov/briefing/statements/2011/178869.htm.

"ultimate weapon of": Joel Fishman "'A Disaster of Another Kind': Zionism = Racism, Its Beginning, and the War of Delegitimization against Israel," *Israel Journal of Foreign Affairs* 3 (2011), 83.

"Live Together in Peace": Available at http://www.artonstamps.org/Countries/Unit-Nat/un-slogans.htm.

"My amended": Ahmed Moor, "My Rights, My Remedy," Sept. 11, 2009, http://electronicintifada.net/content/my-rights-my-remedy/8437.

"Zionism is": *Dailyillini.com*, Feb. 12, 2012.

12 "we will always": "Obama's Speech at AIPAC, March 2012," Council on Foreign Relations, March 4, 2012, available at http://www.cfr.org/united-states/

obamas-speech-aipac-march-2012/p27549. See also Remarks by Barack Obama in Cairo ("A New Beginning"), June 4, 2009, available at http://www.whitehouse.gov/the-press-office/remarks-president-cairo-university-6-04-09 and Condoleezza Rice quoted in *Haaretz*, Oct. 16, 2007.

12 "in international discussions": Bayard Rustin, "Zionism is not Racism," Nov. 13, 1975, Rustin Column, New Release, Folder "United Nations, 1975–1980," Box 13, Bayard Rustin MSS, Library of Congress, Washington, DC.

13 "as equally legitimate": DPM, *Dangerous Place*, 172.
"profound hypocrisy": Noam Chomsky, *Fateful Triangle: The United States, Israel and the Palestinians* (Cambridge, MA, 1983, 1999), 158.
"vague": Edward Said, *The Question of Palestine* (London, 1980), 111.
"I was never": Adel Iskander and Hakem Rustom, *Edward Said: A Legacy of Emancipation and Representation* (Berkeley, 2010), 315.
"it was almost": Fishman, "Disaster of Another Kind," 77–78.

14 "process of debasement": Winthrop D. Jordan, *White Over Black: American Attitudes Toward the Negro, 1550–1812* (Chapel Hill, 1968), 80, 94.
Moynihan eventually accepted: HAK, *Years of Renewal* (New York, 1999), 783, and DPM, *Dangerous Place*, 216.
"We are conducting": TelCon between HAK and William Buffum, Nov. 10, 1975, 4:25 p.m., HAK TelCon.
"the worst of times": DPM eulogy of Henry Jackson, Sept. 11, 1983, *DPM Letters*, 455.

15 "a hard anti-Marxist": DMP TO RN, Dec. 28, 1972, *DPM Letters*, 270–71.
"failure of nerve": DPM, "How Much Does Freedom Matter," Maxwell Kriendler Memorial Lecture, Freedom House, Apr. 12, 1975 in Folder 1, Box 335, DPM MSS.
During his first: "Transcript of Remarks by Ambassador Moynihan on meeting the staff of the U.S. Mission to the U.N. on Tuesday, July 1, 1975," Tap MSS.
"insult to his intelligence": Elie Wiesel OH.
"neototalitarian assault": DPM to Richard W. Lyman, July 3, 1975, *DPM Letters*, 377.
"believe that our": DPM, *Dangerous Place*, 158–59.
"anti-Americans": Norman Podhoretz to author, Dec. 8, 2011.

16 "liberal antiradical": Tevi Troy, *Intellectuals and the American Presidency: Philosophers, Jesters, or Technicians?* (Lanham, MD, 2003), 112.
"them, *them*": Suzanne Weaver Garment OH.
"Zionism issue is": DPM notes, undated, 10, Box 338, UN Subject File: Notes, DPM MSS.
"There will be more campaigns": DPM, *Dangerous Place*, 159.
anti-Zionism and anti-Americanism: Paul Hollander, "Introduction: The New Virulence and Popularity," in *Understanding Anti-Americanism: Its Origins and Impact at Home and Abroad*, ed. Paul Hollander (Chicago, 2004), 45.
"the organic and total": Mr. Kaddoumi (Palestine Liberation Organization), Nov. 3, 1975, 2390th Plenary Meeting, UN GA, *Official Records* 630:40.

17 "this is a society": Suzanne Weaver Garment OH.
"You sound like": Clifford and Evelyn Harkins, Houston, TX, to DPM, Feb. 27, 1975, Folder 3, Box 328, DPM MSS.

17 "crucial topic modern": Kwame Anthony Appiah, *The Honor Code: How Moral Revolutions Happen* (New York, 2010), xv.

"no basis for": Mr. Salim (United Republic of Tanzania), Sept. 16, 1980, 1st Plenary Meeting, 35th Session, UN GA, *Official Records* 3:21.

Historians now appreciate: Samuel Moyn, *The Last Utopia: Human Rights in History* (Cambridge, MA, 2010), 2–3.

"There are those of us": DPM, *Dangerous Place*, 199.

18 "while the UN": Dershowitz OH.

"final solution of": DPM, "Telling the Truth about the Lie," *Moment*, Mar. 1985, 21.

"the delusion, paranoia": James Kirchik, "Pink Eye," *Tablet Magazine*, Nov. 29, 2011, available at http://www.tabletmag.com/news-and-politics/84216/pink-eye/#comments.

19 "What is this": Interview with Ambassador Moynihan on CBS *Morning News*, Dec. 17, 1975, Folder 14, Box 336, DPM MSS.

"to affect history": Garment OH.

"the danger": "Transcript Ambassador Moynihan meeting staff. July 1, 1975," 10, Tap MSS.

CHAPTER 1: FROM "WE THE PEOPLES OF THE UNITED NATIONS" TO "THE UNITED STATES IN OPPOSITION"

22 "the small states are": Stephen C. Schlesinger, *Act of Creation: The Founding of the United Nations* (Boulder, CO, 2003), 101.

"That 25 percent was": "From Where to Where?" *Time*, July 9, 1945.

23 "messianic": Barbara Willner Hartman OH,

"[T]here is now": *NYT*, June 17, 1945, E8.

"TO STOP A THIRD WORLD WAR": *NYT*, July 24, 1945, 22.

"a world government": Gallup Polls, July 1946, Aug. 1947, quoted in Gregory G. Holyk, "U.S. Public Support for the United Nations," *Public Opinion Quarterly* 74:1 (Spring 2010): 183, 170.

"unrealistic": Dean Acheson, *Present at the Creation: My Years in the State Department* (New York, 1987), 6.

24 "battlefield of ideas": "The San Francisco Conference," *Jewish Criterion* (Pittsburgh, PA), Apr. 27, 1945.

"to bind together in peace": *NYT*, Jan. 15, 1946, 6.

"least that Christian civilization": *NYT*, May 10, 1948, 16.

"It is the greatest thing": *Los Angeles Times*, Nov. 30, 1947, 2.

25 "an exercise in": DPM, *Pandaemonium: Ethnicity in International Politics*, (New York, 1993, 1994), 3.

"a sin against": *Times* (London), May 16, 1939, 13.

"We shall be": Efraim Karsh, *Palestine Betrayed* (New Haven, 2010), 86.

"universal process": Rashid Khalidi, *Palestinian Identity: The Construction of Modern National Consciousness* (New York, 2010), 20.

26 "My first feeling": *NYT*, Nov. 30, 1947, 60.

"turning point in": *NYT*, Nov. 30, 1947, 1.

27 "Today's resolution": *NYT*, Nov. 30, 1947, 1.

28 "to date": Holyk, "Public Support for UN," 169.
    Throughout this period: Holyk, "Public Support for UN," 169.

29 "You North Amerikans": Allen J. Matusow, *The Unraveling of America* (New York, 1984), 326.
    "white Western imperialist society": Maurice Isserman and Michael Kazin, *America Divided: The Civil War of the 1960s* (New York, 2000), 176.
    "one oppressor—in the": Matusow, *Unraveling of America*, 333.

30 "the basic problems": "Joint Declaration of the Seventy-Seven," June 15, 1964, in Karl P. Sauvant, *The Group of 77: Evolution, Structure, Organization* (New York, 1981), 3.
    the records reversed: Paul M. Kennedy, *The Parliament of Man: The Past, Present, and Future of the United Nations* (Toronto, 2006), 54.

31 "War of Words": *Time*, Apr. 30, 1973.
    "deeply in the": *NYT*, Dec. 7, 1974, 15.

32 "frustration and disenchantment": *NYT*, Dec. 8, 1974, 2.
    "try to make": Holyk, "Public Support for UN," 171, 173.

33 "there is no country": Walter Isaacson, *Kissinger: A Biography* (New York, 2005), 506, 503, 504.
    "The powers of": DPM notes, Dec. 31, 1973, and Dec. 30, 1973, Folder 4, Box 364, DPM MSS.

34 "Ford has just": Isaacson, *Kissinger*, 601–2, 503.
    "Super K": *Newsweek*, June 10, 1974, cover.
    Baring teeth: Steven L. Spiegel, *The Other Arab Israeli Conflict* (Chicago, 1985), 221.
    "an overall settlement": MemCon, GRF, HAK, BS, Yigal Allon, et al., 12:57 p.m.–2:15 p.m., Dec. 9, 1974, 3, GRF NSA.
    "we're losing control": *NYT*, Mar. 6, 1976, 8.
    "the possible breakdown": MemCon, HAK, Ken Jamieson, et al., Oct. 26, 1973, 10, http://www.gwu.edu/~nsarchiv/NSAEBB/NSAEBB98/octwar-82.pdf.
    "The Middle East": MemCon, GRF, HAK, and BS, 9:00 a.m., Aug. 12, 1974, 9, GRF NSA.

35 "bringing the world": MemCon, GRF, HAK, and BS, 9:21 a.m.–9:54 a.m., Mar. 24, 1975, 4, GRF NSA.
    "outraged at the Israelis": MemCon, GRF, HAK, and BS, 9:21 a.m.–9:54 a.m., Mar. 24, 1975, 1, 3, GRF NSA.
    "fools": TelCon between HAK and Max Fisher, Dec. 10, 1975, 1, HAK TelCon.
    "common thugs": MemCon, GRF and HAK, 9:15 a.m., Jan. 6, 1976, 2, GRF NSA.
    "the basic cause": MemCon, GRF, HAK, and BS, Dec. 9, 1975, 2, GRF NSA.
    "This is terribly painful to me": MemCon, GRF, HAK, and BS, 9:21 a.m.–9:54 a.m., Mar. 24, 1975, 3, GRF NSA.
    "a sick bunch": TelCon between HAK and DPM, Dec. 9, 1975, 2. HAK TelCon.
    "the world's worst": MemCon, GRF, HAK, and BS, 10:00 a.m., June 12, 1975, 1, GRF NSA.

36 "get tough-minded": *NYT*, Nov. 14, 1974, 1.

36 "Their power in": MemCon, GRF and HAK, BS, et al., 9:00 a.m.–10:00 a.m.,
    Dec. 17, 1974, 3, GRF NSA.

"you know how": MemCon, GRF, BS, and Max Fisher, 7:00 p.m.–7:50 p.m.,
    Dec. 12, 1975, 2, GRF NSA.

"such a tiny people": MemCon, GRF, HAK, BS, and Donald Rumsfeld, 9:19 a.m.–
    10:23 a.m., Jan. 7, 1976, 2, GRF NSA.

"The effect on our policy": MemCon, GRF, HAK, and BS, 9:21 a.m.–9:54 a.m.,
    Mar. 24, 1975, 2, GRF NSA.

"Henry and I": MemCon, Max Fisher, GRF, HAK, BS, 3, 10 p.m., Mar. 27, 1975,
    3, GRF NSA.

37 "was so close": Minutes, NSC Meeting, Mar. 28, 1975, 3:15 p.m.–6:15 p.m., 2, 9,
    GRF NSA.

"I know they will hit us": MemCom, GRF, HAK, and BS, 9:22 a.m.–10:18 a.m.,
    Mar. 26, 1975, 3, GRF NSA.

"We are responsible": MemCom, GRF, HAK, and BS, 9:21 a.m.–9:54 a.m.,
    Mar. 24, 1975, 6, 7, GRF NSA.

"you have let Cambodia go": MemCom, GRF, HAK, and BS, 9:21 a.m.–9:54 a.m.,
    Mar. 24, 1975, 6, GRF NSA.

38 "to a wayward": *NYT*, Nov. 18, 1975, 1.

39 "*The United States goes*": DPM, "The United States in Opposition," *Commentary*,
    Mar. 1975.

CHAPTER 2: THE ULTIMATE WARRIOR-DIPLOMAT

42 "A massive ego": DPM diary, Nov. 11, 1973, Folder 9, Box 363, DPM MSS.

"vulnerability": David Riesman to Elizabeth Moynihan, Dec. 30, 1974, Folder 7,
    Box 336, DPM MSS.

"I don't think": Norman Podhoretz OH.

"God I wish": *DPM Letters*, 11.

"Pat was so witty": Podhoretz OH.

43 "Marriage broke up": Godfrey Hodgson, *The Gentleman from New York: Daniel
    Patrick Moynihan* (New York, 2000), 29.

"almost everything": Hodgson, *Gentleman from New York*, 29.

"loved arguing for something": *DPM Letters*, 11.

44 "longshoreman's loading hook": *NYTM*, July 31, 1966, 48.

"needed a good": Hodgson, *Gentleman from New York*, 37.

"nothing and no one": Hodgson, *Gentleman from New York*, 46.

45 "Moynihan was a": Chester Finn OH.

46 "hyper-aware of": Nathan Glazer OH.

"probably most of our": Elizabeth Moynihan OH.

"Catholics, with a claim": DPM Diary, Nov. 22, 1973, Folder 1, Box 364,
    DPM MSS.

"I guess there's": Hodgson, *Gentleman from New York*, 85.

"We'll never laugh again": James T. Patterson, *Freedom Is Not Enough: The
    Moynihan Report and America's Struggle over Black Family Life—from LBJ to
    Obama* (New York, 2010), 11.

46 "that for weeks": DPM Diary, Nov. 22, 1973, Folder 1, Box 364, DPM MSS.
"Very little has": DPM Diary, Nov. 22, 1973, Folder 1, Box 364, DPM MSS.

47 "I don't know *anyone*": Chester Finn to DPM, June 5, 1975, Folder 3, Box 327, DPM MSS.
"coined in": DPM to Peter Steinfels, Feb. 20, 1979, *DPM Letters*, 406.
"tendency": Irving Kristol, "What Is a 'Neoconservative'?" *Newsweek*, Jan. 19, 1976, 17.
"tension between": DPM, notes, n.d., Folder 10, Box 338, DPM MSS.
"practically invent[ed] the role": Nicholas Lehmann, *The Promised Land: The Black Migration and How It Changed America* (New York, 1992), 154.

48 "We have to do": DPM, "The Negro Family: The Case for National Action," Mar. 1965, Office of Public Planning and Research, United States Department of Labor, at http://www.dol.gov/oasam/programs/history/webid-meynihan.htm
"almost physical excitement": Patterson, *Freedom Is Not Enough*, 42.
"The most difficult fact": DPM, "The Negro Family."
"nine pages of": Patterson, *Freedom Is Not Enough*, 43.
"I am now known as": DPM to Roy Wilkins, Jan. 12, 1966, *DPM Letters*, 114.
"If Pat is": Kenneth Clark in Patterson, *Freedom Is Not Enough*, 86.
"It was the worst": Moynihan OH.
Earlier, in July 1965: Glazer OH.

49 "liberal dissenter": DPM to RN, Jan. 3, 1969, *DPM Letters*, 165.
"nihilist terrorism": DPM to John Ehrlichman and Bob Finch, Nov. 18, 1970, 4 (Campus Unrest), 1, Box 20, WHCF: SMOF: DPM, at http://nixon.archives.gov/virtuallibrary/documents/jul10/60.pdf
"the crisis of": DPM to RN, July 17, 1969, 1 Domestic Hours (with the President), Box 23, Subject File 1, WHCF: SMOF: DPM at http://nixon.archives.gov/virtuallibrary/documents/jul10/79.pdf
"educated elite": DPM to RN, Aug. 19, 1969, *DPM Letters*, 195.

50 "shrug off": *Washington Post*, Mar. 21, 1970, D15.
"the position of Negroes": DPM to RN, Jan. 16, 1970, *DPM Letters*, 211, 213, 214.

51 "I am choosing": DPM to RN, May 9, 1970, *DPM Letters*, 225–26. See also Hodgson, *Gentleman from New York*, 154–55.
When he called his wife: Hodgson, *Gentleman from New York*, 178.
"like the work": Hodgson, *Gentleman from New York*, 196.

52 "the same dreary": DPM to George H. W. Bush, Nov. 9, 1971, *DPM Letters*, 256.
"It was probably": DPM to Saul Bellow, Oct. 4, 1972, *DPM Letters*, 268.
"The students hate": DPM Diary, Oct. 6, 1974, *DPM Letters*, 355.
"corpse had already": DPM to William F. Buckley, Dec. 18, 1974, Folder 7, Box 357, DPM MSS.

53 "Is it true": *DPM Letters*, 7–8.
"that the only people": DPM Diary, Folder 3, Box 364, DPM MSS.
Negotiations resulted in: DPM to editors of the *Guinness Book of World Records*, Feb. 25, 1974, *DPM Letters*, 325.
"I *like* to think": DPM to Nathan Glazer, May 25, 1973, *DPM Letters*, 282, 283.
"felt out of": Bernard Weinraub OH.

53 He admired the country's: DPM to Nathan Glazer, Feb. 26, 1974, Folder 8, Box 354, DPM MSS.

   "a semi-secret": Podhoretz OH.

54 "Hawks on Israel": MemCon, GF, Nelson Rockefeller, HAK, BS, Sept. 6, 1974, GRF NSA.

   "I have been thinking": DPM to Nathan Glazer, Oct. 11, 1973, Folder 9, Box 354, DPM MSS.

   "We were alone": DPM Diary, Folder 7, Box 363, DPM MSS.

   "obscene": DPM Diary, Oct. 22, 1973, Folder 7, Box 363, DPM MSS.

   A few weeks later: Moynihan OH. See also: Telegram, DPM to American Consulate Bombay et al., Dec. 17, 1973, at http://aad.archives.gov/aad/createpdf?rid=108313&dt=2472&dl=1345

   The plans included: Hodgson, *Gentleman from New York*, 210.

55 "One doesn't change": Moynihan OH.

   "He found it": Elizabeth Moynihan to author, Jan. 26, 2011.

   "as a stooge": DPM Diary, Folder 7, Box 363, DPM MSS.

   "has got itself": DPM to Nathan Glazer, Feb. 26, 1974, Folder 8, Box 354, DPM MSS.

   "I came here thinking": DPM to William F. Buckley, Dec. 18, 1974, Folder 7, Box 357, DPM MSS.

56 "The more we do": DPM Diary, Apr. 27, 1974, *DPM Letters*, 333.

   "this leftist, 'anti-colonial'": DPM to Richard Nixon, Mar. 21, 1973, Folder 4, Box 362, DPM MSS.

   diagnosed the new: Ernest W. Lefever, "Moralism and U.S. Foreign Policy," *Orbis* 16 (Summer 1972): 404, 399.

   "the powerful upsurge": Paul Seabury to Norman Podhoretz, Nov. 24, 1974, Folder 12, Box 357, DPM MSS.

   "PAPER GOING": DPM to Norman Podhoretz, Telegram, Dec. 26, 1974, Folder 3, Box 357, DPM MSS.

   "Norman Podhoretz is": DPM to Robert C. Christopher, July 29, 1974, Folder 7, Box 357, DPM MSS.

57 "huge manuscript": Podhoretz OH.

   "in all my scribbling": DPM to Donald Rumsfeld, Mar. 17, 1975, *DPM Letters*, 375.

   "Mr. President, we have": DPM Diary, Jan. 27, 1975, *DPM Letters*, 373.

58 Weeks later: Walter Isaacson, *Kissinger: A Biography* (New York, 2005), 666–67.

   "head a group": MemCon, GRF, HAK, BS, Mar. 26, 1975, 9:22 a.m.–10:18 a.m., Box 10, GRF NSA.

   "Do what Henry": *DPM Letters*, 375.

   "had long been": HAK, *Years of Renewal* (New York, 1999), 106.

   "Henry was not": Isaacson, *Kissinger: A Biography*, 666, 667.

   "You do not": DPM, *Dangerous Place*, 3.

   "And to say": George Will OH.

59 "That *Commentary* article": Memcon, GRF, HAK, BS, DPM, Apr. 12, 1975, 10:45 a.m., Box 10, GRF NSA.

   "MOYNIHAN CALLS ON": *NYT*, Feb. 26, 1975, 3.

59 "We must play": MemCon, GRF, DPM, BS, Aug. 27, 1975, 2:00 p.m., GRF NSA.
"Would he carry": MemCon, GRF, HAK, BS, Mar. 26, 1975, 9:22 a.m.–10:18 a.m., GRF NSA.
"a disgrace": MemCon, GRF, HAK, BS, Apr. 15, 1975, 9:23 a.m.–10:04 a.m., GRF NSA.
60 The violence so intensified: "Last U.S. Marines in Saigon during Vietnam War," *Don Moore's War Tales*, Apr. 9, 2010. http://donmooreswartales.com/2010/04/09/randy-smith/
"It is a moral collapse": MemCon, GRF, Nelson Rockefeller, HAK, BS, Mar. 28, 1975, 9:25 a.m.–10:10 a.m., 4, GRF NSA.
"but the money": MemCon, GF, HAK, BS, Apr. 3, 1975, 1, GRF NSA.
"By our self-indulgence": Isaacson, *Kissinger*, 647.
"What we've learned": *Time*, May 12, 1975.
"I have no illusions": MemCon, GRF, DPM, HAK, BS, Apr. 12, 1975, 10:45 a.m., 1–2, Box 10, GRF NSA.
"On your knees, Moynihan": Podhoretz OH.
"One major problem": MemCon, HAK, DPM, BS, Apr. 12, 1975, 10:56 a.m.–11:11 a.m., 1–2, GRF NSA.
61 "intellectual ambitions": Weinraub OH.
"one of the most": *DPM Letters*, 367.
"to shore up the right flank": Podhoretz OH.
62 "in public only": DPM Diary, Dec. 22, 1974, *DPM Letters*, 365.

CHAPTER 3: THE "FASHIONABLE ENEMY"

63 "was not interested": Elizabeth Moynihan OH.
"source": Leonard Garment, notes, ca. 1991, Folder 8, Box 7, Leonard Garment MSS, Library of Congress, Washington, DC.
64 "Big Red Lie": DPM, "Big Red Lie: It Was the Soviets, Not the Arabs, Who Came Up with 'Zionism Is Racism,'" *Washington Post*, Sept. 29, 1991, C7.
"It was these": Norman Podhoretz, "The Abandonment of Israel," *Commentary*, July 1976.
"fashionable enemy": Bernard Lewis, "The Anti-Zionist Resolution," *Foreign Affairs* 55:1, Oct. 1976, 59.
"racism was": DPM, *Loyalties* (New York, 1984), 41.
65 "*Was sind Juden*": Carl Heinrich Stratz, *Was sind Juden?: eine ethnographisch-anthropologische Studie* (Vienna, 1903).
Most Zionists used: Amos Morris-Reich, "Arthur Ruppin's Concept of Race," *Israel Studies* 11:3 (2006): 7, 9.
"our national teachers": Theodor Herzl, *The Jewish State* (Rockville, MD, 2008), 109.
"the epic of two": George Bornstein, *Colors of Zion: Blacks, Jews, and Irish from 1845 to 1945* (Cambridge, MA, 2011), 24.
"only a Jew": Theodore Herzl, *The Old-New Land* (New York, 1987), 170.
"peculiarly": Yehiel Michael Pines, "Religion Is the Source of Nationalism," in Arthur Hertzberg (ed.), *The Zionist Idea: A Historical Analysis and Reader* (New York, 1959, 1969), 412.

65 "human race": *Time*, Aug. 16, 1948.

66 "Purity of Blood Statutes": Eric L. Goldstein, *The Price of Whiteness: Jews, Race, and American Identity* (Princeton, NJ, 2006), 16; also see Yosef Hayim Yerushalmi, *Assimilation and Racial Anti-Semitism: The Iberian and the German Models* (New York, 1982), 17.

"racial conundrum": Goldstein, *Price of Whiteness*, 1–2.

"race suicide": Karen Brodkin, *How Jews Became White Folks & What That Says about Race in America* (New Brunswick, 2010), 27–28.

"Israel has disappeared": Einhorn, Baer, Boaz quoted in Goldstein, *Price of Whiteness*, 27, 174, 193.

67 "unmeltable ethnics": Michael Novak, *The Rise of the Unmeltable Ethnics* (New York, 1972).

"gentiles, heathens and": Jonathan D. Sarna, "Ethnicity and Beyond," *Ethnicity and Beyond: Theories and Dilemmas of Jewish Group Demarcation—Studies in Contemporary Jewry*, vol. 25, ed. Eli Lederhendler (Oxford, 2011), 108.

"normal": Brodkin, *How Jews Became White Folks*.

68 An estimated 600,000: Benny Morris, *Righteous Victims: A History of the Zionist-Arab Conflict, 1881–2001* (New York, 2001), 257. Official Israeli estimates were 520,000, while Palestinian estimates are as high as 900,000 to 1 million.

"too tough, too smart": *Time*, Aug. 16, 1948.

Israel was surrounded: Michael Oren, *Six Days of War: June 1967 and the Making of the Modern Middle East* (New York, 2002), 17, 6.

69 "The thought of the": Robert S. Wistrich, *A Lethal Obsession: Anti-Semitism from Antiquity to the Global Jihad* (New York, 2010), 691.

"Zionist Nazism": Yehoshafat Harkabi, *Arab Attitudes Toward Israel* (Hoboken, NJ, 1974), 176.

"the pillar of imperialism": Wistrich, *Lethal Obsession*, 613.

His Muslim Brotherhood: Jeffrey Herf, "Scapegoat," *TNR*, May 12, 2011.

"third round": Oren, *Six Days*, 28.

"it would be normal": Rashid Khalidi, *Palestinian Identity: The Construction of Modern National Consciousness* (New York, 2010), 146.

70 "racist and fanatic": *Decisions and Actions Related to the Palestine National Charter*, available at http://www.un.int/wcm/content/site/palestine/pid/12361

"complete destruction": Oren, *Six Days*, 78.

"practically no Jewish": Morris, *Righteous Victims*, 310.

"It is about time": Oren, *Six Days*, 79, 50.

"If I had to choose": Chaim Herzog, *Living History* (New York, 1996), 170.

71 Within hours, Israel had: Morris, *Righteous Victims*, 318.

"Let's conquer Cairo": Tom Segev, *1967: Israel, the War, and the Year That Transformed the Middle East* (New York, 2008), 15.

"Israeli aggression": Minutes from the United Nations 1526th Plenary Meeting, Fifth Emergency Special Session, June 19, 1967, available at http://unispal.un.org/UNISPAL.NSF/0/729809A9BA3345EB852573400 054118A. See also: William Korey, *The Soviet Cage: Anti-Semitism in Russia* (New York, 1973), 128.

71 "combined a severe": "Special Assessment on the Middle East Situation: Soviet Premier Kosygin's UN Speech," June 19, 1967," CIA Memorandum, available at http://www.foia.cia.gov/docs/DOC_0000233691/DOC_0000233691.pdf

"the unfolding of the Zionorama": "Minutes from the United Nations 1548th Plenary Meeting, Fifth Emergency Special Session," July 4, 1967, available at http://unispal.un.org/UNISPAL.NSF/0/00829F88026C0884852573440053862A

72 "the American imperialists": "Minutes from the United Nations 1558th Plenary Meeting, Fifth Emergency Special Session," July 21, 1967, available at http://unispal.un.org/UNISPAL.NSF/0/AC195A047EACA776852573450046B4D8

"Israel became an": Edward W. Said, *The Question of Palestine* (New York, 1992), 137.

73 "as the sole": Joseph A. Massad, *Colonial Effects: The Making of National Identity in Jordan* (New York, 2001), 249.

"generalizing tendency": Said, *Palestine*, 143, 140.

They viewed any: Barry Rubin, *The PLO—Between Anti-Zionism and Antisemitism: Background and Recent Developments: Analysis of Current Trends in Antisemitism* (Jerusalem, 1993), 6.

"I have never": al-Quds al-Arabi, Feb. 18, 1992, quoted in Rubin, *PLO*, 6.

"secular democratic state": Yasir Arafat, *International Documents on Palestine*, Oct. 1968, 453–54.

"Our goal is": "Yasir Arafat: An Oriana Fallaci Interview," originally in *L'Europeo* 1970, reprinted in *TNR*, Nov. 16, 1974.

Mein Kampf was: Wistrich, *Lethal Obsession*, 701.

74 "What is the secular": William Korey, *Russian Antisemitism, Pamyat, and the Demonology of Zionism* (London, 1995), 11, 33, 14.

75 "Only the Nazis": Wistrich, *Lethal Obsession*, 139.

"new official demonology": Korey, *Russian Antisemitism*, 13.

"Everyone who believes": Wistrich, *Lethal Obsession*, 147.

76 "a proposition that": DPM, *Loyalties*, 41.

"an enemy of": Korey, *Soviet Cage*, 158, 160.

In the seven years since: Korey, *Russian Antisemitism*, 23, 27.

77 Qaddafi claimed responsibility: Joel Peters, *Israel and Africa: The Problematic Friendship* (London, 1992), 47.

In May 1970: "International Olympic Committee, Structure of the Olympic Movement, part 3/4," Jan. 31, 2002, available at http://www.olympic.org/Documents/Reports/EN/en_report_269.pdf.

78 "legitimacy": Resolution adopted by the UN GA 27th Session, 2078th plenary meeting, page 3, paragraph 6, Nov. 2, 1972.

"crime against humanity": Commission on Human Rights, resolution 16 (XXIX), Apr. 2, 1973.

"the unholy alliance": Robert G. Weisbord & Richard Kazarian, Jr., *Israel in the Black American Perspective* (Westport, CT, 1985), 100.

"Zionism and Israeli": Christopher M. Gacek, "Removing the Stain of the United Nations' 'Zionism is Racism' Resolution," Heritage Foundation, Sept. 12,

1991, available at http://www.heritage.org/Research/Reports/1991/09/
Removing-the-Stain-of-the-United-Nations-Zionism-Is-Racism-Resolution

78 "the United Nations of today": Yasir Arafat's speech before the UN GA, Nov. 13, 1974, available at http://www.mideastweb.org/arafat_at_un.htm.

79 "When the forces": Che Guevara, *Guerilla Warfare* (Lincoln, NE, 1998), 8.
"I have come bearing": Arafat UN GA Speech.

80 "Do you know": Weisbord & Kazarian, *Israel in the Black American Perspective*, 33, 32.
One cartoon depicted: *NYT*, Aug. 15, 1967, 1.
"only": *NYT*, Aug. 15, 1967, 16.

81 "habit": Martin Peretz OH. See also: Jonathan Kaufman, *Broken Alliance: The Turbulent Times Between Blacks and Jews in America* (New York, 1995), 208–11.
"the imperialistic Zionist war": *NYT*, Sept. 3, 1967, 1.
"The importance of": James Forman, *The Making of Black Revolutionaries* (Seattle, 1997), 498–500.
"the Middle East murderers": *NYT*, Oct. 23, 1968, 32.
"racist, ruthless, Zionist bandits": Jay Kaufman, "Thou Shalt Surely Rebuke Thy Neighbor," *Black Anti-Semitism and Jewish Racism* (New York, 1970), 57.
"If the Jews": *The Black Panther*, Dec. 21, 1968, quoted in Seymour Martin Lipset, "The Socialism of Fools," *NYTM*, Jan. 3, 1971, 26.
"same Zionists that exploit": Weisbord & Kazarian, *Israel in the Black American Perspective*, 36, 37.
"the litmus test": Alan Dershowitz OH.

82 "biological": Marty Peretz OH.
"Israeli embassies, tourist offices": Eric Mann op-ed, *The Guardian*, Oct. 17, 1970.
At an anti-nukes: *NYT*, Aug. 14, 1970, 1.
"a criminal Jewish community": Alan Dershowitz, "Can the Guild Survive Its Hypocrisy?" *American Lawyer*, Aug. 11, 1978, 30.
"deradicalized": Nathan Glazer, "On Being Deradicalized," *Commentary*, October, 1970.

83 "the myth of Arab-black": *NYT*, Nov. 1, 1970, 74.
"the Arab nations": Bayard Rustin, "American Negroes and Israel (1974)," Bayard Rustin et al., *Time on Two Crosses: The Collected Writings of Bayard Rustin* (Berkeley, 2003), 320, 318.
"left-wing kooks": Barry Levenfeld OH.
"The Israel of American Jews": Jonathan D. Sarna, "A Projection of America As It Ought to Be: Zion in the Mind's Eye of American Jews," in Allon Gal, *Envisioning Israel: The Changing Ideals and Images of North American Jews* (Jerusalem, 1996), 41–42, 59.
"relatively naïve": Betty Friedan, "Woman as Jew—Jew as Woman," transcription from the "American Jewish Congress Dialogue between American and Israeli Women," Feb. 8, 1984, Folder 45,11, Box 37, Betty Friedan MSS, Schlesinger Library, Radcliffe Institute, Harvard University, Cambridge, MA.

84 "female flunkies": Betty Friedan, "Anti-Semitism as a Political Tool: Its Congruence with Anti-Feminism," [1985] position paper for the "Anti-Semitism in the

Political Arena" workshop, sponsored by the President of Israel's Eighth International Seminar, Folder 12, Box 13, Friedan MSS.

84 "imperialism, neocolonialism": Betty Friedan, "Scary Doings in Mexico City," in *"It Changed My Life": Writings on the Women's Movement* (Cambridge, 1998), 460.

"If Zionism is": Stanley Meisler, *United Nations: The First Fifty Years* (New York, 1995), 205.

"not to speak": Betty Friedan, "Scary Doings in Mexico City," 442.

"microphones were turned off": Betty Friedan, Mexico City Account, Folder 75, 1256, Box 108, Betty Friedan MSS.

"followed by gunmen": Betty Friedan, "Anti-Semitism as a Political Tool."

85 "own background was": Betty Friedan, "Women and Jews: The Quest for Selfhood," *Congress Monthly*, Feb./Mar. 1985, 52:2, 7.

"this American witch": Betty Friedan, draft of speech for "Israel World Meeting," June 1973, Folder 4, 1227a, Box 105, Friedan MSS.

"[It] is the prevention": Betty Friedan, "Woman as Jew—Jew as Woman," transcription from the "American Jewish Congress Dialogue between American and Israeli Women," Feb. 8, 1984, Folder 47, 11, Box 37, Friedan MSS.

"new strength and authenticity": Betty Friedan, "Anti-Semitism as a Political Tool."

"All this has nothing": Bernard Lewis, "The Anti-Zionist Resolution," *Foreign Affairs*, 55: Oct. 1, 1976, 64.

CHAPTER 4: MOYNIHAN ON THE MOVE, OCTOBER 1975

87 "exercise in EGOSAG": *New York Sunday News*, Sept. 14, 1975, Folder 3, Box 327, DPM MSS.

88 "substantive accomplishments": Ambassador [Barbara] White to DPM, July 7, 1975, 3–4, Carton 1, Barbara M. White MSS (80-M235), Schlesinger Library, Radcliffe Institute, Harvard University, Cambridge, MA.

"how, if the Declaration": DPM, *Dangerous Place*, 96.

His colleague Leonard: Leonard Garment, *Crazy Rhythm* (New York, 2001), 301.

"We've got to stop this": Suzanne Weaver Garment OH.

"totalitarian tract": DPM, *Dangerous Place*, 96.

White praised: "Transcript of a Press Briefing, Ambassador Barbara M. White, July 11, 1975," Press Release USUN-79 (75), July 14, 1975, 6, Barbara M. White MSS.

"their job *as*": DPM, *Dangerous Place*, 96.

"Does President Ford": *NYT*, July 4, 1975.

"echoes": DPM, *Dangerous Place*, 77.

89 Abba Eban: Abba Eban, "Israel and the Future of the United Nations Ideal," *NYT*, Aug. 7, 1975, 26.

"the Third World Congress": George G. Higgins, July 21, 1975, Folder 4, Box 328, DPM MSS.

The *Washington Post*: "A Job for Moynihan?" *Washington Post*, Apr. 23, 1975, 4.

89   "Speak high and bold": Theodore H. White to DPM, May 7, 1975, DPM MSS.
      "a florid combination": Garry Wills, "Pat Moynihan: Pixie in Politics." *The Morning Record* (Meriden, June 2, 1975), 6.
      "white Western": St. Clair Drake, "Moynihan and the Third World." *The Nation*, July 5, 1975, 12.
      "I figured this was": *NYT*, June 22, 1975, 5.
90   "state department north": DPM, *Dangerous Place*, 3, 10.
      "be forgiven": *NYT*, Mar. 31, 1974, 69.
      "finale": " 'It's a respectable job,'" *New York Sunday News*, Sept. 14, 1975, Folder 6, Box 331, DPM MSS.
      "the most popular": "New American at UN will heat up debate," *Toronto Star*, Apr. 26, 1975, Folder 7, Box 325, DPM MSS.
      "destructive": DPM For Rel,1, 62.
91   "Is there somebody": DPM For Rel, 301.
      "are we such": DPM For Rel, 60, 301.
      "Moynihan approach": DPM For Rel, 79, 161.
      Most experts: DPM For Rel, 6.
      "This country's standing": DPM For Rel, 166, 300.
      "indispensable": DPM For Rel, 363, 366, 383.
92   "well, after all": DPM For Rel, 389.
      "can't have it": DPM For Rel, 384–85.
      "Onetime Shoeshine Boy": *People*, May 12, 1975, Folder 4, Box 335, DPM MSS.
      "liberal values": Irving Kristol to DPM, June 2, 1975, Folder 9, Box 337, DPM MSS.
      "liberal dissenter": DPM to Richard W. Lyman, July 3, 1975, Folder 7, Box 329, DPM MSS.
      "person of high ideals": Transcript of DPM UN ambassadorship swearing-in ceremony, July 1, 1975, Folder 3, Box 328, DPM MSS.
93   Privately, Moynihan: DPM to GRF, July 3, 1975, Folder 8, Box 343, DPM MSS.
      "liberalism is draining": DPM, *Dangerous Place*, 98, 99. See also Irving Kristol, "The 'New Cold War'," *Wall Street Journal*, July 17, 1975.
      "decline of democratic regimes": Transcript of DPM speech to U.S. Mission to the UN, July 1, 1975, 4, Tap MSS.
      "These were decent people": DPM, *Dangerous Place*, 100–101.
      Chester Finn: Chester Finn to DPM, July 23, 1975, Folder 3, Box 327, DPM MSS.
      "the name of": DPM to Chester Finn, Aug. 7, 1975, Folder 3, Box 327, DPM MSS.
      "a known Israel-phile": Chester Finn to DPM, July 23, 1975, Folder 3, Box 327, DPM MSS.
94   "polite, deferential, civilized": Suzanne Weaver Garment OH.
      "You told me that": TelCon between HAK and DPM, Aug. 6, 1975, 1 in HAK TelCon.
      "a weapon of": Transcript of HAK speech "Global Challenge and International Cooperation," July 14, 1975, 6, Folder 5, Box 337, DPM MSS.
      Kissinger adroitly balanced: Transcript of HAK speech "The Moral Foundations of Foreign Policy," July 15, 1975, 3, Folder 6, Box 337, DPM MSS.

95 "The World's New": Robert C. Christopher, "The World's New Cold War," *Newsweek*, June 16, 1975, 37.

"this nation to contribute": HAK, "Moral Foundations," 11.

"a challenge": Barbara M. White to DPM, July 16, 1975, Folder 5, Box 337, DPM MSS.

"Dear Henry": DPM to HAK, Aug. 14, 1975, Folder 5, Box 337, DPM MSS.

"multilateral countries": DPM to HAK, Aug. 14, 1975, Folder 5, Box 337, DPM MSS.

"Small countries": DPM to Lawrence Eagleburger, Aug. 15, 1975, Folder 14, Box 335, DPM MSS.

96 Kissinger established an: HAK, *Years of Renewal*, 783.

the same official observer: DPM to Lawrence Eagleburger, Aug. 15, 1975, Folder 14, Box 335, DPM MSS.

"imperialist oppressors": DPM to Richard Funkhouser, Sept. 2, 1975, Folder 5, Box 327, DPM MSS.

"We were not about": DPM, *Dangerous Place*, 111.

"unfriendly act": DPM to Lawrence Eagleburger, Aug. 15, 1975, Folder 14, Box 335, DPM MSS.

"Why are we so": DPM to HAK, Aug. 15, 1975, Folder 5, Box 337, DPM MSS.

"Just be brutal": HAK, *Years of Renewal*, 783.

"black-and-white": Malcolm Butler to BS, Aug. 26, 1975, *Foreign Relations of the United States, 1969–1976*, Vol. E–14, Part 1, Documents on the United Nations, 1973–1976, Document 25.

"fudge factory": DPM to Lawrence Eagleburger, Aug. 15, 1975, Folder 14, Box 335, DPM MSS.

"we were far closer": HAK, *Years of Renewal*, 783.

97 "Yes.": DPM, *Dangerous Place*, 111.

"bureaucratic glitch": HAK, *Years of Renewal*, 783.

"U.S WINS A UN": *NYT*, Aug. 21, 1975, 73, 34.

"rude and intimidatory": *New York Post*, Sept. 20, 1975.

Moynihan was shocked: Charles B. Rangel to DPM, Sept. 19, 1975, Folder 11, Box 333, DPM MSS.

"In the name": DPM to William F. Buckley Jr., Sept. 17, 1975, Folder 5, Box 333, DPM MSS.

98 "It was inspiring": Carl Gershman to DPM, Sept. 22, 1975, Folder 22, Box 335, DPM MSS.

"not used to": DPM to HAK, Sept. 6, 1975, Folder 5, Box 337, DPM MSS.

"we showed our teeth": DPM to HAK, Sept. 9, 1975, Folder 5, Box 337, DPM MSS.

In a 12,000-word: *NYT*, Sept. 2, 1975, 1, 21.

Both vengeful and worried: Galia Golan, *Soviet Policies in the Middle East from World War II to Gorbachev* (Cambridge, UK, 1990), 100.

"an interminable catalogue": DPM, *Dangerous Place*, 135, 126–27.

"the broadest development program": DPM, *Dangerous Place*, 136, 139, 141.

99 "class struggle": "UN Debate: Groping for New Relationships," *NYT*, Sept. 4, 1975.

"Scarsdale": DPM, *Dangerous Place*, 143.

99 "Mr. President": DPM, *Dangerous Place*, 139.

100 "the mother of Africa": Benjamin Neuberger, "Israel's Relations with the Third World (1948–2008)," research paper #5, a publication of the S. Daniel Abraham Center for International and Regional Studies, Oct. 2009, 11, 14, available at http://www.tau.ac.il/humanities/abraham/publications/israel.pdf.

"a façade for neo-colonialism": Joel Peters, *Israel and Africa: The Problematic Friendship* (London, 1992), 22, 21.

"the racist aggressive": "Resolution on the Middle East and Occupied Arab Territories," Resolution 76, Article 9, Organization of African Unity, Assembly of Heads of State and Government, July 28–Aug. 1, 1975, available at http://www.au.int/en/sites/default/files/ASSEMBLY_EN_JULY_28_01_AUGUST_1975_ASSEMBLY_HEADS_STATE_GOVERNMENT_THIRTEENTH_ORDINARY_SESSION.pdf

In early September : *NYT*, Sept. 6, 1975.

101 "stressed the importance": Kurt Waldheim to Arthur J. Goldberg, Sept. 8, 1975, Folder 1 Box 336, DPM MSS.

"plea bargaining": DPM to W. Scott Thompson, Sept. 2, 1975, Folder 3, Box 332, DPM MSS.

"extinction of Israel": *NYT*, Oct. 2, 1975, 1.

Finally, he insulted: *NYT*, Oct. 3, 1975, 6.

When reporters asked: DPM, *Dangerous Place*, 155.

"good old days": Suzanne Weaver Garment OH.

102 "Something was going": DPM, *A Dangerous Place*, 154, 156.

"President, a racist murderer": *NYT*, Oct. 3, 1975.

"a form of good": DPM, *Dangerous Place*, 148.

"'Democracy has come'": DPM, *Dangerous Place*, 158–59.

"no accident": DPM, *Dangerous Place*, 159

103 "blew his stack": *Newsweek*, Oct. 20, 1975, 50.

"concern for Israel": DPM, *Dangerous Place*, 168.

"moral lectures": George F. Will, "Right Man at U.N.," *Emporia Gazette*, Oct. 11, 1975, 4.

"undiplomatically": *Newsweek*, Oct. 13, 1975, 51.

"embattled": *Newsweek*, Oct. 20, 1975, 50.

"start raising hell": *NYT*, Oct. 4, 1975, 1.

"Americans at UN": *NYT*, Oct. 5, 1975, 2.

"Ambassador Moynihan's words": Courtney Sheldon to DPM, Oct. 6, 1975, Folder 7, Box 334, DPM MSS.

Seeking more distance: Ambassador Bennett and Courtney Sheldon to DPM, Oct. 6, 1975, Folder 7, Box 334, DPM MSS.

104 "earned wide": DPM, *Dangerous Place*, 162–63.

"international diplomacy": Article clipping from DPM to Henry Grunwald, Oct. 14, 1975, Folder 3, Box 329, DPM MSS.

"uncivil attacks": Statement by the Executive Secretariat of the Organization of African Unity to the UN, Oct. 5, 1975, Folder 5, Box 339, DPM MSS.

"unsolicited advice on how": Statement by Clarence M. Mitchell Jr., Oct. 5, 1975, Folder 7, Box 334, DPM MSS.

104 "not indulge tyrants": Bayard Rustin, "The Amin Controversy," *New America*, Nov. 1975, 1, Box 330, DPM MSS.

105 "ideological counter-offensive": *New America*, Nov. 1975, 1, 8.

105 "the most racist act": Peters, *Israel and Africa*, 76.

"inspired": Anthony Lewis, "For Which We Stand: IV," *NYT*, Oct. 9, 1975, 7, Box 325, DPM MSS.

"Diplomacy is becoming": William Safire, "New Order of Rhetoric," *NYT*, Oct. 9, 1975, 7, Box 325, DPM MSS.

"the proximate": William F. Buckley, Jr. to DPM, Oct. 17, 1975, Folder 5, Box 335, DPM MSS.

since the summer: Malcolm Butler to BS, Aug. 26, 1975, GRF Lib.

"This Moynihan thing": MemCon, GRF, HAK, BS, Oct. 9, 1975, 9:30 a.m., Box 15, GRF NSA.

"I was *his* ambassador": DPM, *Dangerous Place*, 166.

"Israel had become": DPM, *Dangerous Place*, 168.

106 At a cabinet: DPM, *Dangerous Place*, 164.

"You seem to be": DPM, *Dangerous Place*, 164.

"avoid writing speeches": DPM, *Dangerous Place*, 162.

"It has been": George B. Lambrakis to DPM, Oct. 16, 1975, Folder 4, Box 329, DPM MSS.

"turned against": DPM, "The Politics of Human Rights," Aug. 1977, *Commentary*.

107 By December 1975: Aleksandr Solzhnetsyn, *NYT*, Dec. 1, 1975.

"But then—I am": Samuel H. Beer to DPM, Aug. 18, 1975, Folder 8, Box 325, DPM MSS.

"concern with liberty": Suzanne Weaver to Leonard Garment, Sept. 4, 1975, Folder 9, Box 336, DPM MSS.

"in Swahili": Daniel C. Thomas, *The Helsinki Effect: International Norms, Human Rights, and the Demise of Communism* (Princeton, NJ, 2001), 55.

"enshrining human rights": HAK, *Years of Renewal*, 648.

"individual rights": Irving Kristol, *The Neoconservative Persuasion* (New York, 2011), 221.

108 "was the pivotal": Hodgson, *The Gentleman from New York: Daniel Patrick Moynihan*, 243.

CHAPTER 5: OOM, SHMOOM: "WHERE ARE YOUR BLOODY JEWS?"

109 "Where are your": Chaim Herzog, *Living History* (New York, 1996), 197.

110 "one of the worst": Yitzhak Rabin, *The Rabin Memoirs* (Los Angeles, 1996), 261.

111 "both shared": Isaac Herzog OH.

"He was a man": DPM, *A Dangerous Place* (Boston, 1978), 178.

"The Arabs used to talk": Telegram, Israel's New York Mission to MFA, reprint of C.J. Sulzberger's article in the *NYT*, "Shape of Things to Come," Aug. 24, 1975, 7026/1-‎א, MFA MSS.

112 In late September : Telegram, Israel's New York Mission to MFA, Sept. 26, 1975, 5251/1 – חצ, MFA MSS.

"extremist trends": Telegram, Israel's New York Mission to MFA, Sept. 25, 1975, 5251/1 – חצ, MFA MSS.

"definite and clear action": *NYT*, Aug. 1, 1975, 3.

"out of the blue": Address by Chaim Herzog at the farewell meeting of the Presidents' Conference of Major Jewish Organizations, June 28, 1978, 2.21.4 (6), Speeches, 2, 107, 5/1978–6/1978, Chaim Herzog MSS, Chaim Herzog Institute, Herzliya, Israel.

"realized the significance": DPM, *Loyalties* (New York, 1984), 41.

"The goal of this": Pinchas Elias to the MFA, Oct. 2, 1975, 3873/3, MFA MSS.

113 "For Sadat, a": HAK, *Years of Renewal* (New York, 1999), 459.

"The United Nations": Text of the 2390th plenary meeting of the U.N. General Assembly's Thirtieth Session, agenda item 27, Nov. 3, 1975, 632, paragraph 71.

"all decent and": Address by Chaim Herzog to the Fletcher School of Law and Diplomacy at Tufts University, Jan. 28, 1976, 2.22.1, Speeches, 2.110, 1/22/1976-4/28/1976 (146), Herzog MSS.

"embarrassed": Telegram, Israel's New York Mission to MFA, Oct. 4, 1975, 3813/3, MFA MSS.

114 "the peak": James T. Kloppenberg, *Reading Obama: Dreams, Hope, and the American Political Tradition* (Princeton, NJ, 2010), 115.

Delegates representing: Samuel Moyn, *The Last Utopia: Human Rights in History* (Cambridge, MA, 2010), 118–19.

"they would need": Telegram, Israel's New York Mission to MFA, Oct. 3, 1975, 3813/3, MFA MSS.

"in their discussions": Telegram, Israel's New York Mission to MFA, Oct. 10, 1975, 3813/3, MFA MSS.

"are working vigorously": Telegram, Israel's New York Mission to MFA, Oct. 3, 1975, 3813/3, MFA MSS.

"this Israeli thing": TelCon between HAK and DPM, Aug. 6, 1975, 9, HAK TelCon.

115 "In a confrontation": TelCon between HAK and Paul Ziffren, Apr. 25, 1975, 2, HAK TelCon.

"I got a call": TelCon between HAK and Max Fisher, Apr. 2, 1975, 1, HAK TelCon.

"closely": Address by Chaim Herzog at the 70th Annual Meeting of the American Jewish Committee, May 16, 1976, 26–27, 2.22.2, Speeches, 2.110, 5/4/1976-6/26/1976, Herzog MSS.

116 He heard the mutterings: Telegram, Israel's New York Mission to MFA, Oct. 3, 1975, 3813/3, MFA MSS.

"The Jewish public must": Telegram, Israel's New York Mission to MFA, Oct. 2, 1975, 3813/3, MFA MSS.

"community as a whole": Malcolm Hoenlein OH.

During the summer: Morris Fine to Bertram Gold, July 30, 1975, Folder 1–2, Box 206, AJC MSS.

"especially non-Jews": Telegram, MFA to Israeli missions abroad, Oct. 6, 1975, 3813/3, MFA MSS.

117 "nevertheless work towards": Telegram, Israel's New York Mission to MFA, Oct. 13, 1975, 3813/3, MFA MSS.

"had no legal basis": Telegram, Israel's Mexico City Mission to MFA, Oct. 17, 1975, 3813/3, MFA MSS.

"surprise meeting": Telegram, Israel's New York Mission to MFA, Oct. 13, 1975, 3813/3, MFA MSS.

Although the group usually: Telegram, Israel's New York Mission to MFA, Oct. 13, 1975, 3813/3, MFA MSS. See also "Random Thoughts on Selected Delegates," Mar. 23, 1976, 6, Tap MSS.

118 "no monkey business": Ilan Hartuv OH.

"sold and bought": Mark Gayn, "Crucial Votes Sold at UN Delegates Say," *Toronto Star*, Dec. 27, 1975.

"culture of corruption": Rachel Ehrenfeld, "Where Corruption Rules—The U.N. Is Thoroughly Tainted," American Center for Democracy, *National Review Online*, Dec. 14, 2004 http://acdemocracy.org/viewarticle.cfm?category=U.S.%20Policy&id=213. See also Sharon Otterman, "Council on Foreign Relations." *Council on Foreign Relations*, Oct. 25, 2005, http://www.cfr.org/un/iraq-oil-food-scandal/p76.

"The time of the Arab": *NYT*, Oct. 14, 1975, 8.

"petrodollar diplomacy": *NYT*, Oct. 23, 1975, 2.

119 "congratulated": 2120th meeting, ThirdCom, 49, paragraphs 44–45, Oct. 3, 1975.

120 "claiming Jews are": 2132nd meeting, ThirdCom, 105, paragraph 64, Oct. 16, 1975.

"a Jew from Yemen": 2133rd meeting, ThirdCom, 108–9, paragraph 14, Oct. 17, 1975.

"Nazism in the sense": 2118th meeting, ThirdCom, 34, paragraph 44, Oct. 1, 1975.

"a huge Zionist ghetto": 2133rd meeting, ThirdCom, 108–9, paragraph 14, Oct. 17, 1975.

121 "reactionary Tel Aviv": 2118th meeting, ThirdCom, paragraph 27, Oct. 1, 1975.

"single operative paragraph": 2132nd meeting, ThirdCom, 100, paragraph 21, Oct. 16, 1975.

Rather than defend: 2132nd meeting, ThirdCom, 103, paragraphs 44–46, Oct. 16, 1975.

"a pestilence afflicting": 2132nd meeting, ThirdCom, 100, paragraphs 22–24, Oct. 16, 1975.

"intellectual dishonesty": 2133rd meeting, ThirdCom, 107–8, paragraphs 4–8, Oct. 17, 1975.

122 "a vital element": 2132nd meeting, ThirdCom, 104, paragraphs 47–53, Oct. 16, 1975.

"To question the": 2132nd meeting, ThirdCom, 104, paragraph 48, Oct. 16, 1975.

"only the Jewish": 2132nd meeting, ThirdCom, 104, paragraph 48, Oct. 16, 1975.

"for the word": Garment OH 2.

"obscene act": 2134th meeting, ThirdCom, 113, paragraph 23, Oct. 17, 1975.

123 "not only unjust": 2121st meeting, ThirdCom, 54, paragraph 29, Oct. 3, 1975.

"to commit one": 2134th meeting, ThirdCom, 113, paragraph 23, Oct. 17, 1975.

"practical effect will be": *Wall Street Journal,* Oct. 24, 1975.

123 "attack upon Zionism": George V. R. Smith, *Atlanta Journal,* Oct. 3, 1975.

"countries whose regimes": DPM, *Dangerous Place,* 184.

124 "behave with": DPM, *Dangerous Place,* 185.

"pungent words": DPM, Fundraising Letter, 2, ca. 1997, in David Luchins, private papers.

"walked to": *NYT,* Oct. 18, 1975, 1.

"I was very moved indeed": Herzog, *Living History,* 197.

"shameful, benighted and arbitrary": Address delivered to the Knesset, Oct. 20, 1975, United Nations and Zionism, 1975, Box 217, Interreligious Affairs, AJC MSS.

Using Freedom House's classifications: *Wall Street Journal,* Oct. 24, 1975.

"We were facing": Herzog, *Living History,* 196–97.

125 "from various levels": Telegram, Israel's New York Mission to MFA, Oct. 21, 1975, 3813/3, MFA MSS.

"He believes that": Telegram, Israel's New York Mission to MFA, Oct. 23, 1975, 3813/3, MFA MSS.

"he learned more": Telegram, Israel's New York Mission to MFA, Oct. 21, 1975, 3813/3, MFA MSS.

"It would be helpful": Herzog, *Living History,* 197.

"Ruthie, no one": Ruth Wisse, "The Socialist," *Tablet Magazine,* Mar. 8, 2011, available at http://www.tabletmag.com/news-and-politics/60829/the-socialist/; Ruth Wisse OH.

"Where were the": *NYT,* Oct. 25, 1975, 3. Transcript of Chaim Herzog remarks to Conference of Presidents of Major American Jewish Organizations, Oct. 24, 1975, in Telegram, Israel's Washington Embassy to MFA, Oct. 24, 1975, 3813/3 – חצ, 90, MFA MSS.

126 "I am surprised": Telegram, Israel's Washington, DC, Mission to MFA, Oct. 24, 1975, 3813/3, MFA MSS.

The Washington Embassy: Telegram, Israel's Washington, DC, Mission to MFA, Oct. 25, 1975, 3813/3, MFA MSS.

"The activities of the Embassy": Chaim Herzog, personal note to file, Oct. 25, 1975, Political Activist, 5.22, (5), 1975–1977, Chaim Herzog Archives. See also Chaim Herzog to Chaim Barlev, Oct. 30, 1975, 1.64 Correspondence, 9/5/1975–10/31/1975 (33), Herzog MSS.

"wasn't criticizing the government": Telegram, Israel's New York Mission to MFA, Oct. 27, 1975, 3813/3, MFA MSS.

"I did not relate": Message from Simcha Dinitz to Chaim Herzog duplicated in Telegram, Israel's Washington, DC, Mission to MFA, Oct. 28, 1975, 3813/3, MFA MSS.

127 "immediate response": Telegram, Foreign Ministry Director Avraham Kidron to MFA, Oct. 31, 1975, 3813/3, MFA MSS.

The Israelis were: Telegram, Israel's Washington, DC, Mission to MFA, Nov. 6, 1975, 7087/11-א, MFA MSS.

"great man": Jeremi Suri, *Henry Kissinger and the American Century* (Cambridge, MA, 2007), 263.

128 "do you consider": Transcript of meeting by Sadat with the National Press Club, Oct. 27, 1975, 15–16, Anwar Sadat MSS, University of Maryland, available at http://sadat.umd.edu/archives/speeches.htm.

"the very close": Text of GRF's toast to Sadat, Oct. 27, 1975, 1725–1726, *Public Papers of the Presidents.*

"at Salzburg were": MemCon, GRF, HAK, Mohammed Anwar al-Sadat, Ismail Fahmy, Oct. 27, 1975, 12:00 p.m.–12:50 p.m., 1, GRF NSA.

But the Israelis protested: Telegram, Israel's Washington, DC, Mission to MFA, Nov. 6, 1975, 7087/11-א, MFA MSS.

"could report to": Telegram, Israel's Washington, DC, Mission to MFA, Nov. 1, 1975, 7087/9-א, MFA MSS.

"primitive anti-Semitism": Telegram, MFA to Israeli missions abroad, Nov. 6, 1975, 7087/9-א, MFA MSS.

129 But just as Rabin: Anita Shapira, *Yigal Allon, Native Son: A Biography*, translated into English by Evelyn Abel (Philadelphia, 2008), 313. See also http://www.haaretz.com/print-edition/features/the-jordanian-option-the-plan-that-refuses-to-die-1.226164

"it is self-evident": Text of the 2390th plenary meeting of the UN GA, agenda item 27, Nov. 3, 1975, 635, paragraph 101.

"Waging political warfare": Statement by Chaim Herzog at the UN, Apr. 19, 1975, Political Activist, 5.22, (5), 1975–1977, 2, Herzog MSS.

130 "the decent countries": *NYT*, Oct. 19, 1975, 4.

In this latest wallop: *NYT,* Oct. 6, 1975, 1.

"FORD TO CITY": *NYT*, Oct. 30, 1975, 1.

"The people of": *NYT,* Dec. 28, 2006,

131 "Kissinger lost his": Aaron Latham, "Kissinger's Bluff," *New York Magazine*, Apr. 12, 1976, 34.

"serious questions all": *Washington Post,* Nov. 15, 1975, A5.

CHAPTER 6: THE SPEECH

133 "We are conducting": TelCon between HAK and William Buffum, Nov. 10, 1975, 4:25 p.m., HAK TelCon.

by margins of 49: Harris Survey, Nov. 22–29, in *New York Post*, Dec. 15, 1975, 6.

"human rights": DPM, Statement in Third Committee, Nov. 12, 1975, in *Freedom at Issue*, Jan.-Feb. 1976, 7 in Folder 21, Box 335, DPM MSS.

134 "aimed more at": Harris Survey, Nov. 22–29, in *New York Post*, Dec. 15, 1975, 6.

"The United Nations": DPM to William Shawn, Nov. 3, 1975, 2, Folder 5, Box 333, DPM MSS.

A nationalist movement: Bernard Lewis, "The Anti-Zionist Resolution," *Foreign Affairs,* 55:1, Oct. 1976.

"Nonsense": DPM, *A Dangerous Place* (New York, 1978), 185.

135 "Be an anti-Semite": DPM, *Dangerous Place*, 186.

They wondered if: TelCon between HAK and William Buffum, Nov. 10, 1975, 4:25 p.m., HAK TelCon.

135 "Its soul, its whatness": Telegram, DPM to HAK, Oct. 18, 1975, 1, Folder 5, Box 337, DPM MSS.
 "rebelled": Telegram, DPM to HAK, Oct. 18, 1975, 3–4, Folder 5, Box 337, DPM MSS.
136 "the Ford administration's": Walter Burns, Lynne V. Cheney, Donald Rumsfeld, *In Memoriam: Robert A. Goldwin,* Jan. 21, 2010, American Enterprise Institute, available at http://www.aei.org/article/society-and-culture/in-memoriam-robert-a-goldwin/
 "jeopardizes": Robert Goldwin, Draft, ca. late Oct. 1975 in Hal Horan to BS, Oct. 22, 1975, NSC, USUN (8), Box 21, GRF Lib.
 "scrubbed": Handwritten request, BS, Oct. 22, 1975, NSC, USUN (8), Box 21, GRF Lib.
 "must not pass": Hal Horan to BS, Oct. 22, 1975, NSC, USUN (8), Box 21, GRF Lib.
 "strongly": Hal Horan to BS, Oct. 22, 1975, NSC, USUN (8), Box 21, GRF Lib.
 "unanimous": Hal Horan to BS, Oct. 24, 1975, NSC, USUN (8), Box 21, GRF Lib.
 "in the strongest terms": Presidential Statement, Oct. 24, 1975, NSC, USUN (8), Box 21, GRF Lib.
 "horror": Hal Horan to BS, Oct. 23, 1975, NSC, USUN (8), Box 21, GRF Lib.
137 "We have been": TelCon between HAK and William Buffum, Nov. 10, 1975, 4:25 p.m., HAK Telcon.
 "Moynihan got your": TelCon between HAK and William Buffum, Nov. 10, 1975, 6:34 p.m., HAK Telcon.
138 "the very quintessence": DPM, "Address by DPM, United States Representative to the United Nations, to the Appeal of Conscience Foundation, Annual Award Dinner," New York, Oct. 21, 1975, 1–3, Press Release USUN-123 (75) in DPM Vertical File, AJC MSS.
 "one-party states": "Address by DPM," Oct. 21, 1975, 3–4.
 Shortly after the: Excerpts from United Nations advertisements from the Advertising Council's promotional campaign, Folder 5, Box 329, DPM MSS.
139 "There's always been": James F. Leonard to DPM, Oct. 20, 1975, Folder 5, Box 329, DPM MSS.
 "bravos": *People*, Dec. 29–Jan. 5, 1975, 27.
 "the common people": Philip and Olive Tocker to DPM, Oct. 19, 1975, Folder 3, Box 325, DPM MSS.
 "The fine firm": Nick Thimmesch, "The Fine Firm of Moynihan and Garment," *Los Angeles Times*, Oct. 21, 1975.
 "The vote on": W. Tapley Bennett, Jr., to Hubert H. Humphrey, Nov. 12, 1975, Tap MSS.
 "sentiment for postponement": Hal Horan to BS, Oct. 24, 1975, NSC, USUN (8), Box 21, GRF Lib.
 "anti-American pique": *NYT*, Nov. 12, 1975, 17.
140 "voice of the victim": Mr. Kaddoumi (Palestine Liberation Organization), Nov. 3, 1975, 2390th meeting, UN GA, *Official Records*, 627:4, 628:16, 627:9, 631:52, A/PV.2390.

140 "money changing": Mr. Baroody (Saudi Arabia), Nov. 3, 1975, 2390th meeting, UN GA, *Official Records*, 637:119, A/PV.2390.

"Jewish blood by marriage": Mr. Fall (Senegal), Nov. 3, 1975, 2390th meeting, UN GA, *Official Records*, 638:130, A/PV.2390.

"contemptuous rogue waves": Michael Schumacher, *Mighty Fitz: The Sinking of the Edmund Fitzgerald* (New York, 2005), 179.

"not too clear": Mr. Wilson (Liberia), 2400th GA, 771:18, A/PV.2400.

141 Talib El-Shibib of: 2400th GA, 771:23–24, A/PV.2400.

"hard-line Arab tactics": *NYT*, Nov. 12, 1975, 17.

"our positions clear": DPM to Benjamin Bradle[e], Nov. 20, 1975, Folder 1, Box 326, DPM MSS.

"So much for": Suzanne Weaver to W. Tapley Bennett, Jr., Nov. 11, 1975, Tap MSS.

"unanimity" and "consensus": Text of the 2400th meeting of the UN GA, 782:143; 780:118, Nov. 10, 1975.

"racism and racial": Mr. Richard (United Kingdom) 2400th GA, 782: 155, 158, A/PV.2400.

142 "single out": Mr. Sikivou (Fiji), Nov. 10, 1975, 2400th GA, 787: 216, A/PV.2400.

"Is there a single": The Reverend Nunez (Cost Rica), 2400th GA, 778:103, A/PV.2400.

"feverish activity by certain": Mr. Adjibade (Dahomey), 2400th GA, 777:85, A/PV.2400.

"pressure, coercion, threats": Mr. Ramphul (Mauritius), 2400th GA, 781:135, 137, A/PV.2400.

"to equate with anti-Semitism": Mr. Petric (Yugoslavia), 2400th GA, 781:130, A/PV.2400.

"the right to return": Mr. Adjibade (Dahomey), 2400th GA, 777:87–88, A/PV.2400.

"race in the biological": Mr. Al-Sayegh (Kuwait), 2400th GA, 790–791:245, 248, 259, A/PV.2400.

143 "the world that they": Norman Podhoretz, "The Abandonment of Israel," *Commentary*, July 1976.

"The continued existence": Mr. Herzog (Israel), 2400th GA, 776:80, A/PV.2400.

"film of broken glass": Mr. Herzog (Israel), 2400th GA, 773:44, A/PV.2400.

"Zionism": Mr. Herzog (Israel), 2400th GA, 774:57, A/PV.2400.

"For us, the Jewish": Mr. Herzog (Israel), 2400th GA, 776:82, A/PV.2400.

"The filthy huts": Chaim Herzog, *Living History*, 61.

"Lurie's Opinion": Ranan Lurie, *Reporter Dispatch* (White Plains, NY), Nov. 4, 1975, A8.

144 "To prepare 'solutions'": Elie Wiesel, in *Le Figaro*, ca. Nov. 11, 1975, translated in Elie Wiesel, *A Jew Today* (New York, 1979), 41–43.

"a number of countries": B'nai B'rith Advertisement, *NYT*, Nov. 10, 1975, 27.

"the delegitimization of Israel": Shimon Peres, Irwin Cotler quoted in Yohanan Manor, *To Right a Wrong: The Revocation of the UN General Assembly Resolution 3379 Defaming Zionism* (New York, 1996), vii, 69–70.

145 "doing something": Mr. Moynihan (United States of America), 2400th GA, 795:307, 309, 313, A/PV.2400.

145 "call Moynihan and tell": Telecon between HAK and William Buffum, Nov. 10, 1975, 11:04 a.m., HAK Telcon.

"the harm this act": Mr. Moynihan (United States of America), 2400th GA, 795:310, A/PV.2400.

146 "defining deviancy down": DPM, "Defining Deviancy Down: How we've become Accustomed to Alarming Levels of Crime and Destructive Behavior," *American Scholar*, 62:1, Winter 1993, 17–30.

"A great evil": Mr. Moynihan (United States of America), 2400th GA, 795:311, A/PV.2400.

"If this resolution": DPM, *Dangerous Place*, 191.

"symbolic amnesty": Mr. Moynihan (United States of America), 2400th GA, 795–6:312, A/PV.2400.

"It is too much": TelCon between HAK and William Buffum, Nov. 10, 1975, 4:25 p.m., HAK Telcon.

"historians": Mr. Moynihan (United States of America), 2400th GA, 796:313, A/PV.2400.

"In all our postwar": Mr. Moynihan (United States of America), 2400th GA, 796:315, A/PV.2400.

The Harris survey: Harris Survey, 22–29 November, in *New York Post*, Dec. 15, 1975, 6.

147 "lie": Text of the 2400th meeting of the UN GA, Nov. 10, 1975, *Official Records*, 796: 316, A/PV.2400.

"You took that out": "Brawler at the U.N.," *NYTM*, Dec. 7, 1975, 32, 107.

"semantic infiltration": Fred Charles Iklé in DPM. "Words and Foreign Policy," *Policy Review*, Fall, 1978, 1.

"Ur-document": Suzanne Weaver Garment OH.

"To call Zionism": DPM, *Dangerous Place*, 195.

148 "the United Nations has declared": Text of the 2400th meeting of the UN GA, 796, paragraph 317, Nov. 10, 1975.

Now relying on: Herbert Reis to DPM, Nov. 12, 1975, Folder 10, Box 343, DPM MSS.

"racial discrimination is": Mr. Moynihan (United States of America), 2400th GA, 796:319, A/PV.2400.

"racism": Mr. Moynihan (United States of America), 2400th GA, 796:320–21, 322 A/PV.2400.

"a political lie": Mr. Moynihan (United States of America), 2400th GA, 796:322, A/PV.2400.

149 "a lie of Hitlerian size": "Brawler at U.N.," 32.

"discredited": Mr. Moynihan (United States of America), 2400th GA, 796:323, A/PV.2400.

"alien to the political": Mr. Moynihan (United States of America), 2400th GA, 796:324, A/PV.2400.

Showing off his: Podhoretz to DPM, Nov. 6, 1975, Folder 9, Box 339, DPM MSS.

"ancient": Mr. Moynihan (United States of America), 2400th GA, 797:324–30, A/PV.2400.

150 "human rights" to describe: Samuel Moyn, *The Last Utopia: Human Rights in History* (Cambridge, MA: 2010), 149.

Kissinger dismissed: Barbara Keys, "Congress, Kissinger, and the Origins of Human Rights Diplomacy," *Diplomatic History*, Nov. 2010, 34:5, 828, 830.

151 "The terrible lie": Mr. Moynihan (United States of America), 2400th GA, 797:331, A/PV.2400.

"if racism is no": Charles Fairbanks Memorandum quoted in DPM, *Dangerous Place*, 195.

152 "the old extremes": Henry Paolucci, "Moynihan, Solzhenitsyn, and St. Augustine," *State of the Nation*, 7:9, Sept. 1975, DPM MSS.

"If we destroy": Mr. Moynihan (United States of America), 2400th GA, 798: 334–36, A/PV.2400.

"the event did more": Manor, *To Right a Wrong*, 50.

153 "those idiots": Irving Kristol to DPM, Nov. 11, 1975, Folder 9, Box 337, DPM MSS.

"But we are liars": Mr. Baroody (Saudi Arabia), 2400th GA, 801:376, 391, 385, 387, A/PV.2400.

"They knew they": Suzanne Weaver Garment to author, Feb. 14, 2012.

154 "to clear all": W. Tapley Bennett, Jr. to all members of the U.S. Mission, Oct. 31, 1975, Tap MSS.

"I will not put": TelCon between HAK and William Buffum, Nov. 11, 1975, 9:29 a.m., HAK Telcon.

"turning into a": MemCon, GF, HAK, BS, Oct. 25, 1975, 9:30 a.m., 4, GRF NSA.

"pay no attention": *NYT*, Nov. 13, 1975, 11.

"vulnerable": William F. Buckley, *National Review*, Dec. 5, 1975, 1391.

"foolishness": Anthony Lewis, "The U.N. and Zionism," *NYT*, Nov. 13, 1975, 41.

155 "Kissinger raked Moynihan": "An 'Infamous Act' at the U.N." *Newsweek*, Nov. 24, 1975, 51.

"It might please": Press release from the US Mission to UN, Oct. 27, 1975, Folder 7, Box 331, DPM MSS.

"using the United Nations": DPM to William Shaw, Nov. 3, 1975, Folder 7, Box 331, DPM MSS.

"You were so kind": DPM to James Buckley, Nov. 4, 1975, Folder 5, Box 333, DPM MSS.

156 "Less and less": DPM, "America's Crisis of Confidence," *The New Leader*, Oct. 27, 1975, Folder 2, Box 329, DM MSS.

"if it should happen": William F. Buckley, *National Review*, Dec. 5, 1975, 1391.

"as one man": Morton Weinfeld to DPM, Oct. 18, 1975, Folder 7, Box 332, DPM MSS.

"You have done": Frank Church to DPM, Nov. 13, 1975, Folder 8, Box 333, DPM MSS.

157 "security and diplomatic": "Additional Views of Senator Barry Goldwater," Church Committee Interim Report. Available at http://www.history-matters.com/archive/church/reports/ir/html/ChurchIR_0178a.htm

"Dear Dan": Barry Goldwater to DPM, Nov. 14, 1975, Folder 9, Box 337, DPM MSS.

CHAPTER 7: BACKLASH

158 "The vigorous reaction": W. Tapley Bennett, Jr. to Hubert H. Humphrey, Nov. 12, 1975, 2, Tap MSS.

At the same time: Nathan Glazer and Daniel P. Moynihan, *Beyond the Melting Pot: The Negroes, Puerto Ricans, Jews, Italians, and Irish of New York City,* 2nd ed. (Cambridge, MA, 1963, 1970), xxxix.

159 "should not be": *NYT,* Nov. 12, 1975, 16.

"Zionism in its": *Washington Post,* Oct. 26, 1975, 84.

160 "in condemnation of": "The U.N. Vote," *NYT,* Nov. 11, 1975.

"of all people": Eldridge Cleaver, "U.N. hypocritical toward Israel, U.S.," *Waterbury Republican,* Jan. 14, 1976.

"rally against racism": Report of Conference of Presidents of Major Jewish Organizations, 12, Israel Miller MSS, Yeshiva University Library, New York.

161 "youth rally": Ed Prince OH. See also Malcolm Hoenlein OH.

"urgent message": Memorandum from Morris Fine to Bertram H. Gold, Oct. 22, 1975, AJC MSS.

One indication of: Report of Conference of Presidents of Major American Jewish Organizations, 12, Miller MSS. See also, *NYT,* Oct. 26, 1975, 4:11.

162 Glickmans, Rosenbergs, Salzburgs: Pearl Glickman to DPM, Nov. 26, 1975, Theodore Rosenberg to DPM, Nov. 25, 1975, Milton Salzburg to DPM, Nov. 5, 1975, Jane Goldstein to DPM, Oct. 21, 1975, Natalie Cohen to DPM, Oct. 21, 1975, Natalie Kahn to DPM, Oct. 20, 1975, all in Folder 2, Box 333, DPM MSS.

"sea of people": Prince OH.

163 "outspoken yet softspoken": *NYT,* July 26, 1965.

But Miller deferred: Hoenlein OH.

"The voices of hate": "Text of Israel Miller's address at the 'Rally against Racism and Anti-Semitism,'" Nov. 11, 1975, 1, Miller MSS.

"verbal violence": Gordon W. Allport, *The Nature of Prejudice* (New York, 1954, 1979), 49, 14–15.

164 "anti-Zionist propaganda campaign": Judith H. Banki, "The UN's Anti-Zionism Resolution: Christian Responses," The Interreligious Affairs Departments, American Jewish Committee 70th Anniversary Annual Meeting, May 12–16, 1976, iii–iv, AJC MSS, available at http://www.ajcarchives.org/AJC_DATA/Files/740.pdf

"as an American": Natalie Kahn to DPM, Oct. 20, 1975, Folder 2, Box 333, DPM MSS.

"As a natural born": Irwin Guber to DPM, Dec. 3, 1975, Folder 1, Box 333, DPM MSS.

"sexy": Letter to DPM, Folder 1, Box 333, DPM MSS.

"I'm becoming specially": DPM to Stephen Hess, Dec. 8, 1975, Folder 4, Box 328, DPM MSS.

"They must not triumph": " Miller's address," 1, 3.

165 "not only the Soviet": Natan Sharansky OH.

"Zionism is beautiful!": Report of Conference of Presidents of Major Jewish Organizations, 16, Miller MSS.

165 "PROUD TO BE JEWS": *NYT*, Dec. 3, 1975, 29.

"Israel as the": Prince OH.

166 "crash program": *NYT*, Nov. 16, 1975, 16.

New York's Board: Report of Conference of Presidents of Major American Jewish Organizations, 13, Miller MSS.

"our history will not": *NYT*, Nov. 12, 1975, 1, 16.

Some slogans: *NYT*, Nov. 12, 1975, 1, 16.

"I somehow sensed": *NYT*, Nov. 12, 1975, 1, 16.

167 "bone stupid": *JTA*, Nov. 11, 1975.

"black day": *JTA*, Nov. 13, 1975.

The state of the Jews: Yossi Klein Halevi, "War and Atonement," *Jerusalem Post*, Oct. 3, 2003, http://info.jpost.com/C003/Supplements/30YK/new.07.html.

Municipalities changed: "Zionism Vote: Rage and Discord," *Time*, Nov. 24, 1975.

"Zionism gave expression": Nathan Laufer OH, and Dr. David Hartman, "Zionism as a Dialectic between Continuity and Change," Beit Atid, Jerusalem, Dec. 15, 1975, in private collection of Nathan Laufer.

168 Yitzhak Rabin charged: Prime Minister Yitzhak Rabin, "The Government's Response to the Vote in the United Nations on Nov. 10, 1975," in Minutes of 8th Knesset, Third Sitting, Nov. 11, 1975, MFA MSS, 68, 65.

"double game": Meir Talmi (MK, Labor Party), "The Government's Response," 85–86. See also Shneur Zalman Abramov (MK, Likud Party).

"Zionism, Judaism, the State": Prime Minister Yitzhak Rabin, "The Government's Response," 70.

"The United Nations": Telegram, Israel's Foreign Ministry to Israeli missions abroad, Nov. 10, 1975, MFA MSS, 7026/1-א.

"Another one": Mathis Chazanov, "Bomb explodes in Jerusalem, killing six," *The Telegraph-Herald* (Dubuque, Iowa), Nov. 14, 1975.

169 "a heroic and daring": *NYT*, Nov. 13, 1975, 1, 3.

"This assembly confirmed": Barry Levenfeld, "A Farce for Peace," *Harvard Political Review* (IV:3, 1976), 44.

"fitting response": Gershom Gorenberg, *The Accidental Empire: Israel and the Birth of the Settlements, 1967–1977* (New York, 2006), 332.

THE PROPER: Gorenberg, *Accidental Empire*, 332.

"You who see": Yossi Klein Halevi to author, July 15, 2011.

"This is the Zionist": *JTA*, Dec. 5, 1975.

170 "Gush Emunim's greatest": Yossi Klein Halevi, "Demonizing Israel: Political and Religious Consequences Among Israelis," available at http://www.isgap.org/wp-content/uploads/2011/10/halevi-4-2-09-paper.pdf

"The mood of the country": MemCom, GRF, Max Fisher, BS, 1, Dec. 12, 1975, 7:00 p.m.–7:50 p.m., GRF NSA.

"Many people approached": Jonathan Sarna OH.

David Lehrer, a Zionist: David Lehrer OH.

Diplomats from Israel's: "Why Student Groups Matter: The Harvard Committee on American Foreign Policy Claims Victory, 36 Years Later," *Secure Nation*, May 16, 2011, available at http://securenation.wordpress.com/2011/05/16/why-student-groups-matter/

170 "We had nothing": *NYT,* June 27, 1976.

Within weeks, more than: Richard Maas, "Observations on Meetings in Mexico— Dec. 11 & 12, 1975," Box 206, Bertram Gold boxes, AJC MSS.

171 "in no way": "Text of Statement to the Press," Dec. 12, 1975, Box 206, Bertram Gold boxes, AJC MSS.

Feeling pressed: David M. Blumberg to B'nai B'rith leaders, Jan. 26, 1976, Box 206, Bertram Gold boxes, AJC MSS.

"moral loathing": "Thousands in New York City Hit U.N. Attack on Zionism," *Religious News Service,* Nov. 11, 1975, 2.

"deplored the resolution": GRF, "Presidential Statement," Oct. 24, 1975, Folder "United Nations, Moynihan," Box 30, Ron Nessen MSS, GRF Library.

"Your gathering today": "Thousands in New York City Hit U.N. Attack," 2.

"I consider the": Letter of Thomas P. O'Neill, Oct. 21, 1975, Folder: "UN–Zionism Resolution," Box 280, Bella Abzug MSS, Rare Books and Manuscripts Library, Columbia University, New York.

172 Three years earlier: *NYT,* Nov. 12, 1975, 1, 16.

"Wherever Hitler": *NYT,* Nov. 12, 1975, 16.

"the UN is in": *Middlesboro Daily News,* Nov. 13, 1975, 6.

"If I thought": *NYT,* Nov. 25, 1998.

"One more act": Report of Conference of Presidents of Major Jewish Organizations, 14, Miller MSS.

173 "When Pat Moynihan": Report of Conference of Presidents of Major Jewish Organizations, 13–14, Miller MSS.

"ludicrous": Telegram, Israel's New York Mission to Israel's Foreign Ministry, Oct. 31, 1975, MFA MSS, 3813/3.

"morally and historically": *NYT,* Nov. 16, 1975, 16.

"a national home": *JTA,* Nov. 20, 1975.

174 "Smearing the 'racist'": Vernon E. Jordan, "A Setback for the U.N.," *To Be Equal,* Nov. 12, 1975.

"social dislocation and": *NYT,* Aug. 25, 1987.

"an insult to the": Bayard Rustin, "Zionism Is Not Racism," Nov. 13, 1975, Rustin Column, "United Nations File: 1975–1980," Bayard Rustin MSS, Library of Congress, Washington, DC.

"extraneous issue": *JTA,* Nov. 10, 1975.

175 "Shame on them!": "Zionism Vote: Rage and Discord," *Time,* Nov. 24, 1975.

"appalling": "A Statement on the UN Anti-Zionist Resolution by the Executive Committee of the Leadership Conference on Civil Rights," Nov. 4, 1975, Folder 8, Box 332, DPM MSS.

"near unanimity of": Banki, "The UN's Anti-Zionism Resolution," vii.

"some concrete Israeli": Statement by Dr. Phillip Potter, General Secretary, World Council of Churches, received by Telex from Geneva, Nov. 11, 1975, S-1066-0011-12, UN USG for Special Political Affairs, Zionism Resolution, Nov. 10–Nov. 14, 1975, UN MSS.

176 Rabbi Marc Tanenbaum: Marc H. Tanenbaum, "Christians Condemn Anti-Zionism," transcript from his Nov. 16, 1975 radio broadcast on WINS, AJC MSS.

176 "Christian concern for Palestinians": Banki, "The UN's Anti-Zionism Resolution," 82–83, 90.

"We recognize racism": Banki, "The UN's Anti-Zionism Resolution," 8.

"We must reject": Judith H. Banki, "The UN's Anti-Zionism Resolution: Christian Responses," The Interreligious Affairs Departments, American Jewish Committee 70th Anniversary Annual Meeting, May 12–16, 1976, 3, AJC MSS, available at http://www.ajcarchives.org/AJC_DATA/Files/740.PDF

"blunt honesty": Andrew M. Greeley, "Chicago Tribune End of the Year Round Up," ca. Dec. 1975, Folder 3, Box 336, DPM MSS.

"The Tanzanians": DPM, *Dangerous Place*, 259.

177 "immoral and counterproductive": *NYT*, Feb. 4, 1976.

Moynihan would sidestep: DPM to Theodore M. Hesburgh, Feb. 9, 1976, Folder 4, Box 328, DPM MSS.

"My strongest fellow": Report of Conference of Presidents of Major American Jewish Organizations, 16, Miller MSS.

"a forgery of": *JTA*, Nov. 17, 1975, JTA.

Weeks later, a left-wing: *JTA*, Dec. 16, 1975, JTA.

"through tiny slips": Bernard-Henri Lévy quoted in Yohanan Manor, *To Right a Wrong: The Revocation of the UN General Assembly Resolution 3379 Defaming Zionism*, 76.

178 "as a woman": Report of Conference of Presidents of Major American Jewish Organizations, 15, Miller MSS.

"All my life": Bernard Goodwin to Betty Friedan, Dec. 8, 1975, Betty Friedan papers, Schlesinger Library, Radcliffe Institute, Harvard University.

"among the most": Betty Friedan, "Woman as Jew—Jew as Woman," transcription from the "American Jewish Congress Dialogue between American and Israeli Women," Feb. 8, 1984, 45, Folder 11, Box 37, Friedan MSS.

"shame": Betty Friedan, "Ad Hoc Committee for Human Rights," Folder 1885: October–Dec. 1975, Box 149, MC 575, Friedan MSS.

"all human rights": "Ad Hoc Committee of Women for Human Rights," Nov. 10, 1975, Box 280, Folder: United Nations-Zionism Resolution, Bella Abzug Archives, Columbia University, Rare Books and Manuscript Library.

"this passion against": Betty Friedan, "Women and Jews: The Quest for Selfhood," *Congress Monthly*, Feb./Mar. 1985, 52:2, 7.

"I knew the arrow": Letty Cottin Pogrebin, *Deborah, Golda, and Me: Being Female and Jewish in America* (New York, 1991), 154.

179 "a service of concern": *Toledo Blade*, Nov. 13, 1975, 5.

"moral collapse of": *JTA*, Nov. 10, 1975.

"As a sort of": "For Now, Standing Pat at the U.N.," *Time*, Dec. 8, 1975.

The first week alone: *NYT*, Nov. 21, 1975, 3.

180 "Pat, Hang in": Gabriel Hague to DPM, Nov. 21, 1975, Folder 3, Box 328, DPM MSS.

"I'm still hanging": DPM to Gabriel Hague, Folder 3, Box 328, DPM MSS.

"vigorous—not gentle": "Big 50 Press Survey 'Anti-Zionism' and the United Nations," Box 217, AJC MSS.

The Harris poll found: *New York Post*, Dec. 15, 1975, 6.

180 Incorporating Holocaust references: Hasia R. Diner, *We Remember with Reverence and Love: American Jews and the Myth of Silence after the Holocaust, 1945–1962* (New York, 2009), 11, 311.
181 "campaign against Zionism": *NYT*, Nov. 13, 1975.
   "Who would have": "Big 50 Press Survey."
   "Christians seem to know": Marc Tanenbaum to Bert Gold, "Christian responses to UN resolution on Zionism-as-Racism," Nov. 20, 1975, Box 206, AJC MSS.
   "these manifestations of": Marc Tanenbaum, "Christians Condemn Anti-Zionism," transcript from his Nov. 16, 1975 radio broadcast on WINS, "Box 217, AJC MSS.
   a myth developed: See Norman Finkelstein, *The Holocaust Industry: Reflections on the Exploitation of Jewish Suffering* (2000, 2003).
   exaggerating: Diner, *We Remember with Reverence*.
   "perpetual victimhood": Peter Beinart, *The Crisis of Zionism* (New York, 2012), 6.
182 "the victimization Olympics": Peter Novick, *The Holocaust in American Life* (New York, 2000), 195.
   "was as if": "Reagan Pledges His Support for Removal from UN Record of the 'Blot' of the Zionism-Racism Resolution," *Daily News Bulletin*, Nov. 12, 1975.

CHAPTER 8: BACKLASH AGAINST MOYNIHAN

184 "As we were": DPM, *Dangerous Place*, 178.
   "an attack on": *NYT*, Nov. 12, 1975, 16.
   "criticizing them heavily": TelCon between HAK and Olof Palme, Nov. 23, 1975, HAK TelCon.
185 "awful": DPM remarks in "The Effort to Repeal Resolution 3379," An American Jewish Committee Conference, Nov. 8, 1990, USUN, http://www.ajcarchives.org/AJC_DATA/Files/739.pdf, 3–4.
   the US Committee for UNICEF: "U.S. Committee for UNICEF Condemns Vote on Zionism," *Religious News Service*, Nov. 19, 1975, 25.
   "it would embarrass them": *NYT*, Jan. 6, 1976, 2.
   "we may lose the future": United Nations press release, "Statement on Zionism Resolution," Nov. 10, 1975, Executive Office of the Secretary-General, S-0273-0017-08, UN MSS.
   "unnecessary": United Nations press release, "Statement by President Gaston Thorn," Nov. 11, 1975, UN USG for Special Political Affairs (1981–1988 Cordovez), S-0359-0016-07, UN MSS.
   In the charged atmosphere: United Nations press release, "Weekly News Summary (main developments during week Nov. 7–13)," Nov. 14, 1975, UN USG for Special Political Affairs (1981–1988 Cordovez), S-0359-0016-07, UN MSS.
   "wise and sound": Memorandum from Saadoon Hammadi, Nov. 1975, UN USG for Special Political Affairs (1981–1988 Cordovez), S-0359-0016-07, UN MSS.
186 The Arab League's: Jerome Bakst to Arnold Forster, "Comments in Connection with Big 50 Press Survey on 'Anti-Zionism' and the United Nations," Nov. 26, 1975, "UN Anti-Zionism Resolution: Jewish and General Reactions, 1975," Box 217, AJC MSS.

186 "The Arabs have": *NYT*, Nov. 15, 1975, 5.

$9 million: *Time*, June 23, 1975.

El-Messiri insisted: "Zionism and Racism," *NYT*, Nov. 13, 1975, 41.

The Arab League sponsored: *NYT*, Nov. 15, 1975, 5.

The papers also ran: Bakst to Forster, "Comments in Connections with Big 50 Press Survey."

"a universal religious": Position Statements of the American Council for Judaism, available at http://www.acjna.org/acjna/about_position.aspx

187 "Jews Against Zionism": Thomas A. Kolsky, *Jews Against Zionism: The American Council for Judaism 1942–1948* (Philadelphia, 1992).

"useful tools for": Bakst to Forster, "Comments in Connection with Big 50 Press Survey."

"overreaction": "Big 50 Press Survey 'Anti-Zionism' and the United Nations," "UN Anti-Zionism Resolution: Jewish and General Reactions, 1975," Box 217, AJC MSS.

"niggers of the Middle East": Randall Kennedy, *Nigger: The Strange Career of a Troublesome Word* (New York, 2002), 22.

"We smell": James R. Lawson, "SPIT Still Acts as Zionist Tool Against Fellow Blacks," Bulletin #430, Harlem Council for Economic Development, Dec. 6, 1975, 139 1.3 1/56 in Fayez A. Sayegh Collection, Aziz S. Atiya Library for Middle East Studies, Marriott Library, University of Utah, Salt Lake City, UT.

"element of truth": Transcript of Channel 4—NY, "Newsbeat," "Positively Black," Nov. 1975, clipping, AJC MSS.

"neo-colonialist mentality": *Cleveland Press*, Dec. 5, 1975, clipping in 139 1.3 1/50, Sayegh MSS.

188 "decent countries": Dwight Dickinson to DPM, Oct. 19, 1975, 2, Folder 4, Box 334, DPM MSS.

"PERHAPS THE": Doug Marlette, "Perhaps the Third World," *The Reporter Dispatch*, Dec. 3, 1975, A14.

"The Arabs are right": Nathan Glazer, "Zionism Examined," *NYT*, Dec. 13, 1975.

"We have a long-term": MemCon, GRF, HAK, BS, Nov. 11, 1975, 9:15 a.m. 1, GRF NSA.

189 "totally unacceptable": TelCon between Ambassador Buffum and HAK, Nov. 10, 1975, 11:04 a.m., http://foia.state.gov/documents/kissinger/0000BCD4.pdf

"this moment rare": Text of DPM Nov. 12, 1975 speech to the Third Committee of the UN, *Freedom at Issue*, Jan.–Feb. 1976, 21, Box 335, DPM MSS.

Just as the Helsinki Accords: Freedom House press release, "Background for Ambassador Moynihan's United Nations Speech on Political Prisoners," Nov. 13, 1975, Folder 20, Box 335, DPM MSS.

"at his brilliant": *Detroit News*, ca. 21 1975, clipping, "United Nations clips," DPM MSS.

"alienated the Arabs": *Washington Post*, Nov. 20, 1975, 12.

190 "an open political system": Text of Leonard Garment Nov. 12, 1975, speech to the Third Committee of the UN, *Freedom at Issue*, Jan.–Feb. 1976, 21, Box 335, DPM MSS.

"I expect you don't": "*N.O.Tes*," newsletter, Nov. 1975, 4:11, 1, personal papers of Carl Gershman, Washington, DC.

190 "has been badly misunderstood": C. Robert Zelnick to DPM, Nov. 17, 1975, Folder 10, Box 332, DPM MSS.

"Pat, keep on": *Newsweek,* Nov. 24, 1975, 51.

"awful Chinese drink": "Brawler at the U.N.," *NYTM,* Dec. 7, 1975, 32.

"very old and": *Newsweek,* Nov. 24, 1975, 51.

190 "we won a majority": DPM to W. Averell Harriman, Nov. 20, 1975, Folder 3, Box 328, DPM MSS.

"absurd": Text of Ivor Richard speech to the United Nations Association, Nov. 17, 1975, Folder 10, Box 340, DPM MSS.

"I'm haggling in corridors": "Brawler at U.N.," 32.

"whispering campaign": *NYT,* Nov. 23, 1975, 21.

192 "decent": *NYT,* Nov. 21, 1975, 3.

"the United States": William F. Buckley, "Briton Missed Point in Lecturing Moynihan," *Milwaukee Sentinel,* Nov. 29, 1975, 10.

"the one thing": Paul Johnson, "London Diary," *New Statesman,* Nov. 28, 1975, Folder 10, Box 340, DPM MSS.

"undiplomatic diplomat": "The Perils of Pat," *Newsweek,* Dec. 1, 1975, 48.

Ivor Richard's attack: See "Behind the Headlines: The Conflict between Moynihan and the Foreign Policy Establishment," *JTA,* Nov. 28, 1975, 4.

"Ivor took": William Safire, "Henry & Pat & Ivor," *NYT,* Nov. 24, 1975, 35.

"MOYNIHAN'S STYLE IN": *NYT,* Nov. 21, 1975, 3.

193 "utterly preposterous": *NYT,* Nov. 23, 1975, 21.

although one complained: *NYT,* Nov. 21, 1975, 3.

"You could almost": "Perils of Pat," 48.

"that's no way": "Brawler at U.N.," 32.

"There is a lot": MemCon, GRF, DPM, BS, Jan. 27, 1976, 4:32 p.m.–5:15 p.m., 2, GRF NSA.

"about 4 feet": "Perils of Pat," 48.

194 "The President fully": "Perils of Pat," 48.

"Here I am": *NYT,* Nov. 22, 1975, 1.

"no reason to": *Milwaukee Journal,* Nov. 22, 1975, 2.

"Persons familiar with": *Milwaukee Journal,* Nov. 22, 1975, 2.

"pleaded": TelCon between HAK and Bob Anderson, Nov. 22, 1975, HAK TelCon.

"prior American approval": Statement by UK Mission to the UN, Nov. 22, 1975, Folder 10, Box 340, DPM MSS.

195 "*Nobody* in my mission": "Brawler at U.N.," 32.

"It seems that this": TelCon between HAK and Dean Rusk, Nov. 22, 1975, HAK TelCon.

196 "the kids still": TelCon between HAK and Ted Koppel, Nov. 22, 1975, HAK TelCon.

197 "the national spirit": DPM, *Dangerous Place,* 220.

"SINCE WHEN DOES": *NYT,* Nov. 23, 1975, 21.

"personnel changes": Suzanne Weaver to DPM, Nov. 23, 1975, "Notes for Moynihan," DPM MSS.

197 "patterns of appeasement": John St. Denis, "Daniel in the Lion's Den," Nov. 29, 1975, Folder 7, Box 326, DPM MSS.
198 "The President wants it": White House press conference, Nov. 24, 1975, Folder 15, Box 336, DPM MSS.
"His complete confidence": Statement by the Press Secretary, Nov. 24, 1975, Folder "United Nations, Moynihan," Box 30, Ron Nessen MSS, GRF Lib.
"President and Secretary Kissinger": *NYT*, Nov. 25, 1975, 1.
"Kissinger had to eat": "Clouds Over Kissinger," *Newsweek*, Dec. 8, 1975, 36.
"on top of the world": CBS Newsradio, "First Line Report, Daniel Schorr" in BS to GRF, Nov. 25, 1975, Folder USUN, Box 21, NSA Presidential Agency File, GRF Lib.
"FORD LIKES MOYNIHAN'S": *Daily News*, Nov. 23, 1975, 10.
"A Warrior among": *Washington Star*, Nov. 23, 1975, 1.
"I very much want": *Washington Post*, Nov. 22, 1975, 1.
"Everyone leaves eventually": *NYT*, Nov. 22, 1975, 1.
"United Nations has": *NYT*, Nov. 21, 1975.
"Guilt is a weapon": Folder 10: "UN Subject File: Notes," Box 338, DPM MSS.
199 "sanctimonious": *Telegraph-Herald* [Dubuque, Iowa], Nov. 25, 1975, 4.
"retreat": *NYT*, Nov. 26, 1975, 28.
Seventy percent: "Public Solidly Behind Moynihan, Split on U.N. Dollars," North American Newspaper Alliance, Jan. 12, 1976, Folder 8, Box 343, DPM MSS.
200 "I am sure that": *New America*, Dec. 1975, 9.
"shameless": Daniel Patrick Moynihan, *Pandaemonium: Ethnicity in International Politics* (New York: 1993, 1994), 153.
"the wrong man": Paul Good, "The Mask of Liberalism," *Nation*, Dec. 20, 1975, Vol. 221, Issue 21, 654.
201 "Kissinger's Agnew": Frances Fitzgerald, "The Warrior Intellectuals," *Harper's*, May 1976, 58.
"gung-ho junior": "Ideologue of the Reaction," *Harvard Crimson*, May 20, 1976.
"the decline of authority": Fitzgerald, "Warrior Intellectuals," 59, 58.
202 "far right-wing": *NYT*, July 25, 1974, 27.
"Three Structural Problems": DPM, "Three Structural Problems in American Foreign Policy," Feb. 19, 1976, 3, 5, 12, 19–20, 21, 22, 27, Folder 21, Box 335, DPM MSS.
204 "total war": Michael Walzer, "The New Terrorists," *TNR*, Aug. 30, 1975, 13–14.
"conceivable rationality of": Roger Morris, "Terrorism: A Debate," *TNR*, Nov. 22, 1975, 14.
"random murder of": Walzer, "New Terrorists," 12–14.
"record this past": DPM to Michael Walzer, Feb. 26, 1976, Folder 7, Box 336, DPM MSS.
"rejected the apocalyptic": Graham Hovey, "Fog and Worse on Angola," *NYT*, Dec. 30, 1975, 25.
"Power is the basis": DPM notes, Jan. 7, 1976, Folder 10, Box 338, DPM MSS.
205 "you sold out": DPM notes, Jan. 7, 1976, 10, Box 338, DPM MSS.
"profound, even alarming": *NYT*, Dec. 18, 1975, 1.

205 "too much": Homer A. Jack to DPM, Dec. 30, 1975, Folder 7, Box 328, DPM MSS.

Moynihan responded legalistically: DPM to Homer A. Jack, Jan. 14, 1976, Folder 7, Box 328, DPM MSS.

"the American public": DPM to Roscoe Diamond, Jan. 20, 1976, Folder 8, Box 326, DPM MSS.

"it may or may not": MemCon, Jan. 27, 1976, Folder 8, Box 348, DPM MSS.

206 "appeared confrontational": *NYT*, Jan. 28, 1976, 1.

"Pat": James Reston, "What About Moynihan?" *NYT*, Jan. 30, 1976.

207 "I have been": DPM to James Reston, Jan. 30, 1976, Folder 6, Box 333, DPM MSS.

"we did not do": DPM to Richard Cheney, Jan. 31, 1976, Folder 6, Box 333, DPM MSS.

"After an agonizing": DPM to HAK, Jan. 31, 1976, Folder 6, Box 333, DPM MSS.

"Today is the last": DPM to GRF, Jan. 31, 1976, Folder 6, Box 333, DPM MSS.

"I made up": *Time*, Feb. 16, 1976.

"asserted our position": *The Patriot*, Feb. 4, 1976, 16, Folder 12 Box 332, DPM MSS.

208 "institutional loyalty": *Time*, Feb. 16, 1976.

"It is hard": DPM to Michael Segal, Feb. 13, 1976, Folder 7, Box 336, DPM MSS.

"[W]e had changed": DPM, *Dangerous Place*, 278.

"In a very short time": Henry Cabot Lodge to DPM, Feb. 3, 1976, Folder 7, Box 329, DPM MSS.

CHAPTER 9: THE POLITICS OF PATRIOTIC INDIGNATION

209 "the new consciousness": Bruce Schulman, *The Seventies: The Great Shift in American Culture, Society, and Politics* (New York, 2001, 2002), 97.

"Pat Moynihan is": George Putnam, "Moynihan at the U.N.," Putnam at Ten, Channel 9–Los Angeles, Jan. 29, 1976, in Folder 7, Box 330, DPM MSS.

210 "an utterly corrupt": Paddy Chayefsky, draft letter to the *NYT*, 1975, 10, Box 139, Paddy Chayefsky Papers, Performing Arts Library, New York Public Library, New York.

"don't want jolly": *NYT*, May 22, 2011, AR1.

"IMAHAINGTTIAM Midnight": Schulman, *Seventies*, 51. The original movie says "I'm as mad" and "not going to take this anymore" but in popular culture it was frequently rendered as "I'm mad" and "not going to take it anymore."

"redneck revival": Schulman, *Seventies*, 117.

"We have a new": Daniel A. Smith, *Tax Crusaders and the Politics of Direct Democracy* (New York, 1998), 25.

211 "middle class tax revolt": Howard Jarvis, *I'm Mad As Hell*, 128, 12.

Many American WASPs: Carol Zisowitz Stearns and Peter N. Stearns, *Anger: The Struggle for Emotional Control in American History* (Chicago, 1986), 2.

"American politics has": Richard Hofstadter, "The Paranoid Style in American Politics," *Harper's Magazine*, Nov. 1964, 77.

211 "the educated elite": *DPM Letters*, 195.

212 "get down": Schulman, *Seventies*, 24, 23.

In this new world: William Graebner, "America's *Poseidon Adventure*," in Beth Bailey and David Farber, *America in the '70s* (Lawrence, KS, 2004), 158–60.

"age of nonheroes": *US News and World Report*, July 21, 1975, 16, 18.

213 "take me to": *Time*, July 15, 1974.

an embarrassment: DPM, *Pandaemonium: Ethnicity in International Politics* (New York, 1993, 1994), 38.

"it was like a jolt": Jonathan Rauch OH.

"governments became legitimate": DPM, *On the Law of Nations* (Cambridge, MA, 1990), 54.

"to generate excitement": Leonard Garment to Samuel Lewis, July 9, 1976, Folder 8, Box 7, Leonard Garment MSS, Library of Congress, Washington, DC.

Moynihan's claim that: see Leonard Garment, "AT UN (1975)," n.d., "Anti-Semitism," Folder 8, Box 7, Garment MSS.

214 "climate of discussion": Michael Novak to Suzanne Weaver, Feb. 6, 1976, Folder 4, Box 330, DPM MSS.

"the new political": Michael Novak, "The Rise of Unmeltable Ethnics, Part I," Aug. 31, 2006, at http://www.firstthings.com/onthesquare/2006/08/novak-the-rise-of-unmeltable-e.

"gatekeepers": Michael Novak, *Unmeltable Ethnics: Politics and Culture in American Life*, rev. ed. (Piscataway, NJ: 1996), xi.

"I now find it": Michael Novak to Suzanne Weaver, Feb. 6, 1976, Folder 4, Box 330, DPM MSS.

"Pat tried to reawaken": Michael Novak to Suzanne Weaver, Feb. 6, 1976, Folder 4, Box 330, DPM MSS.

215 "I think you": DPM to Michael Novak, Feb. 24, 1976, Folder 4, Box 330, DPM MSS.

"The ambassador": *People*, Dec. 29, 1975–Jan. 5, 1976, 27.

"a Moynihan problem": MemCon, GRF HAK, BS, Dec. 6, 1975, GRF Lib.

"very good news": *Washington Star*, Feb. 4, 1976.

"There are no": *Time*, Feb. 16, 1976.

"OK, so Henry": "Dry Bones," *Jerusalem Post*, Feb. 4, 1976, 8, Box 328, DPM MSS.

"We're not going": *Time*, Feb. 16, 1976.

Secretly, he had already: Michael Barone, "A Renaissance Man in the Senate," in Robert A. Katzmann, *Daniel Patrick Moynihan: The Intellectual in Public Life* (Washington, DC, 1998, 2004), 135.

Having denied interest: Chester Finn to DPM, Feb. 3, 1976, Folder 3, Box 327, DPM MSS.

The cynics and critics: See, for example, William Caldwell, "How About Pat for President," *The Sunday Record* [Bergen Country], Feb. 15, 1976, D1.

216 "insulting behavior": *Chicago Tribune*, Jan. 1, 1976, Folder 8, Box 325, DPM MSS.

"more trouble with the blacks": Chester Finn to DPM, Feb. 3, 1976, Folder 3, Box 327, DPM MSS.

216 "on Saturday I": DPM notes, Feb. 2, 1976, Folder 10, Box 338, DPM MSS.
"Isn't it too bad": *Time*, Feb. 16, 1976.
"I know something": George Murphy to DPM, Feb. 3, 1976, Folder 3, Box 330, DPM MSS.
26,000 letters: See Mark Gayn, "26,000 Letters Back Moynihan's Hard Line," *Toronto Star*, Jan. 5, 1976.
"Your telling it": Michael A. Samuels to DPM, Feb. 3, 1976, Folder 4, Box 334, DPM MSS.
"MOYNIHAN WILL BE": *St. Louis Globe-Democrat*, Feb. 4, 1976, 14.
Michael Segal: Michael Segal to DPM, Feb. 5, 1976, Folder 7, Box 336, DPM MSS.
217 Celebrities like the: *DPM Letters*, 652.
"You look positively": Chester Finn to DPM, Feb. 3, 1976, Folder 3, Box 327, DPM MSS.
"a very sensitive": Michael Novak to Suzanne Weaver, Feb. 6, 1976, Folder 4, Box 330, DPM MSS.
"The Case of the Outspoken": Russell Baker, "Dangerous Case of English," *NYT*, Jan. 31, 1976, 20.
"Clearly, the *New*": DPM to the *NYT*, Feb. 2, 1976, Folder 4, Box 330, DPM MSS.
218 "This was in": George Will OH.
"I'm not a hawk": Excerpt from Henry "Scoop" Jackson for President 1972 Campaign Brochure: "'This man can help America find itself,'" http://www.4president.org/brochures/scoopjackson1972brochure.htm
219 "taking a nap": DPM to Jeane Kirkpatrick, Jan. 29, 1983, *DPM Letters*, 450.
"Mr. Moynihan wore": *NYT*, June 11, 1976, D19.
"Why do you": *NYT*, Sept. 10, 1976.
220 "Nixon's man in": *NYT*, June 11, 1976, D19.
"presented the image": *NYT*, Sept. 15, 1976, 28.
"older, central": *NYT*, Sept. 9, 1976, 41.
"You may want": *NYT*, Sept. 9, 1976, 44.
221 "that rambunctious child": *NYT*, Sept. 10, 1976.
"bigot in a bowtie": *NYT*, Sept. 28, 1976, 1, 53.
Voters generally perceived: *NYT*, Sept. 15, 1976, 28.
"unless": *NYT*, Nov. 3, 1976, 19.
222 "a ghastly and reprehensible": *Albany Herald* [Georgia], Nov. 12, 1975, 20.
"peace is not": Jimmy Carter, "Our Nation's Past and Future," July 15, 1976, transcript available at http://www.presidency.ucsb.edu/ws/index.php?pid=25953#ixzz1OUo883qJ
Moynihan expected Carter's: *DPM Letters*, 402.
223 "dubious tactics": Jimmy Carter, address at the B'nai B'rith Convention, Washington, DC, Sept. 8, 1976, in Jimmy Carter, *A Government As Good As Its People* (Atlanta, 1977, 1996), 143–44.
"boner": *Sarasota Journal*, Sept. 28, 1976, 6A.
"I am proud": GRF, Remarks at the B'nai B'rith Biennial Convention, Sept. 9, 1976, 7, The American Presidency Project, http://www.presidency.ucsb.edu/ws/?pid=6317#axzz1x9Foqy1d.

223 "center-right": William Safire, "A Lot to Learn," *NYT*, Nov. 4, 1976, 39.

"our great shock": *DPM Letters*, 403.

"justice, equity, and": Dominic Sandbrook, *Mad As Hell: The Crisis of the 1970s and the Rise of the Populist Right*, 319.

"persons of the opposite": *DPM Letters*, 403.

224 "weak": *DPM Letters*, 415.

"Could it be": Tom Wicker, "Kissinger's Megalomania Showing" in *Eugene Register-Guard*, Nov. 24, 1979.

"Now you've got it": Kevin Mattson, *What the Heck Are You Up To, Mr. President? Jimmy Carter, America's "Malaise," and the Speech That Should Have Changed the Country* (New York, 2009).

By March 1980: *Time*, Apr. 7, 1980.

"it may take": Andrew Young in Steven F. Hayward, *The Age of Reagan: The Fall of the Old Liberal Order, 1964–1980* (New York, 2001), 544.

"express any": *NYT*, Jan. 3, 1977.

"He's young": *NYT*, Jan. 5, 1977, 65.

225 "individualistic Manicheanism": *Kirkus Reviews*, Nov. 20, 1978, https://www. kirkusreviews.com/book-reviews/daniel-patrick-with-suzanne-weaver-moynihan/a-dangerous-place/#review.

"the brutal sentimentality": *New York Review of Books*, May 3, 1979, http://www. nybooks.com/articles/archives/1979/may/03/timely-griefs/

"the bugler in chief": *New York Times Book Review*, Dec. 10, 1978, 3, 45.

"We've ended the": *NYT*, Sept. 16, 1977, 7.

"didn't need a": *National Public Radio*, May 27, 2005, available at http://www.npr. org/templates/story/story.php?storyId = 4670207

Four days before: The US abstained on Resolutions 446, 452, 476, and 478; approved 465 and 480, but vetoed S/13911 on Apr. 30, 1980.

226 "flagrant violation of": DPM, "Joining the Jackals: The U.S. at the UN 1977–1980," *Commentary* 71:2 (Feb. 1981), 28.

Jewish rights to settle: See Nicholas Rostow, "Are the Settlements Illegal?" *The American Interest*, Mar. /Apr. 2010.

"perfectly into the": DPM, "Joining the Jackals," 28.

knowing that Jews: *Time*, Apr. 7, 1980.

"it was the United": DPM, "Joining the Jackals," 23, 24, 25, 26, 31.

227 "the essential Carter": *Washington Post*, Dec. 21, 1980, C6.

228 "outrageous": *The Day* [New London], Nov. 12, 1975, 5.

"hypocritical": *Milwaukee Sentinel*, Nov. 17, 1975, 7.

"The day of": Ronald Reagan, "To Restore America," Mar. 31, 1976, transcript available at http://www.pbs.org/wgbh/amex/presidents/40_reagan/psources/ps_restore.html.

"When it comes": Hayward, *Age of Reagan*, 466. See also Adam Clymer, *Drawing the Line at the Big Ditch: The Panama Canal Treaties and the Rise of the Right* (Lawrence, KS, 2008), 208.

229 "Negotiations with the Soviet": Ronald Reagan's Announcement for Presidential Candidacy, Nov. 13, 1979, http://www.reagan.utexas.edu/archives/reference/11.13.79.html

229 "Reagan proved to": Hayward, *Age of Reagan*, 441.

"I am paying for": Debate between Ronald Reagan and George H. W. Bush, Feb. 23, 1980, video clip available at http://www.youtube.com/watch?v=OO2_49TycdE.

"we are given": Ronald Reagan, Address Accepting the Presidential Nomination at the Republican National Convention, July 17, 1980, http://www.presidency.ucsb.edu/ws/index.php?pid=25970#axzz1OUBQLA9X.

"Vietnam Syndrome": Ronald Reagan, "Restoring the Margin of Safety," Aug. 18, 1980, http://www.reagan.utexas.edu/archives/reference/8.18.80.html.

"ABC election": *NYT*, Nov. 9, 1980, 28.

230 Moynihan pronounced Carter's: DPM, "Joining the Jackals," 23–31.

"the party of ideas": James A. Patterson, *Restless Giant: The United States from Watergate to Bush v. Gore* (New York, 2005), 133.

"return to a": Hayward, *Age of Reagan*, 441.

"a liberal who": DPM to Arthur O. (Punch) Sulzberger in *DPM Letters*, Dec. 4, 1981, 438.

"countries which have papers": Ronald Reagan, "Remarks and a Question-and-Answer Session with Regional Editors and Broadcasters on Domestic and Foreign Policy Issues," Sept. 21, 1983, http://www.reagan.utexas.edu/archives/speeches/1983/92183f.htm

Reagan's UN Ambassador: *NYT*, Oct. 6, 1988.

"forthright and courageous": Ronald Reagan, "Remarks at the International Convention of B'nai Brith," Sept. 6, 1984, http://www.reagan.utexas.edu/archives/speeches/1984/90684a.htm

"but if they chose": *NYT*, Sept. 22, 1983, 1.

231 "selective morality": *NYT*, Mar. 16, 1982.

"that an elected government": DPM, Gridiron Speech, Mar. 28, 1981, in DPM, *Came the Revolution: Argument in the Reagan Era* (San Diego, 1988), 21. See also DPM, "Reagan's Bankrupt Budget," *TNR*, Dec. 26, 1983, 15–20.

232 "could blow up": Seymour Martin Lipset, "The Prescient Politician" in *Daniel Patrick Moynihan: The Intellectual in Public Life*, ed. Robert A. Katzmann (Baltimore, 2004), 27.

"The Age of totalitarianism": *DPM Letters*, 519, 510.

CHAPTER 10: "WORDS MATTER"

233 "words matter": MemCon between GRF, HAK, and DPM, 3, 10:45 a.m., Apr. 12, 1975, GRF NSA.

"just words": David Luchins, *A Tribute to Senator Moynihan*, Apr. 5, 2003, aish.com, http://www.aish.com/ci/s/48900337.html

"Ideas are important": Tim Russert, *Big Russ and Me: Father and Son: Lessons of Life* (New York, 2005), 261.

"our era's": Elizabeth Moynihan to Arthur O. Sulzberger, Jr., *DPM Letters*, Nov. 27, 2000, 647.

234 "ridiculous because": Yohanan Manor, *To Right a Wrong: The Revocation of the UN General Assembly Resolution 3379 Defaming Zionism* (New York, 1996), 183.

"a resolution born": *Ukrainian Weekly*, Oct. 6, 1991, 11.

234 "Big Red Lie": *Washington Post*, Sept. 29, 1991, C7.

235 "Zionist Racism": Fayez A. al-Sayegh, "Zionism: A Form of Racism and Racial Discrimination," *International Symposium on Zionism and Racism*, Baghdad, Iraq, Nov. 1976, available at http://www.al-moharer.net/falasteen_docs/fayez_sayegh.htm

"the world's colored": Jeane Kirkpatrick, "How the PLO was Legitimized," *Commentary*, July 1989, 22.

Lumping Israel: Ruth Lapidoth, *Some Reflections on Zionism: A Reply to the Baghdad International Symposium of Nov. 1976*, Feb. 6, 1977, Records of the American Jewish Congress, "Zionism is Racism"-U.N. Resolution 3379. 1975–1986, 1991, I-77, Box 715, Folders 28–29, American Jewish Historical Society, New York.

"the world's underdog-lovers": Morton Kondracke, "What to do about the Palestinians," *TNR*, Feb. 7, 1976, 16.

"tantamount to": Kirkpatrick, "How PLO was Legitimized," 26.

236 "against colonial domination": International Convention against the Taking of Hostages, adopted by the General Assembly, Dec. 17, 1979, available at http://treaties.un.org/doc/db/Terrorism/english-18-5.pdf.

"These policies, whether": Text of the 1938rd meeting of the UN Security Council, 9, paragraph 74, June 29, 1976, S/PV.1938.

"Mr. Rothschild": Robert Wistrich, *A Lethal Obsession: Anti-Semitism from Antiquity to the Global Jihad* (New York, 2010), 479, 478.

anti-Zionism and anti-Americanism increasingly: Paul Hollander, "Introduction: The New Virulence and Popularity," in *Understanding Anti-Americanism: Its Origins and Impact at Home and Abroad,* ed. Paul Hollander (Chicago, 2004), 45.

"Israel made a big": George Will OH.

The world's new: Andrei S. Markovits, *Uncouth Nation: Why Europe Dislikes America* (Princeton, 2007), 174, 167.

"the Jews": Letty Cottin Pogrebin, "Anti-Semitism in the Women's Movement," *Ms.,* June 1982, 68.

237 "our true enemies": Pogrebin, "Anti-Semitism in the Women's Movement," 70.

Paralleling the growth: Murray Friedman, *Black Anti-Semitism on the Rise,* *Commentary*, 68:4, Oct. 1979, 31.

"stench": *Morning Record and Journal* [Meriden, Connecticut], Sept. 27 1979, 40.

"how hate-filled": *United States Congress House Committee on Foreign Relations: The U.S. Role in the United Nations: Hearings before the Subcommittee on Human Rights and International Organizations of the Committee on Foreign Affairs, House of Representatives, Ninety-eighth Congress, First Session, Sept. 27 and Oct. 3, 1983,* 80.

"comprehensive": Juliana Geran Pilon, "The United Nations' Campaign Against Israel," *Heritage Foundation,* June 16, 1983, 2.

"I'm in a": Richard Schifter, lecture given at Congregation Adat Shalom, Bethesda, Maryland, Oct. 25, 2009, available at http://www.adatshalom.net/schifter.html

238 "Jim Crowism": William H. Chafe, *Never Stop Running: Allard Lowenstein and the Struggle to Save American Liberalism* (Princeton, NJ, 1998), 44.

"stinking little resolution": Manor, *To Right a Wrong,* 94.

238 At Harvard: Daniel Benson, "'Human Rights' at Harvard Law School," *Commentary*, Sept. 1979, 75, 78.

"purely from a": Alan Dershowitz, "Can the Guild Survive Its Hypocrisy?" *American Lawyer*, Aug. 11, 1978, 31.

239 "Zionism Supports": Friedman, "Black Anti-Semitism on the Rise," *Commentary* 68:4, Oct. 1979, 32.

"the only good": Memo from Mark Pelavin to Phil Baum and Neil Goldstein, July 3, 1987, Records of the American Jewish Congress, "Zionism is Racism"-U.N. Resolution 3379. 1975–1986, 1991, I-77, Box 715, Folders 28–29, American Jewish Historical Society.

"moral purism": Michael Walzer, "Can There Be a Decent Left?" *Dissent*, Spring 2002.

"No Platform": Violet Martin, "'No Platform' and Free Speech," Mar. 23, 2006, http://www.workersliberty.org/node/5904

"justification": Robin Shepherd, *A State Beyond the Pale: Europe's Problem with Israel* (London, 2009), 3.

In the classroom: Naomi Paik, "Education and Empire, Old and New," http://laborculture.research.yale.edu//documents/paik_education_and_empire.pdf.

"postcolonial": Edward William Said, *Orientalism*, rev. ed. (London, 2003), 350.

"a generalized swear-word": Nikkie Keddie interview in Nancy Elizabeth Gallagher, ed., *Approaches to the History of the Middle East*, 144–45.

240 "add Zionism": Tamar Eshel, "The Women's Conference in Copenhagen: A Post Mortem," Oct. 1980, 1, Folder 8, Box 14, Series B. Women's Right, Norma U. Levitt MSS (MSS 720), American Jewish Archives, Cincinnati, OH.

"unprepared": DPM to Warren Christopher at "U.N. World Conference of the U.N. Decade for Women," May 5, 1980, 52, http://ufdc.ufl.edu/UF00088999/00001/66j pp. 58.

"a simple majority": Berlinske Tidende, *American Heritage Report*, Aug. 5, 1980, 7.

Gangs of young: Betty Friedan, "Anti-Semitism as a Political Tool: Its Congruence with Anti-Feminism," 1985, Folder 12, Box 13, Betty Friedan MSS, Schlesinger Library, Radcliffe Institute, Harvard University, Cambridge, MA.

"I cried": Peg Downey, "A Feminist Perspective on Copenhagen," *Graduate Woman*, 12, 13.

"psychological pogrom": Phyllis Chesler, *NewsReal Blog*, Sept. 2, 2010.

"The only way": Letty Cottin Pogrebin, *Deborah, Golda, and Me: Being Female and Jewish in America* (New York, 1991), 156.

"It's just not": Pogrebin, "Anti-Semitism in the Women's Movement."

"I'll tell you what": Pogrebin, *Deborah, Golda, and Me*, 157.

241 In 1975 feminists: Sidney Liskofsky, "A Dismal Anniversary: A Decade of the UN's "Zionism Equals Racism" Resolution, 1975–1985," 7, I-77, Box 715, Folders 28–29, American Jewish Historical Society, New York.

"The real test": Pogrebin, *Deborah, Golda, and Me*, 160.

"I'm an anti": Ellen Willis, "Is There Still a Jewish Question? Why I'm an Anti-Anti-Zionist," *Contested Terrain*, Mar. 1, 2007.

she fought the UN: Jeane Kirkpatrick, "The United Nations as a Political System: A Practicing Political Scientist's Insights into U.N. Politics," *World Affairs* 146:4 (1984): 359.

241 "his campaign to enable": DPM Fundraising Letter, ca. 1997, 4, in David Luchins MSS, private collection, New York.

242 "door to door": DPM to Laurence Tisch, *DPM Letters*, Oct. 3, 1991, 575–76.

"the wording has": Manor, *To Right a Wrong*, 132.

"reminded the world": David Harris OH.

"cover": Malcolm Hoenlein OH.

"generated a life": Harris OH.

"Mission Impossible": Manor, *To Right a Wrong*, ix.

"no resolution": Harris OH.

243 "virtual feminist retirement": Betty Friedan, "Anti-Semitism as a Political Tool," 15.

"our deep commitment": Bella Abzug, "Preparations Payoff," *Jewish Week*, Aug. 2, 1985.

"business of the conference": *Time*, Apr. 12, 2003.

"as feminists about": Betty Friedan, "Anti-Semitism as a Political Tool," 15, 26, 27, 29–30.

244 "removal of this blot": *NYT*, Nov. 11, 1985, A1.

"license to kill": *Chicago Tribune*, Nov. 12, 1985.

Moynihan worried about: DPM, "Letting Go: The United States Edging Out of the United Nations," *Institute of International Education*, May 12, 1986, 11.

"incite anti-Semitism": US Congressional Joint Resolution 385, Oct. 21, 1987, Records of the American Jewish Congress, "Zionism is Racism"-U.N. Resolution 3379. 1975–1986, 1991, I-77, Box 715, Folders 28–29, American Jewish Historical Society.

"Never in history": *Los Angeles Times*, Nov. 11, 1987.

"Finally, there was an": DPM Fund-raising Letter, ca. 1997, 4, in Luchins MSS.

245 "key countries": Martin Raffel to members of the Israel Strategy Committee, Nov. 20, 1987, Martin Raffel MSS, Jewish Center for Public Affairs, New York.

"to see": Manor, *To Right a Wrong*, 226.

"there is no tradition": MemCon, BS, John Wolf, Nancy Bearg Dyke, Javier Perez de Cuellar, Ronald I. Spiers, Alvaro de Soto, John L. Washburn, 3, 3:30 p.m.– 4:10 p.m., June 6, 1990, GHWB MSS.

"the stupidest thing": Manor, *To Right a Wrong*, 226, 227.

"one lonely little guy": *Newsweek*, Sept. 22, 1991.

"anti-Israel": Hoenlein OH.

"Mr. President": Shoshana Cardin, *Shoshana: Memoirs of Shoshana Shoubin Cardin* (Baltimore, 2008), 146–47; and Shoshana Cardin to author.

246 teary-eyed: Hoenlein OH.

"repudiate the odious": *Chicago Tribune*, May 23, 1989.

"Zionist state": *Time*, Nov. 7, 1988.

"undermines the UN's": *New York Daily News*, Dec. 11, 1989.

Quayle then made: *NYT*, Dec. 12, 1989.

"We are in a": Telegram. Secretary of State James A. Baker III to all US missions, Mar. 30, 1990, in "Assistant Secretary of State John Bolton Subcommittee Statement on Repeal of UN Resolution 3379 Equating Zionism with Racism," printed in *Current Policy* #1269, from *US Participation in the UN* (Washington, DC, 1990).

246 "an attempt to foster": Baker to all US missions, Mar. 30, 1990, in *Current Policy* #1269.

"basic UN principles": Text of John Bolton's statement before the Senate Subcommittee on Near Eastern and South Asian affairs, *Current Policy*, Mar. 30, 1990.

"Did we ever tell": Godfrey Hodgson, *The Gentleman from New York: Daniel Patrick Moynihan: A Biography* (Boston, 2000), 258.

"Shame on you": Elie Wurtman OH, Sept. 13, 2011.

"moral victory": Baker to all US missions, Mar. 30, 1990, in *Current Policy* #1269.

247 "a wrong and unfair": Harris O. Schoenberg and Dean Weinrich, "To Rid the UN of Z = R," B'nai B'rith International publication, July 11, 1991, 1975–1986, 1991, I-77, Box 715, Folders 28–29 Records of the American Jewish Congress, American Jewish Historical Society, New York.

"You cannot say": Manor, *To Right a Wrong*, 250.

"actually dead": MemCon, June 6, 1990, 2, GHWB MSS.

"Big Red Lie": DPM, "Big Red Lie," *Washington Post*, Sept. 29, 1991, C7.

"Tell me": Elie Wiesel OH. See also *JTA*, Sept. 16, 1991.

"This is the moment": DPM to George H. W. Bush, Sept. 16, 1991, *DPM Letters*, 574.

"Zionism is not": *NYT*, Sept. 24, 1991, 14.

248 "obnoxious": *Los Angeles Times*, Sept. 25, 1991, 6.

While Arab leaders: Quigley, *The Case for Palestine: An International Law Perspective*, 215.

"You're not doing": *NYT*, Dec. 22, 1991.

"simple *unconditional* resolution": Martin Raffel to NJRAC member agencies, Dec. 6, 1991, Martin Raffel MSS, Jewish Center for Public Affairs, New York.

Egypt opposed: U.S. senators to Hosni Mubarak, "Zionism is Racism," Nov. 19, 1991, Martin Raffel MSS, Jewish Center for Public Affairs, New York.

"irritant": MemCon, June 6, 1990, 2, GHWB MSS.

Chief of Staff: *Sunday Telegraph*, Sept. 22, 1991, 4.

249 "no instructions": Edgar Bronfman, *Making of a Jew* (New York, 1996), 182–85.

"I'm sorry": Stephen Herbits OH.

"mad dialers": John Bolton, *Surrender Is Not an Option: Defending America at the United Nations and Abroad* (New York, 2008), 33.

The president directed: Manor, *To Right a Wrong*, 259.

"Ideological conflict": Lawrence Eagleburger, Statement at the UN General Assembly, Dec. 16, 1991, US *Department of State Dispatch*, Dec. 23, 1991, 908, 909.

Ultimately, on Dec. 16: *NYT*, Dec. 17, 1991, 1.

250 "satisfying moment": Lawrence Eagleburger, "Foreword," in Yohanan Manor, *To Right a Wrong*, ix.

"feel less isolated": Edgar Bronfman to George H. W. Bush, Dec. 18, 1991, GHWB MSS.

Herzog called: Arie Dayan, "The Debate over Zionism and Racism: An Israeli View," *Journal of Palestine Studies* 23 (Spring 1993): 96.

"moment of truth": DPM to Laurence Tisch, Oct. 3, 1991, *DPM Letters*, 576.

251 "pragmatist": *NYT*, Oct. 26, 1991.

251 "Israeli repression": *Kentucky New Era* (AP story), Dec. 16, 1991, 19.

"Naïve student": "Zionism is Racism" *Harvard Crimson,* Dec. 19, 1991.

"paved the way": Manor, *To Right a Wrong,* vii.

252 "Oslo via Madrid": John B. Quigley, *The Case for Palestine: An International Law Perspective* (Duke University Press, 2005), 215.

"our delegation": Chaim Herzog, "Address to the American Jewish Congress," Mar. 16, 1996, Chaim Herzog MSS, Herzog Archives, Herzliya, Israel.

"has never quite": "Zionism Is Racism" *Harvard Crimson,* Dec. 19, 1991.

"Soweto on the Jordan": Elaine Hagopian, "Soweto on the Jordan," *al-Ahram Weekly*, July 2–8, 1998.

"The State Department": Richard Schifter OH.

253 "regrettable impression": Kofi Annan, "Kofi Annan says 'healing of wounds' between Jewish community and United Nations among his priorities as Secretary-General," United Nations press release, Dec. 15, 1999, http://www.un.org/News/Press/docs/1999/19991215.sgsm7260.doc.html

"have all been": Marc Ellis, "Can Jews Abroad Rescue Israel?" *Tablet*, Jan. 17, 1998.

polls in 1998: "1998 Annual Survey of American Jewish Opinion," AJC MSS, 19 Feb.–Mar. 8, 1998, 9, http://www.jewishdatabank.org/Archive/N-AJC-1998-Main_Report.pdf.

"anti-democratic": Yoram Hazony, *The Jewish State: The Struggle for Israel's Soul* (New York, 2000), 47.

these shifts coalesced: Anthony Julius, *Trials of the Diaspora: A History of Anti-Semitism in England* (New York, 2010), 441, 455.

254 "a dog whistle": Jeffrey Goldberg, "How to Listen for Racism on the Campaign Trail," *Bloombergview*, Jan. 31, 2012.

"Zionism is a": Jay Nordlinger, "The Z-Word," *National Review*, Dec. 31, 2011.

255 "wrote more books…": George Will, "Pat Moynihan, R.I.P.," Townhall.com, Mar. 27, 2003.

"sissy kid": *NYTM*, July 31, 1966, 48.

CONCLUSION: "WHAT WE'RE FIGHTING FOR"

256 "the paranoid style": *DPM Letters*, 658–59.

"clean hatred": Kaplan, *Warrior Politics: Why Leadership Demands a Pagan Ethos* (New York, 2001, 2003), 71.

257 "if you define": DPM undated notes, Folder 10, Box 338, DPM MSS.

"Any equation of Zionism": *Globe and Mail*, Mar. 8, 2001.

"the racist practices": Tom Lantos, "The Durban Debacle: An Insider's View of the UN World Conference Against Racism," *Fletcher Forum of World Affairs* 26:1, Winter/Spring 2002, reprint available at http://www.eyeontheun.org/assets/attachments/articles/568_durban_debacle.pdf, 6.

"Israeli racist": Text from WCAR NGO Forum Declaration against conference on racism, Sept. 3, 2001, section 98, 99, 160, 419, 424, 425.

"in the struggle": Address by Ms. Hanan Ashrawi (Palestine) World Conference Against Racism, Racial Discrimination, Xenophoia, and Related Intolerances, Aug. 28, 2001. Available at http://www.i-p-o.org/palestine-ashrawi.htm.

257 "an anti-American": Lantos, "The Durban Debacle," 26:1, 16.

258 "Hitler was right!": Abraham Cooper, "Mary Robinson gave hate a megaphone," Wiesenthal Center news release, Aug. 12, 2009, available at http://www.wiesenthal.com/site/apps/nlnet/content2.aspx?c=lsKWLbPJLnF&b=5711841&ct=7301781.

"finished the job": *Washington Jewish Week*, Dec. 23, 2009, available at http://www.washingtonjewishweek.com/print.asp?ArticleID=12000&SectionID=4&SubSectionID=16.

"a grotesque": Denis MacShane, *Globalising Hatred: The New Anti-Semitism* (London, 2009), xvii.

"Oh, no": *Globe and Mail*, Mar. 10, 2001, A19.

"a disaster": *New York Post*, July 28, 2001.

"Lyin' about Zion": David Greenberg, "Lyin' about Zion: The diplomatic back-story on 'Zionism equals racism,'" *Slate*, Sept. 7, 2001, available at http://www.slate.com/articles/news_and_politics/history_lesson/2001/09/lyin_about_zion.html.

"was criminal then": *New York Post*, July 28, 2001.

"Durban became": *Jerusalem Post*, Dec. 18, 2010.

259 "Today, Jew-haters try": Denis MacShane, *Globalising Hatred*, 82.

260 "earned anti-Semitism": Anthony Julius, *Trials of the Diaspora: A History of Anti-Semitism in England* (New York, 2010), 529.

"a racist state": Julius, *Trials of the Diaspora*, 419.

Few European leftists: Todd Gitlin, "The Rough Beat Returns," *Mother Jones*, June 16, 2002, available at http://motherjones.com/politics/2002/06/rough-beast-returns.

Exploiting Israel's unpopularity: Interview with Osama bin Laden, *Daily Ummat* Sept. 28, 2001, 1, 7. Available at http://www.globalresearch.ca/index.php?context = va&aid = 24697.

"Yankee-phobia": Michael Gove, "The Hatred of America is the Socialism of Fools," Jan. 8, 2003, available at http://www.freerepublic.com/focus/news/818590/posts.

"America had long": Richard Wolin, *The Seduction of Unreason: The Intellectual Roman with Fascism from Nietzsche to Postmodernism* (Princeton, 2004), 283. See also Andrei S. Markovits, *Uncouth Nation: Why Europe Dislikes America* (Princeton, 2007), 11.

261 "wonderful illogicality": Jean-François Revel, *Anti-Americanism* (San Francisco, 2003), 7.

"Why is it": Nick Cohen, *What's Left: How Liberals Lost Their Way* (London, 2007), 9–10.

"No.1 and": *NYT*, Oct. 8, 2002.

Ward Churchill traveled: Ward Churchill, "Zionism, Manifest Destiny, and Nazi Lebensraumpolitik: Three Variations on a Common Theme," lecture given Nov. 27, 2007, UC Davis campus, available at http://dhi.ucdavis.edu/?p=224.

attacked Zionist racism: "Rev. Wright Blames 'The Jews' for Keeping President Obama From Taking to Him" *ABC News*, June 11, 2009. Available at http://

abcnews.go.com/blogs/politics/2009/06/rev-wright-blames-them-jews-for-keeping-president-from-talking-to-him/.

262 "reputation": Robin Shepherd, *A State Beyond the Pale: Europe's Problem with Israel* (London, 2009), 51.

263 "Whether Israel was responsible": DPM, *A Dangerous Place* (Boston, 1978), 177.

"anti-Arab racism": Peter Beinart, *The Crisis of Zionism* (New York, 2012), 26. On apartheid see 20.

"the worst crimes": Raymond Aron, *The Opium of the Intellectuals* (Piscataway, NJ, 1955), xvii.

"Even the oppressed": Michael Walzer, "Can There Be a Decent Left?" *Dissent*, Spring 2002.

"What is the nerve": Ellen Willis, "Is There Still a Jewish Question? Why I'm an Anti-Anti-Zionist," *Contested Terrain*, Mar. 1, 2007, available at http://contested-terrain.net/willis/.

"It would be foolish": "Divesting in Israel" by Steven Lubet, *Baltimore Sun*, Oct. 18, 2002.

"wicked anti-Semitism": Todd Gitlin, "The Rough Beast Return," *Mother Jones*, June 17, 2002, available at http://motherjones.com/politics/2002/06/rough-beast-returns.

264 Yasin defined "Jihad": Zayed Yasin, "My American Jihad," June 6, 2002, http://www.beliefnet.com/Faiths/Islam/2002/06/My-American-Jihad.aspx.

"were not nuclear": DPM Keynote Address at Harvard University's 351 commencement, June 6, 2002. Available at http://www.wilsoncenter.org/article/daniel-patrick-moynihan-delivers-keynote-address-harvards-351st-commencement.

265 "A Letter from": *Washington Post*, Feb. 12, 2002, A16.

266 "fatalism of the appeasers": Kaplan, *Warrior Politics*, 71.

268 "the pragmatic mind": *DPM Letters*, 233.

"unique ability to": Gerd Korman to DPM, Nov. 17, 1975, Folder 3, Box 329, DPM MSS.

269 "My journey from": DPM to Thomas Gleason, Jan. 23, 1976, Folder 8, Box 329, DPM MSS.

"AN ISSUE OF HONOR": DPM to HAK, telegram, Oct. 18, 1975, 5, Folder 5, Box 337, DPM MSS.

SOURCES

The most valuable sources for this study were the voluminous Daniel Patrick Moynihan Papers at the Library of Congress, the illuminating transcripts of Henry Kissinger's conversations and of Gerald Ford's Oval Office briefings, the Israeli Foreign Ministry archives, the American Jewish Committee archives, the witty, candid memoir Moynihan wrote—with Suzanne Weaver Garment—about his time at the UN, *A Dangerous Place* (Boston, 1978), various oral history interviews, and the jewel of a letters collection that Steven R. Weisman edited with such impressive skill, *Daniel Patrick Moynihan: A Portrait in Letters of an American Visionary* (New York, 2010). Particularly valuable monographs included Godfrey Hodgson's biography, *The Gentleman from New York: Daniel Patrick Moynihan* (New York, 2000) and James T. Patterson's superb *Freedom Is Not Enough: The Moynihan Report and America's Struggle over Black Family Life—from LBJ to Obama* (New York, 2010), which inspired me by viewing a different moment from Moynihan's career in its broadest historical perspective.

MANUSCRIPT COLLECTIONS CONSULTED

Bella Abzug Papers, Rare Books and Manuscript Library, Columbia University, New York

Bertram Gold Papers, Interreligious Affairs, 1970s, Blaustein Library Vertical Files "United Nations" and "Daniel Patrick Moynihan" in American Jewish Committee Archives, New York

American Jewish Congress materials, "1975 Resolution" and "1991 Resolution," American Jewish Historical Society, New York

William Tapley Bennett Jr. Papers, Richard B. Russell Library for Political Research and Studies, University of Georgia Libraries, Athens, GA

George H. W. Bush Presidential Library and Museum, College Station, TX

Paddy Chayefsky Papers, Performing Arts Library, New York Public Library, New York

Betty Friedan Papers, Schlesinger Library, Radcliffe Institute, Harvard University, Cambridge, MA
Gerald R. Ford Presidential Library, Ann Arbor, MI
Leonard Garment Papers, Library of Congress, Washington, DC
Chaim Herzog Papers, Chaim Herzog Archives, Herzilya, Israel
Norma U. Levitt Papers, MSS No. 720, American Jewish Archives, Cincinnati, OH
Ministry of Foreign Affairs Papers, Israel State Archives, Jerusalem, Israel
Daniel Patrick Moynihan Papers, Library of Congress, Washington, DC
Israel Miller Archives, Yeshiva University Library, New York
Richard Nixon Presidential Materials Project, National Archives, College Park, MD
Thomas P. O'Neill Papers, John J. Burns Library, Boston College, Brookline, MA
Martin Raffel Papers, Jewish Council for Public Affairs, New York
Bayard T. Rustin Papers, Library of Congress, Washington, DC
Fayez A. Sayegh Collection, Aziz S. Atiya Library for Middle East Studies, Marriott Library, University of Utah, Salt Lake City, UT
United Nations Archives, New York
Barbara M. White Papers, 80-M235, Schlesinger Library, Radcliffe Institute, Harvard University, Cambridge, MA

PRIVATE COLLECTIONS OF PAPERS CONSULTED

Carl Gershman Papers, Washington, DC
Nathan Laufer Papers, Efrata, Israel
David Luchins Papers, New York

ORAL HISTORIES WITH

Shoshana Cardin (correspondence), Feb. 13, 2012, from Baltimore, MD
Alan Dershowitz, Oct. 31, 2011, Cambridge, MA
Chester Finn, Feb. 6, 2012, Washington, DC
Leonard Garment and Suzanne Weaver Garment, July 8, 2009; Nov. 2, 2011 (additional correspondence Feb. 14, 2012), New York
Carl Gershman, Jan. 15, 2010, Washington, DC
Nathan Glazer, May 24, 2011, Cambridge, MA
Yossi Klein Halevi (correspondence), July 15, 2011, Jerusalem, Israel
David Harris, Nov. 5, 2009, New York
Barbara Willner Hartman, Nov. 15, 2011, Jerusalem, Israel
Ilan Hartuv, Oct. 23, 2011, Jerusalem, Israel
Stephen Herbits (correspondence), Dec. 23, 2011 from Miami, FL
Isaac Herzog, Mar. 23, 2011, Jerusalem, Israel
Malcolm Hoenlein, June 13, 2011, New York
Ed Koch (correspondence), Feb. 7, 2012, New York
Nathan Laufer (correspondence), June 7, 2012, Efrata, Israel
David Lehrer, Dec. 16, 2011, phone conversation, from Kibbutz Ketura, Israel
Barry Levenfeld, Oct. 5, 2011, Jerusalem, Israel
David Luchins, Mar. 16, 2010, New York

Elizabeth Moynihan, July 7, 2010, New York (additional correspondence Jan. 26, 2011)

Martin Peretz, Jan. 16, 2012, Tel Aviv, Israel

Norman Podhoretz, Nov. 6, 2009, New York (additional correspondence Dec. 8, 2011)

Ed Prince, July 7, 2011, by telephone from Highland Park, NJ

Martin Raffel, Aug. 15, 2011, New York

Jonathan Rauch, Oct. 27, 2011, Washington, DC

Donald Rumsfeld, Feb. 6, 2012, Washington, DC

Jonathan Sarna, Feb. 17, 2010, Jerusalem, Israel

Richard Schifter (correspondence), May 28, 2012, from Washington, DC

Natan Sharansky, Mar. 25, 2012, Jerusalem, Israel

Don Walker (correspondence), Feb. 5, 2011, from New York

Michael Walzer, June 13, 2011, Jerusalem, Israel

Bernard Weinraub, Apr. 26, 2012, by telephone from Los Angeles

Elie Wiesel, Nov. 3, 2011, New York

George Will, Mar. 28, 2012, by telephone from Washington, DC

Ruth Wisse (correspondence), Nov. 14, 2010, from Cambridge, MA

Elie Wurtman, Sept. 13, 2011, Jerusalem, Israel

INDEX

and United Nations founding,
23–24
and Yom Kippur War, 54
See also Zionism; Zionism as racism
(UN Resolution 3799); *specific*
Jewish organizations
Jews, European, 66, 259
as nation, 64–65, 67, 73, 174
See also Holocaust
Jews, Israeli
loss of faith in UN, 80
self-critique, 13, 262–63
See also Israel; Zionism
Jews, Soviet
American activism on behalf of, 37,
115, 160, 161, 218
emigration to Israel, 76, 245
Israel as hope for, 74
Soviet harassment of, 37, 52, 63, 75,
76, 165
John Birch Society, 98
John, Elton, 213
John Paul, Pope, 59
Johnson, Lyndon B.
civil rights movement, 48
immigration legislation, 67
and Moynihan, 5, 6, 38, 41
resignation, 49
and Vietnam War, 29
War on Poverty, 48
Johnson, Paul, 192
Johnson, Sonia, 240
John XXIII, Pope, 18
Jordan
hostilities with Israel (1967), 70
Jerusalem partition, 68
Madrid Peace Conference, 248
PLO terrorism, 72–73
Six-Day War, 71
See also West Bank territory
Jordan, Vernon, 7, 174
Jordan, Winthrop, 14
Joyce, James, 15, 65, 135
Judaism as a Civilization (Kaplan), 67
Judaism Without Embellishment
(Kichko), 74

Judeo-Christian ethic, 18, 67
Julius, Anthony, 260

Kaddoumi, Farouk, 16, 140
Kahane, Meir, 24
Kahn, Natalie, 164
Kallen, Horace, 67
Kaplan, Mordechai, 67
Kaplan, Robert D., 266
Kapllani, Muhamet, 121
Kassebaum, Nancy, 243
Kaufmann, Johan, 184
Kazin, Alfred, 56
Keddie, Nikki, 239
Kennedy, Eamonn L., 135
Kennedy, John F.
assassination, 46
idealism, 29
as influence on Moynihan, 5, 18, 38,
41, 55, 217
Kennedy, Ted, 226
Khader, Naim, 215
Khalidi, Rashid, 25, 69
Khomeini, Ruhollah, 240
Khouri, Faris, 27
Kichko, Trofim, 74
Kidron, Avraham, 116
King, Coretta Scott, 7
King, Martin Luther, Jr., 83, 174, 212,
224, 237
King, Martin Luther, Sr., 7
Kirchik, James, 18
Kirkland, Lane, 59, 199–200
Kirkpatrick, Jeane, 230, 231, 234,
235–36, 237, 241, 242, 244
Kirschen, Yaacov, 215
Kissinger, Henry
détente policies, 5, 37, 59, 95, 104,
133, 151–52, 202, 228
diplomatic relations with Israel, 35, 54,
105–6, 110, 111, 115, 127, 128,
135, 184
diplomatic relations with Sadat, 110,
111, 127
early life, 33, 35, 40
egotism, 33, 34, 42